OLD TESTAMENT
INTRODUCTION

OLD TESTAMENT INTRODUCTION

WERNER H. SCHMIDT

Translated by
MATTHEW J. O'CONNELL

CROSSROAD · NEW YORK

1990
The Crossroad Publishing Company
370 Lexington Avenue, New York, N.Y. 10017

Originally published under the title
Einführung in das Alte Testament
© 1979 by Walter de Gruyter & Co.
Second edition © 1982 by Walter de Gruyter & Co.

English translation copyright © 1984 by
The Crossroad Publishing Company

Printed in the United States of America

Library of Congress Cataloging in Publication Data
Schmidt, Werner H.
Old Testament introduction.
Translation of: Einführung in das Alte Testament.
Bibliography: p. 345
Includes index.
1. Bible. O.T.—Introductions. I. Title.
BS1140.2.S2913   1984   221.6'1   83-26298
ISBN 0-8245-0606-5
ISBN 0-8245-1051-8 (pbk)

CONTENTS

92262

PREFACE

This book stands within a tradition but at the same time represents a break with it. It has a precursor in Johannes Meinhold's *Einführung in das Alte Testament* (1919, 1932³), but Meinhold's book was structured in accordance with historical considerations, whereas the presentation given here largely follows the order of the Old Testament books themselves. Does not a correlation of the various books, documentary sources, collections of laws, or even psalms with the history of Israel require a surer knowledge of the time of origin of the texts than we now have?

"Introductions" (German: *Einleitung* and *Einführung*) are of several kinds. In contrast to an *Einleitung*, an *Einführung* such as is offered here does not have its character so determined in advance by the history of past scholarship that it cannot allow for various approaches. It is clear, of course, that an *Einführung* must include three thematic areas: "history of Israel," literary criticism (which is the subject of the traditional *Einleitung*), and "Old Testament theology." In the present book, the survey of the history of Israel takes the form of a summary of principal events (§2), although this is supplemented by a review of some sociohistorical data (§3).

We live in an age of textbooks—if you go by what sells in the bookstores. In the sixties there were only a few standard works which everyone had to read; today the offerings are so numerous and varied that it is difficult to choose. But are not these external appearances deceiving?

We do not really live in an age of textbooks—if you judge by the state of things in the scholarly world. How united Old Testament scholarship was at one time, and what deep divisions it now shows! And the change has occurred precisely at key points; what previously seemed more or less obvious and indisputable has become doubtful. The explanation of the Pentateuch in the light of the "short credo" (G. von Rad), the understanding of Israel's early history in terms of the amphictyony (M. Noth), the distinction between apodictic and casuistic law, the reconstruction of the belief in the "God of the

ix

fathers" (A. Alt), as well as older perceptions such as the connection of Deuteronomy with King Josiah's reform or the early dating of the Yahwist—all these are now challenged. Even the legitimacy of the distinction of sources in the Pentateuch is disputed.

Given this situation, any attempt to introduce readers to a basic understanding of the Old Testament as seen today—to the character, development, and theological intention of its books—is a subjective and even risky undertaking. Must one therefore be content simply to set forth the contrasting views on each subject? As a matter of fact, there may at times be more points in dispute than the presentation or even the questions it raises may suggest. Nonetheless I have tried to make my own views secondary and to emphasize the views that are held by the majority or that may even be said to be the prevailing ones at the present time. On the other hand, the very determination of these majority or prevailing views calls for an exercise of personal opinion. For this reason I have been concerned with justifying the opinions put forward so that the reader can judge the soundness of the arguments.

Knowledge of Hebrew is not required of the reader. The latter must decide whether and to what extent I have succeeded in combining three goals not easily rendered compatible: the communication of basic information (with a little biblical scholarship), necessary brevity, and general intelligibility.

I offer my heartfelt thanks to Dr. Georg Warmuth and Mr. Norbert Pusch for their assistance.

Kiel, September 1978

I am happy to say that this book has been well received, even by reviewers. For the second edition I have corrected a few slips and considerably expanded the bibliography.

Marburg, June 1981

For this English-language edition I wish to thank the translator, Matthew J. O'Connell, for his care and expertise, and also Professor J. J. M. Roberts, of Princeton Theological Seminary, who expanded and updated the bibliography with the particular needs of English-language readers in mind.

Marburg, January 1984   *Werner H. Schmidt*

Translator's Note

The Revised Standard Version has been used for quotations from the Old Testament. The asterisk (*) in references to the books of scripture indicates a passage that belongs only in part to the source being considered.

PART I

SURVEY OF
THE OLD TESTAMENT
AND ITS HISTORY

§1

THE PARTS OF
THE OLD TESTAMENT

a) Name and Structure

It is the New Testament that makes the Old Testament "Old." The very name "Old Testament" (OT), which makes sense only in correlation with the New Testament (NT), already implies the problem of the Christian interpretation of this body of traditions. At the same time, however, while the name is determined by Christianity's understanding of itself, it also has a basis within the OT or, more accurately, in the prophetic expectation of what was to come, namely, that after judging his people God would again bestow his favor on them. According to the promises in Jer 31:31ff. a "new covenant" (Latin: *testamentum*) would replace the one that was broken. This one word is an example of how the OT develops beyond itself, as it were, and transcends itself through hope. The Christian understanding of the OT has a basis in this kind of OT expectation, which looks beyond the condition of its time. The NT relates the prophetic promises to the future that has now made its appearance in the person of Jesus (see 2 Cor 3; Heb 8). But the application of the term "old covenant" or "testament" to the books of the OT is not yet found in the NT itself.

The NT cites the Old as an authority (e.g., Luke 10:25ff.), as "scripture . . . inspired by God" (2 Tim 3:16). In fact the OT is regarded simply as "the scripture" or "the scriptures" without qualification (Luke 4:21; 24:27ff.; etc.). This designation reflects its high and even, in a sense, unparalleled standing, but it should not be misinterpreted as meaning that the OT is by its nature a word set down in writing, while the NT is a spoken, living word. To an important extent, the OT, and especially the prophetic message, emerged from oral teaching and was later read and explained in the liturgy (Neh 8:8; Luke 4:17).

The NT speaks of the whole OT also as "law" (John 12:34; 1 Cor 14:21) or, with greater precision, "law and prophets" or "Moses and prophets" (Matt 7:12; Luke 16:16, 29; Rom 3:21; etc.); and on one occasion the OT is described as consisting of "Moses and the prophets and the psalms" (Luke 24:44). The characterization of the OT as "law" is likewise open to misunderstanding, as though the OT were essentially a compilation of laws. But the "law" has by no means only the character of command (see Matt 22:40); it has a prophetic character also (John 15:25; Matt 11:13; etc.). A legalistic interpretation does not reflect the OT's self-understanding.

The bipartite formulas and, even more, the tripartite formula "Moses and the prophets and the psalms" reflect the structure of the OT. A comparable threefold division is already found, ca. 130 B.C., in the prologue to the Greek translation of the (apocryphal) sayings of Jesus the son of Sirach. Alongside such names for the Bible as *miqrā'* ("the reading," "the book to be read"), the abbreviation *TNK* (pronounced *Tᵉnak*) is still customary in Judaism. The abbreviation is made up of the initial consonants of the names for the three basic sections of the OT.

T: *Torah*, i.e., "Instruction," the five books of Moses: Genesis, Exodus, Leviticus, Numbers, Deuteronomy

N: *Nebiim*, i.e., the "Prophets" (including the historical books Joshua through Kings)

K: *Ketubim*, i.e., the (other sacred) "Writings," such as Psalms and Job

In contrast, the Septuagint (LXX) or Greek translation of the OT is divided into four parts and is more inclusive, since it also contains in varying degrees the so-called Apocrypha (such books as Maccabees, Baruch, and Ecclesiasticus or Sirach). The LXX divides its material thus:

legal (five books of Moses)

historical (Joshua, Judges, Ruth, 1–2 Samuel, 1–2 Kings, 1–2 Chronicles, Ezra, Nehemiah, 1–2 Maccabees, etc.)

poetic (Psalms, Proverbs, Ecclesiastes, Song of Solomon, Job, etc.)

prophetic (twelve minor prophets, Isaiah, Jeremiah, Lamentations, Ezekiel, etc.)

If the first two of these groups are combined (i.e., if the five books of Moses are counted as historical books), the result is a threefold division that is clearer than that of the Hebrew Bible and corresponds to a distinction of times: past (historical books), present (Psalms, Proverbs), and future (prophetic books). This temporal structure has passed into our present Bible by way of the Latin translation or Vulgate.

In the first group—the Pentateuch or five books of Moses (see §4a)—the Hebrew and Greek traditions have the same contents. Since the

Pentateuch begins with the creation of the world and then recounts the beginnings (patriarchs, Egypt) and foundation (Sinai) of Israel, it rightly comes in the first place.

In the appraisal of the second group, the Christian tradition differs from the Jewish. Jewish tradition gives the name "latter" or "later prophets" to the books of the so-called major prophets Isaiah, Jeremiah, and Ezekiel (but not Daniel) and to the book of the Twelve Prophets, which includes the prophets Hosea to Malachi (originally in a single scroll). These are preceded by the "former" or "earlier prophets," that is, the books of Joshua, Judges, Samuel, and Kings. The contrast "former—latter" or "earlier—later" can be understood either spatially, that is, simply according to the position of the books in the canon, or temporally, in accordance with the order in which the various prophets appeared, inasmuch as the "former" narrative writings include accounts of such prophets as Nathan, Elijah, and Elisha. Perhaps the combining of the historical and the prophetic books into a single block has a basis also in the view that even the historical books were written by prophets (Samuel).

As a matter of fact, the narrative literature and the prophetic have certain points in common. They are largely in agreement, for example, in their view of history and in particular of the close connection between word (which precedes or follows and interprets) and event. Both narrative literature and prophetic literature give evidence of the same kind of editorial revision (by the "Deuteronomistic" school), which sees the guilt of the people as consisting in their transgression of the first and second commandments. From this point of view, the linking of the historical and prophetic literatures seems to go back to an early period.

The Christian tradition, on the other hand, does not associate the narrative and prophetic literatures but follows the Greek translation and the Latin (which reflects the Greek) in regarding the Pentateuch as a set of historical books, joining it to Joshua–Kings, and then adding still other narrative works (Chronicles, Ezra, Nehemiah, Esther). In this way the Pentateuch loses something of its special character; however, its historical nature and its connection with the book of Joshua emerge more clearly, the settlement being seen as the fulfillment of the promise made to the patriarchs and to Israel. The entire history from the patriarchs, or even from creation, down to the postexilic period is given a continuity that is reflected only partially in the individual books from Genesis to Ezra-Nehemiah.

The third part of the OT canon is not a clearly defined entity in either the Jewish or the Christian tradition. The "Writings" (*Hagiog-*

rapha) were made to include books for which there was no place in the first two groups (these being already regarded as closed); for centuries the order of these works was not fixed. In the Hebrew Bible, the more extensive books—Psalms, Job, Proverbs—are usually followed by the five *Megilloth*, that is, the "scrolls" for the five annual feasts—Ruth, Song of Solomon, Qoheleth (Ecclesiastes), Lamentations, Esther (§26)—and finally by Daniel and the Chronicler's history (Ezra, Nehemiah, 1–2 Chronicles).

Christian tradition—once again following the Greek and Latin translations—gives part of the Writings a separate existence as poetic books (Job, Psalms, Proverbs, Ecclesiastes, Song of Solomon), and it assigns another part (Chronicles, Ezra, Nehemiah, Esther) to the historical books and a third part (Lamentations, Daniel) to the prophetic books.

b) The Formation of the Canon

The fact that no clear principle governs the structure of the OT is due to the historical process whereby it came into existence. The divisions adopted simply imposed a subsequent unity on books already at hand; this is especially true of the Writings. In fact, the phases of the formation of the OT determined the distribution of the material.

The oldest part is the Pentateuch, which after a centuries-long history of growth acquired its present form in the fifth or, at the latest, the fourth century B.C. The Samaritans, who gradually split off from the Jerusalem community (a split that probably became definitive only in the Hellenistic period), recognized and kept only the Torah, that is, the five books of Moses, as their authority (see §12c4). The Pentateuch had long been in existence prior even to the Greek translation that was made in Egypt, beginning in the third century B.C.

To this nucleus the prophetic books were added as a separate entity, probably in the third century B.C. The age of prophecy was regarded as over (see Zech 13:2ff.); the age of interpretation had begun. In about 190 B.C. Ben Sira includes Isaiah, Jeremiah, Ezekiel, and the twelve prophets in his "Praise of the Fathers" (see chaps. 48–49), but the book of Daniel, which came into existence only around 165 B.C. is missing.

Did not the Pentateuch call for a continuation, even if this could not have the same rank and dignity? In both their legal and their narrative sections the five books of Moses often point ahead to Israel's residence in an arable land. Conversely, the historical books and occasionally the prophetic texts as well refer back to the basic traditions stemming from the early Israelite period.

In addition, the custom of reading from both the "law" and the prophets during the liturgy (Acts 13:15) may well be a very ancient one (see §13a3).

The group of books known as the Writings was clearly defined only in the NT period, when the contents and text of the OT were established and canonized, that is, acknowledged as inspired and therefore authoritative for the faith and life of the community. The insertion of Chronicles and Daniel into this third group suggests the relatively late composition of these works, since there was no longer a place for them in the older, already closed collections.

The definitive determination of the contents of the OT as a whole probably came only at the end of the first century A.D. (perhaps at the so-called Synod of Jabneh or Jamnia), when the Jewish community was getting organized again after the destruction of Jerusalem and the temple (A.D. 70). Did a desire to distinguish the Jewish community from the Christian also play a role in the determination of the canon? It was not only the Torah that had long since enjoyed a high regard; the prophets and the psalms too were in practice already viewed as "canonical." Nonetheless the NT does not seem to have known the OT in the fixed form in which we now have it; the NT often cites

The Organization of the (Hebrew) Old Testament

Name	Contents	Probable time of establishment ("canonization")
Torah "Instruction"	Pentateuch 5 books of Moses: Gen, Exod, Lev, Num, Deut	5th–4th century B.C. (Samaritans)
Nebiim "Prophets"	Former (Earlier) Prophets: Josh, Judg, 1–2 Sam, 1–2 Kgs Latter (Later) Prophets: Isa, Jer, Ezek, 12 minor prophets (Hos–Mal)	3rd century B.C.
Ketubim "Writings"	Pss, Job, Prov 5 *Megilloth* (Ruth, Song, Eccl, Lam, Esther) Dan, 1–2 Chr, Ezra, Neh	ca. A.D. 100

writings (Jude 14–15; cf. 1 Cor 2:9; etc.) that were excluded as apocryphal, that is, noncanonical.

The history of the OT canon still continues in the Christian churches, which do not all agree on what is to be included in the OT. Some of them retain the Apocrypha (the Catholics); others exclude them (the Lutherans and, more decisively, the Reformed churches).

§2

THE STAGES OF
ISRAEL'S HISTORY

The OT came into being in the course of a history, and most of what it says has to do with history. At the same time, however, its presentation of history is in the form of a testimony to faith; it does not preserve the tradition in its original, "historically pure" form, but relates it to the present and in the process alters it.

The historian's task, therefore, is to sift critically the data of Israelite history from the OT. From a methodological standpoint this reconstruction requires three steps: (1) analysis of the sources, including the material in the text that had originally been in the form of oral tradition; (2) discovery and evaluation of comparable material from the nonbiblical ancient Near East; and (3) very cautious conclusions regarding the historical events.

An extensive written tradition began in Israel only in the period of the monarchy. Memories of earlier times had been handed on orally, often in the form of sagas. As a consequence of the state of the sources as well as of the divergent methodologies employed to study them, in many instances the results obtained, especially concerning the prehistory and early history of Israel, are often disputed. Only after the migration into Canaan is it possible to deal with Israel as a self-contained subject for historical inquiry; even then, however, its self-understanding is based on traditions from the time before the settlement.

In light of these considerations, the history of Israel may for clarity's sake be roughly divided into five or six periods (the fourth and fifth might well be tied together as a single phase):

a) nomadic antiquity	fifteenth (?) to thirteenth century
b) prenational early period	twelfth to eleventh century
c) monarchic period	ca. 1000–587
d) exile	587–539
e) postexilic period	from 539
f) Hellenistic age	from 333

9

PRINCIPAL PERIODS OF THE HISTORY OF ISRAEL

Periods	Dates	Events	Personages
I. Nomadic antiquity	15th(?)–13th cent.	Promise to the patriarchs Liberation from Egypt Revelation at Sinai	
II. Early period before the state Philistine threat	12th–11th cent.	Settlement Development of the country Age of the judges Wars of Yahweh Tribal confederation: "Amphictyony"?	
III. Period of the monarchy Period of the united kingdoms	ca. 1000	Saul David (capital at Jerusalem) Solomon (building of the temple)	Yahwist?
Period of the divided kingdoms: northern kingdom of Israel, southern kingdom of Judah	926	So-called dividing of the realm (first firm date in the history of Israel; 1 Kgs 12)	
Pressure from Arameans (esp. 850–800)			Elijah, Elisha, the Elohist?
Assyrian domination (ca. 750–630)	ca. 733	Syro-Ephraimite war against Judah (2 Kgs 16:5; Isa 7)	Amos (ca. 760) Hosea (ca. 750–725) Isaiah (ca. 740–700)

Periods	Dates	Events	Personages
Period of Judah	732	Israel loses territory (2 Kgs 15:29), and conquest of Samaria by the Assyrians (2 Kgs 17)	
	722		
	701	Assyrian siege of Jerusalem (2 Kgs 18–20 = Isa 36–39; 1:4–8)	Jeremiah (ca. 626–586)
Babylonian domination (from 605)	ca. 622	Josiah's reform (2 Kgs 22–23; Deuteronomy)	
	597	First destruction of Jerusalem; ten years later:	Ezekiel
IV. Exile	587	Final destruction of Jerusalem by the Babylonians (2 Kgs 24–25; Jer 27ff.)	Lamentations Deuteronomistic history (Deut–2 Kgs, ca. 560) Priestly document Second Isaiah
V. Postexilic period	539	Babylon falls to the Persians (Isa 46f.; etc.)	Haggai, Zechariah
Persian domination (539–533)	520–515	Rebuilding of the temple (Ezra 5–6)	
Hellenistic age	333	Alexander the Great (victory over the Persians at the battle of Issus)	Chronicler's history
	164	Rededication of the temple during the Maccabean revolt	Daniel
	64	Conquest of Palestine by the Romans	

It is not my intention, of course, in this brief survey to discuss the often complex problems of historiography or to present the many details of Israelite history in their ancient Near Eastern context. My intention is simply to sketch a framework in which events indispensable for understanding the OT can be located.

a) Nomadic Antiquity

History, which supposes the existence of some form of writing, had started in the ancient East by the beginning of the third millennium B.C. When Israel came onto the stage of history, the peoples of the ancient East thus already had a long past behind them, and Israel understood itself as taking its place in it (Gen 10). But, despite Gen 11:28ff.; 12:4f., Israel's ancestors can hardly have come from the developed cultures of Mesopotamia and the Nile valley.

Gen 11:20ff. uses proper names such as Nahor and Haran, which are documented as place names in northwest Mesopotamia; Haran, in fact, appears even in the OT as a place name (Gen 11:31f.; 12:4f.; 28:10). But that area, and much less the still farther distant Ur (11:28, 31), can hardly have been the home of Israel's ancestors. The latter rather had relations of kinship with the populations of those areas (27:43; 22:20ff.; 24:4ff.) and with their closer neighbors in the east and the south: Ammon, Moab (19:30ff.), and Edom (36:10ff.), which arose out of the Aramean migration.

Israel's ancestors are rather to be sought among those groups of Arameans which in the course of time emerged in successive waves from the wilderness or steppe and pressed into the fertile arable region. Abraham's relatives are described as Arameans (Gen 25:20; 28:5; 31:18, 20, 24; etc.), and the credo preserved in Deut 26:5 even applies to Israel's own ancestors the statement "A wandering Aramean was my father." It would seem that Israel's ancestors originally spoke Aramaic and only after the settlement adopted Hebrew, the language of their new home.

Even the divine name Yahweh is probably Aramaic (*hwh*, "to be") and most probably means "he is, shows himself (to be effective, helpful)," which the interpretation in Exod 3:12, 14 assumes: "I will be (with you)."

In approximately the second half of the second millennium B.C. there arose three traditions that were constitutive for the self-understanding of the later people of Israel: the promise to the patriarchs, the liberation from compulsory service in Egypt, and the revelation at Sinai. The three have been welded into a historical continuum in the final version given in the OT, by a process of tradition that is complex and difficult to trace in its details. The patriarchs Abraham, Isaac, and Jacob have become father, son, and grandson; the sons of Jacob-Israel grow into the people of Israel in Egypt (Exod 1:7), and Moses becomes the focal figure in a wide-ranging series of events from the oppression in Egypt, by way of the sojourn at Sinai, to the migration through the territory east of the Jordan (Deut 34). Faith understands the past as embodying the activity of the one God in dealing with a single people who together are brought in roundabout ways into the promised land and who henceforth create a history that is presented as more unified than it proves to be to a searching historical analysis.

The traditions recorded in the books from Exodus to Joshua were subsequently "interpreted in terms of Israel as a whole" (M. Noth), but in their original form these traditions were not concerned with the people as a whole. With greater fidelity to the truth the sagas in the book of Judges still describe the later history as a history of separate tribes. A critical inquiry must first of all, therefore, eliminate the interpretation that makes the Pentateuchal traditions refer to Israel as a whole (an interpretation that has now left a profound mark on these traditions). Such an inquiry must then ask: Do not the traditions embodied in the story of the patriarchal families and in the history of the people that begins in the time of Moses, and even in the traditions concerning the Exodus and Sinai, represent in fact various traditions that have differing milieus and contents and that originate in the experiences of independent groups? This is the main problem to be faced in the writing of Israelite history; any reconstruction in this area is no more than a groping in the dark.

1. Especially in treating the religion of the patriarchs only conjectures are possible. The classical solution (A. Alt, 1929), which is being increasingly called into question nowadays, deduced a special kind of family or kinship religion that fits in well with nomadic living conditions: a faith in the "God of the fathers."

The "God of Abraham," the "Fear (Kinsman?) of Isaac," and the "Mighty One of Jacob" (Gen 31:29, 42, 53; 46:1; 49:24f.) were not connected with any sanctuary at which there were priests, but revealed themselves (in each case only) to the leader of a wandering clan and promised him guidance, protection, posterity, and possession of land (12:7; 28:15, 20; etc.). Israel, however, related the promised possession of land to the whole of Palestine and broadened the assurance of children into a promise of nationhood (15:4ff.; etc.).

According to the picture given in Genesis the patriarchs in their travels took up their abodes at certain holy places and there received God's self-revelations (see §5b3). It is likely that ancestral groups did originally settle around such places: Abraham at Hebron (Gen 13:18; 18; 23), Isaac at Beersheba in the south (24:62; 25:11; 26:23ff.), and Jacob in East Jordan at Penuel and Mahanaim (32:2, 23ff.) and in West Jordan at Shechem and Bethel (28:10ff.; 33:19ff.; 35:1ff.). This divergence in settlement locales implies that the patriarchal groups originally lived as separate entities. It is probable, therefore, that only later on were Abraham, Isaac, and Jacob linked together as successive generations; this would have happened when the individual groups and tribes formed a union or even—at the latest, if such a date is not too late—when they came together to form a state.

As a result of trade, removal to different pastures, or visits to pilgrimage sanctuaries—and certainly as a result of the settlement— the seminomadic tribes came into contact with the indigenous Canaanites and then identified their own patriarchal gods with the El-divinities of the local sanctuaries, for example, with El-bethel, "God (of) Bethel" at Bethel (Gen 35:7; cf. 31:13), or with El-olam, "Everlasting God" at Beersheba (21:33; cf. 16:13; etc.).

At a later stage the patriarchal and El divinities alike were identified (Exod 3:6, 13ff.; 6:2f.) with Yahweh, the God of Israel (see Josh 24:23). This process did not mean a foreign infiltration into the Yahwist faith, because the God of the patriarchs with his word that reveals the future was already concerned with human beings and thus with history and, above all, was already venerated in a monolatric way (i.e., within the clan in question).

2. The deliverance from Egypt was regarded as the fulfillment of a promise (Exod 3–4, 6) and became a basic part of Israel's confession of faith (20:2; Hos 13:4; Ezek 20:5; Ps 81:10; etc.). But all the historical evidence indicates that only one group sojourned in Egypt and later merged with the people of Israel—probably in the northern kingdom.

Within these limits, however, the tradition has a reliable nucleus. Israel's ancestors were forced, probably by the threat of famine (Gen 12:10; 42f.), to go down into Egypt, where they were compelled to supply laborers for the building of the storehouse cities, Pithom and Raamses (Exod 1:11). This datum brings us into the thirteenth century B.C., when Rameses II had a new capital (House of Rameses) built in the eastern part of the delta on the northeastern edge of his kingdom. When the contingent of workers fled (Exod 14:5), they were pursued but rescued, perhaps by a natural catastrophe. The earliest witness to the event is a song that presents it not as a victory of Israel but solely as an action of God without any human collaboration: "Sing to the Lord, for he has triumphed gloriously; the horse and his rider he has thrown into the sea" (Exod 15:21; cf. 14:13f., 25).

The two versions of this tradition—one a hymn (Exod 15), the other a prose account (Exod 14)—show two traits of OT faith, which (along with exclusivity and the rejection of images [Exod 20:2ff.; etc.]) would be characteristic of it down to the late period. It appeals for its justification to God's deeds in history, and it proclaims its allegiance to the God who rescues human beings from distress.

In the course of time, however, the memory of these events, both the oppression in Egypt (Exod 1:15ff.; 5) and the deliverance (14:23, 26, 28–29 P; 15:8ff.; Ps 136:13ff.; Isa 51:9f.; etc.), was presented in ever stronger colors. The miracle of the plagues and of Passover night, which compelled Pharaoh to "let Israel go," are in the last analysis symbolic. Children and grandchildren and even the entire world must experience what Yahweh has done (Exod 9:16; 10:2).

When the final destructive blow (the slaying of the firstborn of humans and cattle) is struck in the night, only those are spared who have rendered themselves safe by means of a protective rite. This reveals something of the origin of Passover, which goes back to the nomadic period. At one time Passover had been an apotropaic rite (smearing of the entrance to house or tent with the blood of sheep; consumption of the baked flesh) by means of which shepherds protected themselves and their flocks from a demon of the wilderness, the "destroyer" (Exod 12:23; cf. Heb 11:28).

In Israel Passover took on a new character; it was linked to the feast of Mazzoth, during which people ate unleavened bread for seven days (Exod 13; cf. 23:15; 34:18), and it became an anniversary of the exodus (12:14P; cf. Deut 16:3, 12; etc.) and thus an occasion for proclamation (Exod 12:24ff.; 13:8, 14ff.; etc.).

3. The divine name Yahweh was originally connected with Mount Sinai (Judg 5:4; Deut 33:2); it is said of Moses that he "went up to God" in order to bring the people to God (Exod 19; 24; cf. 33:12ff.; 1 Kgs 19).

Did Sinai, the exact location of which is still unknown, lie in the area where the nomadic Midianites lived? It is possible that Israel's ancestors received their faith in Yahweh through the Midianites (see Exod 18:12) or the Kenites (see Gen 4:15). In any event, the tradition preserved the reliable recollection that Moses had been the son-in-law of a Midianite priest (Exod 2:16ff.; 18) or a Kenite (Judg 1:16; 4:11). Did Moses become acquainted with faith in Yahweh in this manner and then bring it to the people doing forced labor in Egypt (see Exod 3–4)? Since Moses is an Egyptian name (probably meaning "son"), we are justified in regarding him as a connecting link between Egypt, Midian, and East Jordan (Deut 34:5f.). Is Moses' mediatorial role in the revelation at Sinai also a nuclear part of the tradition? But there is disagreement about what "really" happened at Sinai.

The Sinai pericope as we have it contains essentially three themes: the theophany, that is, the manifestation of God in natural events, whether volcanic activity or a thunderstorm (Exod 19:16ff.); the conclusion of a covenant, that is, the establishment of a community embracing God and the people (Exod 24; 34); and the proclamation of God's law (especially Exod 20–23; 34).

In its original form, the tradition certainly included the theophany and, in all probability, the encounter with God, who initiated an abiding relationship, which probably only later on was given the name "covenant." But is the proclamation of the law not an original and independent element in the tradition? In any case, inasmuch as the Decalogue, the Book of the Covenant, and other collections of legal prescriptions and cultic ordinances have been inserted into the Sinai pericope, ethics and laws governing human social life and divine worship are seen as flowing from the relationship with God.

Between the exodus and the revelation at Sinai and then between the revelation at Sinai and the settlement there is inserted the area of tradition known as the "guidance in the wilderness." But this does not form a continuous unit; rather it is made up of all sorts of individual sagas and scenes. These essentially describe the rescue of the people from various troubles and dangers: hunger (the feeding with manna and quail: Exod 16; Num 11) and thirst (water from the rock: Exod 17; Num 20; cf. Exod 15:22ff.), but also threats from enemies (war with Amalek: Exod 17:8ff.). Given the context into which they are placed, these individual traditions illustrate Israel's lack of trust in the divine promise, or the "murmuring" of the people as they look back with longing to the "fleshpots" of Egypt (Exod 16:3; Num 11).

These various local traditions from the deep south of Palestine (especially Exod 17) are grouped around a hidden center, of whose significance the OT has kept only a vague memory (Deut 1:46; 32:51; 33:8; Num 13:26; 20; etc.). Did Israel's ancestors remain for a longer period in the oasis area of Kadesh? Did those who had escaped from Egypt meet other groups that may likewise have come from the region of Sinai? Was this also a decisive intermediate station in the spread of faith in Yahweh, as the people moved toward the arable land? Even in regard to this part of Israel's ancient history, though so close to Palestine, more questions are possible than there are sure answers.

b) The Early Period before the State
(Settlement and Age of the Judges)

At a time when the Hittite kingdom in Asia Minor was going under and the great empires in Egypt and Mesopotamia were experiencing a decline of their power, at about the time of the transition from the Late Bronze Age to the Iron Age, the seminomadic ancestors of Israel made their way into Palestine and there, probably for the first time, formed well-defined tribes. This process of immigration, to which the deliberately neutral name of "settlement" has been given (A. Alt), would hardly (despite Josh 1–12) have taken the form of a military operation in which Israel, united under a common leader, conquered the entire land part by part. It would essentially have taken the form rather of a peaceful, stratified, and seemingly also protracted process in which the newcomers gradually adopted a settled life.

More or less accidentally attested individual cases show us how differently things might have gone from one region to another. The tribe of Dan, which initially tried to settle in central Palestine, was forced into the far north (Judg 1:34; 13:2, 25; 17f.; Josh 19:40ff.). It would seem that Reuben (see Josh 15:6; 18:17; Judg 5:15f.) as well as Simeon and Levi (Gen 34; 49:5ff.) likewise originally settled in central Palestine.

The tribe of Issachar, as its name ("wage-earner") suggests, was apparently able to buy the right to settle only by obliging itself to provide services to the Canaanite towns (see Gen 49:14f.; also Judg 5:17).

The individual groups also probably entered the country from different directions. Was Judah (around Bethlehem) colonized from the south (see Num 13f.), and central Palestine, with the areas settled by Benjamin and the "House of Joseph," from the east (Josh 2ff.)? In any case it was the more hilly and sparsely populated regions that were settled first (see Josh 17:16; Judg 1:19, 34). The strongholds in the plains, which in some cases were politically independent city-states, could not be conquered—as the "negative list of occupancies" in Judg 1:21, 27ff., so important in reconstructing the early history of Israel, bears witness.

In this manner four areas of settlement came into existence, which were only loosely connected with one another: the two centers, namely, the "House of Joseph" in central Palestine and Judah in the south, and two more peripheral territories, namely, Galilee in the north (Asher, Zebulun, Naphtali, Issachar) and the land east of the Jordan (Reuben, Gad). The three regions west of the Jordan were cut off from each other in the north by a cordon of fortified Canaanite city-states that cut across the plain of Jezreel (Judg 1:27; Josh 17:14) and, in the south, by another that stretched westward from Jerusalem (Judg 1:21, 29, 35). Yet this intersecting barrier did not mean an absolute partition of "Israel."

During the age of the judges, which is admittedly somewhat later, it was possible for individuals and tribes from central Palestine and Galilee to meet (Judg 4f.; 6f.). Were there also relations with Judah in the south (compare Josh 7:1, 16; 15:16 with Judg 3:9 and possibly 12:8)?

The settlement, which ended in about the twelfth century B.C., was followed by a gradual development of the land. It is probable that only then, in the period "when Israel grew strong" (Judg 1:28), was there an age characterized to a high degree by military conflicts with the Canaanite city-states, especially in the battle associated with Deborah (Judg 4f.; cf. 1:17, 22ff.; Josh 10f.; Num 21:21ff.; but also Gen 34). Canaanites were subjected to forced labor (Judg 1:28ff.; Josh 9) and thus were gradually assimilated, so that Israel could take over the religious ideas of the indigenous population.

Was it not inevitable that the age-old customs of an agricultural society (see Ps 126:5f.) should continue to be practiced? Were not the life-giving rain and the fertility of the soil due to the gods of the country, especially Baal? The claim of Yahwistic faith to exclusivity ultimately made only one solution possible, although it took a long time for this solution to prevail: Yahweh is also lord of nature's year (Gen 2:5; 8:21J; 1 Kgs 17f.; Hos 2; etc.). At such sanctuaries as Bethel and Shiloh Israel would have become familiar with the agrarian festivals current in the land (Judg 9:27; 21:19ff.; cf. Exod 23:14ff.).

The Song of Deborah (Judg 5) celebrates how a coalition of tribes with the help of Yahweh defeated the Canaanite cities in the plain of Jezreel. In like manner in other emergencies those directly affected banded together with the neighboring tribes under the leadership of a charismatic "judge" for a "war of Yahweh," either to resist the encroachments of hostile neighbors, such as the Ammonites (Judg 11; 1 Sam 11), or to beat back invasions by hostile tribes, such as the Midianites (Judg 6f.; see §11c2).

Just as various tribes joined forces in times of war, so too neighboring tribes met for common worship at various pilgrimage sanctuaries (see Deut 33:19, referring to Tabor). Was there also a permanent and to some extent institutionalized union of all the tribes? Prior to the establishment of the state did Israel form a twelve-tribe federation, the "amphictyony" (M. Noth), and worship Yahweh together?

According to texts both older (Gen 29:31ff.; 49; Deut 33) and more recent (e.g., 1 Chr 2:1f.) the tribes did form a group of twelve; these tribes were personified by the twelve sons of the patriarch Jacob-Israel, and formed subgroups according to their respective mothers:
Sons of Leah: Reuben, Simeon, Levi, Judah, Issachar, Zebulun
Sons of Rachel: Joseph (Ephraim, Manasseh), Benjamin
Sons of the serving-maids: Dan, Naphtali or Gad, Asher
In a later form of the list (Num 1; 26) Levi is omitted; the number twelve is then kept by dividing Joseph into (his sons) Ephraim and Manasseh.

Symbol and reality are certainly intermingled in this system, but what is its historical background? The origin of the number twelve, which (despite changes in the concrete members) is strikingly constant and influential for centuries is hardly to be found in the monarchic period, for the monarchy led to a national and ultimately a territorial state that ranged far beyond the tribal structure. Nor does the order of precedence assigned to the tribes in the later period correspond any longer to historical reality, since the tribes of Reuben, Simeon, and Levi (see Gen 34; 49:3–7) had long since lost their importance or had even disappeared. Consequently, the grouping within the list conceals an older history of the tribes that was, at least to some extent, quite different.

Especially the group formed by the six sons of Leah seems to have had a history of its own; it may have already been settled in central Palestine before Joseph and Benjamin, the sons of Rachel, immigrated, possibly bringing with them—from Egypt—the Yahwistic faith and introducing it into Israel. Is there a recollection of this event in Josh 24?

Since the list of twelve includes tribes from both south and north, it is possible that all the tribes had certain things in common, perhaps even a comprehensive organization.

The more consistent view—that Judah in the south and the central Palestinian tribes of Ephraim/Manasseh with the center of Yahwistic faith at Shechem (see Gen 33:18–20; Josh 24; etc.) had a common history only since the time of David—probably represents too radical a negation of relations between the tribes in the period prior to the state. If that view is retained, it is hardly possible to give a satisfactory answer to the difficult question of how the Yahwistic faith was able to prevail in the south.

The patriarchal traditions presuppose very close relations between Beersheba (Gen 26:23ff.) or Hebron (Gen 18) in the south and Shechem (12:6; etc.) in the north. Are we to say that all the traditions in the books of Joshua and Judges, traditions that include the south (Josh 7; 10; Judg 3:9; etc.), originated only in the monarchic period? After all, even the description in Judg 1 includes the situation of the settlement in Judah. Perhaps the list of "lesser" judges in Judg 10:1ff.; 12:8ff. preserves memories of an office of administration of justice over (northern or even all?) Israel.

In any case, in Palestine the many and varied individual city-states in the plains and the areas settled by the Israelites in the hills gradually formed a more close-knit structure, just as Israel's neighbors—the Ammonites, Moabites, and Edomites in the east and southeast and the Arameans in the north and northeast—established national states.

c) The Period of the Monarchy

The southern coastal plain also saw the rise of a new power that soon became a threat to all of Israel: the Philistines. These were not Semites (this is why the OT speaks of them as "uncircumcised"); they probably entered Palestine as part of the movement of seafaring peoples that is connected with the Doric migration. They ultimately established five city-states (Gaza, Ashkelon, Ashdod, Ekron, and Gath). Whereas the inroads of hostile tribes of peoples during the period of the judges had been limited in place and time, the growing (see Judg 3:31; 13–16) and finally abiding (1 Sam 4ff.; 10:5) predominance of the Philistines with their superior iron weapons (see Judg 13:19f.; 17:7) forced Israel as a whole to take common action under a permanent leader. Thus, external political pressure around the year 1000 B.C. led to the establishment of the monarchy and thereby to the formation of a state (1 Sam 8–12; see §11c3).

1. The Period of the United Kingdoms

The rule of Saul with its initial successes (1 Sam 11; 13ff.) and its catastrophic ending (1 Sam 28; 31) was of short duration. He failed against the Philistine threat; it would take David's efforts to put an end to this.

Once again the question arises of the relation between north and south. Did Saul's kingdom, like that of his son Ishbaal, who ruled during a brief transitional period after Saul's death (2 Sam 2:9f.), embrace only the later northern kingdom and not include Judah? In any event, Saul did extend his sphere of influence into the south as well. David, of the family of Ishai ("Root of Jesse"), from Bethlehem in Judah, was trained at the court of Saul in Gibeah, north of Jerusalem (1 Sam 16:14ff.; cf. 22:6), and Saul enviously pursued the successful David, who had gathered a band of soldiers around him, down into the south (1 Sam 22ff.).

After a short interim David became king: first in Hebron over the House of Judah (2 Sam 2:1–4), then later, by a covenant, over the northern tribes as well (5:1–3). Installation in office was by an anointing which the representatives of the people (2:4; 5:3) and, at least occasionally, a prophet acting in God's name performed (2 Kgs 9; cf. 1 Sam 10:1; 16:13).

For this reason the king is God's "anointed" (*mašîᵃḥ*, "messiah": 2 Sam 23:1f.; Pss 2:2; 20:6; etc.) and therefore inviolable (1 Sam 24:7, 11). In addition, he is regarded as God's son, although a son by adoption (Pss 2:7; 89:26f.; 2 Sam 7:14). To him belongs world dominion (Pss 2; 110), and his "justice" is effective not only in the realm of human society but in nature as well (Ps 72).

David not only united the northern and southern tribes in his person; he also incorporated into Israel Canaanite city-states that were still independent. In addition, by means of his standing army he made the surrounding peoples—the Philistines in the west, the Ammonites, Moabites, and Edomites in the east, and even the Arameans in the north (2 Sam 8; 12:30)—dependent on him in varying degrees, so that he succeeded in building a Syro-Palestinian empire for which he and his successors also created the needed organization (§3c).

In the course of this expansion of power David took a step that was supremely important for the future and for Israel's faith. He had his soldiers capture the Canaanite or, more accurately, the Jebusite city of Jerusalem, which stood in a kind of neutral area between the northern and southern kingdoms. He made this both his own residence (2 Sam 5:6ff.) and also, by transferring the Ark to it (2 Sam 6), the liturgical center of the Yahwistic faith.

As a result of court intrigue and David's authoritative decision, Solomon became his successor (1 Kgs 1). Solomon built a temple in the capital (1 Kgs 6–8). His international trading enterprises proved helpful to him in this undertaking (9:11, 26ff.; 10); they made possible a period of peace and probably created the conditions for the development of Solomon's "wisdom" (3; 4:29ff.; see §27,1).

The temple, which was closely connected with the royal palace, had the rank of an imperial sanctuary (see Amos 7:13), in which priests supplied the official personnel (1 Kgs 4:2). Did not the new conviction that Yahweh dwelt in the temple (8:12f.) or on Zion (Isa 8:18; Pss 46; 48; see §25,4c) cause the memory of nomadic times to be too forcibly repressed? Together with the sanctuaries throughout the land, Jerusalem seems to have been the place where ideas derived from other religions—the mountain of God (Ps 48:2), the heavenly court (Pss 29; 89:7ff.), the kingship of God (Pss 47; 93ff.; Isa 6), the struggle with the dragon (Ps 77:16ff.), but also the creation of the world (Pss 8; 24:2; 104; etc.)—made their way into the Yahwistic faith, there to be transformed into statements expressive of this faith.

2. The Period of the Divided Kingdoms
The Northern Kingdom, Israel

The empire created by David began to crumble along its borders already during the reign of Solomon (1 Kgs 11:14ff., 23ff.); after Solomon's death it fell apart. The old antagonism between north and south, which even in the lifetimes of David and Solomon had been kept alive and had found expression in the saying "What portion have we in David?" (2 Sam 20:1; 1 Kgs 12:16; cf. 11:26ff.), broke out again, and in a definitive way, in the division of the kingdom (926 B.C.; 1 Kgs 12). Barely two hundred years later the prophet Isaiah looked back to that moment as a day of judgment (Isa 7:17). Judah in the south, along with Jerusalem the capital, and Israel in the north were henceforth independent states.

The only data we have on the length of the reigns of David and Solomon assign them forty years each (1 Kgs 2:11; 11:42). A more reliable chronology can be constructed for the period after the division of the kingdom. From that time on only minor disagreements in calculation are possible, since on the one hand the books of Kings keep comparing the reigns of the rulers in north and south (§11c4), and on the other hand Israel's history is more clearly integrated into the known chronology of the ancient Near East (1 Kgs 14:25f.; 2 Kgs 3; etc.).

In addition, literary sources made their appearance with the rise of the monarchy: first, the stories of David's accession and of the succession (§11c3), then the official "daybooks" of the kings (1 Kgs 11:41; 14:19; etc.). Most important, the Yahwist source of the Pentateuch seems to have come into existence in the age of Solomon and, a half century later, the Elohist source.

In the southern kingdom the Davidic dynasty ruled unopposed for more than three centuries; its residence, of course, continued to be Jerusalem, where the royal sanctuary was located. There are no corresponding fixed points for the northern kingdom; for this reason it gives the impression of being less secure. The capital of the northern kingdom kept changing: Shechem, Penuel (1 Kgs 12:25), Tirzah for a lengthy period (14:17; 15:21, 33; etc.), and, finally and for good, Samaria, a previously uninhabited hill that Omri bought in about 880 B.C. in order that the new residence might belong to the king of the north in the way that Jerusalem belonged to the king of the south. As a matter of course, the kings of the north also attempted to establish dynasties (1 Kgs 15:25; 16:8, 29; etc.; see already 2 Sam 2:8f.), but sooner or later these were violently overthrown (1 Kgs 15:27; 16:9; etc.). The prophetic movement seems occasionally to have played a destructive role here by naming the new ruler (Jehu's revolution, 2 Kgs 9f.; cf. the schematic presentation in 1 Kgs 11:29ff.; 14:14; etc.). In any case, harsh critics of the kings arose among the prophets.

Prominent among the rulers of the north were these:
The first king, Jeroboam I (926–907) seems to have made Israel liturgically independent, since he turned Bethel and Dan into royal sanctuaries (1 Kgs 12:26ff.; cf. Amos 7:10, 13).

Omri, in reference to whom the Assyrians could speak of the northern kingdom as the "House of Omri," and his son Ahab (ca. 880–850) promoted syncretism in order to achieve the integration of the Canaanite population. Their sufferance and even support of the religion of Baal (1 Kgs 16:31f.) elicited the resistance of the prophets, especially Elijah (see §13d).

Jehu (845–818) came to power through a revolution in which he had the support of circles faithful to Yahweh. Although he campaigned against the syncretistically inclined court (2 Kgs 9f.), he was later rejected by the prophet Hosea (1:4f.) because of his bloody deeds. Jehu founded the longest dynasty, one that ruled a bare hundred years. To this dynasty belonged Jeroboam II (787–747), who seems to have experienced another golden age in the northern kingdom (2 Kgs 14:25ff.). In the final quarter century there were numerous usurpers (among them Menahem, Pekahiah, and Pekah), until the monarchy was finally destroyed in the reign of Hoshea, 722 B.C. (2 Kgs 17).

In the area of domestic politics the development of the northern state was determined by the important part taken by the Canaanite population with its own political, legal, social, and religious views. In foreign affairs the first need was to keep the borders of the northern kingdom clearly defined against Judah in the south. Only for part of the time was the relation between these sister states a friendly one; there were frequent boundary disputes in connection with the region of Benjamin, north of Jerusalem (1 Kgs 14:30; 15:16ff.; 2 Kgs 14:8ff.).

A much more dangerous and inflexible enemy arose in the north. Even in the time of Solomon the Aramean state of Damascus successfully asserted its independence (1 Kgs 11:23f.); it soon embroiled Israel in border conflicts (15:20) and, during the second half of the ninth century, in difficult wars (20; 22; 2 Kgs 6f.; 8:12; 13; Amos 1:3f.; etc.). Israel was unable to rest until the Assyrians had weakened the power of Damascus. Since the Assyrians themselves then withdrew from the Syro-Palestinian area for a few decades (ca. 800–750), Israel was able to win back lost territories (2 Kgs 13:25; 14:25, 28). But toward the end of this period (from about 760 on) the prophets Amos, Hosea, and Isaiah were already proclaiming the "end" of Israel.

In the ninth century (854/853) the Assyrians had already laid claim to Syria in the battle at Kharkar on the Orontes against a coalition of small states, including Israel. Only from about 740 on did this military power, notorious for its cruelty (Isa 5:26–29; Nah 2), begin the southward advance that was such a threat to Israel. The subjugation of the northern kingdom was accomplished in three increasingly harsh steps that were characteristic of the Assyrian policy of expansion:

1. Payment of tribute by Menahem (738 B.C.; 2 Kgs 15:19f.).

2. Reduction in the size of the state (733/732 B.C.), separation of the northern regions of Israel and conversion of Dor, Megiddo, and Gilead into three provinces (2 Kgs 15:29), as well as installation of a ruler submissive to Assyria (Hoshea).

3. Incorporation of the remaining truncated state (Ephraim) into the system of Assyrian provinces and thus the removal of all political

independence, deportation of the local upper class and introduction of a new foreign one (722 B.C.; 2 Kgs 17).

Thus the efforts of the small states to throw off vassalage only led to an ever greater dependence—to the second stage, then to the third. This is the temporal and material context of the Syro-Ephraimite war (ca. 733 B.C.), which Damascus (Syria) under Rezin and Israel (now centered in Ephraim) under Pekah, the "son of Remaliah" (Isa 7:2, 9), undertook against the southern kingdom of Judah. Their aim was to force Judah to join an anti-Assyrian coalition and to overthrow King Ahaz of Judah, of the Davidic dynasty, who was unwilling to join such a coalition (2 Kgs 16:5; Isa 7). Rezin and Pekah were unsuccessful. The Assyrians made their way into Israel, which fell into the second stage of dependence, and soon afterward the Assyrians destroyed Damascus (2 Kgs 16:9). Judah got off with a payment of heavy tribute and became an Assyrian vassal (16:8, 10ff.).

In 722 B.C., after a siege of three years, Samaria fell; this put an end to the history of the northern kingdom, which had once been the heartland of the Yahwistic faith. The northern Israelite traditions (such as the message of Hosea, probably the Elohist version, and perhaps an early form of Deuteronomy) passed over to the southern kingdom, which kept the name "Israel" in existence. The south now became the focal point of further literary development.

Since the Assyrians, unlike the Babylonians of barely a century and a half later, scattered the deported upper classes (2 Kgs 17:6), all trace of them was lost. The people who were left in the former northern kingdom intermingled with forcibly resettled foreigners (17:24; cf. Ezra 4:2) and later became the Samaritans.

3. The Southern Kingdom, Judah

For about a century the kings of Assyria controlled the history first of the two kingdoms and then of the remaining southern kingdom.

Name	Dates	Mentioned
Tiglath-pileser (III)	745–727	2 Kgs 15:29; 16:7, 10
under Babylonian		2 Kgs 15:19
enthronement name Pul		
Shalmaneser (V)	726–722	2 Kgs 17:3; 18:9
Sargon (II)	721–705	Isa 20:1
Sennacherib	704–681	2 Kgs 18:13; 19:20, 36
		= Isa 36:1; 37:21, 37
Esarhaddon	680–669	2 Kgs 19:37 = Isa 37:38
Ashurbanipal	668–631 (?)	

Although the fate of subjects in the other small states might have served as a deterrent, there were constant disturbances; for example, the movement of rebellion in 713–711 B.C., which started in the Philistine city of Ashdod and involved Judah (Isa 20). In efforts to shake off Assyrian domination, help was sought from Egypt, where the Ethiopian dynasty (Isa 18), with Shabaka as current pharaoh, was in power. This triangular political relationship—the Assyrian empire, Egypt, and the small states including Judah—is the background for the oracles from Isaiah's late period in which he threatens the defeat of Egypt and its protégés (especially Isa 30:1–3; 31:1–3).

When, after the accession of Sennacherib, King Hezekiah became the ringleader of a conspiracy (this context, namely, liberation from dependence on Assyria, may explain the cultic reform mentioned in 2 Kgs 18:4), the Assyrians responded in 701 by occupying the country and besieging Jerusalem. But for reasons no longer fully clear Sennacherib did not conquer the city and was satisfied with the payment of tribute and the renewal of the vassalage relationship (2 Kgs 18:13–16; cf. Ps 46:5?). Amid the general transports of joy Isaiah issued a call for mourning (22:1–14). The land of Judah seems, though only for a short time, to have been separated from the capital and divided among the Philistine states that were loyal to Assyria (thus in Sennacherib's account of his reign; cf. Isa 1:4–8).

Indeed, the Assyrians were able to conquer even Egypt around 670 (see Nah 3:8), but after 650 B.C. their power gradually declined. In the subsequent troubled years the prophet Jeremiah appeared on the scene, as did Nahum, Habakkuk, and Zephaniah.

After the long reign of Menahem, who had been a loyal vassal of Assyria, Josiah (639–609 B.C.) was able to regain political independence as Assyrian power declined. He was even able to win back parts of the former northern kingdom. This brief period of freedom made possible the reform in which Deuteronomy, or an earlier form of it, was turned into a kind of law of the land, the cult was purified of foreign elements, and Jerusalem was elevated to sole sanctuary (622 B.C.; 2 Kgs 22f.). But even though this action is of decisive importance for an understanding of broad areas of the OT, its historical character is disputed (see §10a5).

During the years 614–612 Assyria and Nineveh fell under the combined attacks of the Medes (located around Ecbatana in northwest Iran) and the Chaldeans or Neo-Babylonians (who undertook a restoration of the Old Babylonian kingdom under the aegis of the cult of Marduk). Pharaoh Neco sought to prevent the destruction of the

Assyrian empire. During an expedition of Neco, King Josiah lost his life at Megiddo (609 B.C.), and his successor, Jehoahaz, was shortly afterward exiled to Egypt (2 Kgs 23:29ff.; 2 Chr 35:20ff.; Jer 22:10ff.). But Nebuchadnezzar routed the Egyptian army (at Carchemish on the Euphrates, 605 B.C.) and thus conquered Syria/Palestine for Babylon.

When Jehoiakim (608–598), a son of Josiah, dared to discontinue the payment of tribute, Nebuchadnezzar had Jerusalem besieged. During the siege Jehoiakim died. His son and successor, Jehoiachin, was able to rule for only a few months and after the first conquest of Jerusalem was forced to go into exile with the royal family, the upper classes, and the craftsmen, among whom was the prophet Ezekiel (2 Kgs 24:8ff.). In some circles, nonetheless, Jehoiachin seems to have been regarded still as the legitimate king (see the dating in Ezek 1:2); but the hopes set on him were not realized (Jer 22:24ff.). In any case, the last item of information given in the Deuteronomistic history is that Jehoiachin was pardoned (2 Kgs 25:27ff.).

Nebuchadnezzar treated Jerusalem with indulgence and installed a new member of the Davidic dynasty, Zedekiah (597–587 B.C.), as ruler (2 Kgs 24:17). But when Zedekiah mistook the political situation and canceled the vassalage agreement, letting Jeremiah's warnings go unheeded, Jerusalem was besieged for the second time and captured in 587 (or 586?). This time the Babylonians showed harshness and even cruelty (2 Kgs 25).

This event meant a fourfold profound division: (1) the definitive loss of political independence (until the time of the Maccabees); Judah became a Babylonian and later a Persian province; (2) the end of the Davidic dynasty (despite the prophecy of Nathan in 2 Sam 7); (3) the destruction of the temple, the palace, and the city (despite the Zion tradition, Pss 46; 48); and (4) the banishment from the Promised Land, the deportation of the remaining upper classes (with the temple furnishings). In this way the prophetic oracles of disaster were fulfilled; yet the history of the people of God continued.

d) The Exilic and Postexilic Periods

Unlike the Assyrians, the Babylonians did not install a foreign upper class in Palestine; the result was that no alien religious cults gained access to the southern kingdom as they had to the northern scarcely a century and a half before. In addition, the Babylonians allowed the deported Israelites to live together (see Ezek 3:15). They could build houses, plant gardens (Jer 29:5f.), and, it would seem, be represented by their "elders" (Ezek 20:1; etc.). Despite several deportations the major part of the population probably remained in Palestine (see 2 Kgs 25:12). In any event, Israel (i.e., the Jews) lived on, or, as we can now say after this profound turning point, Judaism lived on in two areas—in Palestine and in the Gola (in exile) or the Diaspora.

Diaspora communities arose not only in Babylonia but, for various reasons, in Egypt as well. After the destruction of Jerusalem the Babylonians appointed Gedaliah, a Judean, as governor (with his residence at Mizpah); after the murder of Gedaliah a group of Judeans fled to Egypt (2 Kgs 25:22ff.; Jer 40ff.).

The external losses of many kinds were spiritually profitable, because the period of exile became one of uncommon literary productivity. Lamentations (and Pss 44; 74; 79; 89:38ff.; Isa 63:7ff.; etc.) grieved over the situation in the country. The Deuteronomistic school was at work there: it conceived the Deuteronomistic history as a kind of confession of guilt, and it transmitted and edited the tradition of the prophets, especially of Jeremiah. The Priestly document, on the other hand, originated in the exile, where the prophets Ezekiel and Second Isaiah (Isa 40–55) exercised their ministry.

The power centers of the ancient Near East had up to this point been in Egypt and Mesopotamia; but from about 550 B.C. on world dominion passed to new forces that penetrated the ancient Near Eastern world from outside. First, for a full two hundred years, it passed to the Persians.

The last Babylonian ruler, Nabonidus, who had opposed the priests of Marduk in Babylon and promoted the cult of the moon-god Sin (in Haran), resided for ten years in the oasis city of Tema in the North Arabian wilderness and left the business of government in the hands of his son Belshazzar, who, in the legendary story told in Dan 5, is regarded as the last king of the Babylonians before the Persians took power.

The brilliant rise of the Persian Cyrus (559–530) was in three stages: the establishment of a Medean-Persian empire (with Ecbatana as its capital); the subjugation of Asia Minor through victory over Croesus, king of Lydia; and, finally, entrance into Babylon (539 B.C.). The second of these three events seems to be reflected in the message of the exilic prophet Second Isaiah (see §21,1).

The early kings of Persia respected the traditions of the subject peoples and promoted the indigenous cults. It is in keeping with this outlook and attitude that after only a year (538) Cyrus ordered the rebuilding of the temple in Jerusalem and the return of the temple furnishings that had been carted off to Babylon. Ezra 6:3–5 (see §12b) preserves his edict in Aramaic, which was the official language for the western part of the Persian empire and was increasingly replacing Hebrew as the language of the people.

The return of the exiles themselves took place only gradually and in waves (according to Ezra 2, under Zerubbabel; according to 7:12ff., under Ezra; cf. 4:12). Many stayed behind in foreign parts, where they had prospered economically. The rebuilding of the temple was completed, at the urging of the prophets Haggai and Zechariah (see §22), only in 520–515 B.C.

In the time of Cyrus, Sheshbazzar was charged with returning the temple furnishings to Jerusalem; he is also supposed to have laid the foundations of the new temple (Ezra 5:14ff.; 1:7ff.). Like Zerubbabel, whose activity came a little later and who was a grandson of King Jehoiachin (banished in 597), Sheshbazzar was a Persian official. Messianic hopes were set on Zerubbabel (Hag 2:23ff.; Zech 6:9ff.), but these were not fulfilled.

The fifth and fourth centuries are a rather obscure period, in which only a few individual events stand out. Around 450 B.C. Ezra and Nehemiah—the former through commitment to a strict observance of the Law, the latter by building the walls of Jerusalem—endeavored to consolidate the community internally and externally; but the price they paid for it was a harsh limitation of membership (for details, see §12b). At about the same time the prophet Malachi must have exercised his ministry (§22,4).

After two hundred years of Persian domination (539–333 B.C.) Alexander the Great inaugurated the Hellenistic period with his victory at the battle of Issus (333). After the death of Alexander (323), as a result of the quarrels of the Diadochoi ("successors"), Palestine became for a century part of the (Egyptian) realm of the Ptolemies (301–198); it then became part of the (Syrian) kingdom of the Seleucids (198–64 B.C.).

An outstanding event that followed upon the accession of the Seleucid King Antiochus IV Epiphanes was the revolt of the Maccabees, who wanted to expel foreign cults. The book of Daniel (§24) came into existence shortly before the rededication of the temple in 164 B.C.

In 64 B.C. Palestine fell under Roman control. In A.D. 70 Jerusalem and the temple were destroyed a second time, and after the rebellion of Simon bar Kokhba (A.D. 132–135) Jews were no longer allowed to enter the city, which became known as Aelia Capitolina.

§3

ASPECTS OF SOCIAL HISTORY

An understanding of OT traditions requires from time to time that we have a certain basic knowledge of their social background. For example: What was the life of the patriarchs like? On what social conditions are the indictments of the prophets based?

On the other hand, the Bible presupposes rather than describes the social situation at each period, since it has no direct interest in this situation as such. Its concern is rather the history of God's dealings with Israel. What is obvious does not have to be explicitly mentioned or described. This means that we must get at the social situation—usually with great effort—by using very diverse and indirect evidences, as well as comparisons, for which a basis is occasionally provided. In consequence, the results obtained by research are often uncertain and turn out to be quite diverse, even in dealing with basic problems. The following survey, which is divided according to the periods of Israelite history, is intended to sketch only a few problem areas.

a) The Nomadic Clans

Israel's ancestors lived in tents or common encampments and moved from place to place (Gen 13:3; 18:1ff.; 31:25, 33f.; cf. 32:1; etc.).

To "pitch" a tent (12:8; 26:15; 33:19) meant to stay at a place for a while; conversely, to "pull up" (the tent-pegs) meant to "start out," "journey on" (12:9; 33:12; and often). Even centuries after the settlement the cry "Every man to his tent!" still echoed and meant a return home (Judg 7:8; 1 Sam 4:10; 2 Sam 20:1, 22; 1 Kgs 12:16; etc.).

1. Israel's ancestors were stock breeders, but, unlike the Arabian Bedouin down to our own day, they did not herd camels. The only camel-riding warriors were the Midianites, who made predatory raids into Israel (Judg 6:5; 7:12; cf. Gen 37:25; also 1 Sam 30:17 on the Amalekites). The patriarchs lived rather as seminomads, with and by means of their flocks of sheep and goats (ṣōʾn, "small livestock"; see Gen 30:31ff.). From the skins of these animals they made their dark

29

brown tents (Song 1:5). The beast used for carrying burdens (Gen 22:3, 5; 42:26f.; 45:23; Exod 23:5; etc.) and for riding (Exod 4:20; Num 22:22ff.; even Zech 9:9) was the ass; only in isolated cases was the camel used (Gen 31:17, 34; 24:10ff.), but camels were not yet being bred in herds. The keeping of cattle, at least on an extensive scale, was made possible only by the settlement.

The raising of sheep and goats called for a special (less warlike) manner of life. Unlike camels, sheep and goats cannot cover such long distances, and they need regular resting places with adequate water and forage. Such herds live only on the edge of the desert and in the rainy steppe.

What the OT calls "wilderness," "steppe" (*midbār*) is a region which, though poor in water, is not completely waterless, that is, does not completely lack springs, cisterns (Gen 16:7; 36:24; 37:22), and rainfall. Here and there a bush or a tree can prosper (1 Kgs 19:4), and sheep and goats can on occasion find pasture (Exod 3:1; 1 Sam 17:28).

The few watering places were the object of frequent conflicts (Gen 26:20f.; 21:25; 13:7; Exod 2:17ff.), but they were also natural meeting places (Gen 24:11ff.; 29:2ff.; Exod 2:15ff.). Justice was even administered at oases (see Gen 14:7; cf. Exod 18).

In addition, the lives of the seminomads seem to have been controlled by transhumance, that is, the regular twice-yearly shift from steppe to arable land and back again. During the rainy period in the winter they remained on the steppe, and in the summer, after the steppe had dried up, they migrated to the cultivated areas where the fields had already been harvested and were now available for grazing.

Because the seminomads traveled back and forth between the fringes of the arable lands and these lands themselves, they were also in closer contact with the rural population; trade and intermarriage were possible (see Gen 34; 38). In fact, Israel's ancestors were apparently already in transition from a seminomadic life to a sedentary life in which they would till the fields and raise cattle (26:12; 33:19; 23 P). It is hardly accidental that most of the stories about the patriarchs have the arable land for their locale, while the promise of possession of a land leaves its mark throughout (12:7; 28:13; etc.).

2. It was barely possible for an individual to survive alone in the hard living conditions of steppe or desert. Consequently, people lived in groups that had to be large enough to support and defend themselves, but not too large, so that they could still find water sufficient for their needs. In any case, nomadic communities differed greatly in size. If one tries to reduce the terminology of the OT, which is by no means fixed, to some sort of unity, one can recognize a division that regulated

communal life until far into the time when Israel had become a sedentary people (Josh 7:14; 1 Sam 10:19ff.; 9:21):

Individual

"House," that is, household
After the settlement this became the term used for the family, with the father of the house at its head. He had tutelary and legal authority (see Gen 38:24ff.; 42:37; 16:5f.; 19:8; Exod 21:7; Judg 19:24; restricted in Deut 21:18ff.). For this reason the household is called also "the father's house."

Clan

The clan was governed by the elders of the clan, probably the heads of families, and seems to have provided a thousand men capable of military service (Mic 5:2; 1 Sam 8:12; 23:23; Judg 6:15).

Tribe

The basic community was not the tribe but the (extended) family. Such a family—perhaps even in the nomadic period, but certainly later on—could embrace three to four generations: wife and secondary wives (1 Sam 1:1f.; Judg 19:1f.; 8:30), married sons, their children and perhaps grandchildren, any unmarried daughters (Num 30:4), and finally sisters and brothers of the father of the house (see Deut 25:5; Ps 133:1; on the family as a whole see Lev 18; Deut 27:20ff.).

The well-known threat in the Decalogue, "I the Lord your God am a jealous God, visiting the iniquity of the fathers upon the children to the third and fourth generation" (Exod 20:5; 34:7; etc.), probably had such an extended family in mind. Its members necessarily experienced and had to bear the blows of destiny together. The promise that follows the threat, "but showing steadfast love to thousands [i.e., of generations]," far transcends the historical reality of the family at any given moment.

The extended family, which was an economic, legal, and religious community, was "a group constituted by blood kinship, in which duties and tasks are regulated for the protection of all members of the community; it is a group, therefore, in which solidarity and mutual responsibility are dominant values; the family property (herds, later land), which is managed by the patriarch, is for the profit and sustenance of all, while the rules and prohibitions established by the father of the family are meant to secure the peaceful coexistence of all" (W. Thiel).

3. The family, the clan, the tribe, and even the people as a whole regarded themselves as the "sons" of a "father," that is, the ancestor of the group, the first ancestor long ago, or some eponymous ancestor (Jer 35:16). The group felt itself to be personified by or incorporated

into this individual (corporate personality). While the tribe was usually the widest possible group based on blood kinship, in the case of Israel this group was the people (see, e.g., Exod 1:1ff., or the lists of tribes in Num 1:26).

Whatever may have been the historical processes by which a nomadic group came into existence or underwent change, the group explained its union and its origin by means of a blood kinship (often fictive)—and this over a period of time. That is, it explained these genealogically. The family tree set forth the unity (the relation between individual and community) and the history of the group.

4. Within the group there was solidarity, and the individual enjoyed protections and rights. There was no higher legal authority. In dealing with outsiders a strict order was observed: the *ius talionis* (law of talion) in cases of bodily harm, according to which retaliation in kind was sought (Exod 21:23ff.; Lev 24:18ff.; also Deut 19:21), and the vendetta in cases of slaying (Num 35:9ff.; Deut 19; 2 Sam 21; etc.). "We are dealing here with a legal norm that was valid in the dealings of individual communities with one another, that is, with an inter-clan law" (V. Wagner, p. 14).

Originally no distinction was made between intentional and unintentional killing (see the addition in Exod 21:13f., compared with the older principle in 21:12). Such an approach, which from the viewpoint of the individual was a horrible one, made sense from the standpoint of the group. The vendetta compensated for what had been lost, so that a balance of power was maintained among the groups following the nomadic way of life. No group was to be allowed, deliberately or indeliberately, to gain superiority over the others. The vendetta thus served ultimately to protect the group and the individual (see Gen 4:14f.).

The individual may have had no rights, but hospitality was shown to strangers (Gen 18f.; Exod 2:20f.; Judg 19:16ff.), and the law governing guests included protection of them.

The overall result of this way of thinking and living was that long after the nomadic age the community continued to take priority, as it were, over the individual. The individual had to emerge gradually from the community (see Ezek 18).

b) Ownership of Land

With the settlement, nomads turned into farmers and villagers. Even in cases in which a whole clan settled in a place or several clans established a colony together, relations with neighbors gradually became stronger than relations with blood relatives. The territorial context was superimposed on, or even suppressed, the clan structure.

1. Real estate became the basis for the existence of clan or family, while at the same time it assured the social position of the free individual (see Mic 2:2: "a man—his house—his inherited property"). He therefore had to have a piece of farmland adequate to supply the necessities of life. In addition, there was probably property owned in common. It is uncertain whether originally the land belonged more or less in its entirety to the group (common land, common pasture) and at regular intervals was divided by lot among the heads of families; a casting of lots for the division of land is reported by the OT only as a one-time act, not as a regularly recurring ritual (Josh 14:2; 18:6, 8; Ezek 45:1; etc.; also Mic 2:5; Ps 16:5f.).

The inheritance went chiefly to the firstborn son (Deut 21:17). Was it possible in earlier times for the father to transfer the right of the firstborn to another son (Gen 48; cf. 49:3ff.; 25:31ff.)? In any case, inherited landed property was inalienable according to Israelite law, which in this respect differed from Canaanite law (Gen 23; 2 Sam 24; 1 Kgs 16:24); the owner could not dispose of it as he wished. Perhaps he could not even lease it out; at the very least he could not sell it (1 Kgs 21; cf. Deut 27:17; etc.).

By its nature the "(family) inheritance" (*naḥălâ*) "of an individual was in any case an ownership of land for his use, which came to him by way of inheritance and thus was distinct from landed property which was acquired by purchase, barter, foreclosure, etc.; it was also distinct from the share in communal land that one might acquire. . . . It is clear from Jer 32 and Lev 25 that the clan had the right of first refusal or redemption when there was question of some kind of alienation (through sale or foreclosure)" (F. Horst, in *Festschrift W. Rudolph*, 1961, pp. 148–49).

Finally, God himself may have been regarded as the owner (Lev 25:23), who at a point in historical time gave the land to the immigrants as an inheritance (see Deut 12:10; Ps 78:55). It did not belong to them from the nature of things and therefore could not be taken for granted.

Israelites acknowledged God's sovereignty over the land by transferring the best of its products, the firstfruits of the animals and of the harvest, to God or the sanctuary (Exod 22:29f.; 23:19; 34:19ff.); the human firstborn was bought back from God (34:20).

2. After the settlement the elders of the clan became the "elders of the place," the free, property-owning citizens who had to make the important decisions in matters of domestic and "foreign" policy (Judg 11:5ff.; 1 Sam 30:26ff.; 2 Sam 3:17; 5:3; 19:11; Ruth 4; cf. Exod 18:12;

24:1, 9; etc.). "Full citizens are those men who occupy their own property, who do not stand under any kind of tutelage and can claim the four great rights—marriage, cult, war, and administration of law" (L. Köhler, p. 134).

The elders were probably the heads of the clans. They were the most prominent sector or representatives of the "men," who, once again, were the full citizens who had legal competency and were capable of bearing arms. These are the people often meant when reference is made to "a man" (Exod 21:12ff.; 1 Sam 11:1, 9f., 15; 2 Sam 2:4; etc.).

Many OT juridical principles and even the ethical part of the Ten Commandments in their still accessible original form (see 9b1) have their origin in this manner of life. Family, freedom, life, and the economic basis for the existence of the free man were protected by the prohibitions against adultery, against the stealing of human beings (Exod 21:16), against deadly blows (21:12; Deut 27:24), and against the coveting of another's "house" (Deut 5:21, the reference being primarily to land and soil). In this ancient understanding of things, women, children, and slaves (captured in war or gotten through trade) were regarded more or less as the "property" of the man (see Exod 20:17).

3. It is not accidental that the prohibition against false testimony in court occurs in this same context of the protection provided for the existence of the free man (Exod 20:16; cf. 23:1ff.; Deut 27:25); for the administration of justice was likewise initially the business of free citizens. Professional judges, officials appointed by the king, make their appearance only at a later time (16:18; etc.; see Macholz). The men of the clan acted both as witnesses and as judges, that is, primarily as arbitrators in disputes, when they gathered "at the gate" to form a court (Ruth 4:1f.; Jer 26; Deut 21:19; 22:15ff.; Amos 5:10, 15; Lam 5:14).

The "gate" means simply the actual passageway that formed the gate of a town or else a small square directly in front of the gate on the inner side, where people could gather (Prov 31:23; cf. Jer 15:17) and also make purchases (2 Kgs 7:1).

The blessing "May the Lord protect your going out and your coming in" (Ps 121:8; cf. Deut 28:5) probably has reference to activity at the city gate. "Going out and coming in" refer to the farmer's going out to his field in the morning and his return from it in the evening; thus it means the day's work (see Ps 104:23).

In this kind of administration of justice those persons were at a disadvantage who did not enjoy the legal protection afforded "men" and did not themselves have legal competency. This accounts for the OT emphasis on not oppressing widows, orphans, and foreigners dwelling in the country (Exod 22:21f.; 23:6ff.; Deut 27:19; 24:17; Lev 19:33f.; Isa 1:17, 23).

c) Changes Brought by the Monarchy

Like the settlement, the coming of the monarchy wrought a gradual but profound change in society and the economy. It caused this change in both direct and indirect ways; by "indirect" is meant specifically the incorporation of the Canaanite cities into Israel and the growing foreign influence.

1. The monarchy added to the tribal structure an administrative entity that embraced the population as a whole (see, e.g., the census in 2 Sam 24:1f.). The raising of the taxes and duties needed for the support of the court and the army meant the need for civil servants, who were doubtless trained in schools (see §27,2).

Three lists (2 Sam 8:16–18; 20:23–25; 1 Kgs 4:2–6; cf. 4:7ff.) enumerate the upper-level civil and military officials in the time of David and Solomon: (high) priests (at the national sanctuary), recorder or scribe (secretary of state; see 2 Kgs 12:10), herald, chief of the levy and chief of the mercenaries, overseer of forced labor, a "friend of the king" (probably an adviser) and someone "in charge of the house," that is, the steward of the palace who may at the same time have been administrator of the crown lands (see 2 Kgs 15:5; Isa 22:15ff.).

2. The conscript army was called up from among the free farmers only when need arose; these men had to provide their own arms and were paid out of booty taken (see Isa 9:3). The conscript army gradually lost its importance with the rise of the standing army. There may have already been the beginnings of a mercenary force in the time of Saul (see 1 Sam 14:52); in any case David formed one (22:2; 27:2; 2 Sam 5:6; see also the Cherethites and Pelethites as the king's bodyguard, 2 Sam 8:18; etc.). From Solomon's time on it was supplemented by a corps of war chariots (1 Kgs 4:26ff.; 9:17ff.; 10:28f.; cf. 1:5; 2 Sam 15:1; 1 Sam 8:11f.).

3. The course of time saw the development, alongside the landed property of the free Israelite, of crown lands (domains), which constantly increased in extent and were augmented by the taking over of property that had become ownerless, by purchase and in other ways (1 Sam 8:12, 14; 22:7; 1 Kgs 21:2, 15f.; 2 Kgs 8:3ff.; 1 Chr 27:27f.; 2 Chr 26:10). The crown lands were a source of supplies for the court, of rewards for the (professional) army, and of fiefs for civil servants.

4. David perhaps (2 Sam 20:24), Solomon certainly (1 Kgs 4:6; etc.)

obliged the foreign (9:20ff.) and even the indigenous (5:13) population to supply forced labor, especially for construction (such as Israel had had to supply in Egypt, Exod 1:11). The obligation of statute labor is to be distinguished from enslavement. A slave could belong to a private individual and be sold, whereas forced labor profited the king or the common good, was perhaps only temporary, and in any case was for a particular purpose.

In many of these new phenomena, such as the establishment of a civil service or the subjection of the people to forced labor, foreign models were exerting their influence on Israel. The powers that the king might claim (probably on the basis of Canaanite practices) are shown in the polemical "privilege of the king" (1 Sam 8:11-17): "He will take" the sons for (lower) positions in the army, the management of the royal lands, and the manufacture of implements; the daughters "to be perfumers and cooks and bakers" for the royal household; "the best of your fields and vineyards and olive orchards" to provide for his officials; and tithes as taxes. How far the discretionary power of the king actually extended in the concrete must, however, remain an open question (see Deut 17:16; 1 Sam 22:7; 1 Kgs 9:22; 21; Amos 7:1).

In addition, there was no uniformity at all times and places during the period of the monarchy. Thus there were certain differences between city and countryside, in the south especially between the city of Jerusalem and the land of Judah. The dominant classes among the rural population, which in the OT is called the "people of the land" (ʿam hāʾāreṣ)—classes made up of propertied citizens possessing full civil rights—sometimes intervened forcefully in politics and in the process remained loyal to the Davidic dynasty (2 Kgs 11:14ff.; 14:21; 21:24; 23:30; cf. 15:19f.; also §17,1).

d) Social Contrasts in the Time of the Major Prophets

As a result of this development, the period of the monarchy saw the gradual development of social distinctions. The process seems to have speeded up in the eighth century B.C. These differences took the form of contrasts between poor and rich that had been unknown to such a degree in the more homogeneous society of the nomadic age or even in the early period after the settlement (see already 1 Sam 25:2; 2 Sam 19:32).

1. There were indeed certain social safeguards and legal prescriptions that sought to maintain the economic and social equality of the

members of the people of God, and in fact these probably worked for
a time. There were, for example:

(a) the fact that inherited property could not be sold (see 1 Kgs 21);

(b) the right and duty of near relatives to "redeem," that is, buy
back landed property and thus preserve it for the rest of the family
(Ruth 4; Jer 32:6ff.; Lev 25:24ff.);

(c) release after seven years from enslavement due to debts (Exod
21:1ff.; Deut 15:12ff.) or the demand in Lev 25 that in a jubilee year,
that is, every fiftieth year, land and soil that had been bought should
be given back and people enslaved for debt should be released (to what
extent was this regulation put into practice?);

(d) the prohibition against charging interest (see Exod 22:25; Deut
23:19f.; Lev 25:35ff.);

(e) and in general the various demands for care of the poor (Lev
19:9ff.; Ruth 2:9, 14ff.; etc.).

2. In the new conditions created by the monarchy and urbanization,
however, such remedies were inadequate. The monarchy, with its
political, military, economic, cultic, and legal jurisdictions, made it
possible for concentrations of power to arise at central locations,
especially in the capitals (Jerusalem, Samaria). As a result, the center
of gravity shifted to the cities, which were the workplaces not of the
rural peasantry but of tradespeople and where, quite early it seems,
the crafts and businesses each had their special streets (Jer 37:15; cf.
1 Kgs 20:34). The king's civil service, which collected the taxes and
were rewarded with crown lands, grew into a new upper class.

The change in the social structure seems also to have had an "ethnic"
aspect, for in this change the Canaanite social and economic order
replaced that of ancient Israel. In Canaanite society there had long
been a more rigid stratification of society, as well as a preeminence
given to trade, city life, and large estates. Since the reigns of David
and Solomon the originally non-Israelite population of the cities had
been incorporated into the state, so that at least from that point on
nomadic and indigenous traditions were intermingled in the social
structure. In the northern kingdom of the eighth century this general
development may have been speeded up by an economic upswing
made possible by a favorable situation in relation to other nations
(2 Kgs 14:25).

With the growth of commerce and communication, buildings became
more splendid (Amos 3:15; 5:11; 6:4, 8; Isa 5:9). In violation of the
prescription in Exod 22:25, rich landowners made loans to simple
farmers and demanded interest so high that the farmers could not pay

their debt; this practice was made easier by the shift from a barter economy to a money economy (initially a weight of precious metal: Exod 21:32; 22:17; Hos 3:2; etc.).

"The rich rules over the poor, and the borrower is the slave of the lender" (Prov 22:7). The dependence created by debt led to the pawning of possessions or the sale of land. This meant the accumulation of properties by a few people (Isa 5:8; Mic 2:2; in contrast Ezek 47:14). The loss of land brought to the former owner the life of a day laborer (see Lev 19:13; 25:39f.; Deut 24:14) or even of a slave to a creditor (2 Kgs 4:1; Amos 2:6; see earlier, 1 Sam 22:2; 12:3; later, Neh 5). The poor, who in earlier times had been few, now became the majority. The loss of social position brought with it the loss of legal rights (see Exod 23:3, 6f.).

"The legal assembly is perfect so long as it is the assembly of free, independent peasants, each approximately equal in possessions, whose affairs it settles justly in such a way as to preserve the life of the community. But the eighth century . . . shows a marked shift in economic circumstances and the beginning of a distinct stratification of Hebrew society. Beside the possessors of property we find those who have no possessions; beside independent citizens we find dependents. At this point the legal assembly fails. The oral and public nature of its conduct of affairs presupposes that each assessor can speak what he thinks right, independently of the others. But fear of those who have economic power and who can do real harm in the narrow common life of the village makes men subservient and lacking in independence" (L. Köhler, p. 142).

3. Oversimplifying greatly, we may say that at least four strata had to be distinguished within the people of Israel: (1) the officials (civil and military), tradesmen and craftsmen, who lived chiefly in the cities; (2) free property owners in the rural areas; (3) the people without property, the poor (a group that included to a greater or lesser extent widows, orphans, and foreigners); and (4) unfree slaves.

Slaves (the institution was taken for granted in the ancient Near East) belonged to their masters and could be sold (see Exod 21; developed in Deut 15:12ff.; 23:15f.). But their situation as individuals need not have been a hard one: they could, for example, practice their religion (Exod 20:10; 12:44; Deut 12:18; etc.) or undertake honorable tasks (Gen 24; cf. 15:2). Moreover, the notion of "slave" was not limited to a particular stratum of the population; for example, high-ranking officials were regarded as "slaves" (ministers) of the king.

e) The Postexilic Situation

With the conquest of Jerusalem and the beginning of the exile the civic and political organization of Israel collapsed. What was left or what arose to fill the void was more familial in structure: on the one hand, the "father's house," a kind of extended family (Ezra 1:5; 2:59f., 68; 4:2f.; 10:16; etc.) and, on the other, the institution of "the elders," who regained the importance they had lost long ago (Jer 29:1; Ezek 8:1; 14:1; 20:1ff.; Ezra 5:9; 6:7; 10:8, 14; etc.).

The upper level of government was in the hands of Persian officials (Neh 2:7f., 16; 5:7, 14f.; Dan 3:2f.; see §12b). Israel formed a community that had the second temple for its center, lived by the Law, and enjoyed independence in matters of religion and worship. At the head of the community stood the high priest, who was even assigned the emblems of royalty (Exod 28; Zech 6:9f.).

Jerusalem was the cultic center of the affiliated communities in the worldwide Diaspora. Moreover, not only did Israel live in spatial apartness; it also began to split internally into various groups (in NT times: Pharisees, Sadducees, Essenes, etc.). But under these conditions the faith of Israel became a hope for the world (Zeph 2:11; Zech 14:9, 16; Dan; etc.).

PART II

TRADITIONS AND DOCUMENTARY SOURCES OF THE PENTATEUCH AND THE HISTORICAL BOOKS

§4

THE PENTATEUCH

a) Name and Structure

In Hebrew the five books of Moses are called *Torah* (or "Torah of Moses," or similar titles), a term that is translated more accurately as "instruction" than as "law." "Torah" meant initially an individual admonition from parents (Prov 1:8; 4:3f.; etc.) or the instruction given by a priest in a concrete case (Hag 2:11ff.). Only later did the term acquire the general meaning of a "law(book)" that included all the ordinances and was connected with the name of Moses (Josh 8:31; 23:6; 2 Kgs 14:6; etc.). The definitive extension of the word to include all five books of Moses is probably not yet attested in the OT, though it is in the NT (Matt 5:17; etc.).

The Greek and Latin name *pentateuchus*, "(the book kept) in five containers" reflects the ancient custom of writing down lengthier texts not in books but on rolls of papyrus or leather and keeping these in their own receptacles. Since a roll was manageable only if limited to a certain size, a division of the complete work (the Torah) was probably necessary. The division into five parts must have been made at a relatively early date, since it is found already in the Septuagint or Greek translation of the OT (third century B.C.). This later occasioned a similar division of the Psalter into five books.

Analogously formed names such as Tetrateuch (four books: Genesis–Numbers) or Hexateuch (six books: Genesis–Deuteronomy and Joshua) reflect particular theories about the original extent and thus the origin as well of the work in question. The idea of a "hexateuch" is based on the view that the book of Joshua is required to bring the "pentateuch" to a real conclusion. The term "tetrateuch," on the other hand, presupposes—with justification—that the fifth book of Moses enjoys a certain independence in relation to the complex formed by the first four.

The Pentateuch is characterized by a close interweaving of narratives and commandments. In the beginning, the narrative style is predominant, with cultic ordinances being introduced here and there (Gen 9;

43

17; Exod 12), but the sections of laws predominate from Exod 20 on. But these laws are not understood in a timeless way; they remain embedded in a historical context and form part of Israel's historical self-understanding.

The five books as a whole are held together by certain themes that run throughout, such as the motif of blessing and promise (Gen 1:28; 9; 12; 15; 17f.; Exod 3; 6; Deut 7:12ff.; etc.). There are also constant references backward and forward, as decisive events are announced in words from the Lord (Gen 15:13ff.; 46:3f.; Exod 3:12, 19ff.; etc.) or retrospectively summarized in confessional statements (Num 20:15f.; Deut 6:20ff.; 26:5ff.; etc.).

The overall history embraces the period from creation and the rise of the nations, through the age of the patriarchs and the sojourns in Egypt and at the mountain of God, down to the beginning of the settlement, when Moses dies in East Jordan within sight of the Promised Land (Deut 34). This historical sequence can be roughly divided into five main sections, which also define the major complexes of traditions (see §4b5).

Gen 1–11	Prehistory	
	1–3	Origin of the world and humanity Irruption of sin
	4	Cain
	5; 11	Genealogies
	6–9	Flood
	10	Table of nations
	11	Tower of Babel
Gen 12–50	History of the patriarchs	
	12–25	Abraham (Lot)
	26	Isaac
	27–36	Jacob (Esau, Laban)
	37–50	Joseph and his brothers
Exod 1–15	Liberation from Egypt	
	1; 5	Israel at forced labor
	2	Moses' youth and
	3–4; 6	Calling
	7–13	Plagues and Passover
	14-15	Rescue at the sea
Exod 19–Num 10:10	Revelation at Sinai (key parts: Exod 19–24; 32–34)	
	Exod 19	Theophany
	20	Decalogue
	21–23	Book of the Covenant

24	Ratification of the covenant
25–31	Instruction for building the tabernacle
35–40	Carrying out the instructions
32	Golden calf
34	Cultic decalogue
Lev 1–7	Laws for sacrifice
8–9	Investiture of priests (8) and first sacrifice (9)
	Offense of Nadab and Abihu
11–15	Rules of purity
16	Ritual for the day of atonement
17–26	The law of holiness

Israel led through the wilderness

Exod 16–18	From Egypt to Sinai	
	Exod 16	Manna and quails (cf. Num 11)
	17	Water from the rock (Num 20); victory over the Amalekites
	18	Meeting with Jethro

Num 10–36	From Sinai to Moab	
(Deut 31–34)	Num 12	Mutiny of Aaron and Miriam
	13f.	Reconnaissance
	16f.	Rebellion of Korah, Dathan, and Abiram
	22–24	Balaam

The theme of occupation or settlement is only alluded to in passing in the Pentateuch (Num 13f.; 32–34) and is developed later on outside the Pentateuch (Josh 1ff.; Judg 1). The promise that Israel will become a people is already fulfilled in the book of Exodus; the promise of possession of a land is fulfilled only in the book of Joshua.

Only in one case does the division of the Pentateuch into five books coincide with the division in terms of theme and tradition history. In Hebrew the books are, as a rule, named after their opening words, but the Greek and Latin names refer in each case to an important event or the main content. The division between the books of Genesis ("origin") and Exodus ("departure") coincides with the passage from the family history of the patriarchal age to the national history of the time of Moses. In contrast, the comprehensive presentation of Israel's sojourn at Sinai is twice interrupted. After completion of the tabernacle (Exod 25–31; 35–40) the book of Leviticus introduces all sorts of

"Levitical (i.e., priestly) ordinances." The information about the census and the organization of the encampment at the beginning of the book of Numbers prepares for the departure from Sinai. Finally, Deuteronomy ("second law"), apart from its containing narrative parts (31–34), is Moses' farewell address and forms a separate unit that includes a further collection of laws (see §10).

b) Stages and Problems of Pentateuchal Scholarship

The approaches and methods of biblical exegesis—literary criticism, form criticism, tradition history, and so on—have generally proved their worth first in connection with the Pentateuch, before being applied to the gospels. As a result, Pentateuchal scholarship has exerted an influence outside its own sphere. The following brief sketch is intended simply as a survey of the principal stages of scholarship and the principal problems raised. A comprehensive survey from the vantage point of the present day would have to do more than consider the problems recognized in the past. Even if in altered form and with limited application the suggested solutions retain a certain value.

1. Criticism of Moses' Authorship

The starting point of all critical reflection was the Judeo-Christian tradition that held Moses to be the author of the Pentateuch. The OT itself ascribes parts of the Pentateuch to Moses, for example, certain laws (see Exod 24:4; 34:27f.) or Deuteronomy (see Deut 31:9, 22ff.), but not the entire work. The ascription of the whole to him is explicitly made only in the first century A.D. in Philo and Josephus and was later accepted by the Christian Church. The NT already uses the name "Moses" to refer to the Pentateuch; it cites the latter as "the book of Moses" (Mark 12:26; etc.) or expressly says, "the law as given through Moses" (John 1:17; cf. Acts 13:39).

Doubts regarding the traditional view of the origin of the Pentateuch were already being expressed in the twelfth century by the Jewish scholar Ibn Ezra; in the Reformation period by Carlstadt; and later, in the seventeenth century, by T. Hobbes, B. Spinoza, R. Simon, and others. In addition to all sorts of other bits of information that became intelligible only in retrospect, that is, when looking back from the vantage point of Israel's residency in Palestine, an important argument was the notice about Moses' death (Deut 34:5f.). Did Moses predict the circumstances of his death, or did some later writer insert them? But did not this kind of historical skepticism also affect the doctrine of inspiration?

The disputes over Moses' authorship of the Pentateuch extended into the eighteenth century and in isolated instances far beyond it. They thus had long overlapped the discoveries of the sources of the Pentateuch. Once Moses could no longer be regarded as the author of the Books of Moses, the effort was made to retain him as legislator and in particular as author of the Decalogue.

2. Discovery and Delimitation of the Pentateuchal Sources

The shift from one to another of the two divine names—Elohim ("God") and Yahweh—had occasionally been noticed in antiquity, but Henning Bernhard Witter, a pastor at Hildesheim, was the first to use it as a way of distinguishing traditions in Gen 1–2 and to discover a separate source in Gen 1. But his publication of 1711 went unnoticed for two centuries.

The first scholar to exert an influence here was Jean Astruc, personal physician to Louis XV. On the basis of the divine name used he separated the whole of Genesis into two (or three) narrative strands. Thus the foundation was laid for literary criticism and increasingly detailed investigations of the matter during the next one and a half to two centuries.

a) *The (older) documentary hypothesis*. Several decades later Johann Gottfried Eichhorn turned to source analysis and carried the project through by showing the differences in style and content between the main sources. (With J. D. Michaelis as a precursor, Eichhorn's publication of his *Einleitung in das Alte Testament* [1780ff., Eng.: *Introduction to the Old Testament*] for practical purposes founded the discipline of OT introduction; at the same time Eichhorn achieved importance by introducing the concept of myth.) Both Witter and Astruc understood the sources they had worked out to be traditions that Moses had at hand; it was in fact only in the course of his life's work that Eichhorn himself came to renounce the hypothesis of Mosaic authorship of the Pentateuch.

Toward the end of the eighteenth century, in his book *Die Urkunden des jerusalemischen Tempelarchivs in ihrer Urgestalt* (1798, Eng.: *The Documents of the Jerusalem Temple Archives in Their Original Form*), Karl David Ilgen discovered a third documentary source, which used the same name for God as the first of the two sources already known. Now three documents or source writings were recognized: two spoke of Elohim and one of Yahweh. The great importance of the dissection of the part of the text that used the name Elohim into two further parts emerged only much later.

b) *The fragment hypothesis*. An increasing alertness to distinctive differences and an eye on the material outside of Genesis helped in the discovery of new documents—more or less independent and self-contained collections, which originated at various times and did not permit of being coordinated, at least in an obvious way, into sources that run throughout the entire work. Consequently, instead of documents, scholars around the year 1800 accepted the existence of widely varying, mutually independent portions of varying extent or, in other words, "fragments," which must have been combined into a continuous story only at a later time (A. Geddes, J. S. Vater, also W. M. L. de Wette).

As a matter of fact, the attempt to separate sources is far less successful for the book of Exodus than it is for Genesis. In particular, there is, even today, no generally accepted answer to the question of the origin of the collections of laws, such as the Decalogue, and their coordination with the documentary sources. Furthermore, the insight that the Pentateuch is made up of individual complexes takes on new meaning when scholars look back beyond the fixing of the text in writing to the oral prehistory of the text and of the complexes of traditions. In any case, without the distinction (made only later) between literary and oral transmission the fragment hypothesis cannot do justice to the longitudinal division of the Pentateuch as this emerges from a structural analysis of the whole or from the shifts in the divine names.

c) According to the *supplementary hypothesis,* which seeks to combine the two preceding solutions, there runs through the entire Pentateuch or Hexateuch (from creation to the occupation of Canaan) a basic document that uses the name Elohim for God (de Wette, H. G. A. Ewald, F. Bleek, F. Delitzsch, and others). The Decalogue and the Book of the Covenant, as well as a more recent document using the divine name Yahweh (and Elohim), were later added by a redactor.

This explanation, in modified form, has likewise been influential down to our day. The origin of the Pentateuch through a combination of individual source documents is easier to conceive if the documents were not mechanically interwoven, but rather if one document served as a basic source into which the others were then intercalated (see §5c).

With these three hypotheses we have in principle all the possible approaches to an explanation of the literary origin of the Pentateuch; the three were subsequently modified or combined.

3. Dating of the Documentary Sources

Once several sources were acknowledged in principle, the temporal relationship between them, especially between the more narrative and the more legislative texts, became a subject of study. A new phase began once there was general acceptance of an idea that had earlier been surmised and was finally put forth by W. M. L. de Wette in 1805: Deuteronomy (the fifth book of Moses) is an independent entity, a kind of special source of the Pentateuch, and is to be connected with the Josianic reform of 622 B.C. (2 Kgs 22f.; see §10a2). This position provided scholars with their first sure date and thus gave them a point of departure for comparison, especially between the legislative parts of the Pentateuch. Where is the centralization of cult, stated in Deuteronomy, presupposed elsewhere? Where do we see an earlier stage in which Israel still had a number of sanctuaries?

The insight into the special character of Deuteronomy was combined with the "new" documentary hypothesis (H. Hupfeld, 1853; A. Dillmann, and others), according to which the rest of the Pentateuch was composed (as the older documentary hypothesis of K. D. Ilgen had surmised) of three originally independent documentary sources. Thus, the division into four sources was essentially given in the basic form it has retained until our own day. But there was still another decisive turning point.

There was a radical change in the appraisal of the sources and therefore in the accepted picture of the history of Israel, when scholars accepted the view that the work regarded as the basic document (one using the divine name Elohim) was in fact the most recent of all the sources, namely, the Priestly document, which came into existence approximately during the exile. It took almost a half century (approximately 1830–1880) for this view, which is called the Reuss-Graf-Kuenen-Wellhausen hypothesis after its originators and chief representatives, to win the day. It was justified, first of all, by a comparison of the cultic ordinances in the Priestly document with the information on Israelite worship that is supplied in the other historical and prophetic books; only later were the narrative parts included in the picture (see §8a4). In the process it emerged that the Priestly document and with it the major part of the OT (cultic) ordinances are to be dated subsequent to the work of the great writing prophets; this realization is summed up in the short formula *lex post prophetas* (the law after the prophets). Because Wellhausen secured general acceptance of this hypothesis and thus projected a new vision of Israel's history, it has been possible to praise him as "the greatest German Old Testament scholar of the past" (R. Smend).

Since subsequent literary criticism has been essentially a continuation and emendation of the position already established by J. Wellhausen, the latter's principal relevant works can still be read with profit: *Die Composition des Hexateuchs* (1876f.; 1885, 1963⁴) and *Prolegomena zur Geschichte Israels*

(1883, 1923⁶, first published in 1878 as *Geschichte Israels I*, Eng.: *Prolegomena to the History of Ancient Israel*, 1885; reprinted 1957).

A comprehensive and at the same time detailed survey of the results of literary criticism that is still remarkable was provided by H. Holzinger, *Einleitung in das Hexateuch* (1893); for a more succinct presentation, C. Steuernagel, *Lehrbuch der Einleitung in das Alte Testament* (1912).

More recent approaches can be found in, for example, M. Noth, *Überlieferungsgeschichte des Pentateuch* (1960², pp. 17ff.; Eng.: *A History of Pentateuchal Traditions*, 1972, pp. 5ff.), or in the appendix of the volume *Wort und Botschaft des AT*, ed. by J. Schreiner (1975³).

4. Results and Still Open Questions of Literary Criticism

The final quarter of the last century saw the completion, for practical purposes, of the theory of literary relationships in the Pentateuch, which has in many ways proved its validity despite older and more recent challenges to it and which in all likelihood will continue to hold the field despite skeptical predictions. All sorts of modifications and complements have of course been offered, but radically new solutions of the Pentateuch problem either have not been proposed or have not been accepted. Despite all doubts the number and sequence of the documentary sources seems firmly established since Wellhausen's day; they are as follows, with the sigla regularly used for them and with the dates that are generally accepted:

J Yahwist	ca. 950 B.C.
	(time of Solomon, before the division of the kingdom in 926 B.C.)
E Elohist	ca. 800 B.C.
	(before the "writing prophets," especially Hosea)
D (original)	ca. seventh century B.C.
Deuteronomy	(beginnings of the Josianic reform in 622 B.C.; subsequent extensive expansions)
P Priestly document	ca. 550 B.C.
	(exile; expansions in the postexilic period)

It is highly likely that the Pentateuch was formed neither by a simple addition of documentary sources nor by a gradual enrichment of the oldest source. We must think rather that there were several redactions, which connected the originally independent individual sources in order to combine the different presentations of Israelite antiquity into a continuous picture. The process unavoidably entailed certain alterations, transpositions, and omissions, as well as additions.

It is uncertain how many stages were required for the final redaction; in principle, however, we must distinguish at least three redactions:

R^JE = the redaction that combined the oldest sources, J and E. This combination, which was made after the fall of the northern kingdom (722 B.C.), was so skillfully accomplished that in various sections it is impossible convincingly to distinguish J and E again. For this reason scholars since Wellhausen's time have even spoken of a Yehowist work, that is, Yahwist-Elohist, J/E (see §7a).

R^P = the (crucial) redaction, which in the postexilic period combined the Yehowist J/E with the Priestly document P, or, more accurately, incorporated J/E into P.

R^D(tr) = the redaction that introduced texts, sentences, and even parts of sentences that resemble Deuteronomy in choice of vocabulary, style, and themes, and thus combined the documentary sources with Deuteronomy or the Deuteronomistic history (Deuteronomy–Kings) (see 4b4e). Whether this redaction preceded or followed the incorporation of J/E into P is disputed (as indicated by the broken line in the following figure).

In greatly simplified form, the origin of the Pentateuch can be presented graphically by the following figure:

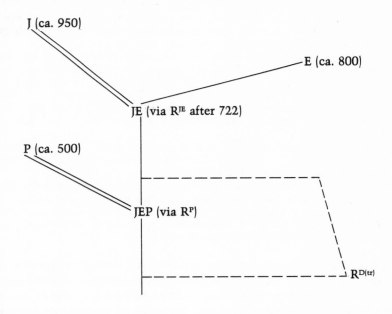

The works that stand at the beginning of a double line are in each case the basic documents into which another work (E into J) or already existing combination (JE into P) is incorporated.

It must be said, however, that the consensus created by Wellhausen seems to be disappearing today; the views being proposed today on the existence, extent, and time and place of origin of the documentary sources are widely divergent. Thus the results of literary-critical scholarship are being generally challenged.

If in our interpretation of the text we want to avoid bias and the seeking of results that are predetermined by a particular approach or conception, we must distinguish four methodological steps in literary criticism:

(1) *Analysis (separation).* As far as possible each text must be investigated on its own terms, with its lack of unity (doublets, joins) and its unity (structure, combinatory elements).

(2) *Synthesis (combination).* The parts of the text revealed by analysis must be carefully studied for their links with one another (agreement in vocabulary, themes, motifs, and intentions) and tested for their internal coherence (structure and course of the action, gaps, and irregularities that remain). The purpose of the study must be to reconstruct story lines that are as intelligible as possible, and that are coherent and internally comprehensible narratives or speeches—not fragments or splinters that could not have existed independently. Thus synthesis provides a kind of cross-check on analysis.

(3) *Comparison.* A further step is needed to combine the units thus elaborated with other (reconstructed) texts, so as to anchor the individual result securely in a larger context and at the same time to form more comprehensive continuities, whether within the more immediate context of the block of tradition or in the more inclusive documentary source.

Occasionally, of course, the criteria for distinction of sources or for the attribution of the text to a source prove inadequate; in these cases the sources of the Pentateuch may have been too fully welded together or the redactor may have played a greater part in giving the text its present form.

(4) *Explanation of the present combination of texts.* How and why were the reconstructed unities combined into the text as we now have it, and how is this text structured?

Literary criticism, therefore, starts with the text as given and returns to it by way of reconstruction. The aim must be to find a theory that explains both the unity and the lack of unity in the present text.

It is possible to avoid bias only if as many viewpoints as possible are taken into account in the study and all arguments are considered in a sympathetic approach to the special characteristic of each text. Finally, the preferred solution should be backed up by various and independent arguments of a linguistic and a material kind (convergence of criteria).

The principal reasons and criteria for distinguishing the sources of the Pentateuch are still doublets (of texts or parts of texts, of sentences, and possibly even parts of sentences) and the variation in the name or designation of God (Yahweh, Elohim). At times, of course, the text is merely using a set formula (e.g., Gen 32:28, "to struggle with God [or gods] and men"), or the theme requires the notion of God instead of the name of Yahweh (e.g., Gen 3:1ff., especially v. 5, "be like God").

But in most cases the variation in the divine name cannot be explained on material grounds. Other indications, such as contradictions, choice of vocabulary, stylistic and theological distinctions, serve to supplement and confirm the principal criteria.

The following figure shows in a rough way the concentrations of the three sources J, E, and P in the first half of Genesis. The broader contours of P show how the Priestly document serves as the framework (it does not show this document as having a greater scope); the sections marked off here with a broken line are those in which more than one source is used (as is the case more or less continuously from Gen 25 on).

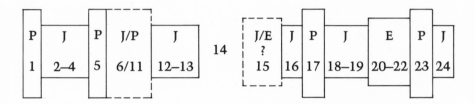

Certain texts that because of their difficulties require the reconstruction of two or even three parallel narratives can serve as typical examples of literary criticism:

Gen 6–9 with its variations in numerical data leads to the analysis of an older and a more recent narrative line (J, P); Gen 28:10ff. and Exod 3 are composed of two older lines (J, E), and Exod 14 probably of three (J, P, and E). The fact that the more recent line (P) in Exod 6 offers a distinct picture of Moses' vocation that is not incorporated into the older double story in Exod 3 shows that it represents not a phase of editorial work but an independent unity (documentary source) (see §8a2).

Only the Priestly and Deuteronomic-Deuteronomistic literatures have a clearly characteristic style. Consequently, it is easier to distinguish this later part of the Pentateuchal text—P and the Deuteronomistic revision—whereas the distinction of the older documentary sources is often less certain, especially from Exodus on. These older sources do not to the same degree have characteristic traits to distinguish them, although the differences are perceptible at times (e.g., Gen 20–22E).

Is literary criticism really worthwhile under these conditions? Are not its results too slight and too uncertain? But the task of literary criticism is not only to ascertain the extent and the time and place of origin of documentary sources; it is to discover their theological intention: What is the work trying to say within its situation? Since every textual statement is integrated into a context and changes as the context changes, it is not possible to extract its theological intention without taking into account its (original and subsequent) context. Consequently, the laborious work of literary criticism cannot be avoided, although it must be approached with caution.

The more recent, often tortuous, history of literary criticism from the turn of the century to the present has been marked by a great variety and range of opinions. There is no room here to trace its stages and its twists and turns. Instead I shall call attention to five problems (a–e) that involve important principles and are repeatedly raised from varying points of view.

a) Do the documentary sources that have been distinguished each form a unit or are there strata within the sources themselves?

In order to explain irregularities within the sources, scholars have dissected them in turn into several strands (especially J but also E and P). This has been done with varying degrees of success but, in the final analysis, without any generally accepted results. To what extent are the authors of the documentary sources collectors of preexisting traditions? To what extent do they arrange the material at will? Have the older sources (especially J) so thoroughly revised the material they pass on that the result has been a coherent unit in which gaps and contradictions are no longer found? At least within the sources incoherencies are to be explained by saying that they took over traditions that were already more or less firmly fixed and possibly written sources as well.

Furthermore, the most recent of the sources (P, but the same can be said of D) is in its present form the result of a lengthy process of growth and therefore the work of several authors. Finally, the literary works may have been supplemented by additions (special material).

The fact that as source analysis becomes more detailed it no longer wins general acceptance is due not only to the situation of the text itself but also to the working of a general law that applies also to literary criticism: The more extravagant and complicated a theory is, the more improbable it becomes. Conversely, the simpler a theory is (i.e., the more facts it explains with the fewest possible suppositions), the more probable it is. The three-source (J, E, P) theory therefore represents a limit beyond which theories become less valuable.

b) How are the common elements in the organization of the documentary sources to be explained?

Did the oldest source, J, give the material in the Pentateuch its fixed form? Did it arrange the major blocks of tradition in a continuous sequence (for example, the patriarchal and Sinai traditions)? Are the later sources dependent on J? It is more likely that the blocks of tradition had already been welded into a unity in the oral tradition, so that the outline of the Pentateuch was by and large already set for both of the older sources. On the one hand, J and E have so much in common in their structure and content that they could not have come into existence in complete independence of one another. On the other hand, as the actual wording shows, they are only loosely related to one another and therefore not directly dependent on one another.

It is true that more and more scholars are inclined to see a literary dependence of E on J, but in fact close contacts between the two are rare. H. Gunkel was right in saying "that there is no literary connexion between J and E; J has not copied from E, nor E from J. If both sources occasionally agree verbally the fact is to be explained on the basis of a common original source" (*Legends*, p. 127).
This conclusion is all the more justified since the two sources are from different geographical areas, J from the southern kingdom, E from the northern.

M. Noth, for example, postulates "a common basis (*Grundlage*, or G) for the two sources, from which both—independently of each other—have drawn the nucleus of the content" (*A History of Penta-teuchal Traditions*, p. 39). But even this assumption of an entity that is not directly accessible has not won universal acceptance and in fact has often been challenged in recent years. Yet it remains a sensible assumption, since it helps to explain both what is common and what is different in J and E. Noth leaves open the question of whether G was written or oral; it is likely, however, that it was a body of oral tradition in which individual traditions, groups of legends, and blocks of tradition had already been molded into the sequence of actions and events to which J and E later bear common witness.

There is disagreement on whether the later Priestly document shows a direct knowledge of the older documentary sources or (rather) only an indirect knowledge.

c) How is the strikingly different scope of the various documentary sources to be explained?

J. Wellhausen observed that the editors of the older sources followed the principle that J was to be taken as the basis and that E was to supply only "what was either not in J at all or not there in the same way" (*Composition*[3], p. 22). If this insight be taken as universally applicable, then by and large a combination of the documentary and supplementary hypotheses as proposed by M. Noth will prove correct. In the process of editing, one source provided the framework and the others were incorporated into this. Thus, the Yahwist provided the foundation, and this was supplemented from the Elohist; much later the combined J/E narrative was inserted into the overall framework provided by the Priestly document (see the diagram above). In this way the fragmentary character of E can be explained; on the other hand, there are occasional lacunae even in J and P.

d) Where are we to locate the end of the Pentateuchal sources?

Is it possible to follow one or more of the sources beyond the Pentateuch? On the one side, there are those who think they find the documentary sources continuing through the book of Joshua into the books of Kings. On the other, in keeping with the hypothesis mentioned in the preceding paragraph, M. Noth is of the opinion that since P ends with the report of Moses' death (Deut 34:7–9), any remaining part of the older sources was lost when these were incorporated into P. In this view, the problem of the Pentateuch becomes, for all practical purposes, the problem of the tetrateuch; apart from a few verses in Deut 34, Deuteronomy and the following historical books belong to another literary complex.

There is presently a great deal of discussion whether J and even P are or are not continued in the description given of the occupation or settlement in the book of Joshua.

e) How extensive is the part played by redaction in the formation of the Pentateuch?

The concept of redaction is not a new one. Its significance, however, has been newly realized and constitutes an important and disputed problem in contemporary discussion. Just as the interpretation of the prophetic message is determined largely by the delimitation of "authentic" material (§13a3), so too the appraisal of the (older) sources, the determination of their age, and especially the understanding of their theological intention depend on determining the part played by redaction or, to put it another way, on the attribution of textual material to the sources themselves.

It is not possible simply to assign all the material to the various sources; account must be taken of the part played by redaction. Thus, there are clearly recognizable additions to the older parts of the text; for example, "And the angel of the Lord called to Abraham a second time" (Gen 22:15–18; also Exod 4:13ff.; 19:3ff.; etc.).

In particular, certain parts of the text in which the themes and language resemble those of Deuteronomy or the Deuteronomistic literature pose a problem of literary criticism. Admittedly, bits of discourse in this style are not so extensive or evenly distributed throughout the Pentateuch as they are throughout Deuteronomy and the books of Kings (or even the book of Jeremiah). To this extent the situation is different in the Pentateuch. We do find, however, the addition of isolated observations of a Deuteronomic-Deuteronomistic kind (as in Gen 50:24; Exod 3:8, 17) and even of lengthier sections (as in Exod 13; 23:20ff.; 32:7ff.; 33; 34:10ff.; etc.). Such additions seem to increase, beginning with the call of Moses—but, then, the Deuteronomic-Deuteronomistic literature has a very special interest in Moses.

In this connection three questions especially remain open:

(1) Was the redactor who combined J and P one who had imbibed the spirit of Deuteronomy? In other words, does $R^{JE} = R^{D(tr)}$? It is more likely that the Deuteronomic-Deuteronomistic redaction represents a second and later phase in relation to the connecting of J and E, because, for stretches at least, the redactional elements can be detached from J/E without disturbing it.

In any case, it is necessary on methodological grounds to make distinctions even among the additions, in order that the Deuteronomistic share in the redaction may remain clearly demarcated.

(2) Do the additions lead toward Deuteronomy, that is, do they present us with a pre- or proto-Deuteronomic language (from the seventh century B.C.)? Or do they not rather belong to the exilic and postexilic periods? May we have to assume a redaction in several stages, reaching from a proto-Deuteronomic to the Deuteronomic proper? But is the linguistic evidence adequate for making such distinctions?

(3) How is the Deuteronomic-Deuteronomistic redaction connected with the incorporation of Deuteronomy into the Pentateuch? Did the two operations take place at the same time, or did the redaction presuppose the incorporation? At least on occasion the redaction reminds us more of the later strata of Deuteronomy or of Deuteronomistic texts.

Did Deuteronomy form the introduction to the Deuteronomistic history, so that for a time there was a single literary work stretching from Gen 2 to 2 Kings? And does the Deuteronomistic redaction of the Pentateuch still bear witness to such a work? Or did the coordination of Deuteronomy with the source strata, and therefore the Deuteronomic-Deuteronomistic redaction, come only after J/E had been combined with P? In any case, here and there even in the P sections there are parts showing Deuteronomistic language (e.g., Num 14:8; also in the Law of Holiness).

There is at present no agreement on whether the formation of the Pentateuch can be roughly summed up in the formula J–E–D–P or whether the formula should rather be J–E–P–D.

5. Form Criticism and Tradition History

A new stimulus to the understanding of the Pentateuch came from form-critical and tradition-historical research. This newer study does not replace literary criticism; rather it builds upon it, prolongs it, and in a measure also modifies it, since it looks back beyond the text as fixed in writing to the world of oral tradition.

H. Gunkel was the pioneer in this area. He applied this new approach (which was no less fruitful for an understanding of the psalms and prophetic texts) especially to Genesis (*Schöpfung und Chaos in Urzeit und Endzeit*, 1895; *Genesis*, 1910³), where he separated out the older individual sagas from the saga cycles (see §5b1). Gunkel's disciple, H. Gressmann (*Mose und seine Zeit*, 1913), made a similar analysis of the book of Exodus. G. von Rad carried the approach further by dealing with the larger continuities, that is, the overall composition and conception into which the original material was incorporated (*Das formgeschichtliche Problem des Hexateuch*, 1938; Eng.: *The Problem of the Hexateuch and Other Essays*, 1966). He explained the traditions about the Exodus, Sinai, and the settlement in terms of their cultic connections. Originally, these were independent traditions attached to various sanctuaries. M. Noth sought to combine analysis and synthesis, detailed investigation and panoramic view (*Überlieferungsgeschichte des Pentateuch*, 1948; Eng.: *A History of Pentateuchal Traditions*, 1972; *Exodus*, ATD 5, 1958; Eng.: *Exodus*, 1962). He found five main "themes" in the Pentateuch: guidance out of Egypt, guidance into the arable land, promise to the patriarchs, guidance in the wilderness, and revelation at Sinai; he regarded the rest of the Pentateuch as a "filling out" or development. Each theme or block of tradition had its own prehistory and had no original historical connection with the others, so that the historical sequence depicted in the Pentateuch must be abandoned (see §2a). More recent scholarship has, to a large extent, been a matter of coming to grips with this view of things.

Is there any real reason for embarking on this uncertain journey beyond the text as we have it into a preliterary prehistory that can only be inferred? For one thing, the date of a text's composition tells us little about the age of its "material" or content; that which was committed to writing at a late date need not itself have been of late origin. Furthermore, the earliest written witness does not by any means have to be a direct reflection of the historical event it reports; as a rule, report and event are separated by a more or less lengthy period of oral transmission. During this intermediate period the memory of events was kept alive in stories, told at sanctuaries or in the family (see Exod 12:26f.; Deut 6:20ff.; etc.) or by a class of storytellers. New and different motifs were added to enliven and serve as illustration, or traditions originally connected with different places were combined to form a single stream of tradition. As a matter of course, experiences from a later age made their way into the tradition being handed on, so that in its final form a story might contain experiences stretching over long periods.

For these reasons, the determination of the prehistory of a text (the question of the origin, progress, and intention of the oral tradition) is not only necessary but also has several advantages, which may be stated roughly as follows:

a) Literary-critical analysis shows up incoherences in the text, discontinuities and contradictions that literary criticism itself is often unable to resolve by its own methods, namely, by increasingly refined and complicated source analysis down to half- and quarter-verses. Here the tradition-historical approach can help us advance further, for it understands individual stories or complexes of stories and even the documentary sources themselves to be the end result of a lengthy process of transmission. Roughnesses that, from the literary-critical standpoint, may be the result of a more or less arbitrary combination of fragments of texts can be explained in an organically meaningful way from the history of the text, the growth of the tradition, and variations in the telling and retelling of the story or stories.

b) Interest thus shifts from the literary work as composed at a particular point in time to a process of transmission that may have required several generations or even larger segments of time. Interest shifts also from the individual author to groups or "schools," that is, usually unidentifiable entities among the people or at a sanctuary or at court. When form criticism seeks to determine the *Sitz im Leben* (the life setting or social context) of a text, it is inquiring into the social relations (institutions) in which the traditions grew.

According to a well-known definition of A. Alt, research into the history of forms or genres "depends on the observation that in each individual literary form, as long as it remains in use in its own context, the ideas it contains are always connected with certain fixed forms of expression. This characteristic connection is not imposed arbitrarily on the material by the literary redactors of a later period. The inseparable connection between form and content goes back beyond the written records to the period of popular oral composition and tradition, where each form of expression was appropriate to some particular circumstance among the regularly recurring events and necessities of life" (*Essays*, p. 111).

In typical, recurring situations, "forms of expression arise which are appropriate to the goal and necessities of these situations." There is thus a connection between form of expression (style, genre, also themes, motifs, principal key words) on the one hand and life situation on the other. The life situation is the place of origin (the *Sitz im Leben*) of the form of expression.

Form criticism therefore supplies information only about the expressions of the life of a community and not about an individual event or the life of an individual person.

Traditions can also be cut off from their original *Sitz im Leben*, be attached to entirely different contexts, and then be passed on accompanied by new intentions. A distinction must therefore be made between the place of origin and the place of use of a form of expression or a tradition.

c) Whereas literary criticism recognized primarily the longitudinal divisions within the Pentateuch, the interest here is in the cross-section (the importance of this had already been glimpsed by the fragment hypothesis). The blocks or complexes of traditions, such as the stories of the patriarchs or the revelation at Sinai, become visible alongside the continuous literary strata. As a result, the problem of the unity of the Pentateuch is posed in a new way: How long did the blocks of tradition exist in independence? Where did they come together (at the sanctuaries?) and how were they welded into continuity? Or is it not possible to separate them to such an extent, that is, were they, historically speaking, originally closely bound up with one another?

Whereas literary criticism starts from the structured text as we now have it, tradition history follows the reverse path: from the smallest unit, through the larger continuities (e.g., saga cycles), to the text as now given.

The two approaches must be combined. But many questions remain open (see R. Rendtorff's objection, based on tradition history, to source analysis). The aim of the explanation must be to present the history of the text (an individual section, a larger complex, or even the Pentateuch in its entirety) as a total intelligible process, from its beginnings insofar as these are still discoverable, through its intermediate stages in blocks of tradition and documentary sources, to the final form in which we now have it. The chief interest in this reconstruction is in tracing the changing intentions of the text.

d) Insofar as the traditional material available to the literary work can be discovered and the part played by tradition can be distinguished from the part played by the author, it is possible to distinguish between the intention that finds expression in the traditional material and the changed emphasis it receives in its literary form. This "redaction-historical" approach seeks to determine the intention with which an author modified the traditions available to him or the intention which he imposed on the ideas he used. Since such recasting is successful only within limits, the original character of the material will mean that not all statements in the text will be in harmony with the conception that dominates the literary work.

e) The appropriation of extrabiblical traditions and ideas by the OT presents a special case in the relation between tradition and interpretation. Only with the application of the tradition-historical method does it become possible to incorporate the history-of-religions approach—and in particular the comparison with parallels in the Near Eastern world—in a way that does justice to the material.

A problem that could not be resolved with the aid of literary criticism and whose full extent was recognized only after the time of Wellhausen is posed by the wealth of relations between OT and ancient Near Eastern texts, for example, between the Babylonian creation myth *Enuma elish* and Gen 1, or between Tablet XI of the Gilgamesh epic and the story of the flood; the situation is comparable in Psalms and in the legal and sapiential texts.

Only in exceptional cases is there direct literary dependence of OT literature on the literature of the ancient Near East; as a rule, the connection is only indirect and of a tradition-historical kind. Once the acceptance and modification of traditions, the borrowing of foreign models, and their corrective reinterpretation are understood, both the impress of foreign influences and the special character of the OT text become clear.

§5

SELECTED TYPES OF NARRATIVE

a) Myth and Primeval History

Myths are "stories of the gods, in contradistinction to the legends [better: sagas] in which the actors are men" (H. Gunkel, *Legends*, p. 14). In myths the gods appear as persons with names; the myth describes their behavior in relation both to one another (marriages among the gods; conflicts among the gods; etc.) and to human beings. Since myth by preference deals with a time that precedes historical experience (prehistoric times: theogony, cosmogony, anthropogony, paradise, flood, etc.), it can be repeated in cult form and thus remain present within history. In this way myth provides the foundation for an interpretation of the world and upholds the cosmic and social order.

When "myth" is thus understood, it must be said that the OT does not, strictly speaking, contain any myths. On the contrary, its concern for history and its conception of God entail great reserve in regard to myth. The OT is indeed able to use the language of myth in giving expression to its faith, and it in fact borrows from surrounding cultures a number of mythical motifs and bits of mythical stories (this is especially the case in the primeval history, Psalms, and the prophets), but it does not itself develop any myths.

The unusual story in Gen 6:1–4 (there is nothing else of the kind in the OT) according to which, in its original form, the giants were the offspring of marriages between gods and human beings, has been stripped of its etiological point and has been made to serve a different intention. In the story as it now stands in the OT the giants are no longer regarded as the offspring of such a union (v. 4), and only the human beings involved are held responsible: their life span is shortened (v. 3). Thus the mythic tradition provides a reflection on objectionable human activity.

When the OT takes over mythic representations, it changes these (essentially in three ways) and integrates them with its own faith and intellectual outlook:

(1) The Yahwist religion "from its very beginning tends toward monotheism. But for a story of the gods at least two gods are essential.

62

. . . The monotheism of Israel tolerates only those myths that represent God as acting alone. . . . Or at the most, the story deals with action between God and men" (H. Gunkel, *Legends*, pp. 15–16). Thus, in the biblical story of the flood (Gen 6:5ff.; 8:20ff.) in contrast to its Babylonian parallel (Gilgamesh epic, Tablet XI), punishment and clemency, anger and repentance are the work of the one God. The exclusiveness of God, which finds expression in the first commandment, does not allow any myths of conflicts among the gods or of the birth and death of gods. An origin can be predicated only of the world and not of God (Gen 1:1; Ps 90:2). In the story of creation (again unlike the *Enuma elish*, the Babylonian epic of the origin of the world) chaos is no longer a personal, independently acting power, but is simply a state of things that ceases when God creates (Gen 1:2). The dragons of the sea are rendered innocuous (1:21; Ps 104:26); the stars are not astral powers (see Ezek 8:16; Deut 4:19) that determine the destinies of human beings, but are simply luminaries created by God that serve only to shed light on the earth and to distinguish various periods of time (Gen 1:14ff.; cf. Ps 136:7ff.). Heavenly and demonic powers are likewise reduced to the status of God's servants (Pss 29; 103:20ff.; cf. Exod 12:23; Amos 9:3; etc.).

(2) Mythic representations are shifted into the future; that is, they do not ground or explain present reality, but rather depict a future reality that is in critical contrast to the present (Isa 1:21–26; 2:2–4, 12–17; 11:1; 24:21ff.; 27:1; 65:17ff.; etc.). In this process myth retains its function of presenting the universal and even cosmic scope of the expected events and thus of OT hope itself.

In this area of futurity the OT has created myths, whereas eschatological myths were almost unknown in the ancient Near East, except among the Persians.

(3) Mythical motifs serve to bring out the meaning of a historical event (the "historicization of myth"). For example, the idea of God doing battle with the sea has the function of rendering vivid the rescue of Israel at the Sea of Reeds during the exodus from Egypt (Isa 51:9ff.; Ps 77:11ff.; etc.). The reference back to the historical past takes the form of remembrance and re-presentation (Exod 12:11, 14; etc.), not of a repetition of the past.

Unlike the "civilization myths," Gen 4:17, 20ff. J does not trace civilizing achievements in the crafts (tools, arts, professions) back to a divine origin (except for the garments in 3:21, which represent a divine act of protection). These achievements are regarded rather as discoveries by human beings. The human person is created as God's "image" and thus in all likelihood as God's representative on earth, given freedom and responsibility along with the commission to subdue the earth (Gen 1:26ff. P; cf. 2:19; Ps 8).

Even the more or less mythical stories in the primeval history are not really independent but are connected with the subsequent presentation of historical events. They are, as it were, a porch leading to it and are dovetailed with it in many ways. This is clear from, for example, the family trees or genealogies (see §3a3), which establish cross-references or connections between various persons and groups of peoples over the course of time:

Descendants of Adam and Cain	Gen 4:1f., 17–24, 25f. J; 5:1ff. P
Descendants of Noah	Gen 10 J/P (Table of Peoples)
Descendants of Shem	Gen 11:10ff.

The genealogies are continued in the story of the patriarchs (Gen 22:20ff.; 25:1ff.; 36:10ff.) and the history of Israel as a people (especially 1 Chr 1–9); their aim, justified or not, is to establish historical continuity.

b) The Saga as a Form of Transmission

In the Pentateuch and even on into the first book of Samuel remembrance of the past takes shape not in strictly historical writing but in the form of sagas, which before being put in writing had been orally transmitted from person to person over a long period of time and had in the process undergone many influences.

1. The Individual Saga

"Saga" is a general notion, and distinctions need to be made concerning it. The distinctions can be made by applying various categories: content, origin, or function (heroic sagas, local sagas, etiological sagas, etc.). But a clear and universally valid explanation is hardly possible.

H. Gunkel divided OT sagas into three groups: the sagas of primeval history (Gen 1–11), in which myth and saga provide material that is combined in reflection on the past of the human race (e.g., the tower of Babel); the sagas of the patriarchs, which deal with Israel's ancestors, their families, and their milieu; and the sagas of tribal or national heroes such as Moses, Joshua, the judges, and even the prophets (§13b1). Like the stages of Israelite history, the sagas can be classified according to changing social structures: stories of nomadic clans, stories of peasant society prior to the formation of the state, stories from the world of the court (H. J. Hermisson).

Consistent with this kind of classification is another that groups sagas according to occasion, background, or principal motif. Stimuli to the formation of sagas may be a historical event, and especially one that concerns the history of a tribe; relations with neighbors (e.g., the description of Cain's special manner of life as ancestor of the Kenites in Gen 4, or the story of the dispute over the wells in Gen 26); some striking natural event (e.g., Gen 19; Exod 16f.); or a cultic ordinance (see below, on sanctuary legends). Along with the principal motifs secondary motifs also may play a part in the formation of sagas.

Names, and especially place names, are readily explained by means of verbal echoes or plays on words. Thus Babel, the name of a city, which in Babylonian means "Gate of God," is connected in Gen 11:9 with the confusion of languages. Or the personal name "Moses," which in Egyptian means "son," is explained in Exod 2:10 by the words of Pharaoh's daughter: "I drew him out of the water" (see also Gen 25:26; Exod 2:22; etc.). In these cases scholars speak of "popular etymologies," although such plays on words are not meant as etymologies in the proper sense.

At times we find motif words or key words (e.g., "see" in Gen 24:4, 13f.).

In one and the same saga several motifs with different origins may be combined and very different intentions may be superimposed on one another, so that the meaning of the story cannot be summed up in a single simple statement. This is already an indication that in addition to general or common traits each saga contains something singular and specific to it; in the final analysis, therefore, each must be studied in its own right, although comparisons with similar stories can be helpful.

Since a shift into another type of narrative is easily made, even the term "saga" is hard to pin down and is therefore ambiguous. Nonetheless, the formal characteristics that A. Olrik long ago identified in sagas originating in the European world (see "Epische Gesetze der Volksdichtung," *Zeitschrift für deutsches Altertum und deutsche Literatur* 51 [1909] 1–12) prove to be surprisingly applicable to OT stories. We may therefore cautiously advance the following as common traits of the sagas (especially those dealing with the patriarchal period):

(1) What is historical or political is put forward as private and personal. A saga reduces the general to the individual, captures the destiny of nations in experiences of individuals, and presents impersonal anonymous situations as direct encounters. Tribes or peoples, who are personified by their ancestors, come on the scene as blood relatives (see §3a3). The patriarchal sagas are "family histories"

(C. Westermann) that tell of relations between husband and wife, father and sons, or brothers. Thus the plight of the people in Egypt is represented by the opposition between Pharaoh and the midwives or— in the case of the unavoidable commitment of the child Moses to the river—in the relations between the mother, the child, and the daughter of Pharaoh (Exod 1f.).

(2) Only two or three persons come on the scene at one time (law of twos or threes). If an additional person enters the stage, one of the others must withdraw into the background (see, e.g., Gen 21, or the relation of mother and sister to the daughter of Pharaoh, Exod 2). Each scene thus remains short and can be taken in at a glance. The action as a whole does not contain manifold juxtapositions and interrelations, nor are numerous motifs and narrative strands commingled and then disentangled; rather, the whole moves toward its goal by means of a simple succession of individual scenes. The clarity of the whole is further increased by the fact that the principal personages stand out sharply over against secondary figures and that unimportant matters are omitted.

(3) A saga emphasizes types. Thus, the Pharaoh who oppresses Israel is not the individual, Rameses II, or any other ruler whose name we know, but simply the king of Egypt (Exod 1:8ff.; cf. Gen 12:15ff.); Moses' rescuer is not just any aristocratic Egyptian lady but the very daughter of Pharaoh (Exod 2). Secondary personages are often given no names. The actors are preferably different in type and origin. This turns a duality into a contrast. Abel and Cain or Jacob and Esau are contrasted as shepherd and hunter and thus as representatives of two different stages of civilization.

(4) Appearance and character are sketched with the utmost brevity, if at all (e.g., Gen 25:25). Characteristics and thoughts are translated rather into actions (16:6; 18:2ff.; 22:3; etc.). But since a saga as a whole is related in as brief a manner as possible, any details not unconditionally required by the main action are omitted; the result is that questions we regard as essential are left unanswered.

This is not simply a universal trait of sagas, but also something peculiarly Israelite. E. Auerbach has made a comparison between the description of the sacrifice of Isaac (Gen 22) and the narrative style of Homer, with its leisurely development and clarification of details. In the story of Isaac, there is "the externalization of only so much of the phenomena as is necessary for the purpose of the narrative, all else left in obscurity; the decisive points of the narrative alone are emphasized, what lies between is nonexistent; time and place are undefined and call for interpretation; thoughts and feeling remain unexpressed, are only suggested by the silence and the fragmentary speeches; the whole, permeated with the most unrelieved suspense and directed toward a single goal (and to that extent far more of a unity), remains mysterious and 'fraught with background' " (*Mimesis*, 1953, 1957, p. 9).

(5) Another trait, likewise especially characteristic of OT sagas, is that motifs which are decisive for the course of the action are expressed in discourse (Gen 26:9ff.; Exod 1:9f.; etc.). God's word in particular often plays a critical role; in advance or after the fact it indicates the culminating point of the action or the change of fortunes of the persons involved. In this respect a theological intention proper to the OT is at work in the shaping of the form or the tradition (e.g., Gen 22:11f.; 18:17ff.); in later sagas discourse may become so extensive and important as to relegate the course of the action to a secondary place (Gen 24).

(6) A saga has a clear beginning and end. The introduction often depicts the situation out of which the action develops (e.g., Gen 18:1b: ". . . as he [Abraham] sat at the door of his tent in the heat of the day," or Exod 3:1: "Now Moses was keeping the flock of his father-in-law, Jethro"). Like the divine discourse, the introduction may also serve as a subsequent interpretation or even correction of the traditional story by means of a title-like summary.

Thus the cult legend of the appearance of the three divine beings at Mamre is explained by the opening title-like summary along the lines of God's exclusiveness: "And the Lord appeared to him" (Gen 18:1). Similarly, the scene of the burning bush prevents the impression that God is visible by saying: "And the angel of the Lord appeared to him" (Exod 3:2). The command to sacrifice Isaac is meant only to test Abraham's faith: "God tested Abraham" (Gen 22:1). A comparable function attaches to the statement that unified the various traditions about creation: "God created the heavens and the earth" (Gen 1:1).

Since a saga's intention is to capture something typical rather than to report a historical nonrecurring event, its relation to history is faulted by our modern standards. It is therefore not possible to eliminate certain traits of a legendary or fairy-tale character and then regard the saga as historically credible; we must rather inquire first into the origin, occasion, and intention of the saga.

"It is not enough, in considering the popular nature of this tradition, to dispute the historical credibility of certain passages according to our own discretion and to stick to the rest as the 'historical nucleus' and incorporate it in the history of Israel. . . . What is important is rather to grasp as precisely as possible the historical assumptions behind these traditions in each individual case from the material of the tradition itself. . . . Only when we have grasped the circumstances under which they arose and what they are driving at, can we answer the vital question as to how they arrived at their particular selection from the wealth of events and why they presented it in the particular way they did. Only when we have answered that can we discern the subjects on which they can be expected to supply information and the weight which may be attached to what they say and what they suppress." The answers to these questions cannot be completely clear but "can only be arrived at by taking all the circumstances into account" (M. Noth, *The History of Israel*, pp. 45–46).

Especially important from the historical viewpoint is the question, Did person and action always belong together? Was the principal figure (Moses, for example) originally connected with the material of the saga, or was he attached to it only later? The relation between history and the formation of a saga cannot be determined on general principles but only in each case and then only with reservations.

Whatever be the origin of the sagas, the historical and especially the theological experiences of successive ages have in any case found expression in the formation of these sagas, as each age used them to interpret their own situation. The sagas gather up and condense the experiences of generations (G. von Rad). To that extent the past and present, which historical writings try carefully to separate, are here intermingled.

"Unlike other (heroic) sagas the Israelite sagas for the most part show no tendency to idealize; the reason for this is that God is the inner subject of the sagas. The longer a saga undergoes the formative influence of the faith of the generations that transmit it, the more theological its content becomes. A saga thus becomes increasingly a prophetic witness which looks back and exteriorizes God's action . . . in images which serve as types" (E. Jenni, *TZ* 12 [1956] 264).

2. Etiological Motifs

A saga often echoes the question, Why a particular name or place or condition or custom? How did reality come to acquire its present form? "The usual answer . . . is that the present relations are due to some transaction of the patriarchs." Existing relations, which suggest the why-question, "are historical, but the way in which they are explained is poetic" (H. Gunkel, *Legends*, p. 26). People conclude from some noteworthy phenomenon to a historical event that can explain it (e.g., Lot's wife in Gen 19 or the conquest of Jericho in Josh 6). The goal to which the analogy leads is historical, but is the point of departure also historical?

As a result of this question the problem of the historicity of the etiologies, especially those in the narratives of the book of Joshua, gave rise at one time to an extensive discussion—although one that has long since slacked off. The problem is that in many instances the etiological motif is not in harmony with the main thrust of a narrative (C. Westermann) and even represents a subsequent addition (B. S. Childs, B. O. Long). The story does not lead up to the concluding etiology ("down to this very day"; "therefore it bears such and such a name"); this conclusion rather introduces a new element, which is precisely the etiological. It does not, therefore, excuse us from the task of inquiring into the historical background and concerns of each story.

3. Sanctuary Legends

By reason of its content and function, though not of its form, the sanctuary legend (*Hieros Logos*) represents a distinct kind of saga and in a sense a special kind of etiology. It is for this reason that the terms "cultic etiology" or "cult-foundational saga" have been coined. The sanctuary legend legitimates a sanctuary as a goal of pilgrimage by telling of a revelation that took place on the spot and thus proving the sacral character of the place. At a prominent place—a well perhaps (Gen 16:7), or a tree or a stone or a ford—a divinity unexpectedly appeared to an individual, whose experience compelled him to say: "How awesome is this place! This is none other than the house of God" (Gen 28:16f.) or "The place on which you are standing is holy ground" (Exod 3:5). The recipient of the revelation responds by building an altar or instituting a cult and by giving a name to this extraordinary place (Judg 6:24; Gen 28:18f.; cf. 12:7f.; 16:13f.; 22:14; 32:30; etc.). Such sanctuary legends, the nucleus of which is probably pre-Israelite (see §2a1), are in the background of:

Gen 18	Visit of the three men to a tree at Mamre near Hebron (cf. Gen 13:18)
Gen 22	Sacrifice of Isaac (originally the redemption of a child by the sacrifice of an animal)
Gen 28:10ff.	Dream of a "ladder" reaching up to heaven at a stone in Bethel (cf. Gen 12:7f.)
Gen 32:30ff.	Wrestling match at a ford of the Jabbok near Penuel (cf. Exod 4:24–26)
Exod 3	Burning bush
Judg 6:11ff.	Apparition at a tree at Ophrah

These and similar stories (e.g., Gen 35:1ff.; 46:1ff.) differ greatly from one another in the details of their construction; in addition to traits shared with the others each has its own proper character. Each case shows clearly, however, the many levels of meaning a story may have: from its original meaning, which can now only be inferred, to its intention in its present context. The cult legends of the OT have lost their former connection with a particular place and have acquired instead a connection with Israel as a whole (Gen 32:27) and an intensified element of futurity. No longer do they simply provide an explanation of an existing reality, but they shift into the mode of promise and point to what is coming (28:14ff.; etc.) in order to inspire human beings with the hope that in reliance on the promise they can go their way into the future.

4. Saga Cycles and Later Form of the Sagas

H. Gunkel laid down the principle that the shorter, tauter, and more compact a saga is, the older it is; the more elaborate its presentation or the less intelligible it is in itself, the later it is. The style changes. Later sagas (such as the wooing of Rebekah, Gen 24) are richer in details. The story or "novella" of Joseph, which is composed on a grand scale, even has a number of intermeshing scenes (see below).

The ancient, originally independent individual sagas undergo a comparable change of meaning when they coalesce into a larger whole, a cycle of sagas. The link between them may be created by geographical contiguity (Josh 2ff.) or by having the same protagonist. In Genesis the most important saga cycles, each revolving around two individuals, are these:

Abraham–Lot	Gen 13f.; 18f.
Jacob–Esau	Gen (25) 27f.; 32f. as framework for:
Jacob–Laban	Gen 29–31

This development raises many questions of a tradition-historical and historical character. To what extent did the saga complexes already form a unity before being taken into the documentary sources? Were there not also narrative complexes that existed as such from the beginning, for example in the exodus tradition?

In addition to the representational form taken by myth and the narrative form of the saga, the Pentateuch itself already contains all sorts of other forms of transmission, such as proverbs, songs, curses, and blessings (Gen 4:23f.; 9:25ff.; 48:15f.; 49; Exod 15; 17:16; Num 6:24ff.; 10:35f.; 21:17f., 27ff.; etc.; cf. §9a3).

Independent fairy tales (*Märchen*) are unknown in the OT, but from time to time traits of a fairy-tale kind do occur. They are to be explained, in part, as residues of mythic-demonic notions (thus the speaking serpent in Gen 3; the speaking ass in Num 22 is a different matter).

c) The Joseph Novella

The Joseph novella, too, tells at first sight a "family history": the vicissitudes of Jacob and his sons, and the enmity and reconciliation of the brothers. But in fact the story takes us considerably beyond this narrow circle of interests. In addition, the story seems much less remote and primitive than the individual sagas of the patriarchal age. It is more intelligible and more genial in its atmosphere. The Joseph novel is "from beginning to end an organically constructed narrative" (G. von Rad), which runs from Gen 37 to Gen 50 (originally without Gen 38; 48f.) and includes all sorts of intermediate scenes and elements which delay the action. The broad narrative style, the clear and purposeful construction, and the imprint of (courtly) wisdom give the story of Joseph a special place.

Since the thematic unity of the whole is obvious, there has been a growing tendency in recent years no longer to separate the story into two strands but rather to understand it by and large as a continuous narrative that as such was inserted into the Yahwist source or even into the combined Yahwist-Elohist work.

There is, however, a series of repetitions and fluctuations that can be explained only in terms of the history of tradition (or as a stylistic device). Thus, even in Gen 37 (especially vv. 22ff.) Judah and Reuben alternate as spokesmen for their brothers, and the Ishmaelites and Midianites both appear as members of the caravan (37:22–24, 28a, 29–31 E). Not only Gen 46:1–5a but also 50:15–26 contains typically Elohist material (e.g., Elohim, "God," as subject of the sentence, or the verbal parallel with Gen 30:2). The central statements in Gen 50:19f. repeat 45:5bff. and prepare for Exod 1:15ff.

Anyone who understands the story of Joseph as a literary unity must come to grips with awkward additions—but is it possible to justify satisfactorily the acceptance of such additions? Thus the traditional view seems more likely, according to which the tensions are to be explained by a combining of two not very dissimilar narrative strata: the Yahwist and Elohist sources, which have here been cleverly interwoven. The share of the Priestly source is quite limited (especially 37:1f.; 46:6ff.; 48:3–6; 49:29–33; 50:12f.). The latest of the source writings contributes only a few sentences and does not present the story line.

Gen 37	Introduction: Conflict between the brothers. Predestination of Joseph as ruler (coat, dreams). Selling of Joseph into Egypt
38	Insert: Judah and his daughter-in-law Tamar First son: Perez, ancestor of David (Ruth 4:12, 18ff.)
39–41	Joseph's rise from prisoner to chancellor of Pharaoh

39	Joseph and Potiphar
40	Dreams of the two court employees
41	Dreams of Pharaoh: seven years of plenty and seven of famine. Joseph (41:38f.), like Daniel after him (Dan 2; 4f.), a wise interpreter of dreams, a man endowed with the spirit of God. Founder of the Egyptian granary system (cf. 47:13ff.). Marriage with the daughter of an Egyptian priest: birth of Manasseh and Ephraim

42–45	Road to reconciliation with his brothers	
	42	First journey of the brothers to Egypt
	43	Second journey, with Benjamin
	44	The cup. Discourse of Judah: substitution for Benjamin, concern for the father (vv. 18–34)
	45	Joseph reveals himself: first reconciliation
46–47	Road to reunion with the father	
	46	Vision at Beersheba. Jacob emigrates to Egypt
	47:1–12	Jacob before Pharaoh. Settlement in Goshen (46:28ff.; 45:11; 47:27)
	47:13ff.	Joseph as steward: the Egyptians become serfs of Pharaoh
48–49	Jacob's last will and testament. Two inserts	
	48	Blessing of Joseph's younger son, Ephraim, before the elder, Manasseh
	49	Blessing of the twelve sons of Jacob. Oracles concerning the tribes, like the blessing of Moses in Deut 33
		Reproaches for Reuben, Simeon, and Levi; prominence given to Judah and Joseph
50	Jacob's death and burial—in Hebron (49:29ff.)	
	After the initial reconciliation (45:5ff.), a definitive reconciliation of Joseph with his brothers (50:15ff)	
	Joseph's death; his burial at Shechem (50:25f.; Josh 24:32)	

In the transition from Genesis to Exodus the story of Joseph is made to show how the sons of Jacob-Israel came to Egypt and thus to establish a link between the time of the patriarchs and the time of Moses. To what extent is this connection original and to what extent is it a later addition (see §2a)? How ancient are the Egyptian elements (e.g., Gen 41:45, 50; 40:1f.; 43:32) in the story? Even if there is no place in the political history of Egypt for the person and office of Joseph, the tradition need not therefore lack all historical basis. In its oldest form the story of Joseph most likely originated in the northern kingdom or in central Palestine (48:22; Josh 17:16ff.; 24:32; Judg 1:22f.), an area that gives evidence of relations with Egypt at a very early date (see Gen 46:1ff.). The name "(House of) Joseph" probably became attached to the descendants of the group that had resided in Egypt.

Was the story thought up at the court in Jerusalem during the early monarchic period? The courtly and sapiential background suggests the "Solomonic Enlightenment" (G. von Rad). This would be consistent with the usual, though controverted, date assigned to the Yahwist. In any case, the story of Joseph, taken in and by itself, is difficult to date.

The Joseph novella says nothing of appearances or discourses of God such as we find especially in the sanctuary legends (an exception: Gen 46:1ff.); localized sagas also play no part in it. As in the stories of David (§11c3), the story of Joseph with all its intertwining of events is understood as a framework within which human beings act. At the same time, however, in all decisions and events God's will is carried out. The sapiential literature already acknowledges that God's ways can remain mysterious and unintelligible (Prov 16:9; 19:21; 20:24; 21:30f.). But the story of Joseph moves beyond this insight and proclaims that God can make use even of human wickedness and injustice in carrying out his plans; his way reaches its destination even despite detours. The brothers use violence in trying to prevent the future revealed in Joseph's dreams, a future in which they will bow down before him (Gen 37), but their very efforts lead to that fulfillment (42:6ff.; 44:14ff.; 50:18). Joseph is rescued but must keep body and soul together as a slave; even his rise to the position of Pharaoh's chancellor (41:40ff.; 45:26; cf. Ps 105:16ff.) involves radical changes. When the brothers fear Joseph's revenge after the death of their father, who had been able to see once more the son he believed dead, Joseph says to them: "Fear not, for am I in the place of God? As for you, you meant evil against me; but God meant it for good" (Gen 50:19f. E; cf. 45:5ff.).

Here Joseph not only refuses to pass judgment, leaving this to God instead (Prov 20:22), but he also views accounts "as already settled by God" (O. Procksch). Joseph need not show any more magnanimity, since by his historical guidance God has already forgiven; he has broken the connection between action and consequences and has turned calamity into salvation. Moreover, the story looks with hope beyond its own limits as a family history: God has turned evil to good, in order "to bring it about that many people should be kept alive" (Gen 50:20; cf. Exod 1:15ff.).

§6

THE YAHWIST HISTORY

a) Introductory Questions

1. Importance. Among the documentary sources for the Pentateuch the Yahwist stratum is rightly regarded as the most important. "Theologically it contains the most important testimony found in the Pentateuchal narrative as a whole" (M. Noth, *A History of Pentateuchal Traditions*, p. 236)—on the one hand, the radical insight into human sinfulness (Gen 6:5; 8:21); on the other, the promise of a blessing upon "all the families of the earth" (12:3). The Yahwist presentation is at the same time the oldest known history that is so extensive and embraces such varied eras of human history, although the ancient Near East was already familiar with the linking of primeval history and subsequent history or of stories from before and from after the great flood. The Yahwist "is the first to conceive the idea of a single world history within which events in Israel play a very definite and indeed decisive role" (J. Hempel).

The Yahwist provides the first written attestation of the Pentateuchal vision that moves from primeval history to the settlement; yet the Yahwist is not likely to have created this vision himself and thus to have welded the blocks of tradition into a single whole (see §4b4b). According to G. von Rad, the Yahwist took over an existing sequence of events—election of the patriarchs, deliverance from Egypt, and settlement (see Deut 26:5ff.)—and expanded it in three ways: by prefixing the primeval history, by developing the patriarchal history (Deut 26:5 mentions only one patriarch), and by including the Sinai tradition. But this view of the matter attributes too much to the Yahwist. Of the three expansions two—the organization of the patriarchs as a series of generations (Abraham, Isaac, Jacob) and the linking of the exodus and Sinai—had already been effected and could therefore also be taken for granted by the Elohist. The special contribution of the Yahwist seems to have been the prefixing of the primeval history (Gen 1–11), in the development of which only the late Priestly

74

document plays a part; the Elohist begins only with the period of the patriarchs and in so doing certainly reflects the older tradition.

2. Scope. The Yahwist's work is generally accepted as beginning with the story of creation and paradise (Gen 2:4bff.), but the point at which his account ends is debated. There are essentially three answers proposed:

(a) According to an older view it is possible to follow the Yahwist through the Pentateuch and the books of Joshua, Judges, and Samuel, down to the separation of the kingdoms or, in other words, to the collapse of the Davidic kingdom after the death of Solomon (1 Kgs 12:19). This was the view of G. Hölscher and others, but neither linguistic usage nor the linking of traditional material reaching so far beyond the Pentateuch suggests an unambiguously single source for all this material.

(b) According to another conception, which has recently been defended once again, the Yahwist presentation embraces the period down to the settlement (inclusively), either to the account, unique in the OT, that is given in Judg 1 or at least to the accounts in the book of Joshua. As a matter of fact, there can hardly be any doubt that the Yahwist recorded at least the settlement of the tribes, for this history not only reports the promise of the land (Gen 28:15; also 12:7; Num 10:29; etc.) but in Num 32 also provides some information about the immigration of the tribes east of the Jordan (see also Num 13f.; 16). To date, however, there has hardly been any convincing proof offered that specific texts outside the Pentateuch are to be assigned to the Yahwist; a few verbal accords (compare, e.g., Exod 16:35 with Josh 5:12, or Exod 3:5 with Josh 5:15) are not adequate proof.

(c) As long, then, as the still open question of where the Yahwist history ends has not been satisfactorily answered, we will do well to prefer M. Noth's view: The end of the Yahwist history (including the account of the settlement) was dropped when this history was incorporated into the Priestly document or into the Pentateuch (see §4b4d). The end as we now have it is formed by the lengthy story of Balaam (Num 22 and 24); after this only a few isolated sentences in Num 25 (vv. 1–5) and 32 belong to the Yahwist. This means that recognizably Yahwistic sections are to be found only in the books of Genesis, Exodus, and Numbers.

The primeval history (Gen 2–4; 6–8*; 9:18ff.; 11:1–9; etc.), the patriarchal period (12–13*; 18–19*; 24; 28:10ff.*; 32:22ff.; 37–50*; etc.) and the exodus from Egypt (Exod 1–17*) are presented in great detail, while the Sinai pericope has been retained only in a short form (at least in Exod 19*). Among the texts usually claimed for J a few, such as Gen 15 (covenant with Abraham), Exod 34 (cultic decalogue) or Exod 4, can be left aside as being especially disputed. Depending on whether or not these are included, our understanding of the overall Yahwist history will be more or less altered.

3. Situation. While there is a dispute over the point at which the Yahwist history ends, most scholars regard the history as having come into existence during the golden age of Solomon, that is, around 950 B.C. It is likely that this period, during which the royal court had a secretarial school for the training of officials, was the first that could provide the material conditions for the writing down of such a comprehensive document. At the same time, conditions at the international level (dependence of neighboring states on Israel; trade) stimulated Israel's reflection on its relations with other peoples.

The principal arguments for this early date are these: (a) The new influences at work in the early monarchic period seem to have stimulated a review of the recent or distant past, for the narratives of David's rise to power and of the succession (1 Sam 16–1 Kgs 2) are approximately contemporary with the Yahwist and congenial to him (see, e.g., the attitude to a "great name":Gen 11:4; 12:2; 2 Sam 7:9; see §11c3). (b) In his work the Yahwist names precisely those neighboring peoples (e.g., the Canaanites, Gen 9:18ff.; the Philistines, Gen 26; the Arameans, Gen 29ff.; Ammon, Moab, Edom) who were important for Israel during the period when David and Solomon ruled over all Israel (especially 2 Sam 8).

(c) The story of Noah the winegrower (Gen 9:18–25), which has for its point the cursing of Canaan and his subjection to Shem (i.e., Israel) and Japheth (i.e., the Philistines)—"Blessed by the Lord my God be Shem; and let Canaan be his slave"—presupposes the relations obtaining in the time of the Davidic empire. The same holds for the indirect reference to David as the "star out of Jacob" (Num 24:15–19) and to the subjection and liberation of Edom in the time of Solomon (compare Gen 25:23; 27:40a with 2 Sam 8:13f.; and Gen 27:40b, an addition based on 1 Kgs 11:14ff.; 2 Kgs 8:20ff.?). (d) The fact that J incorporates all sorts of traditions from Judah (Gen 38) or from the south (Gen 4; 19; also Num 13f.; 16) into his presentation is consistent with the rank held by Judah after David became king (2 Sam 2).

(e) The description of Israel's forced labor in Egypt (Exod 1:11) seems to reflect conditions connected with Solomon's building activity (1 Kgs 9:15, 19; cf. 5:15; 11:28): dependents were compelled to labor on building projects. This means that the origin of the Yahwist history may be assigned more specifically to the period of Solomon's building activity. (f) Finally, this period was one not only of political and economic prosperity; it also saw a spiritual renewal, the "Solomonic

Enlightenment" (G. von Rad). As a matter of fact the Yahwist manifests a high degree of spirituality that betrays an affiliation with sapiential thinking such as may have been cultivated in the school for officials that was mentioned earlier. Does not the primeval history give precisely a storyteller's answer to the sapiential question What is humanity? (Ps 8:4; etc.).

Admittedly, various observations attest only the age of the tradition the documentary source takes over (*terminus ante quem non*). But, contrary to a more recent trend (H. H. Schmid and others), there is no need to date the Yahwist himself in a later period, for he does not suppose the end of the Davidic empire and the split between Judah and Israel, nor the Assyrian threat, nor the prophetic message of judgment, and certainly not the Deuteronomistic demand for the centralization of the cult (Josianic reform) or the exile. Moreover, in individual stories (though not in the overall structure) J often gives an older form of the tradition than E does (see §7a1).

In any case, it is necessary to distinguish carefully between the older basic substance and the later redactional expansions (see §4b4e).

Some of the arguments that are decisive for dating J may also be used in answering the question of where J came from. Because of the traditions originating in the south, the Yahwist is usually regarded as someone who lived in the southern kingdom of Judah. He is perhaps to be thought of as from the countryside (O. H. Steck) rather than as one who lived in the capital, since typically Jerusalemite conceptions are not present.

4. Unity. Once P, E, and redactional additions have been removed, to what extent do the remaining J parts form a unity? This question, which till now has not found a really satisfactory answer, is raised both by literary criticism and by tradition criticism. Many scholars (R. Smend, Sr., among others) have subdivided the basic material into two sources: an older (J¹, Jª; O. Eissfeldt: L[ay source]; similarly G. Fohrer: N[omad source]) and a more recent (J², J) Yahwist. This "most recent form of the documentary hypothesis" is clearly illustrated in O. Eissfeldt's *Hexateuch-Synopse* (1922, 1962), but thus far no one has succeeded in finding a real continuity in the texts that have been separated out and are usually regarded as older. In fact, even the selection made is open to question, so that we would be better advised to renounce this additional division of sources. Nonetheless, literary-critical work on the Yahwist can proceed in two directions: On the one hand, does his work incorporate antecedent written documents? On the other hand, to what extent has J been augmented by means of additions that likewise use the name Yahweh (e.g., Gen 4:25f.; 6:1–4) but detract somewhat from the continuity of the source document?

The latter question of the subsequent history and redactional history of the text is probably the more fruitful of the two.

There is no doubt that important tensions exist within the Yahwist sections of the Pentateuch. For example, the table of peoples in Gen 10 and the story of the Tower of Babel in Gen 11 contradict each other, since Gen 11 once again supposes the unity of humanity. Or are not the early civilizational achievements (Gen 4:17ff.) wiped out by the great flood (Gen 6ff.)? Is it permissible, therefore, to present J as a strongly structured narrative (see §4b4a)?

Are J and E, in fact, "not individual authors" but "schools of narrators" (H. Gunkel, *Legends*, p. 130)? "We may quite readily conceive of J as having a history which began with the matrix of the work shortly after the state came into existence and ended with the prefixing of the primeval history and the incorporation of some passages of a short-story type not very long before the state came to its end" (R. Smend, *EntstAT*, p. 94). But how is it possible to show within the Yahwist stratum a gradual growth (over several centuries) with increasing additions to the text, in other words, the kind of growth that Deuteronomy (for example) underwent?

Certain incoherences are more easily explained in tradition-historical terms; they are "signs of the determination not to relinquish any part of the tradition" (J. Hempel). The Yahwist did not deal as freely with the tradition as the later Priestly document did. Only within limits did he retell his stories as he chose. Rather he accepted traditions without bringing them into complete harmony, and he gave a shape to the complex as a whole but hardly to each part of it.

In any case, it is hardly possible to recognize a single intention running through the entire work and finding expression in turns of phrase that are repeated without alteration. It is indeed possible in the primeval history to discern the Yahwist's purpose from the passages that bind together the individual stories and fit in well with the programmatic statement in Gen 12:1–3. In other blocks of tradition, however, it is more difficult to make a clear distinction between tradition and intention. Only here and there is it possible to determine more accurately the fundamental theological ideas that shape the material.

b) Theological Intentions

1. The work of the Yahwist and, later, the Pentateuch as a whole acquire a universalist dimension as a result of the prefixing of the primeval history to the other blocks of tradition. Inasmuch as the

Yahwist (unlike E and P) uses the name Yahweh from creation on and shows human beings worshiping Yahweh from early times (Gen 4:26, an addition?; cf. 8:20; 9:26), the God of the Israelite people is already being seen as the God of the human race and the Judge of the peoples (Gen 4; 11; cf. 24:3, 7). In the primeval history the Yahwist uses types to present the destiny of humanity with its inner discord, that is, as increasing yet also being diminished, as strong yet weak, graced yet under judgment.

In the tenth century B.C. it was probably not yet self-evident to Israel that Yahweh should be acknowledged not only as a helper in historical needs but also as creator (Gen 14:19ff.; 1 Kgs 8:12; also Ps 24:2; etc.). In any case, the notion that Yahweh determines the rain (Gen 2:5; 7:4), the rhythm of sowing and harvest, summer and winter (8:22), and thus all fertility was still being disputed one or two centuries later (1 Kgs 17f.; Hos 2).

The story of creation that is told in Gen 2:4b ff. is profoundly different in context and course of action from that told in Gen 1 P. The cosmic scope of chap. 1 is replaced by the peasant world of chap. 2. In the first story the waters must be contained within limits (chaos becomes sea), but in the second water gives life, turning the desert into farmland (a Babylonian tradition in chap. 1, a Palestinian in chap. 2?). It is not the human race (Gen 1:26ff.) that is created, but two individuals, one after the other. God passes a judgment of "not good" on his creation (2:18) because the human being he has formed of dust from the ground (2:7; cf. Jer 18:3f.) is alone. But God's effort to remedy the situation achieves true success only on the second try. Not in the beasts, which are subject to the man, but only in woman does he find a partner, "a helper fit for him," and thereby becomes a man (2:19ff.). The story thus emphasizes (contrary to 1 Cor 11:7ff.; 1 Tim 2:11ff.) the equality of man and woman by reason of their creation; woman's subordination to man is the result of the curse (Gen 3:16).

Unlike Gen 1 P, however, the Yahwist story of creation does not have an independent significance but simply establishes the presuppositions for the story of paradise. In contrast to the simple succession expressed in Gen 1:31; 6:13 P, the Yahwist sees creation, guilt and suffering, good and evil, as more closely interwoven from the beginning. It is for this reason that the stories of creation and paradise, which were originally independent traditions, have been tied together. The creatures respond with doubt and disobedience to the creator who has given them the garden as a dwelling and workplace (2:8, 15). Yet God does not carry out his threat, "In the day that you eat of it you shall die" (2:17), but remains merciful even in judgment and preserves human beings from the worst by giving them his protection (3:21 versus 3:7), despite the severity of the punishment (curse on human labor, closing of the access to everlasting life, and expulsion from the garden, 3:14ff., 22f.). The curses give rise, etiologically, to the present distressful conditions of human life, such as woman's pain in giving birth and man's difficulty in earning his bread, but they do not bring either immediate death or even (contrary to Rom 5:12) mortality itself. The very origin of the human person from "dust"—and a divine breath—tells us from the outset of human finiteness (compare 2:7 with 3:19; also Eccl 12:7; Job 10:9).

The story of Cain and Abel in Gen 4 incorporates a tradition that, from the

Israelite standpoint, explains the phenomenon of the Kenites, who also are worshipers of Yahweh but possess no land. Their ancestor or representative, Cain, carries a mark made by Yahweh, but he is restless and a wanderer (4:14f.; cf. Judg 1:16). By its inclusion in the Yahwist primeval history this tribal story is given a universal human bearing, and—according to Gen 2f., which depicts the relationship between God and humanity and between husband and wife—it presents in an archetypal way a further basic possibility inherent in human existence, namely, the relationship between brothers, and this in the form of hostile opposition. Cain's behavior is that of a type: anyone who sheds human blood kills his brother. Thus, Gen 4 is in all likelihood reporting an intensification of human wickedness. Both stories (the first sin; Cain and Abel) are related to one another by common structural elements ("Where are you?"—"Where is your brother?" 3:9; 4:9; curse on the ground or on Cain, 3:17; 4:11). Just as God does not send Adam defenseless from the garden, neither is the murderer Cain driven mercilessly from God's sight, but receives a sign to protect him from being slain.

2. The Yahwist achieves critical insights into the limitless malice that marks human activity, insights that will be reached again only by Jeremiah (13:23) or the psalmist (51:5; cf. also 1 Kgs 8:46; Prov 20:9; etc.): "The imagination of man's heart [i.e., his thinking and willing] is evil from his youth" (Gen 8:21; 6:5).

Like Gen 3f., the story of the flood in Gen 6–8* contains the motif of preservation. God can annihilate what he has created, but one man is mercifully saved. The Yahwist thus imposes a twofold interpretation on a tradition found all over the world.

First, in an introduction and conclusion that are free formulations of his own the Yahwist explains the flood as the result of the wickedness of human beings (6:5–8; 8:21f., after the traditional ending in 8:20). These passages acknowledge God's justice, for they understand the disaster as a consequence of humanity's godless will. The event thus becomes a judgment and punishment that human beings can perceive as such, because the event is caused by their own behavior.

Second, the popular tradition of Noah's "righteousness" (Ezek 14:14, 20; cf. Gen 6:9 P; 5:29 J) is reinterpreted as something passive: Noah "found favor" (6:8), was (literally) "perceived as righteous" (7:1; cf. 18:3; 19:19). This approach avoids making Noah's special position as a "remnant" amid the *massa perditionis* the result of his morality and piety (a line of thinking that is continued in Heb 11:7).

Elsewhere too the Yahwist does not turn his chief personages into idealized figures: neither Abraham (Gen 12:10ff.; 16) nor Jacob (Gen 27) nor Moses (Exod 2) is presented as virtuous and justified in his actions.

God's judgment does not improve human beings; they remain what they are (Gen 8:21; cf. 18:20f., and the following, probably later conversation on God's justice). This insight, which is developed in a narrative way by J without his having a special concept of "sin," by no means applies only to Israel; the Yahwist is rather making a judgment, in the light of his faith, about human beings as such (cf. Rom 7).

Throughout the diversified individual stories of Gen 2–8 there is visible a basic structure or framework of action that can be summed up in these stages: saving solicitude of God—guilt of humanity—punishment—merciful preservation and thus a new beginning.

3. As in his primeval history, the Yahwist likes to interpret the traditions he has received by introducing speeches of Yahweh at decisive points and using these to express theological intentions (Gen 2:16f.; 3:14–19; 4:6f., 11ff.; 6:3, 5–8; 8:21f.; 11:6f.; 12:1–3; 13:14–17; 18:17ff.; 26:24; 28:13–15; 31:3; etc.). While the divine oracles take the form of promises in the history of the patriarchs, in the primeval history they consistently express threats or punishments—with one important exception: the promise not to curse, that is, devastate, the earth again (8:21f.). There seems to be an echo here of ancient Near Eastern tradition according to which the flood put an end to the primeval period. But the sequence of sin and punishment does not cease at this point (Gen 11); rather the older view is overlaid by the specifically Israelite conception of history, according to which only the beginning of the patriarchal age with the call of Abraham puts an end to the primeval epoch.

The blessing in Gen 12:1–3, then, marks the end of the primeval history; it is the objective sought in the curses of that time (3:14, 17; 4:11; 5:29; 9:25) and the beginning of a coming time of salvation. The human race, which of itself is in a state of ruin, needs the salvation that God offers to it in Abraham: "The so-called primal history explains beforehand why all the families of the earth need this blessing" (H. W. Wolff, p. 53). The promises of posterity and a land, which are motifs from the faith of the patriarchs (see 12:6; 28:13f.) are echoed here only in a very generalized form and prepare the way for the more comprehensive promise: "I will bless those who bless you, and him who curses you I will curse; and by you all the families of the earth will bless themselves" (12:3).

The destiny of the human race is to be decided by its attitude to Abraham; all are to have a share in his blessing. Is the Yahwist opposing this promise to the lust for power and the arrogance of his own time? Nothing is explicitly said about his historical situation; the promise is of a future that is not coextensive with the political reality of the Davidic-Solomonic age, a future that has not yet arrived. May we discern here the hope cherished by the Yahwist, who, like the other documentary sources, is extremely chary of eschatological statements? In any case, the programmatic words in 12:1–3 give a new and universal meaning to the tradition of the patriarchs. This begins the history of the patriarchs in the final redaction of the Pentateuch as we now have it and thus provides a kind of "overall meaning" for the patriarchal tradition—assuming that we may look for such an overall meaning when formerly independent strands of tradition and source documents have been formed into a unity.

The promise of blessing recurs from time to time in the Yahwist story (Gen 18:18; 28:14; cf. 22:18; 26:4; Num 24:9), and no less a personage than Pharaoh is compelled to acknowledge its fulfillment: "The people of Israel are too many and too mighty for us" (Exod 1:9). Yet even in the stories of Isaac, Jacob, and Joseph the promise of divine assistance becomes more prominent than the blessing motif, "I will be with you" (Gen 26:3, 24, 28; 28:15; 31:3; 39:2f., 21, 31), and then returns in the stories of David. Did the Israelites of that time (relying, undoubtedly, on earlier tradition) interpret intrahistorical prosperity and success as a consequence of Yahweh's "being with them" (see §11c3)?

4. An independent intention of the Yahwist emerges when he turns Exod 5–14 into a single great unity and reworks the popular stories of the plagues so as to make of them an expression of the relation of foreign oppressors to Yahweh. The theme is introduced by the question in which Pharaoh challenges Yahweh: "Who is the Lord, that I should heed his voice and let Israel go? I do not know the Lord." Subsequent events will force Pharaoh to "know" Yahweh as true God (7:17; 8:10, 22; cf. 10:3; etc.). Pharaoh voices such an acknowledgment when he confesses himself guilty (9:27; 10:16) and asks Moses to intercede with Yahweh for him (8:8, 28; 9:28; 10:17; 12:32). Just as the salvation or doom of humanity is determined by its relation to Abraham, so Pharaoh might share in the blessing of Israel, provided he not remain obdurate. In his own downfall he is forced to acknowledge (14:25) and experience Yahweh's superior power.

As in this account of rescue from oppressors (14:13f., 30), so too in his use of other traditional material the Yahwist brings out Yahweh's exclusive power (he blesses, Gen 12:3; leads out of Egypt, Exod 3:16f.; hardens Pharaoh's heart, 10:1; sends the plagues and strikes Egypt, 12:23; Gen 12:17) and transcendence. God does not dwell on earth, even in the burning bush or on Sinai, but "comes down" (*yārad*, Gen 11:5, 7; 18:21; Exod 3:8; 19:11, 18, 20; etc.) in order to intervene in what is happening. When, finally, we see the Yahwist using as an introduction to a speech the words "The Lord said to Abraham" (Gen 12:1; cf. 26:2) but not saying whence and how God revealed himself, we may conclude that the author was exercising a certain freedom in regard to the anthropomorphic representations (e.g., in the paradise story) that were set before him by the tradition. Or did he perhaps even have a twinkle in his eye when he repeated the tradition that God walked in the garden in the cool of evening (Gen 3:8; cf. 8:21; etc.)?

§7

THE ELOHIST HISTORY

a) Introductory Questions

The Yahwist provides us with the first written form of the outline of the Pentateuch. But this was not the only attempt made to depict the early history of Israel. It was supplemented by another portrayal, that of the Elohist, which was so closely interwoven with the first that scholars even speak of a "Yehowist" (J/E). In fact, even in the story of Joseph, but in any case from Exodus on, it is often difficult to distinguish between the two sources and to determine clearly which is being used. It is therefore frequently necessary to be cautious about attribution to the one or the other source: "The separation of J from E is the most difficult task faced by text analysis and in many cases is simply impossible" (H. Holzinger, *EinlHex*, p. 485, etc.).

1. Independence. Because of the situation just described, the Elohist document is a subject of dispute in literary-critical, historical, and theological research. Not only is its extent judged differently, but even the very existence of an Elohist is denied by some (P. Volz, W. Rudolph, S. Mowinckel, and others).

There are, nonetheless, various reasons for regarding the Elohist as an independent storyteller: (a) There is a series of obvious doublets of the same material—especially, for example, the story of the threat to Israel's ancestor Sarah (Gen 20 E; 12:10ff. J; 26:7ff. J) or of Hagar's flight (Gen 21:9ff. E; 16:1ff. J). (b) There are parallel accounts in which the Yahwist and Elohist versions have been combined. Important examples are the accounts of Jacob's dream (Gen 28:10ff.), Moses' vocation (Exod 3), and the theophany at Sinai (Exod 19:16ff.)—and probably the section on Balaam as well (Num 22–24). Within these blocks a division of the pre-Priestly material into two strands seems to provide the best explanation; with these established it is then possible to determine linkages. (c) In these principal texts the separation of sources is compatible with a decisive criterion, namely, the use of the divine name "Elohim" for "Yahweh."

There are some further arguments, of a corroborative rather than a demonstrative kind, which show the distinction of sources to be objectively well founded: (d) The Elohist history is characterized here and there by peculiarities of style and, to a lesser degree, by a special vocabulary.

There is, for example, this characteristic sequence: address by God, in which the person's name is repeated, with the person then answering "Here am I" (with variations: Gen 22:1, 7, 11; 31:11; 46:2; Exod 3:4b).

There are common factors which admittedly do not run through the Elohist work in its entirety but which do, however, link individual passages. For example: the question "Am I in place of God?" (Gen 30:2; 50:19) or the phrase, Moses "brought forth the people" (Exod 3:10, 12; 19:17).

Instead of the place name "Sinai," E seems to prefer the concept "mountain of God" (Exod 3:1b); the proper name Jethro and the title "Pharaoh" (instead of "King of Egypt") are hardly typical.

(e) Occasional reflections contain references to events of past and future, thus linking the two periods. Thus, the conclusion of the story of Joseph—"As for you, you meant evil against me; but God meant it for good, to bring it about that many people should be kept alive, as they are today" (Gen 50:20, anticipated in 45:5, 7)—explains Joseph's destiny after the fact and also looks forward both conceptually and materially to the next pericope (Exod 1:15ff.), in which the midwives, because of their fear of God, carry out God's plan that "many people should be kept alive." The reflection, then, brings out a thematic connection between different units of text, even when connectives of a literary kind are lacking. In fact, Gen 50:20 seems to have an articulatory function in the Elohist story as a whole; Joseph's words conclude the family history of the patriarchs and introduce the history of the people as a whole. Other utterances of a similar kind (e.g., Gen 31:13, with reference back to Gen 28:10ff.) bear witness to "a high degree of theological reflection and narrative skill" (H. W. Wolff, p. 80).

(f) Finally, it is possible (but, from a methodological standpoint, only in consequence of the previous observations) to recognize certain peculiarities in ethical and theological statements.

A special refinement is often discernible in the ethical outlook of the Elohist. For example: (1) While the Yahwist has Abraham tell a white lie, namely, that Sarah is his sister (Gen 12:11ff.; cf. 26:7ff.), the Elohist avoids charging Abraham with a lie by turning Sarah into his half-sister, a relationship that the author insists actually existed (Gen 20:2, 5, 12). (2) Whereas in the Yahwist version Joseph is sold to Ishmaelites (Gen 37:27, 28b), in the Elohist account he is "only" abandoned in a cistern—or left there for a while—but found and taken off by Midianite traders (Gen 37:22–24, 28a, 29). (3) According to Gen 16:6 J Abraham without scruple lets Sarah have her way with Hagar, but according to Gen 21:11f. E he dismisses her only after being ordered by God to do so, and he provides her with food and water.

These examples show also that the Elohist often gives individual traditions in a later and more rigorously shaped form; but this is not always the case (see Gen 28:10ff.), and in the overall structure of the Pentateuch E has preserved the older form (see below).

Among the theological characteristics of E is especially the theme of fear of God, which runs almost throughout his entire presentation.

Despite the existence of many uncertainties, especially in Exodus and Numbers, these various arguments are conclusive for the original independence of the Elohist. He is indeed often taken to be simply a "new editor" (P. Volz) who revises and supplements the Yahwist, but in fact E seems originally not to have had the Yahwist in mind but to have been independent of him (see §4b4b). This, indeed, must necessarily have been the case with a revisory stratum. Moreover it is possible to trace links between the Elohist parts of the text.

In any case, of this source "only scattered fragments remain" (H. Holzinger, p. 173), for the editor who combined J and E used the Elohist history only to supplement the Yahwist history, which he took as his basis (see §4b4c).

2. Scope. Despite this editing process, which did not favor E, whole stories from this history have been preserved. The most extensive complex of texts, and the one that best reveals the Elohist's approach, is Gen 20–22*. The precise point, however, at which the Elohist's work starts is disputed. This point is usually located in Gen 15, but this chapter combines older and more recent traditions, so that the assignment of the parts of the text to one or another source continues to be disputed. "Apart from a few traces—and even these are still uncertain—in Gen 15 there is nothing from this source in Gen 12–19" (H. Holzinger, p. 174). Even if an Elohist strand provides a basis in Gen 15, the real beginning of this history has not been preserved, in contrast to the sonorous opening of the Priestly document in Gen 1 and of the Yahwist document in Gen 2:4b ff. Did the Elohist originally begin by bringing Abraham on the scene? In any case there is no evidence of E in Gen 1–11 (though efforts have been made to find it); E therefore contains no primeval history but opens with the history of the patriarchs.

There are also various opinions on where the Elohist history ends. Some find the ending in Josh 24, others in Deut 31ff. The last major Elohist text is usually thought to be the Balaam pericope, Num 22f.

Familiar texts that are more or less unanimously assigned to E are the following:

Gen 15*?	The call of Abraham
Gen 20:1–22:19*	Abraham and Abimelech, Isaac's birth, Hagar's dismissal and the sacrifice of Isaac
Gen 28:11f., 17f., 20f.	Jacob's dream of the ladder to heaven
	Parts of Gen 30–33; 35 (especially vv. 1–5, 7f.); 37; 40–42 (predominantly); 47f.
Gen 46:1b–5a	Appearance to Jacob
Gen 45:5b–15; 50:15–26	Joseph's forgiveness
Exod 1:15ff.	Disobedience of the midwives (also 2:1–10?)
Exod 3f.*	Call of Moses (specifically 3:1bβ, 4b, 6, 9–14)
Exod 14*	Miracle of the Sea of Reeds (especially 13:17–19; 14:5a, 19a)
Exod 18*	Moses' meeting with his Midianite father-in-law: joint sacrifice, appointment of judges
Exod 19*	Revelation at Sinai (especially 19:16f., 19; also 24:[9–]11?)
	Parts of Num 20f.
Num 22f.*	Balaam

From various unevennesses or incoherences scholars have concluded to a subsequent revision of the Elohist or to the linking of several Elohist strands, but sound arguments are lacking on which to base such delicate operations. In any case we must allow for additions in an Elohist or even a Deuteronomic-Deuteronomistic style; probable additions of this kind are Exod 20:18–21 or parts of Exod 32. Extremely important in determining the theology of the Elohist is the decision whether to attribute or (with greater justification) to deny to the Elohist such texts as Gen 15:6; Exod 32; Num 12:6ff. or even the Decalogue and the Book of the Covenant (Exod 20–23). A reliable judgment on this theology requires that we restrict ourselves to the critically assured minimum.

3. Situation. Those who accept the existence of an Elohist history are largely in agreement on the place and time of its origin, although there are dissenting views (M. Noth, among others). Its place of origin is probably to be sought in the northern kingdom (an easy mnemonic: E from Ephraim, J from Judah). But the evidence takes the form of clues more than of sure criteria. The chief argument is an argument from silence: The patriarchal tradition in E lacks such stories from J as have their locale in the south, for example, the Abraham-Lot cycle of sagas.

The patriarchal tradition is thus preserved here in an older form in which the sanctuaries of central Palestine—Bethel (Gen 28:22; 35:1ff.), Shechem (Gen 33:19f.; 35:4, 8; 48:22; cf. 50:24f.; Exod 13:19 with Josh 24:32)—and Beersheba (Gen 21:31ff.; 22:19; 46:1ff.), which was in the south but had close ties with the north (cf. Amos 5:5; 8:14), play a decisive role. In the same way, the spokesman for the brothers in the story of Joseph is not Judah, as in J, but Reuben, as befits an earlier stage of the tradition (Gen 37:22–24, 29–30 E, versus 37:21, 26–27 J).

In addition, there are certain connections, though hardly obvious ones, of the Elohist history with the prophets of the northern kingdom— perhaps even Elijah, more clearly Hosea (cf. Exod 3:14 with Hos 1:9; also Exod 3:10ff. with Hos 12:14)—and with Deuteronomy, whose oldest traditions seem to go back to the north (§10a3). It is possible, therefore, to trace a chain of tradition from the Elohist through the prophet Hosea and "Ur-Deuteronomy," which may later be taken up by Jeremiah in the southern kingdom, but caution is called for in this area.

M. Noth has challenged not only the usual geographical location of E but also its assignment to a time after the Yahwist: "On the whole E represents rather an earlier stage in the history of tradition than J" (*A History of Pentateuchal Traditions*, p. 38 n. 143). Thus E lacks both the primeval history and the traditions of the southern kingdom that form part of the patriarchal complex of sagas. But this objection of Noth does not necessarily hold, since a later document can preserve an older tradition. More important, however, in many individual stories E obviously provides us with a later, more theologically conscious form of the tradition than J does (see above, this chapter, a1f). If we give proper consideration to the links between E and the northern kingdom, we must conclude (this is the commonly accepted view) that the Elohist's work emerged between the dividing of the kingdom in 926 B.C. and the appearance of the prophet Hosea, and therefore before the mortal danger from the Assyrians, which E does not seem to know about. The most likely date is around 800 or the first half of the eighth century B.C.

The intellectual and spiritual situation reflected in E fits well into such a temporal framework. E is evidently closely related to the (earlier, which means northern Israelite) prophetic movement. On the one hand, it contains elements of prophetic tradition. Thus, the call of Moses (Exod 3:10ff.) is described in accordance with a formulary that underlies Judg 6, 1 Sam 9f., and Jer 1. Above all, Abraham is called a "prophet" in Gen 20:7, because he practices intercession. On the other hand, Hosea's announcement of judgment, "I am not there for you" (1:9, literally), seems to accept the explanation of the divine name Yahweh, "I am (there for you)" (Exod 3:14, 12 E), and to deny this presence of God.

On the other hand, there are no detectable influences of the early writing prophets—for example, Hosea—on the Elohist history. "Elohim" ("God") as the subject of a sentence is utterly unprophetic. E knows nothing of the criticism leveled at the northern sanctuaries and certainly nothing of the judgment pronounced upon Israel. Dreams, which the Elohist uses as a stylistic device in the patriarchal stories, become unimportant in the writing prophets; they are superseded as a means of revelation and later on even criticized (Jer 23:28f.; cf. Deut 13:1–5; etc.).

In its subsequent destiny the Elohist history has one final point in common with the message of Hosea: after the fall of the northern kingdom in 722 B.C. both migrated to the south. There, perhaps in Jerusalem, E was combined with J.

Exod 3:15 may perhaps be offered in support of this last conjecture. The verse that the redactor has introduced between Exod 3:14 E and 3:16 J seems to belong to Zion and, to be more specific, probably to the Jerusalem liturgy (see Pss 102:12; 135:13).

The fact that E arose in a time and place different from the setting of J makes the relation between the two sources intelligible. Agreements in the overall structure and differences in wording are most easily explained if J and E were only indirectly in contact through oral tradition.

b) Theological Intentions

The literary fact that the Elohist offers no primeval history has substantive significance: he lacks the universalist orientation of the Yahwist. In E Yahweh has not already been at work ever since creation but reveals himself for the first time when he calls Moses (Exod 3). We may conclude from this silence that E is concerned exclusively with the people of Israel and the special position assigned to them. The conclusion is confirmed by the oracle of Balaam: "Lo, a people dwelling alone, and not reckoning itself among the nations!" (Num 23:9).

These words seem to offer an earlier testimony to Israel's self-understanding. Israel's separation from the nations is hardly to be taken as merely geographical; it is also something essential—under the blessing of Yahweh (Num 23:8, 10, 20ff.). At the same time, however, it is hardly possible to reproach the Elohist with particularism, since he also gives evidence of contrary tendencies (see God's conversation with the foreign king in Gen 20:3ff.).

1. How could E have regularly used not the proper name "Yahweh"

but the generic concept "Elohim" (and this without adding any recognizable distinguishing sign and even without using the article)? This, in the northern kingdom of about 800 B.C., and thus in a situation in which as the Elijah stories and the preaching of Hosea tell us, Yahweh and Baal stood in harsh opposition! No really satisfactory explanation has been found of the fact that this documentary source avoids the name for God that was specific to Israel. We certainly may not shift the responsibility to a polytheism that Israel had formerly practiced or simply (a vaguer solution) to an existing tradition. Again, E's intention was hardly to distinguish, as the later Priestly document would, different stages in the understanding of God. E does introduce the name Yahweh into God's answer to Moses' question, and at the same time explains the name: "I will be (am), who I will be (am)" (Exod 3:14), but even after that he sticks, as a rule, to the general name "Elohim."

There is a dispute about whether after Exod 3:14 E uses "Elohim" exclusively or only in most passages. But the very state of the tradition already renders foolhardy any attempt to distinguish two strata in E on the basis of the use or nonuse of Elohim (C. Steuernagel and others). At least at times, the mention of the name of Yahweh in Elohistic parts of the text is due to the secondary influence of the Yahwist or even of the Priestly document, and thus to editorial handling of E (e.g., Gen 22:11, 14, prior to the addition of vv. 15–18). If Exod 3:15 is itself an editorial addition, it is easier to understand that even after 3:14 E uses "Elohim," at least as its predominant word for God.

The most likely reason for the use of "Elohim" is the author's intention of emphasizing God's transcendence and thus indirectly a certain universalism about his own faith. Yahweh, the God of a single people, is God in the unqualified sense. Does E not seem to presuppose the decision made in the episode on Carmel between faith in Yahweh and faith in Baal: "The Lord [Yahweh], he is God [Elohim]" (1 Kgs 18:39) (O. Procksch)? At the same time this would explain why in the texts certainly belonging to it this source gives so little evidence of anti-Canaanite polemics.

2. In any case, the tendency to emphasize the transcendence of God emerges quite strongly in the Elohist. There are no more stories telling of a direct encounter between God and a human (as in Gen 3; 18–19 J). Instead, God keeps a greater distance. He "speaks" with Abraham (Gen 22:1), but no express mention is made of any appearance. Or he "calls" Moses (Exod 3:4b) as from a distance, without it being clear just where the call is coming from. God seems to dwell in heaven, since according to the picture given of the patriarchal period it is from there that he sends his messengers to earth or from there that his

messengers speak (Gen 28:12 or 21:17; 22:11; cf. 22:15; Exod 14:19; 20:22). Through his messengers God acquires a presence in the visible world without becoming an object of direct experience (cf. Gen 28:12 E with 28:13 J). In like manner, the relationship of God to humanity is no longer "objectifiable" when God appears (again only in the period before Moses) in a dream (Gen 20:3ff.; 28:12; 31:24; 46:2; cf. 37:5ff.; 40:9ff.; 41:17ff.).

The two modes of revelation, through messengers and in dreams, may also be combined (31:11; 28:12). A dream has no intrinsic importance but is introduced for a theological purpose and almost as a literary device, in order to allow God to speak. The important thing is not the vision but what is said (Gen 20:3, 6; etc.). In general, discourses occupy a great deal of space; they provide continuity and interpretation for the sequence of actions (31:13; etc.). The Elohistic presentation of Moses' call (Exod 3:1bβ, 4b, 6, 9–14) is almost entirely a conversation in form. The Elohist's intention emerges also in the description of Moses' activity. While in the older tradition the liberation from Egypt is presented as God's own doing (Exod 3:8, 16–17 J; etc.), E seeks to avoid direct contact between God and humanity by having Moses lead the people out of Egypt (3:10, 12; cf. 19:17). "E has pushed Moses much more into the foreground as the instrument of God in effecting the deliverance" (G. von Rad, *Old Testament Theology*, vol. 1, p. 292). In comparison with the Yahwistic account of the story the Elohist presentation seems therefore to show, on the whole, a greater degree of theological reflection. Yet it is hardly appropriate to characterize E as marked by a dematerialization or spiritualization of the image of God, especially since speaking and hearing play so decisive a role.

3. In addition to this indirect determination of the Elohist's special approach through comparison with parallel texts, it is also possible to discern his theological intention more directly by examining the concepts he uses. J. Becker and H. W. Wolff have found in the idea of human beings' being tested for their fear of God a motif that keeps recurring in the individual stories. The theme of temptation or testing that already sounds in Gen 20:11 is taken up in the story of the sacrifice of Isaac, although the focus here is different. This originally pre-Israelite cult legend (see §5b3) of the replacement of the sacrifice of a child with the sacrifice of an animal (v. 22) is interpreted by the Elohist as a test of faith: "God tested Abraham" (22:1). Abraham shows that he indeed fears God (v. 12), that is, is ready to give back to God the gift that God had promised and given him and thus to trust in God without reservation (see Deut 8:2; 13:4). Again, out of fear of

God (Exod 1:17, 21) the midwives will not obey Pharaoh's barbarous command to kill the newborn sons of Israel and allow only the daughters to live (cf. Acts 5:29); without realizing it the midwives are carrying out God's will "to bring it about that many people should be kept alive" (Gen 50:20). Fear of God thus finds varying expression in a diversity of situations: through the obedience of faith (22:12), through reliance on the word (42:18; Exod 18:21), through protection of those in need of protection, be it the foreigner (Gen 20:11) or the newborn child (Exod 1:17, 21; cf. also 20:20). In fear of God, then, religion and ethics, faith in God and behavior toward one's fellow human beings are inseparably intertwined.

Is the Elohistic presentation intended to provide examples and models, at least to the extent that it calls Israel to fear of God during the critical encounter with the Canaanite religion (thus, e.g., H. W. Wolff and K. Jaroš)? But would we not expect the emphasis to be on "fear of Yahweh" rather than on the more general "fear of God," if the issue were a clarification of positions in the face of the danger represented by faith in Baal and the threat coming from syncretism? It is more likely, then, that sapiential circles provided the Elohist with the "fear of God" as a key concept. A proverb such as "By fear of the Lord a man avoids evil" (Prov 16:16; cf. 14:26f.; 19:23; etc.) seems to express in a direct way the intention that guides the Elohist's stories. Is E therefore drawing on the prophetic and sapiential traditions and thus announcing the later linking of prophecy and wisdom?

§8

THE PRIESTLY DOCUMENT

a) Introductory Questions

1. The quite different spirit that animates the Priestly document is already clear to us when we examine its three outstanding characteristics:

a) None of the source documents is as clearly recognizable from its vocabulary and stylistic peculiarities as the Priestly document is. A comparably specific linguistic usage is to be found elsewhere only in the Deuteronomic and Deuteronomistic literature. Some of the turns of phrase used predominantly by P are "Be fruitful and multiply" (Gen 1:28, and often), "remember the covenant" (9:15f.; etc.), or "Pharaoh king of Egypt" (41:46; etc.). In particular, the laws are introduced by typical and to a large extent set formulas (Exod 16:16; Lev 1:1f., and often). In addition to the "preference for stock phrases" T. Nöldeke long ago saw as characteristic of P "a great prolixity along with frequent repetitions. At every point the basic document lacks vitality, vividness, detailed description and warmth of language. . . . The personages who come on the scene are only sketchily described; no detailed characterizations are given" (p. 133). As a matter of fact, the narrative element is insignificant when compared with the older sources. But the monotony of tone gives rise to contrary impressions. It can awaken a sense of the sublime (e.g., Gen 1), but it can also suggest rigidity and stiffness and seem schematic and even pedantic. The lack of vividness can signify a tenacious reserve in regard to mythical conceptions (e.g., Gen 1:14ff.) but also a keener sense of the miraculous (e.g., Exod 14; 16). In any case, there is a definite purpose at work in the circumstantial style with its numerous additions. The aim is to produce an accurately drawn description of the phenomenon in question (e.g., Gen 1:11f.; 29f.) and a concentration on theological statements, so as to direct "the attention of the reader beyond what is immediately said to what lies in the background" (K. Elliger, p. 189).

b) Far more than the older sources the Priestly document provides a great many numbers: from the measurements of Noah's ark (compare

Gen 6:15f. with 7:20) down to the review of the people (Num 1). In particular, P contains an exact chronology (though one created through retrospect), beginning with a circumspect numbering of the days of creation and running through the dating of the flood (Gen 7:11; 8:13; etc.), which was unknown to the older tradition, down to the later exact details regarding year, month, and day (Gen 17:1, 24f.; Exod 12:2, 18, 40f.; 19:1; etc.). Numbers and names are often combined in lists and genealogies. These lists and genealogies are derived in part from a *tôlĕdōt* book, or record of generations, which was probably an originally independent entity. It began with Gen 5:1, "This is the book of the generations of Adam," and was incorporated into P's presentation at significant points marking a new phase in the course of action (6:9; 10:1; 11:10; etc.).

Even before making use of the book of generations P uses the concept *tôlĕdōt* for the creation of the world (Gen 2:4a); here he broadens the term to mean "history of origins."

We find J already using genealogies to link individual stories into sequences (Gen 4:1f., 17ff.; etc.), but P almost inverts the relationship. The historical presentation is "often reduced to genealogies" (H. Holzinger, *EinlHex*, pp. 369–70). Especially in its version of the patriarchal history (or, more accurately, the story of Isaac, Jacob, and Joseph), P is extremely limited, since it reduces the story essentially to a set of genealogical notices. Only two chapters, Gen 17 and 23, report action in detail; it is remarkable that neither of the two stories is told in the older sources.

c) The trait that has given the Priestly document its name is a strong focus on proper worship, in regard both to its location, the "tabernacle," and to its intention, which is the preservation of purity and holiness. This accounts for the transmission of laws governing cult and for the interest in the priesthood as represented by Aaron and the Levites. Aaron takes his place beside Moses and even acts as mediator between Moses and the people (Exod 7:1f.; etc.).

Probably because of the upheaval caused by the exile, P is thus much freer than J had been in dealing with the existing tradition. Its style moreover doubtless shows an even greater degree of theological reflection than is to be found already in E. P does follow the main lines of the older source documents but deliberately seeks conciseness through selection and even elimination of traditional material.

Not only does P lack the colorful stories of the primeval history and the patriarchal history; it even, for example, passes over Moses' childhood and thus his connection with Midian (Exod 2–4; 18 JE). Most notable are the corrections P introduces into the story of the flood and the history of the patriarchs, on the basis of its presupposition that the cult came into existence only at Sinai. On the basis of ancient Near Eastern tradition J tells of a sacrifice that Noah offers after his deliverance (Gen 8:20–21 J), but P says nothing about a sacrifice and the building of an altar, nothing about a distinction between clean and unclean animals (6:19f. and 7:15–16 P as compared with 7:2 and 8:20 J). Cultic information on the time before Moses is omitted in P because it contradicts P's general view that legitimate sacrifice first became possible as a result of the revelation at Sinai (Exod 25ff.).

2. Even though P at times gives only a skeletal picture of an action, it was nonetheless at one time an independent document. This view has, of course, been disputed in favor of the idea that P is identical with the final redaction of the Pentateuch or represents a revision of some parts of the Pentateuch (I. Engnell, R. Rendtorff, F. M. Cross, and others). But even though it is difficult now and then to distinguish clearly between P and a later redaction (R^p), there are important reasons for considering P an independent document.

a) In particular, the doublets in the two older sources and the later source (especially the meshing of the stories of the flood [Gen 6–9] and of the crossing of the sea [Exod 14], as well as the successive accounts of the Abrahamic covenant [Gen 15 and 17] and of the call of Moses [Exod 3f. and 6]) point to the original independence of P. Otherwise could P not have expressed its intentions by means of a redactional revision of Exod 3f.? The fact that Exod 6 sounds like a halting repetition of Exod 3 is more naturally explained if Exod 6 was originally independent of Exod 3 and the two texts were only subsequently combined.

b) I. Engnell and others have not yet been able to determine in a precise way the relationship between P and the two older sources. P did know the Yahwist design in one form or other, since in addition to correspondences in structure there are verbal similarities (e.g., Gen 6:9 P; 7:1 J). But all of these taken together do not justify seeing J/E as the written basis for P. In fact, if P came into being during the exile, there were no written sources available. Concurrences and differences are probably best explained by taking a process of oral tradition as the sole mediating factor, in the same way that the gospel of John takes over the synoptic traditions.

How can we explain the fact that P seems to have taken over only a tradition influenced and enriched by J and E? Did P know the older sources only from recollections of the time before the destruction of the temple? Were these older documents already being read in the Jerusalem liturgy (compare Exod 3:15 with Ps 135:13)? Did P attempt "to supplant the older tradition" (H. Gunkel, *Legends*, p.

158), or did he simply attempt during the exile to supply a kind of replacement for what had been lost? In any case P represents a new interpretation.

c) In addition, the texts of P are intelligible in themselves and thus, despite their varying degrees of fullness, have an independently comprehensible continuity, with only small gaps, which may be due to the subsequent redactor (R^P).

d) Finally, the texts of P are interconnected by a series of related themes or motifs. Thus, the promise of divine blessing runs through Genesis from the story of creation on (1:28; 9:1, 7; 17:2, 20f., etc. down to the fulfillment in 47:27; Exod 1:7) and is then picked up and continued in the promise of the land and the assurance of God's closeness to his people (Gen 17:7; Exod 6:7; 25:22; 29:43; etc.).

The originally independent P later formed the basic document into which the already combined sources J/E were incorporated (see §4b4d). Precisely because P was often so schematic, it made sense to fill it out by fitting the older texts into it; in this way the redactors of the Pentateuch were able to counter the reserve that P exhibited toward the tradition.

3. Since the time of T. Nöldeke (1869) there has been a good deal of agreement on the extent of P, the judgment being based on peculiarities of style and content and on inner coherency. Yet on closer examination P does not give an impression of great unity. In Genesis it does present itself as an almost continuous, planned whole, but from approximately the beginning of Exodus there are roughnesses and even doublets in increasing numbers.

If we leave aside more extensive complexes, especially the so-called Law of Holiness (Lev 17–26; see §9b) or the prescriptions on sacrifice (Lev 1–7) and purity (Lev 11–15), the basic material is not left free of contradictions. Scholars have therefore been compelled to explain the origin of P with the help of a kind of supplementary hypothesis: a more or less clearly definable basic Priestly document, P^G, was augmented in the course of time with all sorts of material that is summed up as P^S, that is, secondary expansion of P. The latter material consists chiefly of cultic law (e.g., Exod 12:43ff. after 12:1–20). But the narrative sections also contain additions, for example, genealogical information (e.g., the list of the sons and grandsons of Jacob in Gen 46:8–27; again Exod 1:1b, 5b, and also 6:14ff.). These additions show the same or at least a very similar style, are usually even more detailed, and thus intensify the tendencies in P^G.

In the case of many of the additions, especially in the book of Numbers, it is difficult to determine whether they are supplements to the originally independent Priestly document or additions made after the combining of the sources.

The purpose of setting aside the secondary material is to get back to a basic document that is as free of contradictions as possible. The guiding principle followed in the process of elimination is "that laws and lists are to be accounted part of the P-narrative (i.e., the basic document) only insofar as they seem to form an organic element in it" (K. Elliger, p. 175). The result of the procedure is that here, as in the older sources, a (continuous) historical narrative is obtained and not just a collection of laws set in a historical framework. This last is the impression given by P in its present final state, in which the secondary material has been integrated into it.

The distinction between the various Priestly strata—a basic content and later additions—means at the same time that in its present form P, like the Deuteronomic-Deuteronomistic literature, is not the work of a single writer but rather of a school, that is, a group of priests who thought in like manner (therefore the great similarity of language) and gathered, revised, and wrote down traditions.

G. von Rad (*Die Priesterschrift im Pentateuch*, 1934) attempted to carry these basic literary-critical insights a step further by dissecting the basic document into two parallel narrative strands, but this hypothesis won few supporters and was later abandoned by von Rad himself. P. Weimar made a new attempt along the same lines by trying to find in P's story of the exodus a written document that would have predated P, but despite sophisticated arguments this procedure too has hardly proved convincing. P, with a taste for resumptions and repetitions, was not able despite all its freedom in handling tradition to weld the different historical traditions into so homogeneous a unity as to eliminate all roughnesses.

4. Because of the gradual literary growth it is not easy to determine the precise time when P first came into being. Since about 1875 the (Reuss-Graf-Kuenen-) Wellhausen hypothesis (see §4b3) has won acceptance, according to which the "Priestly Code" is the last source and came into existence during the exile. This is the common view; others regard a date in the early postexilic period as more likely (fifth century B.C.).

The decisive arguments for assigning a late date to this source were drawn not so much from its language as from the history of ideas: (a) The centralization of cult, which is called for in Deuteronomy (12:13ff.) and according to which the people of God acknowledged only one sanctuary, is taken for granted in P. "In that book [Deuteronomy] the unity of the cultus is *commanded*; in the Priestly Code it is *presupposed*"; the tabernacle (Exod 25ff.) is "the sole legitimate sanctuary for the community of the twelve tribes prior to the days of Solomon, and so in fact a projection of the later temple" (J. Wellhausen, *Prolegomena to the History of Ancient Israel*, pp. 35, 37). The permission that Deuteronomy (12:15f.) gives for "profane" slaughtering in the context of its demand for unity of cult is presupposed in Gen 9:1ff. P (although it is withdrawn again in the Law of Holiness, Lev 17:3f.). Accordingly, it is hardly possible that P came into existence before the publication of Deuteronomy (621 B.C.). The two have further points in common: it is hardly accidental that both see Moses' work as chiefly that of mediator in the giving of the Law.

b) P represents a late stage in the history of cult as this is derivable from the OT. This is reflected in the precise dating of feasts, the differentiation of types of sacrifice, and the divisions within the priesthood (sons of Aaron and Levites; place of the high priest).

"The sons of Aaron are the privileged members of the priestly class, while the Levites are nonpriestly members of the tribe of Levi which includes both classes. . . . Eventual claims (of the Levites) to specifically priestly powers are unequivocally rejected. . . . But nonetheless the Levites are given various secondary competences; above all, in the plan of P they are to have a secure livelihood. To this end P makes provision for their income: they are to have the tithes. There can therefore be no question of demoting the Levites; P seeks rather to stabilize the Levitic class" (A. H. J. Gunneweg, p. 223).

c) P substitutes the concept "community" (*ʿēdâ*) for that of "people" (*ʿam*)—"probably because as a member of the postexilic community, which had lost its civic independence, he regarded the connection with the sanctuary, the *ʾōhel môʿēd*, as the decisive factor" (L. Rost, *Die Vorstufen von Kirche und Synagoge im AT*, 1938, p. 59). Anointing and other symbols of royalty now become the distinguishing marks of priesthood (Exod 28f.).

d) The importance P gives to circumcision and sanctification of the sabbath as "signs" and thus as distinguishing marks of the Yahwistic faith becomes intelligible only in the conditions of the time in exile. The certainly very ancient practice of circumcision, which was customary among Israel's eastern neighbors as well (Jer 9:25f.), was unknown in the Babylonian world and could therefore become a criterion of the Jewish religion amid the other religions of that environment. According to P it was not Moses (see Exod 4:24) but Abraham long ago who was given the precept of circumcision as sign of an "everlasting covenant." Every newborn male child was to be circumcised on the eighth day (Gen 17:9ff.; cf. Lev 12:3). Observance of the sabbath, on the other hand, was announced at the very time of creation when God rested on the seventh day and blessed and hallowed it (Gen 2:2f.). Be that as it may, the people of antiquity and of the patriarchal age knew nothing about the sabbath. Israel discovered the special character of the seventh day almost accidentally during the sojourn in the wilderness.

When Israel collected the bread sent from heaven, the manna did not keep from one day to the next. Only on the seventh day did the people find a two days' ration given and could store up some of it for the seventh day. In this way Israel was more or less compelled to observe the sabbath rest (Exod 16:22ff.). Since by reason of the divine solicitude work on the sabbath was both superfluous and impossible, there was not yet a need for a sabbath commandment in the strict sense. This commandment first occurred as a later addition in connection with the instructions on the building of the tabernacle; here it stands out clearly as the only commandment directed to the community (Exod 31:12–17 P^s). The day of rest, which was to be strictly observed, was a "sign" for all generations that Yahweh "hallowed" Israel, that is, set it apart (Ezek 20:12, 20).

On the basis of such considerations as these we may come to a compromise in the question of the date of P. The basic document (P^G) arose during the exile, while the additions (P^s) were made rather during the postexilic period. In any case, in its narrative sections and certainly in the legal sections as in the lists, P is based on previous traditional material, which it recast. Consequently the date of the fixing of the material in writing still tells us little of the age of the tradition itself; the latter must be determined in each individual case.

There is disagreement over whether P was written in Jerusalem or (this is the usual and probably correct view) among the deportees in Babylon and later—perhaps first by Ezra (Ezra 7:14, 25f.; Neh 8)?—brought to Palestine.

5. While P clearly begins and has its first focal point in the story of creation (Gen 1:1–2:4a), there is less agreement about where P ends. Older and more recent attempts to trace P beyond the Pentateuch (see 11c1) must deal with weighty objections. First of all, after Deut 34:1a, 7–9, the last text in the Pentateuch to be assigned to P, there would be a gap, since no continuous Priestly strand is to be found in the book of Joshua (see 14:1; 18:1; etc.). Furthermore, either the linguistic characteristics have later become less marked, or the vocabulary must have been heavily revised. It is advisable, therefore, to adopt the view offered by J. Wellhausen (*Prolegomena*[6], pp. 355f.) and supported with further arguments by M. Noth: The end of P is to be found in Deut 34:7–9, so that this history runs from the creation of the world to the death of Moses.

Important texts in the Priestly presentation are the following:

Gen 1:1–2:4a	Creation
6–9*	Flood, covenant with Noah
17	Covenant with Abraham
23	Acquisition of the cave at Machpelah
Exod 1:1–5:7, 13f.; 2:23–25	Formation of a people, oppression in Egypt, complaint (God's answer to this being:)
6f.	Call of Moses, promise of "deliverance"

7–14*	Plagues, Passover, departure, rescue
16	Murmuring, manna, sabbath
19:1f.; 24:15ff.	Revelation at Sinai
25–29	Instructions regarding the tabernacle
Lev 8f.	Consecration of priests (according to Exod 29) and first sacrifice
Num 10:11f.	Departure from Sinai
13f.	Scouts. Disbelief of the people
20	Incredulity of Moses and Aaron. Aaron's death
27:12ff.	Appointment of Joshua
Deut 34:1a, 7–9	Death of Moses

6. This determination of the scope of P raises a problem with regard to content: Why does P lack its own account of the settlement when it has reported the repeated renewal of the promise of a land and even given this promise greater importance than it had in the older sources?

The promise to Abraham, "I will give to you, and to your descendants after you . . . all the land of Canaan for an everlasting possession" (Gen 17:8; cf. 28:4; 48:4), begins to be fulfilled at once in the legal purchase of the cave at Machpelah and the surrounding field. The acquisition is a partial anticipation of what is to come (Gen 23; cf. 49:29; 50:12f.). In connection with the call of Moses the promise is confirmed (Exod 6:4, 8; cf. Num 13:2; 14:31; 20:12). But when Moses at God's command sends scouts from the wilderness of Paran to reconnoiter the Promised Land, the scouts return disappointed (here P differs from the older tradition) and, except for Joshua and Caleb, are so critical that the people begin to murmur. This murmuring brings a divine judgment: The generation now alive will not see the Promised Land (Num 13f.). When even Moses and Aaron fall into sin (Num 20), they too are refused entry into the new land. Aaron dies on Mount Hor, after his son Eleazar has been appointed his successor in office (20:25–29). Moses is allowed only to look over into the Promised Land from the mountains of Moab (27:12ff.) before he too dies (Deut 34:7f.). He dies, however, with the assurance that the community will listen to Joshua his successor (Num 27:15ff.; Deut 34:9) and—may we conclude?— that the promise will be fulfilled in the next generation. Does not this presentation recall Jeremiah's letter to the exiles (29:5ff., 10)? Not the present generation but only a future generation will be allowed to set foot in the land again.

Just as the patriarchs only pass through the Promised Land and find their burial place in it, so the community in the wilderness is constantly in transit—a *communio viatorum* that hears the promise and heeds it (Exod 12:28; 14:4; 35:21; etc.) but also doubts and rebels (6:9; 16:2; Num 14:2; 20:2, 12; 27:14). Animated by God's pledge but dissatisfied with the way in which he leads them, the community always has the goal before its eyes but never reaches it; it abides in the not-yet. Is this historical picture meant simply as a record of the past or is it also transparently meant for the present, that is, for the time of exile, during which the community again dwells outside the land? If Israel in the wilderness was not allowed to set foot in the land because of its sins, then the Israel of the exile must also leave the land because of its sins. "Because Israel is once again subject to one of the great powers and dwells far from its inherited country, it is given this terse reminder of ancient history and especially of what is to be learned from that history. The covenant and the promise of the land of Canaan still abide" (K. Elliger, p. 196).

Does P intend that this review of the past should rouse hope for the future? Is the community to expect a new fulfillment of the ancient promise? In point of fact, P nowhere offers a direct exhortation to hope and contains no eschatological statements or at least none that are explicit (Num 14:21b is an addition). It is therefore possible to pass contrary judgments on the presentation given in P. Does it belong, like Chronicles, to the group of exilic and postexilic literary works that have abandoned expectations of salvation and are satisfied with a present existence as a cultic community, thus stirring opposition to the late stage of the prophetic movement or, as the case may be, to the dawning apocalyptic movement (O. Plöger)? Or, on the contrary, does what is said about the past contain a sketch of what is to come, and is the past portrayed in the light of this future? "The exiles are in the same position now as the ancients were before the settlement: occupation of the land is refused them now, but it is promised to them" (R. Kilian, p. 247). "The Sinai pericope is at the same time a program for the future; as things once were, so must they be again" (K. Koch, *ZTK* 55 [1958] 40). If the "tabernacle" is to be the one future sanctuary, then does P hope that the community will live in the land under the leadership of a high priest and without a king, and are the laws meant for such a situation? It is difficult to decide between these two types of interpretation, because the second and far more widespread view has only indirect support. It distinguishes between what the text says and what it intends, and this is a difficult, perhaps justified, but certainly dangerous undertaking.

P seems to echo the radical message of disaster that is found in the writing prophets. God's judgment on the sinful human race, "I have determined to make an end of all flesh" (Gen 6:13), universalizes, as it were, the "end" announced by Amos (8:2) and Ezekiel (7:2ff.) and sees this end as already accomplished in the flood that is long past. A hardly less severe judgment is passed later on the entire community of Israel: all must die in the wilderness, except for Joshua and Caleb. The latter are, like Noah, a remnant who bear witness to the extent of the guilt and the punishment (Num 14:26ff.). Where can we find corresponding echoes of the prophetic promise of salvation? Or is the wilderness at the same time the place of a new beginning after the judgment (Hos 2:14; cf. Jer 29:10), and Joshua, like Noah, a "holy seed" (Isa 6:13)?

b) Theological Intentions

Wellhausen, who won acceptance for the late date of P, also introduced Q as a symbol for the Priestly document, Q being an abbreviation for *Liber quattuor foederum,* "The Book of the Four Covenants." And in fact P divides the course of history into four periods. At the beginning of each epoch a decisive event occurs, and an action that is important from the cultic-ritual standpoint is placed or a cultic instruction is given: (1) in connection with creation (Gen 1) God's rest on the seventh day (as well as the allotment of the plants to humanity and beasts as food); (2) in the time of Noah after the flood (Gen 9) the prohibition against the consumption of blood (the eating of flesh is now presupposed) and against the killing of human beings; (3) in the time of Abraham (Gen 17) the command to practice circumcision; (4) at Sinai (Exod 19:1f.; 24:15ff.) the introduction of laws for cult (Exod 25ff.), including that of the sanctification of the sabbath (16:22ff.; cf. 31:12 Ps).

It was soon recognized, however (J. J. P. Valeton, 1892; continued by W. Zimmerli and E. Kutsch), that P knows of only two covenants, that is, he applies the notion of *běrît* ("covenant") only to the second and third of the four events, namely, the divine promises to Noah and Abraham (see the chart on p. 103).

1. Despite its great interest in the cultic community, P, like the Yahwist and perhaps even more so, is universalist in outlook. History begins with the creation of the world. Not only Israelites but all human beings are, as creatures, images of God; they are, as it were, God's representatives on earth. They are commissioned to rule and are blessed by God (Gen 1:26ff.).

The tradition behind Genesis is closely related to the Babylonian epic of creation, the *Enuma elish,* and presents creation as a sequence of eight works (light, firmament, sea/land, plants, heavenly bodies, animals of water and air, land animals, humanity). It is probable that the tradition consisted originally simply of an account of actions, which later had an account of words and a counting of days imposed on it and was corrected from a theological viewpoint (W. H. Schmidt; for another view, O. H. Steck). When plants and animals are created "each according to its kind" (Gen 1:11f., 20f., 24f.), an organization that is important for the later cult has already been established, since it makes possible the distinction between clean and unclean (see Lev 10:10; 20:25; 11:13ff.). By means of the divine blessing (Gen 1:28; 9:1, 7) P explains the

The Historical Periods in the Priestly Document

Gen 1	Creation of the world (The human being, as image of God, is ruler of the earth)	Assignment of plants as food God's rest on the seventh day	Elohim "God"
Gen 9	Noachic "covenant"—with the human race	Noachic commandments: avoidance of blood as food and of killing Rainbow as "sign"	Elohim "God"
Gen 17	Abrahamic "covenant"—with the future people of God (promise of posterity and land; covenant formula in v. 17. Abram = Abraham, Sarai = Sarah) Gen 23: a share in the land	Demand for "blamelessness" in God's sight Circumcision as "sign"	El Shaddai "God Almighty"
Exod 6 Exod 24:15ff.	After fulfillment of the promise of posterity (Exod 1:7): Time of Moses Sinai	Passover (Exod 12) Sanctification of the sabbath (Exod 16; cf. 31:12ff.) Tabernacle and cultic ordinances (Exod 25ff.)	From the call of Moses (Exod 6): Yahweh At Sinai (Exod 25) and after the building of the tabernacle (Exod 40; Lev 9): Yahweh's $k\bar{a}b\hat{o}d$, "glory"

103

existence of the earth's population as springing from the divine word author-
izing its spread. The fulfillment of this authorization is confirmed in sober
form by the genealogies scattered in the text before and after the story of the
flood (Gen 5; 10; 11:10ff.*).

While the promise of increase has its roots in the tradition about the
patriarchs, P sees the promise given to Abraham and Jacob (Gen 17:2ff.; 28:3;
35:11; 48:11) as in turn a renewal of the blessing given at creation and to
Noah. The promise given to the human race as a whole is fulfilled exemplarily,
prototypically or even representatively in Israel's becoming a people (compare
also Exod 1:7 with Gen 1:28).

In God's eyes all of creation fulfills its assigned task: "And behold, it was
very good" (Gen 1:31). But in this judgment the spilling of blood is not
included (Gen 1:29f.; cf. 2:16 J, and the eschatological reversal in Isa 11:6ff.,
etc.). "Violence" enters the world only through human beings and causes God
to alter his first judgment: "Now the earth was corrupt in God's sight" (6:11–
12 P).

Like the world, time too is divided; creation takes the form of a history.
The end and goal of the six days' work are marked by the rest that initially
is reserved to God alone (Gen 2:2f.). This rest is an intimation and anticipation
of what human beings are to imitate later on (Exod 16). Thus, the sabbath of
creation does not yet have the character of a "sign."

It is not surprising, therefore, from the viewpoint either of the
tradition or even of the intention of P that creation is not regarded as
a covenant. On the other hand, P has indeed turned into a "covenant"
the promise God makes after the flood not to curse the earth again
(Gen 8:21 J). It has been turned, that is, into an unbreakable promise
that is independent of human defection (see Isa 54:9f.). It is confirmed
by the rainbow, which is a "sign" reminding God to maintain the
"covenant" (Gen 9:11–17).

According to the Yahwist picture the flood comes through a steady, heavy
rain, but P reports a cosmic catastrophe in which the waters of the primeval
sea, which had been divided at creation (Gen 1:6f.), come together again (7:11;
8:2). Does the flood therefore bring a return to chaos (1:2)? The created world
is doubtless not canceled out; the firmament remains even though its windows
are opened and all living things perish. The flood does not annihilate the
created, orderly world, but only its corrupt part, its guilty inhabitants (6:12f.).

After the flood God renews his blessing on creation; but now a profound
change has taken place within creation. The killing of animals has become
possible (9:2 versus 1:29f.). Only the consumption of blood, which is the seat
of life, is not allowed (9:4; cf. Lev 17:11, 14; Deut 12:23; Acts 15:20; 21:25),
while the killing of a human being, the image of God, is severely punished
(Gen 9:6). Thus the dominion of humanity over the earth (1:28) is restricted;
humanity is protected against itself.

While God's promise to Noah is meant for all human beings, the
second promise of covenant is restricted to a narrower circle—Abraham
and his posterity. In this case P may have been able to rely on a

tradition about a "covenant" with the patriarchs (Gen 15), but at least he develops it and introduces new theological emphases. The "everlasting covenant" goes beyond the promise of a countless posterity and possession of a country, for it contains the general promise, the so-called formula of covenant: "I will be your God" (see Exod 6:4ff.; 29:45f.). This covenant too is formulated unconditionally, although an obligation is placed on those concerned. The "sign" this time involves man himself: circumcision and a declaration of allegiance to God's "covenant" (17:9–14) and thus of "walking before God" (17:1; see below).

P understands the covenant with Abraham to be a "covenant with Abraham, with Isaac, and with Jacob" (Exod 2:24; cf. 6:4; a different view in Lev 26:42). Nonetheless, Isaac and even Joseph remain in the background in P's picture, which goes into detail only with regard to Jacob. At Bethel (Gen 35:6a, 9–13; 48:3f.) Jacob receives once again the promise (of land and posterity), which begins to be fulfilled in his sons (Exod 1:7).

If we expect that after the covenants with Noah and Abraham P will apply the term "covenant" to the revelation at Sinai and the establishment of the cult, we find ourselves disappointed (the concept of "covenant" is introduced only in a later stratum of the Law of Holiness, Lev 26:39ff.). Perhaps the two older sources (J, E) do not yet know anything of a "covenant" being concluded at Sinai or Horeb, but the redaction of these does (Exod 24:7f.; 34:10, 27f.; cf. 19:5) as does Deuteronomy (5:2f.). Is the striking silence of P due only to reliance on an older tradition regarding events at Sinai, or is there an express criticism of the form tradition had taken in the meantime? Like the call of Moses (Exod 6:2 as compared with Gen 17:1), the Sinai pericope lacks the proclamation of God's rights, to say nothing of an announcement of curse and blessing. P does mention, almost in passing, the tables of the Law but gives them the name "tables of the testimony" (Exod 31:18; 25:16, 21) and thus testifies not only to the obligations incumbent on human beings but also to God's promise. What is the point of such shifts of emphasis? Is the tradition being shaped by the situation of exile, in which the threats have already become a reality? That is W. Zimmerli's view: "For P the Sinai covenant in its old form has become questionable as a basis for relations with God. Therefore the whole basis of the covenant condition has been shifted back to the covenant with Abraham" (p. 215).

2. P's division of history into four stages corresponds only in part to changes in the name of God; the two principles of division coincide, strictly speaking, only for the time of Abraham (see the chart given above). During the first two periods, those of creation and of antiquity

after the flood, P sees only Elohim, "God," at work. Elohim does not "appear" to Noah, nor does he present himself to Noah with an "I am." Abraham is the first to whom God reveals a new name in a solemn self-description: "I am God Almighty (*El Shaddai*): walk before me, and be blameless" or, if the last phrase be translated as a consecutive, "then you will be blameless" (Gen 17:1).

This divine name, linked with the promise of increase and of a land, is repeated several times later on (Gen 28:3; 35:11; 48:3 P), until the call of Moses brings a review of this period (Exod 6:3).

P seems influenced here by the memory that the El divinities were indigenous to the arable land (see §2a1). *El Shaddai* first reveals himself in Canaan, although there is no trace left of any link with a particular place. The Priestly document or at least the age that produced it (see Ezek 10:5) seems to have formed the double name from two older components, *El* and *Shaddai* (Num 24:4, 16; cf. Gen 43:14; 49:25), in order thus to combine the various traditions of the patriarchal age and at the same time retain the distinction between these traditions and those of antiquity and of the subsequent age of Moses. Perhaps the name *Shaddai*, so difficult to explain, suggested to P God's transcendence and power.

God's condescension to Moses is really not "a covenant of pure grace" (W. Zimmerli), since the divine self-presentation issues in an exhortation. This programmatic appeal sounds very much like an "anticipation of the Decalogue" (K. Elliger, p. 197), in which the divine self-description is followed by the communication of a commandment. P, which contains no Decalogue, seems to have summed up the fundamental commandments of the "first table," and especially the first commandment, in the exhortation "Walk before me!" and in the demand for blamelessness (see Deut 18:13; 1 Kgs 8:61; Ps 15:2; etc.). The turning of God to Moses is to be matched by a complete turning of Moses to God. The relationship of the patriarchs to God is already marked by the exclusivity that is essential to the Yahwist faith, while the "second table" with the ethical commandments is already contained in a nuclear way in the prohibition against killing that is given to Noah (Gen 9:6). P seems, as it were, to divide the Decalogue into its two principal parts: the ethical demands are directed to the human race in its entirety; but the heart of the Decalogue, the theological part, is reserved for Abraham and his descendants.

P begins the final period, that is, the age of Moses, as it did the age of Abraham, with a self-presentation of God. This time, however, it is not followed by an exhortation. "I appeared to Abraham, to Isaac, and to Jacob, as God Almighty (*El Shaddai*), but by my name the Lord (Yahweh) I did not make myself known to them" (Exod 6:3).

Does P understand the sequence of periods of revelation as a simple succession or does he see it as marked by growth or intensification? In any case we seem to see a difference between God and God in his revelation. P acknowledges the identity of the one God in the various names and forms of revelation, that is, through the changing times, and tries in this way to do justice both to history and to the unity of faith.

In the age of Moses, on the other hand, P does not speak of "Yahweh" throughout, but later on, with the appearance of the "glory of Yahweh," he introduces a distinction in the manner of God's self-revelation (see below).

3. Like J before him (see §6b4), P creates a single great unity that runs from the call of Moses through the plagues to the miracle at the Sea of Reeds (Exod 6–14). As a leitmotiv introducing the entire sequence of events stands the promise: "I will redeem you . . . with great acts of judgment" (6:6; cf. 7:4; 12:12). The Egyptians must learn to know Yahweh (7:5; 14:4, 18). In particular, P tells the story of the plagues as one of conflict between the Egyptian religion and the Yahwist faith, with the miracle at the Sea of Reeds as the definitive judgment in which Yahweh glorifies himself.

As Elijah with the prophets of Baal (1 Kgs 18), so Moses and Aaron come into conflict, in the name of Yahweh, with a large number of Egyptian soothsayer-priests, in a "contest with magicians." The miracle that the two men perform, at Yahweh's behest, of changing a rod into a serpent is duplicated by the Egyptian magicians with "their secret arts" (Exod 7:11f.). The effectiveness of the latter powers is not denied outright, but a distinction is made. The Egyptians use magic, while the representatives of Israel appeal to the word of Yahweh. The exclusiveness of Yahweh does not admit the use of magic and sorcery (Num 23:23; Deut 18:10; etc.). This distinction by its nature "does not reveal itself outwardly and can only be believed and thereafter expressed" (M. Noth, *Exodus*, p. 72). It does nonetheless find expression in the realm of the experiential or the miraculous, since in the course of the dispute the superiority of Yahweh's delegates or rather of Yahweh's own word emerges clearly (Exod 7:12). Twice more the sorcerers manage to hold their own (7:22; 8:7); then their arts fail them and they are forced to admit to the king the superiority of Yahweh. The "finger of God" is at work here, and not any magic arts (8:18f.). Finally, the priests themselves are struck with a plague; they "cannot stand" before Moses and Aaron (9:11) and they withdraw. Although it is not expressly said that the magic powers of the sorcerers are based on the power of their gods, the motif of the story is given again in Yahweh's threat: "On all the gods of Egypt I will execute judgments" (12:12).

Is the scene again meant to reflect the current situation in which P arose, that is, is it expressing in an obscure manner the superiority of the Yahwist faith over the religion and sorcery of the Babylonians (see Dan 1:20; 2:2ff.; Gen 41:8, 24)? In any case, for P even more than for J (Exod 10:1), the failure of the negotiations is willed by God. Before any action taken by Pharaoh God announces, "I will harden Pharaoh's heart" (7:3; cf. 9:12; 10:20, 27, along with 7:13, 22, etc.), and before the miracle at the Sea of Reeds, which is the real climax of the stories of the plagues, God's word again anticipates the event: "I will get glory over Pharaoh and all his host . . . and the Egyptians shall know that I am the Lord" (14:4, 17f.; cf. 7:5; regarding Israel, 16:6, 12).

4. The key word in these last announcements of the future, "glorify myself" (*kbd*, Exod 14:4, 17f.; Lev 10:3), becomes in substantive form "glory (*kābôd*) of Yahweh," the leitmotiv of the Priestly description of the sojourn in the wilderness and the revelation at Sinai.

Canaanite religion was already familiar with the idea that "honor," "glory" is to be given to God (see Pss 29:1f., 9; 19:1; etc.). This notion, probably communicated through the cultic tradition of Jerusalem (Isa 6:3), was developed into a way of presenting the theophany of Yahweh. "This majesty can manifest itself in a phenomenon involving fire, but it is not identical with this phenomenon" (C. Westermann, p. 133). The prophet Ezekiel too (1:28; etc.), whose message has much in common with the priestly-cultic tradition, is able to make use of the same ideas.

When the community on its journey through the wilderness begins to complain—"Would that we had died . . . when we sat by the fleshpots [of Egypt]!"—then "the glory of the Lord appeared in the cloud" (Exod 16:10). This single manifestation on the way to Sinai is an exceptional anticipation of the events on the mountain, where in three revelations of the "glory of Yahweh" (Exod 25; 40; Lev 9) Israel's cult is established and confirmed and the community is thereby constituted.

When Israel came to Sinai (Exod 19:1–2a), "the cloud covered the mountain" and "the glory of the Lord settled on Mount Sinai," "like a devouring fire" (Exod 24:15ff.). Moses enters the cloud and receives God's instructions for the building of the "tent of encounter" (a linking of tent, ark, and Jerusalem temple) and the appointment of a priesthood (Exod 25–29). The "glory" of God fills the newly erected sanctuary (40:34; cf. 25:22; 29:43ff.). It comes a second time after the consecration of the altar and the offering of the first sacrifice or, in other words, after the first liturgy (Lev 9:6, 23). The decisive point is that this revelatory event is not limited to the sacred space on the mountain, although according to the arrangement of the camp in P (Num 1ff.) the people are protected from the sanctuary by the priests and Levites. Even after the departure from Sinai, when "the cloud was taken up" (Num 10:11), the "glory of God" intervenes in moments of need. It intervenes to help but also to judge, and the punishment is more severe now that the revelation has been given (Num 14; 20; cf. 16f.). By means of the concept "glory of Yahweh," the way for which has already been prepared in the story of the exodus (Exod 14), P connects the revelation at Sinai with the sojourn in the wilderness (Exod 16; Num 14; etc.). The event at Sinai is thus not left isolated, and instead P preserves continuity. The God who rescued Israel from Egypt reveals himself at Sinai. God's speaking and acting in cult and history alternate; they cannot be separated.

5. The "glory" is Yahweh himself (see Lev 9:4, 6; Num 14:14), of course, but as he reveals himself on earth. The "glory of the Lord appeared" (Exod 16:10; 27:17); Yahweh himself speaks (16:11; 25:1; etc.). In this way P introduces theological intentions that already have a place in Deuteronomy when the latter seeks to apprehend God's presence in the concept of the "name." Is not this distinction (between God himself and his glory or name) due to an effort to speak of God in such a way that he remains beyond representation or comparison or control—thus, an effort to be responsive to the second commandment? In any case, P is attempting to assert both God's transcendence and his power in the world and at the same time his freedom in revealing himself (see Gen 17:22; 35:13).

The same tendency comes to the fore in quite diverse contexts. P has a special word for God's creative act (*bārā'*, Gen 1:1; etc.), so as to avoid any analogy between this act and human activity. In its presentation of history P seeks to maintain the same understanding of God's word that it has shown in the story of creation (1:3ff.). God's command and its execution by human beings are often reported in a strictly parallel way involving repetition, so that the complete correspondence between the two may be perfectly clear (Gen 17:11f./23; Num 13:2/3, 17; etc.). Thus, whether human beings obey or disobey, history becomes the carrying out of God's word.

§9

OLD TESTAMENT LAW

The Pentateuch contains not only narratives but also extensive tracts of legislation. In fact, these predominate in the section on Sinai (from Exod 20 on) and in Deuteronomy (Deut 12 on). OT law is, of course, integrated into the historical narrative, closely connected with the person of Moses, and taken as the set of rules that organize the life of God's community as established at Sinai. At the same time, however, law is a relatively independent domain that has developed its own idiom and is presented in special collections, such as the Decalogue or the Book of the Covenant.

An introduction to the subject is given in H. J. Boecker, *Recht und Gesetz im Alten Testament und im Alten Orient* (1976). Even the study of the types of law has been to some degree independent of the rest of the scientific study of the OT—a sign of how difficult it is to date the various laws and assign them to their proper place in the history of Israel. In the history of research into OT law A. Alt's "The Origins of Israelite Law" (1934) holds a preeminent place; it introduced the distinction between casuistic and apodictic law, which has since been greatly modified but was nonetheless groundbreaking and is still helpful.

a) The Forms of Legal Statement

1. "Casuistic" law describes a legal situation in all its detail (with the many and varied circumstances that may occur in daily life) and also determines the penalty. For example:

"When men quarrel and one strikes the other with a stone or with his fist and the man does not die but keeps his bed, then if the man rises again and walks abroad with his staff, he that struck him shall be clear; only he shall pay for the loss of his time, and shall have him thoroughly healed" (Exod 21:18f.; similarly, 21:2–11, 20ff.).

This type of law has three characteristics: it is conditional; it is couched in impersonal and general terms (i.e., in the third person); and it bears the marks of an ancient Near Eastern background. A conditional clause (usually introduced by *kî*, "given the case," "if,"

110

"when") gives the facts of the case in the first part of the sentence (also called the "protasis"); further conditional clauses (usually introduced by ʾ*im*, "if then") may specify the facts even further. The subsequent principal clause (also called the "apodosis") then states the legal consequences: freedom from punishment or determination of punishment, as, for example, a simple or complex liability or even death (e.g., Deut 22:23–27). Ancient Near Eastern laws are cast mainly in this form. They probably came into Israel through contacts with Canaan—unless, of course, Israel simply took over Canaanite legal principles as a whole.

These three traits are easily recognizable, but a fourth characteristic, the function of this type of law, can only be inferred. Presumably this casuistic law—better, conditionally formulated law, which is perhaps the specific referent of the OT term *mišpāṭ* (Exod 21:1)—was meant to provide norms for the proper exercise of justice. Was it therefore in Israel the basis for the legal community made up of the elders at the gate (see §3b3)? Did these various legal principles arise out of the concrete administration of justice and subsequently acquire general applicability (G. Liedke)?

A. Alt distinguished an "apodictic" law from the casuistic law just described. Apodictic law is unconditional; it is formulated in metrical-rhythmical language and it is often found in series. Apodictic/unconditional means that on the one hand there is no introductory conditional clause that gives a precise statement of the facts in the case. On the other hand, this law either always states the same punishment, namely, exclusion from the community by curse, excommunication, or death, as the case may be, or, like the Decalogue, says nothing about legal consequences.

The laws thus described became an important stimulus to further discussion. What A. Alt groups under the name "apodictic" does not in fact form a unity at all but embraces various forms calling for separate designation. It is possible to distinguish two basic types. On the one hand, there are participial or relative sentences, with a determination of legal consequences; for example, death sentences and curses. On the other hand, there are commands and prohibitions unaccompanied by any sanction: "You shall (not)." Strictly speaking, each type of formulation must be studied with a view to its life or social setting (*Sitz im Leben*).

2. In Exod 21:12, 15–17 there is a series of death sentences that gives the impression of great antiquity; by "death sentences" I mean legal principles that assign the death penalty to certain crimes committed against human beings. In the first part of each sentence a case is described:

V. 12: Whoever strikes a man so that he dies
V. 15: Whoever strikes his father or his mother

V. 16: Whoever steals a man, whether he sells him or is found in possession of him

V. 17: Whoever curses his father or his mother.

In each case the punishment is prescribed in the same words: "shall be put to death" (*môt yûmāt*).

In Hebrew these sentences consist of only five words and are more rigidly structured than the translation shows. The legal case is described with the help of a participle and without any "if (when)" and "but," and to this extent it is "apodictic." On the other hand, determination of legal consequences is added, although this remains constant (see Exod 22:19). The statements have to do with the adult male, who, along with parents, is the object of protection. This series of laws thus goes back to early—perhaps even nomadic—times, in which the adult male was the most important member of the community (see §3b2). The rigid form, which probably goes back to early oral tradition, is relaxed in the course of time (compare, e.g., Exod 21:12, 17, with the parallels in Lev 24:17 and 20:9), while additions within the series show that these principles needed interpretation at a later time.

Since Exod 21:12 describes the simple fact of the killing, without reference to whether it was deliberate or accidental, the law needed to be qualified later on (in vv. 13f.).

In content these death sentences recall the "second table" of the Decalogue (Exod 20:12–15), but there is no overall explanation of how the laws that define the facts of the case and add the legal consequences are related to sanctionless prohibitions of the "You shall not" type. In the particular case to which I am calling attention here the commandments of the Decalogue clearly belong to a later form of tradition.

Even at a later period, series of similar kinds of laws were formed (Lev 20:2, 9–16; also 24:10ff.; 27:29); but individual laws formulated in the same or a like way were not lacking (Gen 2:17; 4:15; 26:11; Exod 19:12; Judg 21:5; 1 Sam 11:13; etc.).

With regard to these (more recent) isolated laws in narrative contexts it may be observed that persons in authority use them to require or exclude particular forms of behavior (see Gen 26:11; 2 Kgs 11:8, 15; etc.). But what authority stands behind the ancient series in Exod 21:12ff., the father of the family (G. Liedke) or the nomadic group?

3. In the liturgy contained in Deut 27:16–25 there is preserved a series of ten curses, which again have to do chiefly with crimes against fellow human beings.

When this series, probably made up originally of independent individual blocks, was incorporated into Deut (27:14) it had added to it two verses using a different style and a different set of concepts: a specifically theological commandment (prohibition of images, v. 15) and a comprehensive warning to observe "the words of this law" (v. 26). The result was a dodecalogue of curses. Only by means of these additions are the social regulations brought into relation with the specific character of the Yahwist faith.

All these texts begin with a "cursed be" (*ʾārûr*), which is followed by a description of the deed (masculine participle with an object). The texts each end with the same words: "And all the people shall say, 'Amen.' " Once again it is the males who are addressed, and specifically those who are of age, married (vv. 20–23), competent to share in the administration of justice (vv. 19, 25), owners of property (v. 17), and thus citizens possessing full rights. The curses do not threaten the death penalty for particular crimes, but a kind of self-curse in the face of any such actions, a promise of sanction should such cases occur. The penalty would probably take the form of exclusion from the community. Do these curses reflect a nomadic way of life (see Gen 4:11f.; see also W. Schottroff)?

In addition to series there are also individual, variously constructed curses, for example, in the Yahwist primeval history (Gen 3:14ff., 4:11; also Judg 21:18; Jer 17:5; 20:14f.; etc.). In addition, there are execrations (with a curse formula) that consist in the calling down of sicknesses or plagues (Deut 28:20ff.). A curse, which originally was probably a magical command, is probably understood everywhere in the OT to be an act of God.

The counterparts of curses are blessings (*bārûk*, "blessed be"; compare Deut 28:3–6 with 28:16–19). These are to be distinguished from beatitudes or macarisms, which in the OT are really good wishes (*ʾašrê*, "happy"; 1 Kgs 10:8; Pss 1; 128); their counterpart is the woe cry (*Weheruf*) (see §13b3b).

Contrary to a widespread false impression, OT criminal law is by no means based universally on the principle of talion, that is, "the principle of requital for an injury by an exactly similar injury done to the offender" (Alt, p. 135). Requital of like with like—a life for a life, an eye for an eye, a tooth for a tooth—comes into play only in connection with particular crimes among particular persons (Exod 21:22f.; Lev 24:17ff.; cf. Deut 19:15ff.). This was already the case in Babylonian law (Code of Hammurabi, §196ff.), though it was restricted even more in Israelite law. In the case of bodily injury to a slave the principle is expressly not applied (Exod 21:25f.). Both the exceptional character of the talion principle and the strict form in which it is expressed betray the fact that it came into the OT from an earlier, probably pre-Israelite time. In nomadic society, which had as yet no regular system for the administration of justice, the principle of strict requital may have checked the arbitrary exercise of unimpeded retaliation (see Gen 4:23f.) or the endless continuation of vendettas and thus provided some degree of protection (see §3a4).

With A. Alt (*KlSchr*, vol. 1, pp. 134ff.) we may conjecture that the talion formula or some comparable mode of expression may also have been used in substitutional sacrifice, for example, the ransoming of the firstborn (Exod 34:19) by means of an animal (see Gen 22:13).

b) Collections of Laws

1. *The Decalogue*
In comparison with the forms of law I have been reviewing, the unique characteristics of the Ten Commandments (Exod 20; Deut 5) emerge clearly. The Decalogue is the principal representative of those series of taboos or prohibitions that are addressed directly to the individual: "You shall not" (see Lev 18:7ff.; also Exod 22:18, 21f.; 23:1ff.).

The Ten Commandments are categorical and unconditional, that is, they say nothing about the particular circumstances of the action but rather remain deliberately general and axiomatic, and thus make an unqualified claim on the human being. In order to be applicable to everyone, they are formulated with great conciseness, and in order to embrace various areas of life they are made into a series, as though intended to be counted off on the fingers—like the curses in Deut 27, which originally were ten in number. There is, however, no assignment of a penalty, so that the Decalogue cannot be used for the administration of justice. Do sanctionless prohibitions and commands really form a category of legal statement? The commandments of the Decalogue warn of deeds that have not yet taken place; they are instructions for life, ethics rather than law.

The age of the Decalogues—of the two literary attestations and especially of their previous oral form—is disputed. In Deut 5 the Decalogue fits nicely into the account of the theophany and the striking of the covenant, but it became part of Deuteronomy as a whole only at a later stage (see §10a4). In Exod 20 it is really an isolated entity unattached to the rest of the Sinai account. The Decalogue is "from a literary aspect . . . a secondary passage in the account of the theophany on Sinai. . . . It represents in any case a self-contained and independent entity which originally certainly had its own tradition-history" (M. Noth, *Exodus*, pp. 154–55).

Different methods have been tried for reconstructing the development of the Decalogue—comparison of Exod 20 with the more recent form of the

Decalogue in Deut 5, investigation of the form of the commandments, or comparison with parallel laws and prophetic utterances.

Not only do the justifications given for a particular commandment vary (compare, e.g., the sabbath commandment in Exod 20:11 and Deut 5:13ff.), thus showing that they are at least to some extent secondary. Even the formulation of the law itself is not fixed once and for all (compare the priority given to woman in the tenth commandment in Deut 5:21 with Exod 20:17). The series of prohibitions is interrupted by positive formulations in the commandments regarding the sabbath and parents. Moreover, the commandments differ notably in length. In addition, only the first commandment and the justification for the second (Exod 20:3–6) are marked by the presence of the divine "I." This commingling of styles suggests a more recent date for the Decalogue.

Despite a frequent assumption, the Decalogue can hardly have grown out of a "primitive Decalogue," which supposedly already contained all ten commandments. It is more likely that the series of ten is made up of originally independent short series containing one to four commandments. But only two such subgroups can now be determined with a good degree of clarity. The first and second commandments (see Lev 19:3f.; Exod 34:14ff.), on the one hand, and the three prohibitions against killing, adultery, and theft (see Exod 21:12ff.; Hos 4:2; etc.), on the other, probably represent two independent units. As in the dodecalogue of curses in Deut 27 and in other legal texts, it is probable that from a tradition-historical (and even a literary?) viewpoint ethical commandments and theological commandments were joined only secondarily.

There is still disagreement about whether the prophet Hosea (3:1; 4:2; 13:4) in the eighth century and Jeremiah (7:9) only a few decades before the exile knew the Decalogue and freely cited it or whether they are simply located within a stream of tradition from which the Decalogue later emerged.

The Ten Commandments are meant for the group of people that had experienced God's encouragement (Exod 3) and help, as the pronouncement "I am the Lord your God" with its reference back to the past and God's act of deliverance expressly indicates. The commandments are thus not meant to create communion with God but at most to keep this communion alive. Being for the most part negatively formulated, they cannot even describe the relationship of humanity with God but can only assert the boundaries whose transgression breaks the relationship.

The Ten Commandments indicate the uniqueness of this God and of humanity's relationship to him (connection with history, exclusiveness, lack of images). On the other hand, they also serve to protect the neighbor. Parents who have grown old are to be protected from harm and encroachments by their grown children (Exod 21:15, 17; Prov 19:26; 28:24; etc.). The life, freedom, marriage, and property of the neighbor are put off limits as far as alien intrusion is concerned. The prohibition against killing has to do only with the unlawful shedding of blood by an individual and not with killing done by the community either in the form of a death penalty or of war. In contrast, the prohibition against "covetousness" seems already to look beyond the violent appropriation of another's property (see Mic 2:2) and to forbid a kind of thinking and willing (see Prov 6:25). The Ten Commandments are thus not content with forbidding reprehensible conduct; they also call for reflection on how, for example, parents are to be honored and the neighbor protected. At least later on, and down into the NT period, the Decalogue had a set place (also) in the liturgy (see Pss 50:7; 81:8ff.).

In addition to the formal characteristics listed earlier (a1) A. Alt listed two further criteria that have to do with the origin and function of the kind of law he describes as "apodictic." This kind of law, he says, "is related exclusively to the Israelite nation and the religion of Yahweh" ("The Origin of Israelite Law," p. 160). It is therefore unique in the world in which Israel lived. Its proper place is the recitation of the Law before the assembled community, or, in other words, its social setting is the liturgy. But since Alt wrote, ancient Near Eastern parallels have been discovered. Moreover, the addendum (31:9–13 in Deuteronomy), according to which "this (deuteronomic) law" is to be read every seventh year at the feast of Booths is not a solid argument for the view that apodictic law is by its very nature sacral law. Whatever the "social setting" of the death sentences and curses may have been, the Decalogue for its part suggests the conclusion that the cult was hardly the place of origin of particular laws, but became only subsequently a domicile for these (see the admittance liturgies, Pss 15; 24:3f.). But in any event the laws have been integrated with astonishing thoroughness into the Yahwistic faith.

Far more than comparable series (Exod 34; Deut 27; Lev 19f.) the Decalogue embraces the most important theological and ethical commandments, these being ordered according to their objective importance and expressed in a form that gives them the greatest possible general validity. The surpassing significance of the Decalogue is brought out by the fact that it was understood to be God's word (Exod 20:1; Deut 5:4) and, in the Sinai account as in Deuteronomy, was given priority over the other laws, which are presented as being (only) the words of Moses. As a result, from the Book of the Covenant on (Exod 20:22), the very arrangement gives these other commandments the character of being further determinations of the application of the Decalogue.

2. The Book of the Covenant
The collection of laws in Exod 20:22–23:19(33) has been introduced at a later date into the Sinai pericope by means of preceding and following narrative devices; it is from this new setting that the collection gets its name (24:7). Both formally and thematically the

Book of the Covenant is a composite entity. As a result, its structure and especially its origin make it a subject of ongoing debate.

As in the dodecalogue of curses (Deut 27:15, 26) and the Law of Holiness (Lev 17; 26:1), so here the body of laws is set within a— probably late—framework that is either theological or based on cult law and that seeks in various ways to effect a clear differentiation from Canaanite religion (20:22–26; 23:10–19). The prologue, with its more recent form of the prohibition against images (one that contrasts God in heaven with gods made of metal, 20:22f.) and its law regarding the altar, precedes the superscription or title (21:1). The calendar of feasts (23:10ff.) shows close contacts with the so-called cultic decalogue (34:10ff.). In addition, a differently structured concluding section, a speech of dismissal by Yahweh (23:20–33), has been added.

The main section is in two parts. The first half (21:2–22:16) contains chiefly casuistic laws, among which the death sentences (21:12–17) have been introduced. The second and far less unified part (22:17–23:9) is notable (like the prologue, 20:22–26) for the prohibitive "You shall" (22:17, 27ff.; 23:1ff.) and for the (probably more recent, but theologically important) paraenetic justifications, such as "You know the heart of a stranger, for you were strangers in the land of Egypt" (23:9; 22:20) or "I will surely hear their [the needy] cry" (22:22, 26). We have, then, the following broad division:

III. Narrative framework	20:(18–)22
II. Theological framework	20:23–26
	Prohibition of images; law regarding the altar
I. Legal nucleus	21:1–23:9
A) 21:2–22:16	
21:2–11	Law regarding slaves
21:12–17	Death sentences
21:18–36	Bodily injuries
	21:23ff. (Lev 24:20): law of talion
21:37–22:14(16)	Liability, compensation
B) 22:17–23:9	
22:17–19, 27ff.	Religious laws
22:20ff.	Social behavior
23:1ff.	Respect for rights
II. Theological framework	23:10–19
	Sabbatical year, sabbath, three annual feasts
Appendix: 23:20–33	
III. Narrative framework	24:3–8

This complicated structure can hardly have been due to the will of a legislator seeking to give shape to his thought, but is rather to be explained by the gradual growth of the Book of the Covenant. It presupposes a sedentary way of life (see 22:4f.) but implies nothing about the monarchy and its effects. Thus, the core of the material may go back to the time of the judges or, at the latest, to the early monarchic period. As a comparison of laws shows (e.g., of Exod 21:2 with Deut 15:12ff.; Lev 25:10), the Book of the Covenant is in any case older than Deuteronomy, and the latter in turn is older than the Law of Holiness, so that the sequence is Bc—Deut—H.

3. The Law of Holiness

If the Book of the Covenant is the oldest collection of laws, then the Law of Holiness (= H) is the most recent and is usually dated in the time of the exile. It too combines diverse themes and had a gradual growth with several strata. Both very ancient (e.g., in Lev 18; 19) and recent materials were assembled, often revised, and reinterpreted. There is a much greater element of paraenesis in H than in the Book of the Covenant; like Deuteronomic-Deuteronomistic sermonizing, these exhortations recall the historical past and warn the hearers to obey (Lev 18:2ff., 24ff.; etc.). There is disagreement about whether H (the usual view) was originally independent and was only subsequently incorporated into the Priestly document (P^G) or whether on the contrary it was from the beginning conceived of as an appendix to P (K. Elliger). At times H takes over Deuteronomic regulations and extends or corrects them (A. Cholewinski). Apart from cultic ordinances there are the following important regulations:

Lev 17   Extension of Deut 12: central sanctuary, prohibition against consumption of blood, but also (unlike Deut 12; Gen 9:2ff. P) a prohibition against profane slaughtering. "For the life of the flesh is in the blood" (vv. 11, 14).

Lev 18   Sexual intercourse (within the extended family). "Such a thing is not done in Israel" (2 Sam 13:12).

Lev 19   Theological and ethical commandments, like the Decalogue: commandments regarding parents and sabbath, first and second commandments (vv. 3f.; cf. 26:1f.); commandment of love (vv. 17f., 34; cf. vv. 14, 32).

Lev 23   Calendar of feasts. Cf. Exod 23:14ff.; 34:18ff.; Deut 16.

Lev 25   Sabbatical year (cf. Exod 23:10f.) and jubilee year. Release of the land of Israel every fiftieth year instead of every seventh year (as in Deut 15). "The land is mine; for you are strangers and sojourners with me" (v. 23).

Lev 26   Blessing and curse (cf. Deut 28).
         Vv. 40ff.: Promise of salvation in the exile.
         V. 46: Concluding formula.

There is a tendency to ground this diversified material with the "self-presentation formula," that is, "I am Yahweh" or, in a fuller form that adds God's encouragement, with the "benevolence formula," that is, "I am Yahweh, your God." The text that has given the Law of Holiness its name is an exhortation that understands the behavior of the community as a response to and a reflection of the behavior of God toward it: "You shall be holy; for I the Lord your God am holy" (19:2). This text gives the individual laws a common intention (20:26; 21:8, 23; 22:32; etc.).

Taken as a whole, the phenomenon of "law" takes various forms and is conceptualized in various ways in the OT. The common purpose of all the laws is not to create a communion with God, since this is based on an action of God, but to preserve it and thus to show that God's gift calls for a corresponding human task.

§10

DEUTERONOMY

The NT answers the question about the first of the commandments (Mark 12:28ff.) by citing, first of all, Deut 6:4f. This same passage also forms the first and fundamental part of the Jewish profession of faith, the *Shema:* "Hear, O Israel: The Lord our God is one Lord; and you shall love the Lord your God with all your heart, and with all your soul, and with all your might."

This passage sums up in thematic form the principal intention of the fifth book of Moses—undivided devotion to the one God. There is probably no other book of the OT that, on the one hand, so impressively speaks of God's love and, on the other, so tirelessly bids Israel love God and rejoice in his gifts. Deuteronomy, the "second law" as compared with the first, which was given on Sinai (the name resulted from a mistaken interpretation of the term "a copy of this law," in Deut 17:18), tries to win the people to allegiance to this law.

As a matter of fact, the book acquired immense importance, took deep hold on the life of the people, and placed its mark on many areas of the OT. Following more or less in the footsteps of this book the Deuteronomistic history came into existence, while the Deuteronomistic redactors did their work in its light (these redactors intervened here and there in the Pentateuch [see §4b4c] and more extensively in the prophetic tradition [see §19,1, etc.]). The book of Deuteronomy becomes even more important when we take into account the far-reaching indirect influence it exercised. Thus, after Deuteronomy the OT writings know of only a single center where the cult may be carried on. This means that, without Deuteronomy's call for centralization, P in its present form would have been inconceivable.

a) Introductory Questions

1. The collections of laws in the Pentateuch are usually in the form of an address of God to Moses, but Deuteronomy is an address of Moses to the people and thus only indirectly is it the word of God.

Its promises and ordinances are presented as the testament of the man who led Israel out of Egypt, through the wilderness, and to the very borders of the Promised Land. They constitute Moses' farewell addresses.

The nucleus of laws (Deut 12–26) is surrounded by an inner (5–11; 27–28) and an outer (1–4; 29–30) framework of speeches, and the concluding chapters (31–34) bring together Moses' "song" (32) and "blessing" (33) as well as accounts of the appointment of Joshua (31) and the death of Moses (34), among other things. The broad lines of the book's structure can therefore be presented as an ascending and descending stairway:

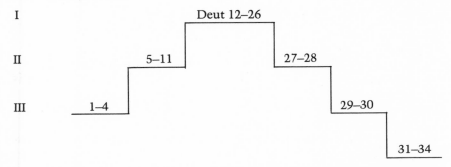

Like the Book of the Covenant (Exod 20:24ff.), the Deuteronomic law begins with regulations about the place of cult or, in this case, about the centralization of the cult (12–16). The central portion of the law consists of regulations for persons in office, such as kings and priests, which remind us of the book of Jeremiah (21–23). In the third and final part (19–25) various themes are commingled.

III. Deut 1–4	First introductory discourse
	1–3 After a description of the situation (1:1–5), a look back at the forty-year journey from Horeb (= Sinai) to Moab, with a repetition of the traditions in Exodus and Numbers
	4 Expansions of 1–3: exhortations to keep the commandments, especially the prohibition against images
	The "canon": add nothing, take away nothing, 4:2; 12:32
II. Deut 5–11	Second introductory discourse on the essence of the commandments
	5 Decalogue (versus Exod 20: social justification for the sabbath commandment),

	prefixed to the discourse of Moses as God's own words
6:4f.	The *Shema:* "Hear, O Israel" (Vv. 8f.: a sign on hand, forehead, and doorpost)
6:20ff.	Catechesis, instruction of children (cf. 4:9f.; 6:7; Exod 12:26f.; 13:14; Josh 4:6ff., 20ff.): maintenance of proclamation and profession down the generations
7:16ff.;	9:1ff.; etc. Exhortations to war (cf. Exod 14:13f.; Isa 7:4ff.)
8	A good land 8:15; 9:4–6: unmerited possession of the land

I. Deut 12–26		Individual commandments, body of law
a) 12–16		Commandments on unity and purity of cult
	12	Call for centralization
	13	Enticement to worship of alien gods
	14	Commandments regarding food (cf. Lev 11)
	15	Remission of debts
	16	Festal calendar, especially Passover (cf. Exod 23:14ff.; Lev 23; Num 28f.)
b) 16(:18)–18		Decrees about persons in office: Judges (16:18–17:13), king (17:14–20), priests (18:1–8), prophets (18:9–22; cf. 13:1–5).
c) 19–25		Commands on various subjects, especially social relations
	19	On sanctuary (cf. 4:41ff.; Num 35; Josh 20)
	20	Laws for war (cf. 21:10ff.; 23:9ff.; 24:5f.)
	21f.; 24f.	Laws on marriage and other matters
	23:1–8	Law on membership in the community (cf. Isa 56)
d) 26		Liturgical appendix (firstfruits, tithes, creed)
II. Deut 27–28		First concluding discourse
	27	Curse (vv. 15ff.: dodecalogue of curses) Ebal and Gerizim (cf. 11:26ff.; Josh 8:30ff.)
	28	Blessing and curse
III. Deut 29–30		Second concluding discourse (paraenesis)
	29:1	Covenants at Horeb and in Moab
	30:11ff.	Nearness of the law
IV. Deut 31–34		Conclusion of the Pentateuch. Additions
	31:9ff.	Reading of the law every seven years
	32	Song of Moses
	33	Moses' blessing, consisting of a hymn (vv. 2–5, 26–29) and oracles for the tribes (vv. 6–25; cf. Gen 49)
	34	Death of Moses (P: vv. 1a, 7–9)

2. After growing doubts about Moses' authorship of the Pentateuch, which presents Deuteronomy as a discourse of Moses, and after the gradual development of the source theory, the beginning of the last century (W. M. L. de Wette, 1805) saw the acceptance of a realization that was in fact not new, namely, that Deuteronomy is an independent entity and connected with the reform of the cult that had been undertaken by Josiah in 621 B.C. As a matter of fact, there are extensive correspondences between Deuteronomy and the account given in 2 Kgs 22f. of the finding of the law and of the ensuing reform. The demands made in this law make it possible to explain:

(a) the centralization of cult undertaken by Josiah (compare 2 Kgs 23:5, 8f., 19, with Deut 12). This centralization goes far beyond the aim of any reform hitherto known, which was to purify the cult of foreign elements; for now even other sanctuaries of Yahweh are eliminated.

(b) the Passover celebrated in common (2 Kgs 23:21ff.; Deut 16).

(c) the abolition of veneration of the heavenly bodies (2 Kgs 23:4f., 11; Deut 17:3), of sacral prostitution (2 Kgs 23:7; Deut 23:17f.), of *maṣṣēbôt* (pillars) and asherahs (sacred poles), of child sacrifice, of soothsaying, astrology, and other alien religious practices (2 Kgs 23:4f., 10ff., 24; Deut 12:2f., 31; 16:21f.; 18:10f.). This does not at all mean, of course, that all of its ordinances were put into practice (see, possibly, 2 Kgs 23:8f. as compared with Deut 18:6ff.). Even the fright that the king experienced at the finding and reading of the law (2 Kgs 22:11, 13, 16f.; cf. Neh 8:9) may have been caused by the curses that Deut 27 (f.) threatens in the case of disobedience.

Did the Josianic reform seek originally only to purify the cult of Yahweh of Assyrian elements? If so, the discovery of Deuteronomy would not have caused the reform but would have given a new and more comprehensive goal to a work already begun (see this chapter, a5).

Despite its own claim, Deuteronomy is not a discourse of Moses but reflects conditions under the monarchy or even later. It is not by chance that it appreciates the risks of having a king (17:14ff.) or warns against false prophets (13:1ff.; 18:9ff.). It is on the basis of this historical background that the questions of the origin and unity of the book arise; to date these questions have received no definitive answer.

3. When and where did Deuteronomy come into existence? As far as many of its laws are concerned it is later than the Book of the Covenant (9b). But what does this mean in terms of an absolute chronology? The opinion that Deuteronomy was composed just before its discovery or that the "discovery" was a pious deception intended

to force the king to institute reforms was sometimes put forward in the past but has now been abandoned. Scholars generally agree that in a basic form the book goes back to the seventh century or even the second half of the eighth century—hardly before the appearance of the first writing prophets around 750 but possibly just before the destruction of the northern kingdom ca. 722 B.C. A variety of indications suggest that certain traditions, ideas, or even parts of Deuteronomy, though not Deuteronomy as such, had their home in the (still existing or already destroyed) northern kingdom.

Some of the arguments (not all of equal weight) are the following:

(a) certain links with the traditions regarding Elijah and Elisha (Moses tradition; zeal for the first commandment);

(b) links with the prophet Hosea (resistance to the Canaanite religion; critical attitude toward the monarchy; a common idiom, e.g., "love"; cf. Hos 11:1, 4; 14:5, and Deut 7:8, 13; etc.);

(c) links perhaps also with the Elohist (e.g., the idea of "seeking"; cf. Gen 22:1 E and Deut 8:2, 16; 13:3);

(d) the conception of the monarchy, including the warning against making a foreigner king (Deut 17:15)—a warning hardly relevant in the domain of the Davidic dynasty, namely, Jerusalem/Judah;

(e) the warning against the apostasy of a whole city from the Yahwist faith (Deut 13:13ff.)—which again seems more applicable to conditions in the northern kingdom.

The northern Israelite heritage—for example, the message of Hosea and probably that of the Elohist as well—may have passed into the southern kingdom after 722 B.C. and been amalgamated with the traditions native there.

Other scholars look in Deuteronomy for traditions more characteristic of Jerusalem. But the typical Zion theology (as in Pss 46; 48; Isa 6) is hardly to be found there. Do not certain points of contact with Jerusalem belong to more recent strata? Jerusalem is the place of application for the Deuteronomic laws rather than their place of origin. Even the characteristic Deuteronomic phrase "the place which the Lord will choose" (see below) was probably applied only subsequently to Zion; see Ps 132.

4. Deuteronomy is thus not a single self-contained design but an astonishingly complex entity. In its present form it is certainly not the law discovered in the time of Josiah. What part, then, of our Deuteronomy did the primitive Deuteronomy found in the temple, the so-called temple document, contain, and how did it grow into its present final form?

On the one hand, the account of the discovery speaks in 2 Kgs 22:8 of a "book of the law." But Deuteronomy contains far more than the content indicated by such a title; it also contains extensive paraenetic discourses along with narrative accounts. On the other hand, the frequent new discourses and the multiplication of superscriptions (1:1;

4:44f.; 6:1; 12:1; 29:1; 33:1) show that Deuteronomy is not a homogeneous document. Did it originally begin with chap. 4 (v. 45) or chap. 6 (v. 4) and go down to chap. 28, or did it in its oldest form include only the legal nucleus, Deut 12–26, and then gradually have further parts added to it? But even such a division is still too unrefined, for not only the narrative sections but even the individual laws themselves lack internal unity. Thus the demand for the centralization of cult in Deut 12 finds expression in no fewer than three, perhaps even four, distinct and more or less identical formulations (vv. 2–7, 8–12, 13–19, 20–27).

Deuteronomy itself provides us with a specific tool for distinguishing various strata within the prose sections and the laws—the change in number. The people are addressed sometimes as "you" in the singular, sometimes as "you" in the plural. This criterion has of course long been used (by C. Steuernagel and others) for distinguishing sources, although its usefulness has occasionally been called into question. Nonetheless, the principle has repeatedly proved its value as a rule of thumb: the version using the singular number is older and formulations using the plural are later additions, although it must be admitted that there are also additions using the singular.

The laws were therefore originally addressed to the people in the singular (see below on Deut 12, and as an example from the discourses, see below on Deut 7:6–8).

Are the sentences using the plural in Deut 5ff. to be ascribed to a Deuteronomistic redaction (G. Minette de Tillesse)? In any case, it is not always possible to separate the sections in the plural from those in the singular, so that recourse must also be had to stylistic considerations.

In the individual chapters the stratification is often clearly discernible, but the interrelation of the strata in the various sections and their chronological succession are difficult to determine. Only with serious reservations is it possible to sketch out a developmental history. It is likely that the growth of the book was from the center outward in a slow process containing at least three main stages (a–c), to which further stages might easily be added as a result of a more careful division of the text:

a) "Ur-Deuteronomy" (the original or primitive Deuteronomy) is chiefly, if not exclusively, to be looked for in the central section containing the laws (Deut 12–25). This oldest collection itself is made up of smaller bodies of law and interpretative additions. Within this earliest stage, then, there is already a variety of existing documents or traditions, which may be quite different in age, that need to be distinguished from the stratum that shapes the individual materials into a unity. The main goal of this section is the centralization of cult. But there is yet no agreement on the precise boundaries of the collection.

b) A Deuteronomic redaction (in the time of Josiah?) revised the laws and added chiefly the inner framework as made up of the introductory discourses in Deut 5–11* and perhaps parts of 27f.

In the law of centralization, Deut 12, the two sections using the plural, vv. 2–7, 8–12, are more recent than vv. 13–19, which in the supplementary verses 20–27 (using the singular), are already given a first interpretation and material restriction. This addition, with its implied geographical extension (12:20; cf. 19:8), may presuppose Josiah's policy of expansion into the territory of the former northern state (2 Kgs 23:15ff.). If this be the case, then the prior stratum, which is already a "collection," would stem from the period before Josiah.

Even more difficult than the question of age is the question of the scope of the redaction. On the one hand, it is possible to start with the (older) superscriptions in 4:45; 12:1 (cf. 6:1). Because of the doublet "statutes and ordinances" these seem to lead us to 26:16. Was this at one time a conclusion, so that the complex had an introductory discourse but not a concluding discourse, or did parts of 27f. already belong to the whole?

On the other hand, Deut 6:4–9 may be taken as the starting point, especially since the Decalogue (Deut 5) was probably prefixed at a later date. Perhaps these various hypotheses are all justified, since the book underwent a gradual growth.

c) The post–Deuteronomic Deuteronomistic redaction, which presupposes the exile (587 B.C.), brought further additions in the body of law (e.g., in the law regarding kings and prophets, Deut 17:18; 18:19–22), and even more so in the inner framework of discourses (Deut 5–11; 27f.). Most important, it added the outer framework of discourses, Deut 1–4 and 29ff. These various supplements were certainly not from a single hand, so that it is possible to make further distinctions between older and more recent Deuteronomistic strata. These strata are connected with the incorporation of the book into the Deuteronomistic history.

Thus, Deuteronomy seems already to have had a history even before its discovery and influence in the time of Josiah; the decisive event of the discovery was then followed by an extensive later history. The details of this reconstructed history are very uncertain; it is clear, however, that Deuteronomy is to be explained by means of a supplementary hypothesis and not a documentary hypothesis. A genesis of this kind is intelligible, of course, only if the book is understood as the work not of a single author but of a school. More precisely, one may try to distinguish between a Deuteronomic and a later Deuteronomistic school. But since these two are connected, as the closely related and even identical language shows, it is also possible to speak of a Deuteronomic-Deuteronomistic school, the activity of which begins in the preexilic period and then stretches deep into the exilic and postexilic periods. But for methodological reasons the exile should be kept as the boundary between "Deuteronomic" and "Deuteronomistic."

5. The view here presented of the connection between the Josianic reform and Deuteronomy represents the more or less "traditional" solution, which has been under increasing attack in recent years. For one thing, the account of the centralization of cult as based on a "book of the covenant" (2 Kgs 23) is taken as a historical fiction that originated in a Deuteronomistic program of the period of exile (E. Würthwein and others). For another, the existence of an (Ur-)Deuteronomy that would go back to the prereform period is doubted, either because in the so-called Ur-Deuteronomy there is no discoverable unity that would connect the varied traditional material, or simply because the book of Deuteronomy is assigned a later, postexilic date (G. Hölscher, O. Kaiser, and others). These objections are not concerned with a mere peripheral problem; they raise a question that is fundamental to the understanding of the OT and in particular to the dating of the sources of the Pentateuch.

If we look for criteria that at least in part lie outside the disputed area and can serve as bases for deciding the question, we may consider the following:

a) From the Josianic reform to the writing down of the Deuteronomistic history (ca. 560 B.C.) approximately six decades passed, so that witnesses to the original events could still have been alive. This means that a simple fabrication of the events, with no historical basis, would have been difficult. Is it not also an indication of the historicity of the reform that final success of the king's work remained out of his reach, or that act and consequence were not in harmony?

b) It is a fact, of course, that the contemporary prophet Jeremiah, like the somewhat later Ezekiel, took no explicit position in regard to the reform (see Jer 22:15f.; but perhaps 8:8). Nonetheless, his attack on the temple at the time when Josiah's successor Jehoiakim took the throne (Jer 7; 26) becomes more intelligible if the reform caused the sanctuary at Jerusalem to be given a heightened value.

The criticism of the cult by the young Jeremiah (Jer 2) and by Zephaniah (1:4ff.) seems to be a denunciation of conditions prior to the reform. Are other texts (Jer 13:27; 17:1ff.) adequate evidence of no reform? Does not the vision of Ezek 8 bring together as though present and contemporary things that may have occurred in succession in the past? Or did cultic abuses prevail again quickly after the death of Josiah?

c) The journey made by pilgrims from Samaria to the ruins of the temple in the razed city of Jerusalem is easier to explain if Josiah's reform had extended the idea of a centralized cult to the north.

d) How could P assume the centralization of cult as obvious (see §8a4) if this centralization were simply a demand made by Deuteronomy and not a historical reality?

e) If an early stratum of interpretation (formulated in the singular) in Deuteronomy speaks of a geographical expansion of Israel (12:20; 19:8), this is best connected with Josiah's policy of expansion (2 Kgs 23:15ff.). In addition, the mention of Passover in Deut 16 is probably to be ascribed to an early stratum of revision that may be connected with the celebration in 2 Kgs 23:21f.

Such considerations, among others, suggest that the traditional dating be maintained, at least for the time being.

6. In addition to the literary-critical and historical approaches, the turn of the century saw the beginning of the form-critical approach. A. Klostermann noticed that in Deuteronomy legal text and interpretation of law alternate; he explained this succession as reflecting the public oral reading of the law. Later on, G. von Rad (following A. Bentzen) interpreted the paraenetic element as indicating a preaching of the law: "This is the most basic distinction between the Book of the Covenant and Deuteronomy that emerges here and there in a special way despite, or really because of, the amount of material both books have in common: Deuteronomy is not codified divine law, but a preaching on the commandments" (*GesStud*, vol. 2, p. 112). This book transforms law that makes demands or even condemns ("You shall . . ." or "Whoever does . . . shall be put to death") into admonitions that seek a loving adhesion; obedience to the commandments is humanity's answer to God's loving solicitude.

It is hard to determine what group was responsible for this preaching of the law. Like others before him, G. von Rad sees Deuteronomy as originating in (rural) Levitical circles in the northern kingdom; they would be responsible for the priestly and the militant spirit of the book, and it would have been their task to instruct the laity (Deut 33:10; Neh 8:7; etc.). But since "Levi" in the OT is something complex and hard to pin down to particulars, it can hardly serve to shed light on the origin of the book. There must, however, have been some connection between Deuteronomy and the Levites (cf. the additions in 27:9ff.; 31:9, 24ff.), since Deuteronomy is concerned for their welfare (12:12, 18f., and often) and includes them among the unfortunate who need protection and help (14:27ff.; 26:11ff.).

Or are the agents of transmission—later on—to be looked for among the sapiential scribes at the royal court in Jerusalem (Prov 25:1; so M. Weinfeld)?

Notably enough, G. von Rad explains the (certainly late) overall structure of the book with its four main sections—historical presentation and exhortation, Deut 1 or 6–11; reading of the law, 12–26; sealing of the covenant, 26:16–19; blessings and curses, 27ff.—not in terms of Levitical instruction of the laity but in terms of the cultic ceremony associated with the covenant, the structure of which is already reflected (he says) in the Sinai account, Exod 19ff. In any case, according to von Rad, this form "had long been used freely for literary and homiletic purposes" (*Deuteronomy*, pp. 21–22).

Others have compared the structure of the book or of individual sections with the formulary used in vassalage treaties, especially among the Hittites. It is true that some remote contacts cannot be excluded, because the influence of contractual thinking became possible once the Assyrians achieved predominance in the seventh century. But we may not overlook the differences in form and even more in content (relation between God and people instead of among peoples); above all, we know too little about a cultic ceremony connected with "covenant" in the OT.

It may be taken as certain, however, that at least at a later time laws were read out in the liturgy (Deut 31:10ff.; 2 Kgs 23:2; cf. Exod 24:7; Neh 8; Ps 81; etc.).

b) Theological Intentions

Strict method would require an investigation of the theological intentions of each separate stratum of interpretation in Deuteronomy. But the distinction between the stages of the book's growth, and especially the differentiation between them in terms of the history of theology, has, with some exceptions, hardly produced certainty as yet. Is there not also a danger of exaggerating differences, since the expansions often closely imitate the traditional material in language and intention? Conversely, an all-embracing or summarizing approach may too easily look upon the book as being a unified entity. In the following remarks, differences in the date of origin are only occasionally indicated.

The intention of Deuteronomy may be summed up in a three-member formula: one God, one people, one cult. And we may add: one land, one king, one prophet.

1. Up to this point Israel had taken for granted a plurality of sanctuaries (Exod 20:24), some of which were highly regarded as pilgrimage centers. Now Deuteronomy demanded exclusivity: "Take heed that you do not offer your burnt offerings at every place that you see; but at the place which the Lord will choose in one of your tribes, there you shall offer your burnt offerings" (12:13f.).

Strictly speaking, even the typical Deuteronomic formula which gives theological justification for the centralization of cult, "the place which the Lord will choose," could refer to various places that the Lord might successively determine. However, both the indication of place, "in one of your tribes," and the different ways in which burnt offering and sacrificial slaughter are treated show that the oldest version of the law of centralization (12:13–19) is already concerned with linking the Yahwistic faith exclusively to a single sanctuary. That is the sense in which the Josianic reform understood and applied the law. The identification with Jerusalem is hardly indicated in the older strata and does not emerge directly even in the later strata, since the book makes no mention at all of the city or of Zion; but the mode of reference is taken over in the Deuteronomistic history and clearly connected with Jerusalem (1 Kgs 9:3; 11:36; etc.).

The short and probably oldest form of the centralization formula, "the place which the Lord will choose" (Deut 12:14, 18, 26), soon had a motive attached to it, "to put his name there" (12:21), or (probably later), "to make his name dwell there" (12:11; etc.). According to this expansion the divine name singles out one place of worship (see already Exod 20:24). It is the place that belongs to Yahweh and in which he is present. At least later on, however, a different, more critical note comes in; God himself dwells in heaven (see Deut 26:15; 4:36), and "only" his name dwells on earth. This distinction between God and God's presence on earth—a distinction that reminds us of the introduction of the concept "glory" into P (see §8b5)—means a qualifying of the older view according to which God himself "dwells" in the sanctuary (compare 1 Kgs 8:12; Isa 8:18; etc.; with 1 Kgs 8:29; etc.; on this point, see R. de Vaux).

The call for concentration of the liturgy in a single place brought radical changes in the cultic and religious life of Israel, especially for the rural population outside of Jerusalem. The principal result was the permission to engage in the "profane" slaughtering of animals (12:15f.). As compared with the burnt offering (holocaust), which was entirely conducted in the holy place, a slaughter-sacrifice or community sacrifice—at least (according to vv. 20ff.) in places far from the one sanctuary where alone sacrifices might be offered—became a simple meal (zābaḥ, "to sacrifice," Deut 15:21, acquired the limited meaning of "to slaughter," 12:15, 21). Was every act of slaughter originally a sacrifice, that is, a sacrificial meal (compare 1 Sam 2:13; 9:13 with Gen 18:7f.)? If so, then the new regulation in Deuteronomy was for the ancient mind a colossal act of secularization. Only the blood received ritual protection: "you shall pour it out upon the earth like water" (Deut 12:16, 23f.; repeated by P in Gen 9:4f.; otherwise in Lev 17:3ff.).

In addition, the demand for centralization affected the regulations on tithes, firstborn and firstfruits (Deut 14:22–27; 15:9–23; 26:1ff.), the festal calendar (16:1ff.), and judges and priests (17:8–13; 18:1–8). Thus the regulations regarding centralization certainly represent a later stratum in this legal material, but they also provide the interpretation that links the diverse antecedent traditions under a single intention.

2. In Deuteronomy as we now have it the unity of cult is simply a consequence of the unity of God, which was given programmatic expression beforehand in the *Shema:* "Hear, O Israel, the Lord our God is one God" [or: "alone is God"; or: "is sole God"] (6:4).

The profession of faith is so worded that it does not reflect something incidental and is not related simply to a provisional situation but is universal and a matter of principle. For this reason it can move in various directions and has several levels of meaning. In its original intention it is hardly to be interpreted as voicing a strict monotheism (Yahweh alone is God; see 4:19, 35, 39; 32:39). On the one hand, it may, in relation to the outside world, be meant to reject the attractions of the Canaanite religion and to appeal to the oneness and singleness of Yahweh over against the many forms taken by the cult of Baal. On the other hand, and in terms of Israel's own life, it can be understood in the context of the call for centralization as "a confession of the oneness of Yahweh in face of the multiplicity of divergent traditions and sanctuaries of Yahweh" (G. von Rad, *Deuteronomy*, p. 63). The two interpretations are convergent as far as their consequences are concerned, since the emphasis on the oneness of the form of the Yahwistic religion serves to set this religion off from the many manifestations of the religion of Baal.

Deuteronomy has, then, a very important place in the history of the Yahwistic faith, because it gives new expression to the first commandment. In its older forms (Exod 22:20; 34:14; etc.) this commandment determines the relation between God and humanity but makes no direct statement about God himself. It is precisely in this direction that the confession in Deut 6:4 moves (cf. Zech 14:9; Mal 2:10). Because it derives the oneness or singleness of God from Yahweh's claim to exclusive veneration it turns a statement about the relation of humanity to God into a statement "about" God himself (like Exod 34:6f. and other passages, it does so without reference back to history). Insofar as the call for centralization is a practical conclusion drawn from this insight, the centralization of the cult can be conceived as a phase in the history of the influence exercised by the first commandment.

In a manner typical of the OT such a statement defining God's "nature" is not left to lie there, as it were; instead, Deuteronomy immediately draws from it a conclusion regarding human behavior. "And you shall love the Lord your God with all your heart, and with all your soul, and with all your might" (6:5; cf. 5:10; 7:9; 10:12; 11:1, 13, 22; 13:3f.; 19:9).

Here the first commandment is once again given a new interpretation. Older negative formulations simply excluded worship of alien gods but said nothing positive—or at least nothing explicit—about the "inner space" of Israel's relationship with Yahweh. Deuteronomy, on the other hand, now conceives the exclusivity anthropologically as the totality of behavior. The unity of God must be matched by the undivided, unreserved turning of the whole person to God. Because "love," like "fear" (i.e., the reverent acknowledgment of God, 6:2, 13, 24; etc.), points to a kind of behavior, it can be commanded (6:5f.; 10:12f.)—and commanded as a grateful response to God's love (7:8; 10:15; etc.).

In exhortations the unlimited scope of the relation to God can be described by the terms "adhere to," "serve," "follow" God or "not forget," "be mindful of" him (6:12ff.; 8:18f.; 10:20; etc.). Do these concepts, and in fact the whole development of the first commandment, reflect prophetic influence (see Hos 2:13; 3:1)? As a matter of fact, prophetic influence is probably nowhere so marked in the OT as in Deuteronomy and the subsequent Deuteronomistic literature. Not only are there individual regulations dealing with a prophet, a blood relative, or even an entire city calling for the worship of alien gods (13:1–18) or themselves worshiping such gods (17:2–7; cf. 12:30f.; 18:20). In addition, the earlier general considerations of the significance of the law (7:4ff.; 8:9; 11:16ff.; etc.) assign decisive importance to the first commandment. The descent into idolatry and the loss or "forgetting" of past history are two errors against which Deuteronomy issues warnings, because these errors rob the Yahwistic faith of its very essence.

It is hardly accidental, therefore, that the Decalogue, which combines the reference to history and the demand for exclusiveness (5:6f.), should have pride of place among the commandments. As in the Sinai story (Exod 20), so in Deuteronomy—though at a later stage of development—the Decalogue comes before all the "statutes and ordinances" and is introduced not as the word of Moses but as directly the word of God (Deut 5:4, 22ff., compared with 5:5). Consequently, all the subsequent laws become, as it were, instructions for carrying out the Decalogue; they explain or develop the Ten Commandments. Even the "covenant" is interpreted in terms of the Decalogue (4:12f.; 5:2; 9:9ff.), and the Ark becomes the receptacle for the two stone tablets containing the Ten Commandments (10:1ff.; cf. 31:26). Deuteronomy may therefore be reproached for giving too much importance to the commandments in the life of the people, but no one can say that Deuteronomy takes a casuistic approach and puts all the commandments too much on the same level.

3. While older laws are addressed to the individual, Deuteronomy addresses itself to the people of God as a whole, both in the sections using "you" in the singular and those using the plural. Is this once again due to the influence of the prophets, who seldom address the individual but regularly address the people as a whole (Hos 2:2ff.;

Amos 3:2; etc.)? In any case, the oneness of the people corresponds to the oneness of God: Yahweh confronts "all Israel" (Deut 5:1; etc.).

In Deuteronomy there is no division of the people into tribes or into a northern and a southern kingdom. Does this fact reflect not only the literary situation (Israel in the time of Moses before the settlement) but also the historical situation in the time of Josiah, who sought to unite north and south, or even a prophetic hope (Hos 1:10–2:1; Ezek 37:15ff.; etc.)?

On the one hand, Deuteronomy impresses on its hearers and readers that Yahweh is "your [sing. or pl.] God"—and this with an emphasis far beyond what is commonly found in the OT—so that this apposition can be taken as a stylistic trait of Deuteronomic and Deuteronomistic literature. On the other hand, Israel is called God's "possession," a "holy people" (7:6; 14:2; 26:18.; etc.). Thus the distinction between Israel and the other peoples, already grasped in the older tradition (Exod 8:22f.; 9:4–5 J; Num 23:9 E), is emphatically highlighted in a new set of concepts.

Both sides of the relationship between God and the people are summed up by Deut 26:17f. in the "covenant formula," which in its linguistic form is late but in its substance can be called the "beginning and abiding principle" (J. Wellhausen) of Israel's history: "Yahweh Israel's God; Israel Yahweh's people."

Deuteronomy expressly seeks to avert the danger of a misunderstanding of this privileged place, for it attributes Israel's holiness solely to the relationship established by God and thus eliminates any otherwise discoverable rationale for it: "You are a people holy to the Lord your God; the Lord your God has chosen you to be a people for his own possession, out of all the peoples that are on the face of the earth" (7:6).

This pledge, at a later time (there is a shift from the singular to the plural, which is characteristic of additions), is explained as follows: "It was not because you were more in number than any other people that the Lord set his love upon you and chose you, for you were the fewest of all peoples; but it is because the Lord loves you, and is keeping the oath which he swore to your fathers" (7:7–8).

The relation between God and people is created by a prior act of God, the "election" (*bāḥar*), which is based on God's "love" (4:37; etc.) and is promised without qualification along with the oath sworn to the patriarchs (this too is a characteristic element in the Deuteronomic and Deuteronomistic literature, 6:10; etc.). Israel therefore possesses the land not by reason of its own abilities and merits but, in the final analysis, because of God's promise: "Not because of your righteousness [right behavior] or the uprightness of your heart are you going in to possess the land; but because of the wickedness of these nations the Lord your God is driving them out from before you, and that he may confirm the word which the Lord swore to your fathers, to Abraham, to Isaac, and to Jacob" (9:5; cf. 8:17).

Since the holiness of the place of cult (12:14; etc.) or of the Levite class (21:5; etc.) also depends on God's "election," the intention of Deuteronomy can be summed up in the term a "theology of election" (Th. C. Vriezen).

4. Deuteronomy seeks to use the unity of the people of God as the basis for conclusions regarding the social life of human beings. The occupants of the highest offices are to come "from among the brethren"—thus, the promised prophet (18:15, 18) and even the king (17:15), whose rights are sharply curtailed so that "his heart may not be lifted up above his brethren" (17:20). Is there not perhaps an intimation here that despite the diversity of roles all are equal before God? The relationship of the brethren to one another likewise yields social consequences. Even the impoverished fellow believer is "your poor brother" (15:2f., 7ff.; etc.; also Lev 25:35ff.), whom the Israelite is not to treat hardheartedly but whose debts he is rather to remit, so that the poor may have a share in God's gift. Not only "widows and orphans" (Exod 22:22–24; Isa 1:17, 23) but also "strangers" or "citizens in need of protection" (*gērîm*), who live far from home and relations, who do not own land and therefore lack certain rights, as well as the Levites—all these are included among the needy (Deut 14:29; 16:11, 14; 26:12f.; etc.). Did this group include the refugees who were accepted into the south after the fall of the northern kingdom?

The same humane spirit is at work in the various laws that are summed up as "humanitarian laws" (15:1–18; 22:1–8; 23:15–25; 24:6, 10–22; 25:1–4). Among them the regulations regarding freedom from military service are exemplary. These regulations may have their roots in earlier magic, but in the OT their only purpose is to permit the individual to enjoy his new possession, whether this be a house, a vineyard, or even a wife (20:5–7) and thus to rejoice in God's good gifts to him (12:7, 12, 18; 16:11, 14f.; etc.). "When a man is newly married, he shall not go out with the army or be charged with any business; he shall be free at home one year, to be happy with his wife whom he has taken" (24:5).

Such regulations (which surely remained "theoretical"), in which the rights of the individual or the family may be put before the tasks of the community, have earned for Deuteronomy the criticism that it is "utopian" in the sense of being remote from reality (G. Hölscher).

But to what extent is practical applicability a suitable criterion for a theological design? Moreover, in another respect Deuteronomy in fact profoundly altered reality.

According to the laws for war (20:10ff., 19f.), the same humane attitude that shows itself in the treatment of foreigners (10:18; 24:14; but cf. 23:20f.) calls for a certain generosity even toward enemies. Only Canaanites (not in reality, but in retrospect from a later vantage point!) are excluded from this more friendly treatment, for their religion represents too dangerous a temptation to the Israelites' own faith (7:4f., 25; 12:2ff., 30f.; etc.).

5. The unity of the people of God does not find expression only in the common life of Israel at any given time, but in a vision of successive generations as living in a common "today." The re-presentation (rendering present) of the past takes precedence over regard for strict historical non-repeatability: "The Lord brought you" (4:20)—or: "us" (6:20ff.; 26:6ff.)—"out of Egypt." The discourse of Moses is addressed, across the centuries, directly to the living of today; in fact, the past is in danger of being swallowed up by the now: "Hear, O Israel, the statutes and ordinances which I speak in your hearing this day" (5:1). Just as the prophet in exile can contrast the "former" and the "new," what was and what is to be (Isa 43:18f.), so Deuteronomy is able to set past and present side by side as mutually exclusive: "Not with our fathers did the Lord make this covenant, but with us, who are all of us here alive this day" (5:3f.). Is the preacher here trying to bring a point home to his hearers? This remarkable "today" has as yet hardly been adequately explained.

Deuteronomy (like P) has no real eschatological expectations, but it does look beyond the present in that it promises that the obedience of faith will be rewarded with "long life" (5:16; 6:2; 11:9, 21; etc.), "rest" from enemies (12:9f., 15; 25:19), the fertility of nature, and the cessation of all sicknesses (7:13ff.; etc.). Are these blessings to be understood as already given and present? Hardly. Thus, the true fulfillment of human life is a possibility not yet realized.

§11

THE DEUTERONOMISTIC HISTORY

a) Introductory Questions

In passing over to the historical books we enter a different world. Yet the realization of the difference in the literary situation outside the Pentateuch (or Tetrateuch) is a relatively recent phenomenon. It was the insights gained in commenting on the book of Joshua (1938) that led M. Noth to the hypothesis of a Deuteronomistic history that runs from Deuteronomy to the second book of Kings (*Überlieferungsge-schichtliche Studien*, 1943, 1957 = *ÜSt*). A. Jepsen reached similar conclusions independently (*Die Quellen des Königsbuches*, 1953).

In the past, scholars used to explain this part of the OT historical books as they did the Pentateuch, in which the source documents already provided continuous narrative strands. True enough, the Deuteronomistic sections from the book of Joshua to the books of Kings had not been overlooked since their characteristic language gives them an unmistakable idiom and style. They were regarded, however, as redactional additions to an already existing continuous narrative; only in the books of Kings were the choice and shaping of traditions ascribed in a larger measure to the redactional stage.

Until very recently attempts were repeatedly made to follow the strata of the Pentateuch (especially J and P, sometimes E) at least into the book of Joshua or even beyond into the books of Kings, but the results achieved varied and in any case have not yet won general recognition. The linking of the texts with one another to form a single narrative work embracing the various periods and, even more, the identification of this with one of the older Pentateuchal sources were enough to rouse opposition. By and large M. Noth's thesis won acceptance, although distinctions and modifications were introduced into it.

M. Noth saw the Deuteronomist as the author of the entire voluminous literary complex. This author (like the Yahwist?) created a work that is "unparalleled in the surrounding world. . . . It follows the course of approximately seven centuries of Israelite history from the time of Moses to the Babylonian exile. With scrupulous care, it assimilates both literary traditions and facts which were experienced directly, and, in the process, achieves an astonishingly unified design" (H. W. Wolff, p. 83).

1. Prior to the Deuteronomist's work, then, there existed no continuous sketch of history that embraced these centuries as a whole. There would, however, have been collections of individual stories into narrative cycles, such as the collections of stories from the age of Joshua and of the judges, or even independent presentations of shorter time periods, such as the story of David's rise to power and of the succession to his throne in 1 Sam 16–1 Kgs 2. Also independent were the cycle of stories about Elijah and Elisha in 1 Kgs 17–2 Kgs 13, and other stories about the prophets. In addition, the Deuteronomistic history brings together diverse materials: traditions about sanctuaries or about the court, lists (e.g., of officials: 2 Sam 8:16ff.; 20:23ff.; 23:8ff; 1 Kgs 4), excerpts from chronicles, and so on.

If various continuous presentations of this type existed prior to the Deuteronomistic history, it is easier to understand why the Deuteronomist did not have to revise all the traditions in the same degree and why, consequently, the specifically Deuteronomistic share in each book varies. These unevennesses are therefore hardly evidence against the existence and unity of the history. On the contrary, according to Noth there are above all two reasons that show the continuity of the stretch of literature from Deuteronomy or Joshua to 2 Kings:

a) A continuous chronology is more or less clearly recognizable (see the summary statement in 1 Kgs 6:1: Solomon built the temple in the 480th year after the exodus).

b) Retrospective and prospective reflections are introduced at historical climaxes and turning points; these reflections take the form either of narrative statements or a discourse of the principal personage involved. They do not simply report a new action but rather attempt to interpret and evaluate history. In the process they give expression to similar basic views on the theology of history and show the same characteristic style. Consequently these connecting pieces resemble sermons—a rhetorical form on which the proclamation of the prophets may have had an influence. The beginning, the divisions, and the end of the Deuteronomistic history are thus clearly marked:

I. The Age of Moses

Deut 1–3(4)   Moses looks back to the migration from Horeb to Transjordan; anticipation of the appointment of Joshua as his successor

Deut 31:1–8; 34	Moses' farewell discourse, appointment of Joshua, Moses' death and burial

II. The Age of Joshua

Josh 1 and 23(24)	Beginning and end of the settlement in Cisjordan
1	Leadership passes to Joshua
12	Results of the conquest of the country
21:43–45	Concluding notice on the fulfillment of the promise
22:1–8	Return of the tribes to Transjordan
23	Joshua's farewell address (analogous to Deut 31)
24:28ff.;	
Judg 2:6ff.	Joshua's death and burial (cf. Deut 34:5f.)

III. The Age of the Judges

Judg 2; 1 Sam 12	Beginning and end of the age of the judges
1 Sam 8; 12	Discourse of Samuel

IV. The Age of the Kings

2 Sam 7	Prophecy of Nathan (Deuteronomistic revision, with retrospect, v. 1)
1 Kgs 3:9	Divine revelations to Solomon
1 Kgs 8 (vv. 14ff.)	Solomon's prayer at the dedication of the temple
1 Kgs 11	Solomon's apostasy
2 Kgs 17	Fall of the northern kingdom (with retrospective judgment, vv. 7–23)
2 Kgs 25	Destruction of Jerusalem (with brief judgment, 21:10ff.; 24:3f.; cf. 22:16f.; 23:26f.

Only at the beginning, that is, in the age of Moses and Joshua, does the later division of the entire work into the books of Joshua, Judges, Samuel, and Kings coincide with the division as originally planned.

At the same time, however, our modern division of books seems indicated at a very early stage, since there are at the end of the books of Judges and 2 Samuel (Judg 17–21; 2 Sam 21–24) and perhaps also at the beginning of the book of Judges (Judg 1) what are probably subsequent additions that break the original narrative thread. On the other hand, the division of Samuel and Kings into two books each is attested only since the late Middle Ages.

Along with the scope, the earliest date for the origin of the work is also determined: it must have been written down after the last events described in 2 Kgs 25:27–30 (the deported king of Judah, Jehoiachin, is released from prison by Evil-merodach [Avil Marduk, 562–560 B.C.], the successor of Nebuchadnezzar, and given a place at the royal court) and probably during the exile, ca. 560 B.C. In any case the work in its substance comes down to this point of time. Where is there even the slightest indication of the new mood caused by the accession of the

Persians (539 B.C.)? There is disagreement about the place of composition, but (as in the case of Lamentations) it is more likely to have been Palestine than (as in the case of P) Babylonia and, more specifically, perhaps Mizpah, which acquired a certain importance after the destruction of Jerusalem (2 Kgs 25:22ff.).

2. A variety of observations requires, however, that M. Noth's view of the history be corrected in one respect: There must have been a Deuteronomistic school rather than a single Deuteronomist. This hypothesis, on the one hand, explains unevennesses and additions within the Deuteronomistic history—even though these are marked by a closely related style and a similar spirit. The editor changes but the school abides. On the other hand, the broad influence of the history, an influence that reaches far beyond the historical books from Joshua to Kings and extends, for example, to the shape taken by the prophetic books, becomes intelligible. The school transmitted and commented on—under the influence of Deuteronomy?—the historical and prophetic tradition.

Was Deuteronomy the catalyst, as it were, for the origin of the Deuteronomistic school? In any case there is disagreement about whether Deuteronomy itself was always part of the Deuteronomistic history or was incorporated into it only secondarily.

Because of certain unevennesses in the books of Kings it is also hypothesized that there was an older, preexilic version of the Deuteronomistic history.

In recent times there has been a growing, and more justified, conviction that parts of the books of Samuel and Kings are Deuteronomistic. At the very least, the Deuteronomistic revision intervened more fully in tradition and texts than scholars used to think. But is there not a danger of exaggerating the Deuteronomistic role and claiming too much as "Deuteronomistic"? As in the Pentateuch, so here a distinction must be made between short connective and interpretative redactional remarks of a general kind and specifically Deuteronomistic material that can be linguistically pinpointed. Such a distinction is important for determining the age of the material and stories.

An effort has been made to reconstruct a Deuteronomistic redactional history chiefly by distinguishing two later revisional strata from a basic stratum: "the basic conception of the history (DtrH), a revision that introduced prophetic texts (DtrP), and a further revision that focused its interest on the law (DtrN)" (R. Smend, *EntstAT*, p. 123; cf. W. Dietrich; T. Veijola; E. Würthwein, ATD 11).

As in the case of Deuteronomy (10b), an investigation of theological intentions would have to take as its starting point the individual strata of the Deuteronomistic history—provided these can be more or less clearly distinguished.

3. In its reverence for the past the Deuteronomistic history cites various traditions that are important for the modern historian and gives their sources, especially the "daybooks" or "acts" of the kings

(1 Kgs 11:41; 14:19, 29; etc.), to which interested readers can go for further information. "The Deuteronomist's intention was not to construct a history of the people of Israel but to give an objective presentation of it based on the material available to him" (M. Noth, *ÜSt*, p. 95). But is not the second part of this judgment at least open to misunderstanding?

To begin with, the Deuteronomistic history makes a selection from the traditional material available, since, on the basis perhaps of its own theological intentions, it gives preference to traditions dealing with Israel's relation to God and its cult over reports of political and military events. In addition, the tradition is filled out and corrected by means of additions; the tradition may, however, be passed on even when it does not properly correspond to the theological intention of the work (e.g., 1 Sam 8–13 on the origin of the monarchy). Finally, the work passes judgment on events in the light of its own key ideas. Accordingly, the work's aim is certainly not to present the past "as it actually was"; its intention is not simply to gather, organize, and present facts, but to interpret them. It presents history for the sake of faith: a history that in the final analysis is the story of humanity's relation to God and his law. Therefore, the same Deuteronomistic history which some scholars have ranked as the work of a historian can with equal justification be characterized as "a piece of tendentious writing" (J. A. Soggin).

b) Theological Intentions

1. Israel as a whole was affected by the fall of the northern kingdom and even more so by the catastrophe that led to the Babylonian exile. The Deuteronomistic history has therefore to answer a question that none of the preceding individual stories or cycles of stories had raised: the question of the existence and destiny of the people of God as such. Unlike the later Chronicler (2 Chr 10ff.), this work traces the history of the two states; its concern is "with the history of the Israelite people as a whole" (M. Noth, *ÜSt*, p. 95). Were not the northern and southern kingdoms part of the one people of God, both of which fell into comparable sin and therefore had to suffer the same fate, even if successively rather than simultaneously (2 Kgs 17; 21; 24:3f.)? This conception of the unity of the people of God is not only an insight springing from the situation; it also represents the acceptance of the starting point of the prophetic message and a principal concern of Deuteronomy (see §10b3).

The Deuteronomistic history not only urges obedience, fear of God, and love of God; it also shows from past history what little heed Israel paid to such admonitions. The work thus provides during and after the catastrophe a kind of self-awareness and even confession in the form of a historical retrospect. Israel's past, from the occupation of the country down to the period just over, is a history of continuous apostasy from God, who repeatedly warned, chastised, and finally exacted a harsh punishment for this continued disobedience. This history therefore has a concrete aim: to show that in the national catastrophe Israel alone was at fault and that God was justified.

"The first conclusion from contemplation of this question was that the fault was not Jahweh's: it was Israel herself who by her own fault had forfeited her salvation. Jahweh's judgment in history was justified. Thus, the Deuteronomist is concerned with Ps. LI. 6[4] and its 'so that thou art justified in thy sentence'; his work is a great 'doxology of judgment' transferred from the cultic to the literary sphere" (G. von Rad, *Old Testament Theology*, vol. 1, pp. 342–43).

Without the preceding prophetic movement such a confession would hardly have been possible. Thus Isaiah's Song of the Vineyard (Isa 5) contrasts God's action for Israel's salvation with Israel's ingratitude. Even more do the critical historical retrospects of the prophets (e.g., Hos 11f.; Isa 9:8ff.; 43:27f.) sound like concentrated anticipations of the Deuteronomistic history. History is a judgment on guilt—the guilt of the people, not (yet) of the individual. Punishment may be delayed for generations, but it will not be called off (compare 1 Kgs 13 with 2 Kgs 23:15ff., or 1 Kgs 21:23 with 2 Kgs 9:36).

2. From Deuteronomy the Deuteronomistic history takes over the concentration on the principal commandment and is skilled in highlighting, in varied language, both this first and the second commandment. The observance of all that the law commands is not all a matter of casuistic fulfillment of commandments, but rather has ultimately but one meaning: not to serve the gods of the neighboring peoples (Josh 23:6f.). Thus, the motivating force in the history is actually a single question: To what extent was Israel faithful to the exclusivity and imagelessness of its faith?—two questions seen as forming a single whole (1 Kgs 14:9; 2 Kgs 17:16; etc.). Israel is tested down the centuries by whether or not it "cleaves" to Yahweh (Josh 23:8) or by whether or not the king is "undivided" (see 1 Kgs 11:4; etc.) in allegiance to Yahweh. The resultant judgment is a negative one, both for the period of the judges (Judg 2:10ff.) and for the period of the kings, although differently for each of the periods.

The Deuteronomistic history depicts the age of the judges as basically an age of the people, one in which they drift back and forth between Yahweh and the Baals (Judg 2:10ff.). But in the following period the entire focus shifts to an individual. The king alone possesses power and responsibility (despite the restrictions on royal authority in Deut 17:14–20); on him falls the judgment that really applies to his whole generation.

In any case, the opportunity the monarchy had was quickly squandered; its swift rise under David was followed by a gradual decline and not by a cyclic rise and fall as in the age of the judges. Already on Solomon the judgment is passed that his heart was not wholly true to the Lord (1 Kgs 11:4; cf. 8:58, 61). Precisely the same judgment is true of almost all his successors. In the process, the criterion not directly brought to bear in the story of David himself is repeatedly applied, since David's behavior serves as a standard: "His heart was not wholly true to the Lord his God, as the heart of David his father . . . because David did what was right in the eyes of the Lord, and did not turn aside from anything that he commanded him all the days of his life, except in the matter of Uriah the Hittite" (1 Kgs 15:3, 5; cf. 9:4; 11:34, 38; 14:8; etc.).

In addition to David himself various kings (of Judah) are praised: for example, within limits Asa (1 Kgs 15:11, 14), Hezekiah without reservation (2 Kgs 18:3ff.), and most of all Josiah: "Before him there was no king like him, who turned to the Lord with all his heart and with all his soul and with all his might, according to all the law of Moses; nor did any like him arise after him" (2 Kgs 23:25; cf. 22:2).

The behavior of the king with respect to God or, more accurately, with respect to the law of Moses as contained in Deuteronomy, determines the weal or woe of his age. By this standard the northern kingdom must be condemned, since the political separation from the south meant a separation from the Jerusalem sanctuary, the only one chosen by Yahweh. The northern kingdom could indeed have won salvation if it had obeyed the commandments as David did (1 Kgs 11:38f.), but in fact the first northern king, Jeroboam, had already strayed from the right path by reason of his quest for cultic independence and had thus set subsequent ages on the wrong course (compare 1 Kgs 14:7ff.; 2 Kgs 17:21ff. with 1 Kgs 12:26ff.). As a result of the "sin of Jeroboam" (1 Kgs 14:16; etc.; 2 Kgs 17:21), namely, the establishment of separate cult, which remained in effect throughout the entire history of the northern state, the ultimate fall is seen as already confirmed. Nonetheless there are differences in the judgments passed on the rulers of Israel (see 2 Kgs 17:2).

On the whole, then, the standards applied in the Deuteronomistic history are quite narrow. Nothing is said of ethical or political offenses or of the social injustice that the prophets attack. As a rule, only cultic lapses are mentioned: apostasy to alien gods, violation of the first and second commandments, offenses against the unity and purity of the cult. The history is nonetheless comparable to the prophetic message in that it is more concerned with pointing out deviations than with urging right behavior. Even the "worship of God is seen less from the standpoint of the development of its own various possibilities than from that of the various possible and historically actualized deviations"; and in fact the history shows little interest in the actual performance of the cult (M. Noth, *ÜSt*, pp. 103ff.). Oversimplified and even unjust though this historical picture may be, it does give expression to the insight that salvation or destruction within history depends on fidelity or infidelity to the Israelite faith with its demand for exclusivity.

3. The unprophetic reduction of evidence of guilt to religio-cultic offenses is all the more striking in that the Deuteronomistic history, at least in its present final form, gives a good deal of space to stories about the prophets and even assigns the prophets an important place when it comes to the interpretation of the course of history. The word of God, which according to the prophetic message is forthcoming here and there in the course of history (Isa 9:8), now becomes an actor in the total story, just as for the approximately contemporary Priestly document the word of God creates the world in the beginning (Gen 1) and shapes subsequent ages (see §8b5). The Deuteronomistic history is based on the word of God, which breaks into history both as promise and as threat (1 Kgs 11:29ff.; 14:7ff.; etc.) and controls the future (cf. the many references to fulfillment, e.g., Josh 21:43ff.; 23:14; also 1 Kgs 15:29; 16:12; etc.).

While the stories about the prophets report that prophets like Elijah announced the deaths of individual kings (1 Kgs 12; 2 Kgs 1), the Deuteronomistic history generalizes this prophecy (doubtless under the influence of the writing prophets) and sees the fall of the northern kingdom (2 Kgs 17:23) as well as that of the southern kingdom as the fulfillment of the prophetic proclamation of disaster. Thus, Judah is destroyed "according to the word of the Lord which he spoke by his servants the prophets" (2 Kgs 24:2, after 20:12ff.; 21:10ff.; 22:16f.; 23:27).

Nonetheless, it is remarkable that the great prophets of disaster such as Amos, Hosea, or Jeremiah, are not mentioned by name (for Isaiah see 2 Kgs 19f.).

While Yahweh's "servants the prophets," as they are frequently called in a stereotyped phrase in the Deuteronomistic literature (2 Kgs 17:23; 21:10; etc.), threaten disaster, according to 2 Kgs 17:13 their role is also to be admonishers who call people to repentance: "Turn from your evil ways" and to obedience to the (Deuteronomic) law. Both conceptions of the prophets are facilitated by the fact that the Deuteronomistic history is in an entirely different situation relative to the prophets from that of their hearers. The prophetic announcements of disaster had meanwhile become a reality and thus confirmed the truth of the prophets' claims. Thus the prophetic proclamation, both in its (now fulfilled) predictions of the future and in its call for repentance (which had gone unheard), serves as proof of guilt. The people cannot be excused, because they had been warned. But does this not represent a shift of emphasis or even an entirely different conception of prophecy from the self-understanding of the writing prophets who in their certainty about coming disaster pronounce judgment and give the reason for it in their indictments? Admittedly, the prophetic message, like the Deuteronomistic history, aims to show the guilt of the people—but did the prophets want to warn them?

4. According to M. Noth (*ÜSt*, pp. 107f.), the theme of the Deuteronomist was "the past and, from his point of view, now finished history of his people"; he leaves unanswered and does not even expressly raise the obvious question of "whether the meaning of the history he narrates may not be found in the future, in things that will manifest themselves only as a result of the collapse of the old order." Thus the Deuteronomist "evidently saw something definitive and conclusive in the divine judgment that was fulfilled in the external collapse of the people of Israel as depicted by him [the Deuteronomist], and he did not express any hope for the future, even in the very modest and simple form of an expectation that the scattered deportees might someday be gathered again."

In fact, the Deuteronomistic history often threatens deportation as punishment for disobedience (Josh 23:13ff.; 1 Kgs 9:7ff.; 2 Kgs 17:18, 23; 21:14f.; etc.), but we hardly find any expectations with regard to the period after the judgment (we miss them especially in 2 Kgs 17; 25). Like the approximately contemporary Priestly document the Deuteronomistic history has at least no direct statements about a future salvation; in this respect, too, it does not make the prophetic proclamation its own.

G. von Rad has expressed the view that the Deuteronomistic writer "had continuously present in his mind the picture of the perfect anointed one." Not only the prophetic threats but also "the promise of salvation in the Nathan prophecy . . . was effective as it ran through the course of history." Thus the history with its concluding notice of the favor shown to Jehoiachin (2 Kgs 25:27ff.) points to a possibility that is still open to God (*Old Testament Theology*, pp. 345, 343). But the concluding notice makes no reference to the prophecy of Nathan and hardly has the noble function of hinting at a messianic future. But given the open conclusion, is salvation or disaster in the future still undecided? Is the possibility still available and the exhortation still applicable to walk "faithfully with all your heart" before God (1 Sam 12:24, 14f.; 1 Kgs 2:4; 9:4; etc.)?

According to H. W. Wolff the Deuteronomistic history has many hidden and indirect statements about the future; this is because the theme of conversion (*šûb*) sounds in almost all the important passages (Judg 2:6ff.; 2 Kgs 23:25; etc.). 2 Kgs 17:13 explicitly sums up the message of all the prophets in the exhortation "Turn from your evil ways!" But the response to the call for repentance is: "But they would not listen, but were stubborn, as their fathers had been, who did not believe in the Lord their God" (17:14ff., 19; 21:9). The offer of repentance thus relates to a past situation, a lost opportunity; in this there is again a parallel to what the prophets say (Isa 9:13; 30:15; etc.).

Only Solomon's prayer for the dedication of the temple—but only in later additions to it (1 Kgs 8:46ff.)—expressly considers that even after the judgment Israel in exile might be converted and confess its guilt, so that Yahweh would hear their prayer, forgive their sins (v. 50), and not reject his people. "The Lord our God be with us, as he was with our fathers; may he not leave us or forsake us; that he may incline our hearts to him, to walk in all his ways, and to keep his commandments, his statutes, and his ordinances, which he commanded our fathers" (1 Kgs 8:57f.; cf. Lam 5:21f.; Lev 26:44). Part of this hope is that all peoples will acknowledge Yahweh (1 Kgs 8:60, 41ff.).

With greater confidence the later framework of discourses added to Deuteronomy looks to a time of salvation after and during the dispersal; it even hopes for a gathering of the Diaspora Israelites and the return of the people to the Promised Land (Deut 4:29–31; 30:1ff.). Thus, only in the additions to the Deuteronomistic history, which extend what is said in the history itself, is there expressed a glimpse into a future beyond the execution of judgment and thus a glimpse of a new historical goal. The history proper seems to have been satisfied with looking to the past and with confessing the guilt of Israel and the justice of God's judgment.

c) From the Book of Joshua to the Books of Kings

1. The Book of Joshua

The appointment of Joshua to office before the death of Moses (Deut 31:2ff.; cf. 3:21ff.; Num 27:15ff.) is presupposed by the book of Joshua, which runs from the confirmation of this commission (Josh 1) to the death of Joshua (Josh 24). Its contents describe the settlement of Israel in two main stages: the conquest (chaps. 2–12) and the apportionment of the land (chaps. 13ff.).

I. Josh 1		(Deuteronomistic) introductory discourse
		Joshua's commission to cross the Jordan with undoubting faith; order given by Joshua, especially to the already settled tribes of Transjordan (Reuben, Gad, and the half-tribe of Manasseh), to take part in the conquest of the territory west of the Jordan (cf. 22:1–6)
II. Josh 2–12		Conquest of Cisjordan
	2–9	Collection of previously independent etiological sagas originating in the territory of Benjamin and perhaps transmitted at the sanctuary of Gilgal near Jericho (M. Noth and others):
	2; 6	Jericho (Rahab the harlot)
	3–4	Gilgal at the ford of the Jordan (the twelve stones)
	5	Circumcision, Passover, vision of "the commander of the army of the Lord"
	7–8	Ai (Achan's theft)
	8:30ff.	Building of an altar and reading of the law at Shechem; cf. Deut 27; 11:28f.
	9	Gibeon, covenant with the four cities
	10–11	Two reports of war, which, after the occupation of central Palestine as told in examples in 2–9, bring us to the Judean south (10) and the Galilean north (11):
	10	Battle at Gibeon against a coalition of cities under Adoni-zedek of Jerusalem; cf. Judg 1:5ff. "Sun, stand thou still" (vv. 12f.)
	11	Battle at the waters of Merom toward Hazor; cf. Judg 4:2
	11:16ff.; 12	Summary. List of conquered kings
III. Josh 13–22		Apportionment of Transjordan (13:7ff.; cf. 22; Num 32; Deut 3) and Cisjordan (14–19; cf. Num 34)
	13–19	Determination of the tribal areas by descriptions of boundaries and lists of villages (15:21ff.; etc.)
		The age of the two traditions is variously assigned
	20–21	Selection of the cities of refuge (20) and the Levitical cities (21); cf. Deut 4:41ff.; 19; Num 35
	22	Return of the Transjordanian tribes (vv. 1–6; cf. 1:12ff.) and building of an altar for them at the Jordan (vv. 9ff.)

IV. Josh 23 (22:1–6)   (Deuteronomistic) farewell address of Joshua
V. Josh 24   Appendix: The Assembly at Shechem. Profession by the tribes of faith in Yahweh (see §2b) "As for me and my house, we will serve the Lord" (v. 15). Pledge to observe the law (vv. 25ff.). Joshua's death and burial

The discourses in Josh 1 and 23 (with 22:1–6) form the interpretative framework of the book of Joshua; some other more or less Deuteronomistic sections are 8:30–35; 14:6–15 (cf. Deut 1:22ff.), and also 24.

Since Joshua's discourses in 23 and 24 are to some extent parallel and would hardly have stood side by side originally, and since chap. 24, which reports not only speeches but also action, has at least undergone Deuteronomistic revision, we must in any case reckon with two Deuteronomistic redactions in the book of Joshua.

In addition, there are some Priestly verses or, better, verses that resemble P (which ends with the death of Moses) in language and intention; see especially the account of the Passover in Josh 5:10–12, the mention of priests and the Ark of the Covenant in 4:15ff.; 14:1f.; 18:1; 19:51; 21:1f.; also 9:15ff.; etc.

Even the narratives of the main part of the book (2ff.) do not seem to form a literary unity. On the other hand, it is not possible to show with certainty that a part of the text of Joshua belongs to one or the other of the two older Pentateuchal sources (e.g., the accord of the formulaic expression in Josh 5:15 with Exod 3:5 J).

The local sagas (chaps. 2–9), which explain particular facts (see §5b), and the battle stories (chap. 10f.), which report or anticipate incidents in the period of the judges, were probably connected with one another only at a later time, turning Joshua into an army commander and a link between various traditions that were now connected with Israel as a whole.

Like the charismatic heroes of the age of the judges, Joshua, an Ephraimite (see Josh 24:30; Num 13:8), may have been active in central Palestine (see Josh 10), although he hardly played the exceptional role ascribed to him in the book of Joshua (Judg 1:22ff. knows nothing of him).

In any case, his name, in which the name of God is certainly attested for the first time in a proper name ("Yahweh helps"), seems to show that Joshua also devoted himself in a special way to the spread of veneration of Yahweh (see Josh 24). Is this the occasion and the justification for the tradition that Joshua was the servant and successor of Moses (Exod 33:11; Num 11:28; 27:15ff.; Deut 31:14, 23; 34:9; Josh 1)?

The book of Joshua explains various events and traditions as a single process (see 10:42) based on the will of Yahweh. The seizure of the land is done at his behest (1:2ff.) and at times with the aid of his miraculous intervention (10:12f.; cf. Judg 5:20f.). Thus it is ultimately

Yahweh himself who gives the land (Josh 1:11, 15; 9:24; 24:13). In the second, extensive main part of the book of Joshua Yahweh's claim to ownership finds expression in the apportionment of the land by lot (18:8ff.; 14:2; etc.), that is, as Yahweh wishes (cf. 7:14ff.; 1 Sam 10:20ff.). In this way, the right of the people to vote on the matter and their right to act without authorization are denied.

In addition, the settlement is the fulfillment of the promise already sworn to the patriarchs and confirmed in connection with the vocation of Moses (Exod 3:8, 17R^Dtr): "Not one of all the good promises which the Lord had made to the house of Israel had failed; all came to pass" (Josh 21:43–45). Because possession of the land is not assignable to the nature of things, it is not something to be taken for granted. Like the prophets one may say that God can withdraw his good gift if Israel proves disobedient (23:13ff.).

2. The Book of Judges

After the conquest of the country, the age of the judges introduces an era that is radically different in the eyes of the Deuteronomistic history. The difference is due to the change in Israel's attitude and behavior. While Israel was faithful to Yahweh during the lifetime of Joshua (Josh 24:31; Judg 2:7), now it falls away from Yahweh. Because of turning to alien gods, the Baals, Israel falls into danger, which the judges are able to ward off—but only for a time, until Israel again becomes disobedient (2:11ff.; cf. 3:7ff.; 4:1ff.; 6:1, 6; etc.).

I. Judg 1	Introduction (perhaps prefixed later on)
	Report or possibly a set of short notices on the conquest of the country; unlike the book of Joshua with its "all Israel" perspective, the conquest is here described with greater historical probability as undertaken by individual tribes without the leadership of Joshua
	The "negative" list of conquests (vv. 19, 21f., 27ff.; cf. Josh 15:63; 16:10; 17:11ff.)
	2:1–5, progress of the angel of Yahweh (see Exod 23:20; 33:2) from Gilgal to Bochim
II. Judg 2–16	Main section
2:6–3:6	Introductory historico-theological (Deuteronomistic) reflections on the relationship to God of all Israel—with various additions at the end, in contrast to the stories of individual tribal heroes (3:7–16:31).
3:7–11	Othniel (see 1:13; Josh 15:17)

3:12–30 Ehud from Benjamin against Eglon of Moab for the liberation of Jericho

3:31 Shamgar (see 5:6) against the Philistines

4–5 Deborah and the battle in the Plain of Jezreel (Tabor) against the Canaanite cities. Deborah from Ephraim and Barak from Naphtali against Sisera (Jabin of Hazor). Assassination of Sisera by Jael the Kenite

5 Song of Deborah. Victory through a theophany of Yahweh from Sinai (vv. 4f.; cf. Deut 33:2), with Israel's help (v. 14). Participation of tribes from central and northern Palestine. Praise of the participants, rebuke of those who stayed away

6–8 Gideon (Jerubaal) from Ophrah in Manasseh against the Midianites (the first camel-raising nomads); cf. Isa 9:4

6:11ff. Vocation formulary (as in Exod 3:10ff. E; 1 Sam 9f.; Jer 1) with sanctuary etiology

8:22f. Refusal of royal rank (cf. 1 Sam 8; 12). In contrast:

9 Abimelech, son of Gideon, king of the city of Shechem (anticipation of the formation of a state)

9:7–15 Jotham's fable (critical of the king)

10–12 Jephthah of Gilead against the Ammonites. Both tribal hero and judge (12:7)

10:1–5; 12:8–15 List of the "lesser" judges

13–16 Samson of Dan against the Philistines. Sagas of a folk-hero

III. Judg 17–21 Two appendixes (?)

These depict the situation prior to the monarchy (17:6; 19:1; 21:25)

17–18 Micah's veneration of images. Establishment of the sanctuary of the tribe of Dan. Migration of the Danites to the north

19–21 The crime at Gibeah

War of all Israel (originally only Ephraim?) against Benjamin. Other disputes among the Israelite tribes in 12:1ff.

The Deuteronomistic interpretation of history finds expression, first of all, in the introductory section in 2:6ff., which corresponds to the concluding discourse in 1 Sam 12. It also finds occasional expression in somewhat lengthy sections (Judg 10:6–16), or in a prophetic oracle (6:7–10), and finally in all kinds of short observations (8:33ff.). This presentation of history seems to have been based, above all, on two

quite different traditions from Israel's early period between the settlement and the formation of the state.

a) Just as the book of Joshua incorporated an older collection of sagas
that was already in existence (Josh 2–9:10f.), so the book of Judges
contains a collection of stories about tribal heroes with charismatic
vocations. These heroes came on the scene as rescuers in distress or
"deliverers" (thus in the later framework, Judg 3:9, 15; cf. 1 Sam 11:3).
When a tribe was threatened by foreign enemies, these heroes summoned the tribe in question and the neighboring tribes to arms. These
"major" judges, who were raised up by the spirit of Yahweh (6:34;
etc.), had careers that were limited in both space and time. They led
certain tribes in a specific military action and then, after the expedition
of liberation, returned home, removed now from their office as it were.

W. Richter has characterized this collection of sagas in more precise terms
as a "Book of Deliverers" that includes Judg 3 (vv. 12f.)–9 and originated in
northern Israel in the ninth century.

b) A list transmits the names, places of origin, periods of activity,
and places of burial of the "lesser" judges (Judg 10:1–5; 12:7–15), who
"judged Israel." In a way different from that foreseen in Deut 16:18
they exercised office as individuals and, unlike the tribal heroes just
mentioned, seem to have had an influence that extended beyond the
neighboring tribes. Their role hardly involved foreign policy and
military undertakings but was concerned rather with domestic affairs
and peace. Did their activity include the administration of justice,
whether as arbiters (see 1 Sam 7:15f.; 2 Sam 15:4, 6) or even as
pronouncers of judgment? Over what territory did they hold authority—
only over what would later be the northern kingdom, or over the south
as well? As a matter of fact, there is even disagreement about whether
the list really transmits recollections of the period prior to the state
or simply projects into the past the (all-Israel) relations of the monarchic
period.

The two groups (a) and (b) overlap in the person of Jephthah, who
acts both as a "lesser" judge (Judg 12:7) and as a charismatic commander
(see Deborah as well, 4:4f.).

Probably under the influence of this tradition, the Deuteronomistic
history identifies the two phenomena. Perhaps it was precisely through
identification with the (lesser) "judges" that the tribal heroes were
transformed into (major) "judges" (so M. Noth).

While the incidents of which the heroic sagas tell us are originally
transient and limited, their significance is given greater extension in
the course of the tradition-history. As in the process to which the

sagas and sanctuary legends of the patriarchal period were subjected, the tribal stories of the period of the judges are set in relation to all Israel and in this way become, either for the first time or in an increasing measure, testimonies to the Yahwistic faith. Human initiative is played down, so that Israel may not boast, "My own hand has delivered me" (7:2). This (later) theological interpretation culminates in Gideon's rejection of royal rank, "I will not rule over you, and my son will not rule over you; the Lord will rule over you" (8:22f.; on the history of this tradition, see W. Beyerlin).

In addition, the Deuteronomistic history fits the traditions into its own overall framework and turns what according to the tradition happens now here, now there, into a typical event that is repeated in an almost identical way—apostasy from Yahweh, oppression by enemies, cry to Yahweh for help, deliverance, new apostasy. A critic has therefore asked "whether, in this theological conception of history in the Book of Judges, Israel was not paying a dangerous tribute to the ancient East's cyclical way of thinking" (G. von Rad, *Old Testament Theology*, vol. 1, p. 330). Admittedly, the book of Judges does describe the frequent repetition of the same or a comparable situation. But—to use an image—what looks like a cycle is rather a spiral that is moving in a definite direction. The sequence of events involves not only repetition but a forward movement. From the start, the period of the judges is moving toward the period of the kings.

3. The Books of Samuel

Despite the title, the books of Samuel do not have Samuel (1 Sam 1–3; 7–16; 28) for their central figure, but rather, after a short prehistory, the fate of the first two kings, Saul (1 Sam 9–31) and David (1 Sam 16–2 Sam 24; 1 Kgs 1f.). In the process, the relationship of Saul and David (1 Sam 16–2 Sam 1) and later of David and his sons (2 Sam 13–19) gets a great deal of attention. If we approach the books in terms of their theme, then, the Septuagint and the Vulgate (the Greek and Latin translations of the OT) are correct in designating the books of Samuel as the first and second books of Kings, and then the two succeeding books of Kings as 3 and 4 Kings.

From the standpoint of literary units the books of Samuel may be subdivided as follows:

I. 1 Sam 1–15   Samuel and Saul
      1–3   Story of Samuel's childhood (at Shiloh)
               Eli and his sons
          2   Hannah's song of praise
                  "The Lord kills and brings to life" (vv. 6f.)

4–6 & 2 Sam 6		Story of the Ark: From the temple at Shiloh through its capture by the Philistines (the god Dagon) and its return to Israel (Kiriath-jearim) to its placement in Jerusalem
7–12		Origin of the monarchy Two versions are distinguished (with J. Wellhausen): a) an older version favorable to the kings: 1 Sam 9–10:16; 11 b) a later (primarily Deuteronomistic) version, critical of the kings: 1 Sam 7–8; 10:17–27; 12
13–15		Saul's deeds in wars with the Philistines (13f.; Jonathan) and Amalek (15; cf. Exod 17). Conflict between monarchy and tradition (regarding holy wars): conveyance of the entire booty to Yahweh by means of the ban Rejection of Saul by Samuel: "To obey is better than sacrifice" (15:22)
II. 1 Sam 16 —2 Sam 5(7–8)		Story of David's rise to power
	16	Anointing of David (cf. 1 Sam 9f.: anointing of Saul) David as minstrel at the court of Saul
	17	Single combat with Goliath (cf. 2 Sam 21:19)
	18ff.	Saul's jealousy (song: 18:7; 21:12) Friendship with Jonathan
	21ff.	David as guerilla and mercenary chieftain (22:2; 27:2f.). Receives Ziklag as a fief (27:6f.)
	28	Saul and the witch of En-dor
	31	Death of Saul and his sons in battle with the Philistines (mountains of Gilboa)
	1	David's lament over Saul and Jonathan
	2–4	David and Ishbaal
	2	David anointed king over Judah at Hebron
	5	David anointed king over Israel Conquest of Jerusalem. Victory over the Philistines
	6	Transfer of the Ark (continuation of the story of the Ark in 1 Sam 4–6)
	7	Prophecy of Nathan: the House of David will rule "for ever." Rejection of the offer to build a temple. The older part of the text is to be looked for in the unconditional promises of continuity for the House of David (vv. 11b, 16) or at least of a successor (vv. 12, 14a) Echoes: 2 Sam 23:5; Pss 89; 132; Isa 55:3
	8	Subjection of neighboring peoples. David's officials (8:16–18; 20:23–26; cf. 1 Kgs 4)
III. 2 Sam (6) 9–20; 2 Kgs 1f.		Story of the succession to David
	10–12	War against the Ammonites (cf. 1 Sam 11)
	11	Bathsheba. Birth of Solomon
	12	Nathan's parable of the rich man and the poor

man (story of a suit, like the song of the
vineyard in Isa 5:1–7)
"You are the man" (v. 7). "I have sinned against
the Lord" (v. 13; cf. Ps 51)

13ff.   David's sons Amnon and Absalom
15–19   Absalom's rebellion
20   Sheba's rebellion
        "We have no portion in David" (v. 1; 1 Kgs 12:16)

IV. 2 Sam 21–24   Supplements (?, insertion into the succession story)
22   = Ps 18
23   "Last words" of David (picture of the ideal
        sovereign)
        David's champions (23:8ff.; 21:15ff.)
24   Etiological explanation of the location of the
        temple? Census of the people. Gad, "David's
        seer." Choice of punishment. Building of an
        altar on the threshing floor of Araunah. Place
        of cult taken over from previous inhabitants,
        reinterpreted in secular terms (as a threshing
        floor)?

Apart from isolated stories (as in Judg 9; 2 Kgs 9f.), the two books
of Samuel contain the earliest extended pieces of Israelite historical
writing. This kind of writing apparently came into existence after the
emergence of the monarchy and, in all likelihood, precisely as a result
of this new institution, which had previously been alien to Israel's
life, since the administration of the state created a need for officials
who could write (see §3c1). In keeping with its origin, this writing of
history concerned itself initially with contemporary events, although
soon after it turned, in the work of the Yahwist, to a broad and
comprehensive survey of Israel's past.

Is it possible to trace further the development of Israelite historical
writing within the books of Samuel? It is noteworthy that in the
gradual construction of the books of Samuel there is also a gradual
growth of freedom in the handling of existing individual traditions.
Beginning with the still quite disparate traditions about Samuel and
Saul, through the history of David, which is loosely made up of all
sorts of heroic sagas and popular tales, down to the methodical and
purposeful story of the succession to David's throne, the composition
becomes increasingly careful, as does the way in which existing
material is fitted into the context and intention of the broader picture
(R. Rendtorff, p. 40).

If we look at the first section of the books (1 Sam 1–15, in the
outline above) and single out the many-leveled tradition about the
origin of the monarchy, we can easily see the various ways in which

the transition to the new situation is seen and judged in retrospect. Strictly speaking, we have as many as five different accounts given:

a) 1 Sam 8: The failure of the sons of Samuel to administer justice properly— or, in other words, internal reasons—gives rise to the desire to have a king "like all the nations."

Inserted here is the "royal privilege" (vv. 11–17), which sets forth in a polemical way the privileges of the king in relation to the free Israel (military service, forced labor, expropriations, tithes).

b) 1 Sam 9–10:16: Saul is anointed *nāgîd* ("prince") by Samuel (see the anointing of David, 1 Sam 16).

"How a man went out to look for asses and found a royal crown" (H. Gressmann).

c) 1 Sam 10:20-24: Choice of a king by lot (at Mizpah).

d) 1 Sam 10:23b–24: Within the previous scene there is reported an original tradition according to which Saul was proclaimed king because he towered over all others by a head (cf. 9:2).

e) 1 Sam 11: the threat from the Ammonites (Jabesh-gilead). Saul as charismatic leader like one of the major judges. At Gilgal Saul is raised up as king "before the Lord" (v. 15).

According to the addendum in vv. 12–14, which, in order to harmonize accounts, speaks of "renewing" the kingship, Samuel played a part in the enthronement.

This last (e) and perhaps oldest account rightly sees military conflicts as the reason for the origin of the monarchy (see also 1 Sam 8:20; 10:1). But, despite 1 Sam 11, the threat hardly came from the Ammonites but in all likelihood from the Philistines (see (9:16; 13f.; 28f.; 31), whose constant pressure on Israel made necessary a counterpressure and therefore a monarchy and not simply a series of charismatic judges who would be called to deal with a series of limited crises. It seems, therefore, that the immediate occasion for the rise of the monarchy did not find literary expression.

A special historical question concerns the extent to which Samuel, who originally was probably a "lesser" judge (1 Sam 7:15f.), had a share in the revolutionary innovations. His importance grows in retrospect (anointing of Saul, 10:1; assembling of the people, 10:17; additions in 11:7, 12–14; see §13d).

Though the several accounts give varying reflections of the event, they are nonetheless close in their theological intention. What 1 Sam 11:15 means by the words "before the Lord" is developed by means both of the symbolic act of anointing and by the choice through lots. Despite all critical reservations the choice of the new officeholder ultimately reflects the will of God, with whom the "chosen" one (10:24) is linked and must remain linked.

1 Sam 8 and 12 form a framework that bears the mark of the

Deuteronomist and surrounds and interprets the older traditions. These chapters pass a very skeptical retrospective judgment on the monarchy and may even be opposing the sovereignty of God to the king's claim of leadership (8:7; 12:12; cf. Judg 8:23). God himself claims to be the true deliverer in time of need (see 1 Sam 10:18f.).

The surprisingly wide-ranging traditions about the time of David (1 Sam 16–2 Kgs 2) are usually subdivided into two large units: David's rise to power (1 Sam 16–2 Sam 5) and the succession to the throne (2 Sam 9–10; 1 Kgs 1f.).

According to the standard analysis by L. Rost (1926) the goal of the succession story, which tells in detail of the changing fortunes of the sons of David, can be formulated in interrogative fashion by asking, Who is to sit on the throne of David (1 Kgs 1:27)? Solomon!

There is, however, no complete agreement on what precisely is to be included in each of the two stories. Especially disputed is the literary place of the transitional chapters (2 Sam 5 and possibly 6–8), which continue the first story, prepare for the second, and thus link the two together. In addition, the final part of the once independent story of the Ark (1 Sam 4–6; 2 Sam 6) has been inserted into this transitional section. As a result of this skillful linking of sources (a linking that preceded the Deuteronomistic history?), a major part of the books of Samuel offers a more or less consecutive narrative that is wide-ranging in scope and embraces a variety of individual scenes. Consequently, a more unified impression is given than in the books of Kings with their constant shifting from one person and action to another.

Since the stories manifest a detailed knowledge of events at the court of David, they have certainly preserved a good many historically reliable recollections (along, possibly, with freely developed speeches or even scenes?). But there are also uncertainties: the age of various individual traditions, the time when the whole was put in writing (as early as the time of Solomon or only after the division of the kingdom in 926 B.C.?), the part played by later redaction, and especially the intention that governs the presentation. The more complex a historical account is, the more difficult it is, of course, to gain a clear grasp of its tendency. Is the story of David's rise pro-Davidic? Is the story of the succession anti-Solomonic? Or is it critical of the hereditary monarchy? (E. Würthwein).

Is the dynastic principle being criticized because Solomon gained his office without the participation of other free Israelites (see 2 Sam 2:4; 5:3; 1 Kgs 12:20)? There may have been opposition to the monarchy at a very early period (1 Sam 10:27; 11:12f.; also 2 Sam 15:3f.; Judg 9:7ff.; etc.).

On the whole, the ambiguity of the story emerges rather clearly. The presentation seems remarkably "secular." Any theological illumination is reserved, almost hidden; thus the somewhat later story of David's appointment as king by anointing (1 Sam 16:1–13) is prefixed to the (presumably) original introduction to the story of David's rise to power, an introduction that tells of how young David from Bethlehem came to Saul's court as a minstrel (16:14ff.). The internal connection between the two stories, which are not easy to bring into historical harmony, is created by the idea of a transfer of charism. The spirit of Yahweh passes from Saul to David, while an evil spirit, likewise sent by Yahweh, descends upon Saul (vv. 14f.). The real intention of the story of David's rise is to be found in the assertion that Yahweh was "with" David (1 Sam 17:37; 18:12, 14, 28). The story begins with this assertion (16:18) and probably ends with it: "And David became greater and greater, for the Lord, the God of hosts, was with him" (2 Sam 5:10; cf. also 7:3, 8f.; 1 Sam 10:7). It would seem that Israel's success in the Davidic-Solomonic age was explained by Yahweh's "being with" these rulers; in this way, the (indirect) action of God was acknowledged in the "natural" course of events, and success was not attributed simply to human prowess. Does the more or less contemporary Yahwist adopt this same view in interpreting the patriarchal sagas (Gen 26:3; 28:15; etc.)?

Generally speaking, the books of Samuel confess human unworthiness and helplessness and assign deliverance to God (1 Sam 9:21; 14:6; 15:17; 16:11; 17:45, 47; 2 Sam 7:18).

There is disagreement about whether early experience or only subsequent hindsight is responsible for the theological judgments in the succession story that see the tangle of guilt and suffering at the court as a divine dispensation: "The Lord has ordained" (2 Sam 17:14; cf. 11:27f; 14:14; etc.). Once again, a comparison with the oldest Pentateuchal source is suggested. With good reason the character portrayal in the succession story, embracing as it does the heights and depths, the strengths and weakness of humanity, reminds the exegete of the realistic view of humanity in the Yahwist history (Gen 4; 8:21).

4. The Books of Kings

The story in the books of Kings runs from the death of David and the establishment in office of Solomon, his successor (1 Kgs 1f.), through the history of the two kingdoms, down to the destruction of Jerusalem and the Babylonian exile (2 Kgs 25). The period of about four centuries that the story covers falls almost automatically into three parts:

I. 1 Kgs 1–11   Reign of Solomon

1–2	End of the story of the succession
	Coronation of Solomon (instead of Adonijah)
3:4ff.; 9	Divine revelations
3; 5:9ff.	Solomon's wisdom
4	Solomon's high officials (cf. 1 Sam 8:16ff.; 20:23ff.) and administrators for the twelve districts of Israel
5–8	Building of the temple and the palace
10–11	Commercial undertakings (9:26ff.), international relations, foreign politics
	Solomon's apostasy, prediction of the dissolution of his kingdom

II. 1 Kgs 12–
2 Kgs 17   History of the divided kingdoms of Israel and Judah (926–722 B.C.)

12	Division of the kingdom. Jeroboam (I) and Rehoboam.
	Two golden "calves"

17–19; 21;
2 Kgs 1   Elijah

18	Divine judgment at Carmel
	"How long will you go limping with two different opinions?" (v. 21)
19	Theophany on Horeb (cf. Exod 33:18ff.)
	Call of Elisha (vv. 19ff.)
21	Naboth's vineyard
1	Ahaziah's appeal to Baalzebub
20	An anonymous prophet in the war with the Arameans

22   Micaiah son of Imlah

The court prophets vs. a single prophet of disaster with his two visions

2 Kgs 2–9; 13   Elisha

2	Assumption of Elijah
	Elisha receives two thirds (cf. Deut 21:17) of Elijah's spirit (2:9)
2; 4; 6ff.	Miracles
3	War against Mesha of Moab
5	Cure of Naaman the Syrian. A cargo of earth
9f.	Rebellion of Jehu (cf. 1 Kgs 19:16ff.)
11	Athaliah of Judah
17	Conquest of Samaria by Sargon (II)
	Resettlement of the country

III. 2 Kgs 18–25   History of the southern kingdom, Judah (to 587 or 561 B.C.)

18–20	= Isa 36–39. Hezekiah and Isaiah
	Siege of Jerusalem by Sennacherib (701 B.C.)

158   *Traditions and Documentary Sources*

20–23	The reform of Josiah (622 B.C.)
	Cf. earlier reforms, 18:4ff. (Hezekiah);
	1 Kgs 15:11ff. (Asa)
24	First conquest of Jerusalem (597 B.C.)
	Deportation of Jehoiachin
25	Second conquest of Jerusalem (587 B.C.)
	Babylonian exile. Gedaliah. Reprieve of
	Jehoiachin

The books of Kings tell a story of guilt, accompanied by forceful theological judgments; consequently, they do not provide a neutral and certainly not a complete picture of the monarchic period. We hear of the usually tense relations between prophets and kings, peaceful or violent changes of regime, cultic measures, and wars, but hardly anything of social problems and problems of domestic politics, although these became increasingly important during the monarchic period.

In addition to all sorts of individual materials there are two main sources on which the presentation in the books of Kings is based, and these two sources are quite different in kind:

a) A rigorous and official character attaches to:

1. the "Synchronistic Chronicle," which in recording the accession of a king indicates the year of the reign of the ruler in the neighboring kingdom (1 Kgs 15:1, 25 to 2 Kgs 18:1), as well as

2. the length of the reign and often the place of residence (1 Kgs 2:11; 11:42; 14:20f., and frequently).

These data allow modern historians to construct, although only with great difficulty, a relative chronology, which needs to be turned into an absolute chronology through comparison with fixed dates in other parts of the ancient Near East.

A. Jepsen, whose work has been carried on by J. Begrich and who himself wrote frequently on methodology (especially BZAW 88, 1964; *VT* 18 [1968] 31–46), drew up a clear chronological table for ancient Near Eastern and especially Israelite history. I have taken this as my basis here (see the appendix to W. Rudolph's commentary on the minor prophets or A. Jepsen and others, *Von Sinuhe bis Nebukadnezar*, 1976²).

These two regularly given pieces of information are supplemented, for the kings of Judah, by notices on:

3. the age of the ruler at his accession, and

4. the name of the queen mother (1 Kgs 14:21; etc.), who as "Mistress" (*gĕbîrâ*) exercised certain functions of government (see 15:13; 2 Kgs 10:13; Jer 13:18).

Finally, information is generally given regarding the death of the king and regarding his successor (1 Kgs 14:20, 31; etc.).

This official information, and perhaps other data as well (12:25;

etc.), may have come from the annals that are likewise cited almost everywhere in the books of Kings: "the book of the acts of Solomon" (11:41), "the Book of the Chronicles of the Kings of Israel" (14:19 to 2 Kgs 15:26, 31), as well as "the Book of the Chronicles of the Kings of Judah" (1 Kgs 14:29 to 2 Kgs 24:5). These references to sources come, of course, from the redactor or redactors of the books of Kings. He or they are also responsible for the regularly recurring judgments on the godliness of the kings (1 Kgs 14:22; 15:11, 26, 34; etc., to 2 Kgs 14:19; see §11b2).

b) From these more or less stereotyped pieces of information are to be distinguished the more loosely structured stories about the prophets, which, it is surprising, take up a goodly space in the books of Kings. There are stories about unnamed prophets (1 Kgs 13; 20) as well as about

Ahijah of Shiloh	1 Kgs 11:29ff.; 14
Micaiah son of Imlah	1 Kgs 22
Elijah	1 Kgs 17–19; 21; 2 Kgs 1
Elisha	2 Kgs 2–9; 13 (1 Kgs 19:19ff.)
Isaiah	2 Kgs 18–20 (= Isa 36–39)

Like the patriarchal sagas of Genesis, the stories about the prophets had to some extent already been joined into saga cycles (e.g., the cycles of Elijah and Elisha) before being taken into the Deuteronomistic history. Once again, a problem of literary history is created by the redactional and specifically the Deuteronomistic revision which fills out the prophetic predictions and statements in the light of the subsequent course of history. Where precisely do we have ancient tradition, and where a post-factum rewriting? It can be said nonetheless that the redactors make their own theological intention, which already characterizes the stories about the prophets—to show the efficacy of God's word.

§12

THE CHRONICLER'S HISTORY

a) Chronicles

It is remarkable that alongside the books of Samuel and Kings the OT has a second description of the period of the kings: the books of Chronicles, which are essentially parallel to the first description but with different emphases. The Hebrew title, "Daybooks," "Annals" (*dibrê hayyāmîm*), was translated as "Chronicles" by Jerome, and Luther followed him.

. Is the Greek and Latin name *Paralipomena*, "What was passed over" or "left out," intended to imply that the two books of Chronicles supply much that had been "omitted" in the books of Samuel and Kings? Or does the title really refer only to the Greek translation, in which precisely because of their parallelism with the books of Samuel and Kings the books of Chronicles may have been first "left out" and later included?

According to the usual but by no means undisputed view, the two books of Chronicles originally formed the first part of a comprehensive work that included Ezra and (in whole or in part) Nehemiah. How did this idea of a Chronicles-history, the author of which is usually called "the Chronicler," arise?

1. The two books of Chronicles follow the story down to the exile, while Ezra and Nehemiah describe the subsequent period. The important edict of Cyrus, which was the turning point in the exile, is given both at the end of 2 Chronicles and at the beginning of Ezra. The repetition (or more accurately the anticipation in 2 Chr 36:22ff.), which goes back to the time when the complete work was divided, makes clear the original connection or continuation of the story.

2. Chronicles and Ezra and Nehemiah show to a large extent the same choice of words, style, basic ideas, and intention, even if there are unmistakable differences.

For example, does the great importance assigned to the Davidic monarchy and to prophecy in Chronicles completely disappear in Ezra and Nehemiah, simply because the latter are describing a period in which the monarchy and prophecy played no decisive role?

160

3. Finally, the breakup of the Chronicler's history can be explained. Because only Ezra and Nehemiah contain information that goes beyond what is in the books of Samuel and Kings, they were separated from 1–2 Chronicles and introduced into the canon at an earlier date. This also makes it understandable that in the Hebrew text Ezra and Nehemiah precede Chronicles (which was only subsequently introduced into the canon).

This sequence, which contradicts the course of the events described, has been corrected in the Greek and Latin translations and similarly in modern translations. These place Chronicles among the "historical books," whereas in the Hebrew text it is placed among the "writings," which come at the end of the Bible. The place of Chronicles in the Hebrew text is a further sign of its late origin.

But despite these arguments the view has also been maintained that Chronicles and Ezra and Nehemiah were distinct works from the beginning, whether or not the authors may have been the same.

The final events narrated in the Chronicler's history occurred about 400 B.C. But even though the story does not include the expedition of Alexander the Great and shows, it seems, no Hellenistic influence, there is disagreement about whether the work was composed in the fourth century or only in about 300, after the end of Persian rule, or even in the third century B.C.

In any case, the work as we have it is not a unity; lengthy sections are generally regarded as later additions. As in P, it is especially various lists (1 Chr 2–9; 23–27; also Neh 7; 11f.; etc.) that were introduced later on.

Were several redactors involved, or should such additions be assigned to a single hand? Extending his earlier analyses K. Galling (ATD 12) had divided the Chronicler's history between two authors: an earlier Chronicler (ca. 300) and a later one who added material. This two-author solution has found little acceptance, but additions could have been made even at so late a time.

The two books of Chronicles carry the story from Adam to the Babylonian exile. It falls naturally into four parts. The first, which includes everything before David, consists simply of a genealogy from Adam to David (with all kinds of genealogical and historical notices being introduced). The Chronicler thus shows how the people of God has its roots in the human race as such, or, if you will, how the history of humanity was leading up to the one true community.

1 Chr 1–9   Genealogy from Adam to David
            with special attention to Judah (2–4) and Levi (6; 6:1ff.)
1 Chr 10–29 Reign of David—from the death of Saul (10; 1 Sam 31) to the
            accession of Solomon (29)
            David's crowning as king of all Israel (11), extensive preparations

for the building of the temple by Solomon, and for the
furnishings of the cult (17; 21ff., with additions)

2 Chr 1–9   Reign of Solomon and the building of the temple
2 Chr 10–36 The kings of Judah/Jerusalem
from Rehoboam to Zedekiah (nothing about the northern kingdom), with special attention to Asa (14–16), Jehoshaphat (17–
20), Hezekiah (29–32), and Josiah (34–35)
36   God's anger (v. 16), the exile (v. 20), and the turning point
(vv. 22ff.)

The Chronicler mentions a profusion of (no longer extant) sources,
both for the kings (2 Chr 16:11; 20:34; especially 24:27) and for the
prophets (1 Chr 29:29; 2 Chr 9:29; 32:32; etc.). Did the Chronicler
really have sources that went beyond the Pentateuch (in 1 Chr 1–9)
and the Deuteronomistic history (in 1 Chr 10ff.)? As a matter of fact,
in essentials he could not have based his account on anything but the
books of Samuel and Kings. Even the various special traditions, in
particular accounts of construction and of wars (e.g., 2 Chr 20), are
with few exceptions (such as the list of fortifications in 2 Chr 11:5b-
10a; cf. 26:6, 10; 35:10ff.; etc.) not historically reliable testimonies
from the time before the exile but originate in the age of the Chronicler
himself (P. Welten).

b) Ezra and Nehemiah

The Chronicler had quite diverse sources at his disposal for the story
he tells in Ezra and Nehemiah, which narrate the return of the exiles,
the building of the temple and the wall, and the reestablishment of
the community at Jerusalem.

1. The most extensive and important document is Nehemiah's own
story (Neh 1:1), or the "Nehemiah source" or "Memoirs of Nehemiah,"
which is generally regarded as a highly valuable historical work (see
U. Kellermann). It tells chiefly of Nehemiah's commission and of the
measures taken for the building of the wall, Neh 1:1–7:5a; 12:27–43
(with small additions), and more briefly of certain reforms, 13:4–31*.
Not only do the memoirs stand out from the third-person account of
the Chronicler by reason of the use of the first person; they also show
all sorts of stylistic peculiarities (e.g., reference to the months by
names, 1:1; 2:1, instead of by numbers, 8:2).

At times there are departures from the first person singular form, as in the
we-account (4:6ff.) or in the list of builders of the wall (3:1ff.)—a list that may
have preceded Nehemiah.

Major sections are concluded with a prayer or "founder formula": "Remember for my good, O my God . . ." (5:19; 13:14; cf. 13:22, 31). Nehemiah thus makes bold to present his deeds to God as meritorious, but he also knows that without God's kind help he would not have completed his task (2:8, 18, 20; 6:16; etc.). The first-person report in Nehemiah's memoirs is already notable for its extent. Scholars have asked whether ancient Near Eastern royal inscriptions, or votive or founder's inscriptions, or memorial pillars, or—in view of the appeal to the divinity that was just mentioned—prayers of defendants may have served as models. In any case, the modification of these prayers by the petition that enemies receive retribution for their actions (6:14; 13:29; 4:4f.) shows the difficult conflicts with Israel's neighbors (2:10, 19; etc.) and with his compatriots (6:10ff.), amid which Nehemiah had to carry out the building of the wall. Thus the memoirs, which are conceived of as a kind of personal statement of accounts, show us "how Nehemiah understood his work and wanted it to be understood by the public and before God" (U. Kellermann, p. 88).

The Latin Bible calls Ezra and Nehemiah "1 and 2 Ezra." 3 Ezra—or 3 Esdras—is an apocryphal book which, in the part that has survived, runs from the Passover of Josiah in 2 Chr 35 to the reading of the law in Neh 8 and includes nonbiblical material (competition of Darius's pages regarding the riddle about the strongest thing in the world—wine, the king, women, truth?). 4 Esdras is an apocalypse that is important for its distinction between the present and the future eons and for its messianic expectation.

Since 3 Esdras (which is also used by Josephus in his *Antiquities*) bypasses the Nehemiah source in Neh 1–7, some have asked whether this translation may not preserve an older stage of the tradition and whether the Nehemiah source may not therefore have been introduced into the Chronicler's history only later (e.g., K.-F. Pohlmann). But does not the absence in 3 Esdras represent rather a deliberate omission?

2. Scholars like to think of there having been an Ezra source or memoir comparable to the Nehemiah source; it would have included Ezra 7–10; Neh 8(–10). As a matter of fact, the Ezra story also takes the form of a first-person account, but only in part, so that the shifting use of "I" (Ezra 7:27–9:15) and "he" (7; 10; Neh 8) needs to be explained. In addition, the first-person account is not marked by stylistic idiosyncracies as is the Nehemiah account. It seems, therefore, that the Chronicler himself composed the Ezra account with the Nehemiah source as a model.

"This dependence is an argument . . . for composition by the Chronicler, who knew and assimilated the Nehemiah-source. Furthermore, there is nothing in Ezra 7–10 which the Chronicler himself could not have derived from the sources he used (Ezra 7:12–26; 8:1–14) and from his own resources. The outline of the entire section, Ezra's journey from Babylon to Jerusalem, and his sojourn in the latter place in order to enforce God's law: these were clear from Ezra 7:12–26. The fact of mixed marriages, which were a long-standing abuse, could be gotten from Neh 13:23–25 and must have been regarded by the Chronicler as so gross a violation of the divine law that Ezra, who bore responsibility for this law, could not have overlooked it; it was thus easy for the Chronicler to make opposition to mixed marriages Ezra's first action in Jerusalem" (M. Noth, *ÜSt*, p. 147; cf. U. Kellermann; W. Th. In der Smitten).

Instead of using a self-contained Ezra source, then, the Chronicler probably just presented various pieces of older material, as, for example, the (presumably "authentic" in essence) decree of Artaxerxes in behalf of Ezra (7:12ff.), perhaps also the list of returning exiles (8:1–14).

3. Another important source was the Jerusalem Chronicle (Ezra 4:6–6:15[18]), which, like Dan 2:4ff., was written in Aramaic and was essentially a collection of letters. When this document deals with the age of Xerxes and Artaxerxes (485–424) before speaking of the earlier reign of Darius (I, 522–486 B.C.), it does so because of a transposition by the Chronicler, "who wanted to report first the disruptions, then the successful outcome" (K. Galling on this passage). The collection of letters is noteworthy for two reasons. First, it mentions the prophets Haggai and Zechariah, who urged the building of the temple (5:1; 6:14). Second, it contains (6:3–5) the edict of Cyrus on the building of the temple (538 B.C.). The letter, composed in Imperial Aramaic (the official language in the western part of the Persian empire), fits in with the aim of the early Persian kings, as this is known from other sources—namely, promoting the cultic and legal individuality of subject peoples. It can therefore be regarded as "genuine" because (in Ezra 1:2ff.) it is supplemented by the permission to return and in this way is corrected—on the basis of the view that only the exiles form the true community.

While events in Ezra 1–6 (except for 4:6ff.) take place in the period 538–515 B.C., chap. 7 jumps ahead several decades into the middle of the fifth century and only then introduces the man who gave the book its name: Ezra. The book of Nehemiah, on the other hand, begins with the "I" that is Nehemiah; Neh 8 continues the account of Ezra.

Ezra 1–6	From the edict of Cyrus (538) to the building of the temple (515)
1	Edict of Cyrus on the rebuilding of the temple, and—going beyond what the older text (6:3–5) says—the return. (First) return of those "whom God had inspired" (1:5, NAB). Restoration of the temple furnishings to Sheshbazzar (cf. 5:14ff.)

2	Cf. Neh 7. List of exiles (register of families) returning with Zerubbabel, the grandson of King Jehoiachin, who had been deported in 597, and with Jeshua, the grandson of the last high priest of Jerusalem. Individuals of uncertain ancestry (vv. 59ff.). Donations for the temple (vv. 68f.)
3	Resumption of the cult: rebuilding of the altar of holocausts, sacrifices, feast of Booths, laying of the foundation of the temple by Zerubbabel (whom the Chronicler mistakenly identifies with Sheshbazzar; cf. 5:2, 16) and Jeshua (cf. Hag 1:12ff.)
	But "the people of the land" (= the Samaritans) prevent the building of the temple (for almost two decades, until 520 B.C.; cf. 4:24)
4:6–6:18	Aramaic Chronicle of Jerusalem. (Revised) collection of official letters with connecting text, in an inverted temporal sequence:
5	At the urging of the prophets Haggai and Zechariah, Zerubbabel and Jeshua (520 B.C.) begin or continue the building of the temple. Tattenai, Persian satrap of Syria, inquires of Darius (521–485 B.C.) about the legality.
6	Darius's response, based on the edict of Cyrus (vv. 3–5), which had been found at Ecbatana (summer residence of the Persian kings). The building of the temple to be supported by public funds
4:6ff.	Complaint to Xerxes. Ca. 450 B.C. prohibition against rebuilding the city walls of Jerusalem under Artaxerxes (I)
6	After the completion of the temple (vv. 14ff.; 515 B.C.) first Passover and feast of Unleavened Bread (cf. 2 Chr 30; 35)
Ezra 7–10	Ezra's story
7	Introduction of Ezra, "the scribe of the law of the God of heaven," and his appointment to depart from Babylon by decree (vv. 12ff., in Aramaic) of King Artaxerxes (I?): repatriation, law, temple offerings, and temple furnishings
8	Return of Ezra with groups of exiles, unprotected by weapons (for a different version, see Neh 1:7ff.) and accompanied only by God's blessing
9–10	Ezra's prayer of repentance (9:5ff.); dissolution of mixed marriages with the approval of the people (10:9ff.). Cf. Neh 9f. 10:18ff. (Added?) list of those involved in mixed marriages
Neh 1–7	"The words of Nehemiah the son of Hacaliah" (1:1). The main part of Nehemiah's memoirs is in the first person
1	Nehemiah as cupbearer in the Persian court in Susa. Report of the situation in Jerusalem. Prayer (obedience to the law, gathering of the people)
2	At his own request Nehemiah is commissioned by Artaxerxes (I) to rebuild the city walls of Jerusalem (vv. 1–10). Preparation—secret inspection of the walls—and beginning of the work (vv. 11-20)

3	List of builders of the wall (in the third person; an official document?)
	Sections of the walls assigned to families from Jerusalem and Judah (cf. 12:31ff.). Resistance, and Nehemiah's prayer for vengeance (4:1ff.)
4	External difficulties created by hostile neighbors: Sanballat the governor of Samaria, Tobiah the Ammonite, and Geshem the Arab (cf. 2:10, 19f.; 4:1ff.). The builders accompanied by armed men (vv. 16f.). Their complaint (v. 10)
5	Domestic difficulties. Nehemiah's social policy
	The lower classes oppressed by the burdens of the building: mortgaging of their property and children (cf. 2 Kgs 4:1) to the upper classes. In a plenary assembly remission of debts, confirmed by oath and Amen (vv. 12ff.). Nehemiah's renunciation of income from taxes, despite an extensive household (vv. 14ff.)
6	Despite persecutions the wall is finished in fifty-two days (6:1, 15; 7:1)
7	Securing of the city gates. Resettlement (*synoikismos*) in Jerusalem (cf. 11:1f.)? List of returnees (= Ezra 2)
Neh 8(–10)	Ezra's story (picks up after Ezra 7–10)
8	Reading of the law by Ezra at the desire of the people. A kind of synagogue service in the open air: Ezra on a dais (cf. 2 Chr 6:13), collaboration of the laity, instruction (in Aramaic?). Feast of Booths (vv. 13ff.; cf. Deut 31:10)
9	Ceremony of lamentation with penitential prayer (cf. 1:5ff.; Ezra 9; Dan 9)
10	Commitment of the people to the law (avoidance of mixed marriages, observance of the sabbath, temple tax, firstfruits, etc.). Cf. Neh 13
Neh 11–13	The Jerusalem community
11	Resettlement (cf. 7:4f.). List of inhabitants
12	List of priests and Levites. Dedication of the city wall (vv. 27ff.)
13	Reform measures of Nehemiah (delimitation of the community, provision for the Levites, observance of the sabbath, mixed marriages)

The account of Ezra (Ezra 7–10; Neh 8) thus serves to frame the main part of Nehemiah's memoirs (Neh 1–7); this can hardly be unintentional. The Chronicler gives precedence to Ezra both materially and in time; as a priest (Ezra 7:12; cf. the genealogy, 7:1ff.), Ezra is called to do a work that surpasses Nehemiah's and makes it less important. Since the picture given of Ezra has in large measure been fashioned by the Chronicler, we have little reliable historical information about Ezra, whereas the Nehemiah memoirs provide us with substantial and, despite the first-person approach, reliable knowledge of Nehemiah. There is sharp disagreement about whether the Chronicler is justified in having Ezra come on the scene a good decade before Nehemiah and whether in fact Ezra did not rather come after Nehemiah. Why does Nehemiah not mention Ezra in his memoirs? Is Nehemiah's warning against future mixed marriages (Neh 13:23ff.) still intelligible after Ezra's drastic dissolution of past ones (Ezra 10:11f., 44; cf. Neh 9:12; 13:3)?

Nehemiah, cupbearer at the Persian court in Susa, asks for and receives in 445 B.C. (Neh 1:1; 2:1) authorization to rebuild the wall of Jerusalem. The work succeeds, though the Samaritans must be excluded. Later Nehemiah becomes "governor" (5:14; cf. 8:9; 10:1) of the province of Judah, which is thus separated from Samaria and becomes independent. Did the accusation of political ambitions (6:6f.) have a real basis?

Ezra too is in the service of the Persians, probably with the title "Scribe of the Law of the God of Heaven" (Ezra 7:12). As a special delegate for religious affairs he is dispatched to Judah with a group of repatriates (in 458 B.C., according to 7:7f.). A well-known question— but one that can hardly be answered now—is, What work is meant by "the law of the God of heaven," which Ezra apparently brings with him from Babylon (7:14, 25) and (according to Neh 8) reads to the people as "the book of the law of Moses"? Is the reference simply to Deuteronomy, or to the Priestly document along with certain laws (especially the Law of Holiness), or to the entire Pentateuch? In fact, how far can we credit the account in Neh 8? But Ezra's official title, which the Chronicler seems to understand as meaning "scribe" (Ezra 7:6, 10f.), indicates at least that Ezra played a decisive role in the acceptance (with the backing now of the state) of the law in Israel. For this reason Ezra has been seen precisely as "the founder of Judaism."

c) Theological Intentions

The Chronicler's aim was "to tell the story of the origin of the postexilic community in which he was living" (M. Noth, p. 172). This makes his work the successor of the Deuteronomistic history and, in parts, the "interpreter" of the latter (T. Willi). Here again the interpretation of events is often given by means of the exhortatory and predictive utterances of the prophets (2 Chr 12:5ff.; 15:2ff.). On the other hand, the Chronicler depicts the past as seen by his own age; he recasts, judges much more radically, corrects, and idealizes. In good measure his intention can be determined by comparison with the books of Samuel and Kings: What does he omit? What does he add?

1. The decisive standard that the Chronicler applies is the connection between action and consequence, the "personal retribution," which helps make clear the contingent character of history. Thus, the leprosy of King Uzziah is explained by his encroachment on priestly privileges (2 Chr 26:16ff. as compared with 2 Kgs 15:5). While in the case of Uzziah the author distinguishes an early good period from a later bad period, in the case of Manasseh the reverse happens: a period of wickedness is followed by a self-humbling before God (the change of heart is due to a—fictitious—experience of Assyrian imprisonment). This conversion makes intelligible the exceptionally lengthy reign of the king (2 Chr 33:1, 10ff.). Behind this kind of approach to history stands the often expressed principle: He who adheres to God will be sustained; he who abandons God will be abandoned (1 Chr 28:2; 2 Chr 15:2; etc.).

2. As in the Deuteronomistic history so in the Chronicler's history David has a very prominent place. He is "the man of God" (2 Chr 8:14), the model of fidelity to the law (7:17; etc.); in an allusion to the name given God in the patriarchal period, Yahweh is even called "the God of David your father" (21:12; 34:3). Less gratifying incidents, such as the affair with Bathsheba or the rebellion of Absalom, are passed over. David's reign was indeed a time of great wars (1 Chr 18f.; 22:8; 28:3), but it was also a time of extensive preparations for the building of the temple by Solomon: David acquires the building site and plans the cult (1 Chr 21ff.; 28:19). Nathan's prophecy (2 Sam 7) focuses on Solomon, the builder of the temple (1 Chr 17:11ff.; cf. 22:6ff.; 28:5ff.). At the dedication God himself acknowledges the sanctuary by sending fire from heaven onto the altar (2 Chr 7:1; cf. 1 Chr 21:26; Lev 9:23f.; 1 Kgs 18). Thus the election of the Davidic dynasty and that of the Jerusalem sanctuary coincide.

3. In general, the cult at the Jerusalem sanctuary plays a fundamental role. The Chronicler gives extensive accounts of the great feasts, especially Passover (2 Chr 30; 35; Ezra 6:19ff.) and the feast of Booths (2 Chr 7:9f.; Neh 8:13ff.). The reading of the law by Ezra, followed by an instruction (in Aramaic?) seems to be a kind of anticipation of the synagogal liturgy (Neh 8). Do such descriptions reflect the manner of life of the Jerusalem community? The execution of the cult also involves the music of the temple, the Levitical singers (1 Chr 15:16ff.; 2 Chr 5:11ff.; 29:25ff.), and the priests who offer sacrifice (1 Chr 23:13; 24:1ff.; etc.). In particular, the temple personnel were highly differentiated, with a variety of functions that underwent certain changes in the course of time. These changes can be seen from differences in

relation to the Priestly document and also in the redaction history of the Chronicler's history itself.

How tradition-oriented the Chronicler is can be seen from the free quotations of scriptural passages, whether from the Torah or the historical books or the prophets. Especially in the discourses that are inserted into the text (e.g., 2 Chr 15:2ff.) prophetic utterances are altered to fit the present (compare 2 Chr 20:15, 20 with Exod 14:13f.; Isa 7:9; or 2 Chr 15:2 with Jer 29:14; etc.). Does this approach "with its recourse to prophetic utterances and its theological retrospect to some facet of the history of the people reflect the style of preaching used by the Levites" (G. von Rad, p. 252; cf. 2 Chr 17:7ff.; 35:3; etc.)?

The hymn inserted in 1 Chr 16:7ff., which uses various psalms (105; 96; 106) to form a new hymn, may be evidence of the later use of the psalms in the liturgy.

4. While the establishment and continuance of the cultic community in Jerusalem is the Chronicler's theme, the preservation of its special character is his goal. This character seems to make separation from foreigners a real necessity (see the attack on mixed marriages in Ezra 9; Neh 9:2; 10:28ff.). Is separation from the Samaritans, the successors to the northern kingdom (2 Chr 13:5ff.; 19:2; 25:7; 30:6ff.; Ezra 4:1ff.; also Neh 2:19f.; etc.) but no longer regarded as orthodox, actually a principal reason for the work's being written? The Chronicler's purpose (according to W. Rudolph) is to "show that, in contrast to the Samaritans, Judah, which possesses the only legitimate monarchy and the only legitimate place of worship, is the true Israel." Or does the Chronicler's history simply document the opposition that intensified in the course of time and finally led to a definitive separation?

5. The starting point of the Chronicler's history proper (1 Chr 10ff., after the genealogy) already gives a glimpse of the importance of the monarchy. Monarchy and the rule of God are much more closely bound together than in the older tradition (but cf. Ps 110:1). The Davidic monarch "on the throne of the Lord" seems to be God's representative, and the reign of the king in Jerusalem seems to be the reign of God on earth (1 Chr 17:14; 28:5; 29:11f., 23; 2 Chr 9:8; 13:8). Behind such statements about the past does there lurk an unspoken hope of the messiah in whom God's power will manifest itself?

In his description of the postexilic period down to his day the Chronicler does not refer to such a messianic expectation; in fact, he passes over in silence the messianic movement that had begun under Haggai and Zechariah. The age of the kings ends in a catastrophe (2 Chr 36:11ff.); after seventy years of atonement (36:21), the edict of the Persian king Cyrus, who has been inspired thereto by God (36:22f.

= Ezra 1:1ff.), brings the return of the exiles, the rebuilding of the city and the temple, and a new possibility of salvation. Just as Second Isaiah, a prophet of the exile, could see Cyrus as God's "anointed," who says to Jerusalem and the temple, "Be built!" (Isa 44:28f.), so now the favor of the Persian king (Ezra 3:7; 6:14; 9:9; etc.) guarantees the cult in Jerusalem and assures "the protection of the cultic community in Jerusalem. For the Chronicler the postexilic theocracy has no room for a legitimate Messianism or a Davidic monarchy" (U. Kellermann, p. 97). Does this mean that foreign policy is left in the hands of the foreign ruler, and does the community that is gathered around the sanctuary in fidelity to the law need only its faith and nothing more? Or does the Chronicler share "the hope of a future reestablishment of the throne of David" (M. Noth, p. 179)? Does the desire for political independence, a desire that will become a reality only in the time of the Maccabees, live on, though concealed (Ezra 9:7ff.; Neh 9:32, 36f.)?

As in the interpretation of P (see §8a6) there is disagreement about whether the Chronicler still cherishes crucial eschatological hopes, or whether on the contrary he means to oppose the eschatological currents of his time.

PART III

THE PROPHETS

§13

THE FORM OF PROPHECY

a) Prophetic Utterance and Prophetic Book

1. Distinction between oral proclamation and written record

A prophet may be called and given the commission "Go and speak!" (Amos 7:15f.; Isa 6:9; cf. Jer 1:7; etc.), and he may then introduce what he says with the words "Hear the word of the Lord!" (Isa 1:10; etc.). Under these circumstances the hearer trusts the prophet—but with the proviso that the word he communicates is not one that he devised on his own but one that he received. Since the reception of the word is taken as a sign of an authentic prophetic mission, Jeremiah's opponents are met with a divine oracle saying, "If they had stood in my council, then they would have proclaimed my words to my people. . . . Let him who has my word speak my word faithfully" (Jer 23:22, 28; cf. 20:8f.; 27:18; 28:8f.; etc.).

The "false" prophets of salvation are accused of "stealing" words from God (Jer 23:30). For this reason there is, on the one hand, an appeal to others not to trust "lying" prophets (23:16; 27:14, 16) and, on the other hand, the complaint that the words of the "true" prophets meet with disbelief, doubt (17:15), and disobedience (29:19; Isa 28:12; 30:10, 12; Ezek 2:7f.; Amos 2:11f.; 7:16; Hos 9:7; etc.). In fact, the prophet himself may suffer because of the word entrusted to him (Jer 20:8; 23:9; cf. Isa 50:4ff.).

In the light of what has thus far been said, the usual notion of "(classical) written prophecy" is unsatisfactory and even highly misleading as applied to the prophets who exercised their ministry from about 750 B.C. on—Amos, Hosea, Isaiah, or, later on, Jeremiah. These men were not writers but speakers or messengers. Their original situation was one of oral proclamation in direct contact with hearers. Only later on were their words gathered, put into writing, to some extent revised, supplemented with other oracles or stories, and combined to make books (see Jer 36).

The fact that the prophetic oracles have been preserved only in written form was for a long time the cause of important misunderstandings. It struck Martin Luther, for example, that the prophets "have an odd way of doing things . . . they [seem to] observe no order but ramble along from one subject to another. This seems incomprehensible to all; people cannot get used to it" (*German Lectures on Habakkuk*, in *Luther's Works*, vol. 19, p. 152). In fact, the reader sees an obvious contradiction between the claim of the prophetic oracle to be living speech and the present form in which this same oracle has been transmitted to us—long, disorganized sections in which the sequence of ideas is noticeably incoherent. The reason for this disparity we learn from form criticism, which came into existence around the turn of the century (H. Gunkel), namely, that a prophetic book, like the synoptic gospels later on, is made up of many small units. These units are independent of one another in form and content; they represent meaningful and independently intelligible structures of oral speech that were uttered each in a particular set of circumstances. Previously the units of prophetic discourse had been gauged on much too large a scale; it was not recognized that a unit might consist of a very brief saying, perhaps no more than a verse or two in length. For example: "You only have I known of all the families of the earth; therefore I will punish you for all your iniquities" (Amos 3:2; cf. 5:2; 9:7; Isa 1:2f.; etc.).

At times lengthier compositions occur, for example, the cycle of visions (7:1–9; 8:1–3) and the oracles against the nations (1:3–2:16) of the prophet Amos or the historical retrospect of the prophet Isaiah (9:8–21; 5:25–29) and his series of woe cries (5:8ff.). In each such case we must ask whether we are dealing with a unit that had always existed as such, even in oral proclamation, or whether the series was formed only at the redactional stage when the prophet's words were written down. The later prophets, like Ezekiel, seem more often to make use of lengthier speech units.

How was the passage from the oral utterance of individual oracles to the composition of prophetic books effected? This question, which for a time was the subject of heated dispute, must in the last analysis be asked anew for each prophetic book; in most cases no fully clear answer is possible. Was the prophetic message written down only in the postexilic period and after long existence in a primarily oral tradition (thus the so-called Uppsala School; see E. Nielsen, *Oral Tradition*, 1955)? Certainly oral tradition played an important but on the whole limited role in the origin of the prophetic books, especially the book of Jeremiah. There are indications now and then (especially Jer 36) that the prophets themselves (see Isa 8:1; 30:8) had already written down parts of their message or had had a scribe write it down for them (see Jer 36:4). Pointers in this direction are the many autobiographical passages, which go back to the prophets themselves (e.g., Amos 7f.; Hos 3; Isa 6; etc.), and the strict metrical form in which the majority of the prophetic oracles have been transmitted. In many instances, then, it is possible to distinguish between the original wording and subsequent revision.

Another and probably even larger portion of the prophetic utterances would have been collected and transmitted by friends or disciples of the given prophet. Such persons are rarely mentioned directly (Isa 8:16; cf. 50:4; 2 Kgs 4:34ff.; 6:1), but their activity can be inferred. Who, apart from disciples of the prophets, would have composed the third-person reports about them that at times seem so contemporary with the events (Amos 7:10ff.; Hos 1; Isa 7; 20; etc.)?

What purpose did the writing down of the oracles serve? Since the judgment the prophet proclaims has not yet occurred (see Isa 5:19) and since he meets with scorn and rejection from his hearers, the prophet sees to it that his teaching is "sealed"—in the hope that the future will confirm what he says and prove him right (Isa 8:16f.; 30:8; cf. 8:1f.; also Hab 2:2f.). Thus the word is, as it were, put on record during the interval between its proclamation and its future fulfillment; the written copy, as a further form of proclamation, continues to attest the future significance of the prophet's words. Once a prediction has been fulfilled there is a new motive for writing the message down: the fulfillment means that the truth of the prophetic claim has been proved by the course of events (see already Amos 1:1; etc.).

The various collections of prophetic oracles were later joined together and supplemented with further traditional material. The prophetic books, therefore, did not originate with the prophets themselves but developed in a lengthy and, in part, obscure process of growth. The need is to recover the prophetic oracles themselves and reconstruct the original situation in which they were spoken.

2. Distinction between individual utterance and composition

The combining of originally independent individual utterances ordinarily occurred under the influence of more or less accidental norms, such as connection by catchword. At times there may have been an effort at chronological succession and to some extent thematically related texts were associated (e.g., on the prophets, Jer 23; Ezek 13), which might result in "kerygmatic units."

We understand prophetic utterances in an objectively valid way only when we identify the original demarcation of the small units, that is, the point at which an utterance or speech begins and ends. Among the helps to this end are, first of all, the introductory and concluding formulas. Among these, in turn, special importance attaches to the "messenger formula": "Thus says [or: said] the Lord" (Amos 1:3; etc.), which shows the prophet to be God's delegate, the authorized transmitter of a particular message to a concrete addressee. The "call for attention," "Hear [sing. or pl.]!"—in the expanded form, "Hear, be attentive!" which is called also the "call at the beginning of instruction"—was familiar in sapiential teaching (see Prov 1:8; 4:1; etc.) and also appears as an exhortation to be attentive just before the singing of a song (Gen 4:23; Judg 5:3; etc.) or in cultic situations (Deut 6:4; Pss 17:1; 50:7; 81:8; etc.). Either the prophet himself (Isa 1:2, 10; 32:9; Mic 1:2) or a later redactor (see Hos 4:1; Amos 3:1; etc.) may use this call to emphasize that what is about to be said is God's word. In the same way, formulaic phrases are used to claim the authority of God for what has been or is about to be said: "pronouncement (nĕ'um) of Yahweh" (Amos 2:16; etc.), "for Yahweh has said/decreed it" (Isa 1:2; 22:25; etc.), or "for the mouth of the Lord has spoken" (Isa 1:20; 40:5). In a formulation characteristic of the book of Ezekiel a comparable assurance even appears as an assertion made by God himself: "I the Lord have spoken, and I will do it" (Ezek 5:15, 17; 17:24; etc.).

Even in the absence of such pointer formulas, the presence of new units of speech may be shown by a change of addressee or of theme or of formal structure. The small units often have common stylistic or structural characteristics, for example, an introductory "Woe . . . ," which allow us to distinguish various genres (see below). Finally, prophetic speech is consistently poetical and metrical in its form; thus it is characterized by parallelism (*parallelismus membrorum*) (see §25, 1). This pattern is so strictly and consistently observed that prose passages, especially when they occur in the midst of metrical speech, are to be suspected of being later additions (e.g., Amos 3:7 within 3:3–6:8). This insight creates special problems for the understanding of the book of Jeremiah, in which large sections of the prophet's words are preserved in prose form.

Being poetic speech, the utterances of the prophets, like the psalms, are characterized by a wealth and vividness or even boldness of images (see Amos 5:19; Hos 5:12, 14; Isa 1:2f.; 28:20; Jer 8:7; and many other passages). These simply allude to an event and yet they make it vivid in the hearer's mind. In exceptional cases a comparison, "And it shall be as . . ." (Isa 17:5; cf. Amos 3:12; 9:9; etc.), may be developed into a parable (Isa 5:1–7; cf. 2 Sam 12).

Since the individual utterance in its formal and material differentiation stood by itself in its original setting (which can now only be conjectured), it follows that its meaning may have been distorted by the context in which it is now found. It is the task of exegesis to investigate such changes as far as this is now possible. The question of the intention of a text in its context and ultimately in the framework given by the entire book is also tackled in what is now called "redaction history."

3. Distinction between original prophetic utterance and later redaction

The pronouncements of the prophets were written down and transmitted not for inclusion in an archive but on account of their importance for the future. Later generations read the collections of prophetic utterances as God's word that was still valid for them. With the aid of these texts they interpreted their own present time, and they looked at the future through eyes supplied by these same texts. As a result, they were able to introduce their own thoughts into the prophetic traditions. Just as the primitive Christian community in its gospels did not preserve the message of Jesus in a "historically pure" form, so too the pronouncements of the prophets were supplemented or even revised in the light of the experiences of later years. Redactional expansions thus indicate something of the continued life of the prophetic message, of its subsequent history, or the history of its influence. They represent an early interpretation that can offer important helps for understanding but can also be misleading. The unfortunate, but now established, terminology "authentic—inauthentic" is meant to express not an evaluation of content but a historical judgment. "Authentic" utterances are those which, with such probability as historical-critical analysis can provide, may be attributed to the prophet himself. But even "inauthentic" material, that is, material coming not from the prophet but from a redactor, can contain "authentic" material, that is, true statements worthy of consideration.

That the additions made need not be of a purely literary kind becomes clear from the fact that use of the prophetic message in the liturgy influenced at times the shaping of a prophetic book. When the prophetic word was read, the community, which saw itself included among the prophet's addressees and expressed its acknowledgment and confession, responded with statements using the plural "we" (e.g., Isa 1:9; 2:5; Mic 4:5) or with a doxology that was then introduced into the prophetic book (Hos 12:7; Amos 4:13; 5:8f.; 9:5f.; cf. Isa 12; Mic 7:8ff.; also Zech 2:13; etc.). In the later Jewish liturgy the reading from the Torah was, at an early date, supplemented by a reading from the prophets, known as the *Haftarah* (see Acts 13:15; Luke 4:17).

The distinction between "authentic" and redactional utterances might be rather insignificant or inconsequential, if it did not reveal differences in content and therefore in the intention of what is said. But as a matter of fact it does reveal such differences. The additions come for the most part from a time in which the disaster predicted by the prophet has already come to pass, and the concern expressed by the additions is completely different from that of the original prophetic utterance.

On the one hand, the redactors, caught in the midst of disaster, are on the lookout for deliverance: When all is said and done, does not God want his people to live? The prophetic announcements of judgment are therefore supplemented by promises of salvation (e.g., Amos 9:11ff.). In fact, as a result of this basic concern, the prophetic books are consistently structured according to the same pattern: first disaster (for Israel and the foreign nations), then deliverance (for Israel). This structure—which was probably suggested by the prophetic proclamation itself (Isa 1:21–26; etc.)—seems to presuppose and imply a two-phase sequence of eschatological events through judgment to salvation.

On the other hand, those affected by the predicted disaster ask themselves, How could this happen? And they bear witness that the judgment they have experienced was a just one. Thus, reflection on the reasons for what happened and the confession of guilt take precedence over the prophetic announcement of punishment. Those concerned see the guilt of the people as consisting in their disobedience to the command of God (e.g., Amos 2:4f.), and they now understand the prophets to have been preachers of repentance whose exhortations went unheard. To this extent the activity of the prophets takes on a new look in retrospect, or at least the emphasis is shifted. They announce an imminent future, but to later eyes they look like men who issued warnings in vain (see especially 2 Kgs 17:13; Zech 1:4; etc.; on this point see §11b3).

The Deuteronomistic school (§11a2) seems to have played an especially important role in collecting and organizing the utterances of the prophets, since Deuteronomistic elements are found in almost all the prophetic books (at least in the superscriptions) and predominantly so in the book of Jeremiah.

Sapiential circles, too, played a part in the redaction of the prophetic books (Hos 14:10; Jer 17:5ff.; cf. Amos 1:1; etc.).

We can now see that the distinction between original prophetic utterance and redactional additions is by no means a marginal and purely historical question but that it raises a problem of substance or content, on the "solution" of which depends the overall understanding of the prophets—the relation between threat of disaster and promise of salvation, the announcement of a "remnant," and so on. Although the distinction is fundamental, it is also the subject of much dispute.

In this situation might we not find a remedy and put exegesis on a surer footing if we changed the basic challenge: not to prove the inauthenticity of what comes later but, on the contrary, to prove the authenticity of the original traditional material?

"The real problem is no longer to prove that something is late and to separate it from a basic substance which would then without further discussion be regarded as authentic, but on the contrary to demonstrate the prophetic nucleus in the tradition. . . . The quest of what is genuinely prophetic must in a strictly methodical way be guided by this criterion: only that material is to be regarded as authentic which can be understood solely in the light of the concrete circumstances of the age in which a particular prophet lived; in the process the individual utterances accepted as authentic must also be shown to be harmonized by an intention specific to the prophet in question" (W. Schottroff, *ZTK* 67 [1970] 294).

Obvious though such a principle may be by reason of its methodical rigor, it is nonetheless difficult to apply. No objectively compelling reason can be given for the necessity, which this presupposition entails, of excluding as redactional all texts that can be explained in the light of later circumstances.

If the redaction-historical explanation is overemphasized, especially in comparison with the tradition-historical question of the form a tradition had before it was committed to writing, there is a danger that the text as a whole will be judged too much as though it were a homogeneous unity and that recognizable differences in the course of the text will be overlooked. Prophetic texts in particular show (redactional) strata of development that betray something of the history of the text. Will not the origin of a prophetic book with all its complexity be more readily intelligible if we reckon with the gradual enrichment of a basic substance that comes from the prophet himself and from his disciples? In any case, the distinction between original and redactional often cannot be clearly drawn. Arguments drawn from the history of ideas are of only limited value for determining what is "authentic" and what is "inauthentic" in a text, since we have hardly any knowledge of what ideas and convictions were possible or not possible in the eighth or seventh century. Only radical upheavals such as the exile leave behind them traces that are fairly easily recognizable.

Admittedly, the authenticity of a text is generally not demonstrable. But the difficult task remains of carefully weighing the pros and cons with the help of all available arguments (linguistic, substantive, historical). Yet in many cases—and not rarely in the very cases that are important for interpretation—objective criteria do not permit a sure judgment. Therefore, after eliminating what is recognizably "inauthentic," we are forced to turn to the subjective criterion of coherence: Do the texts in question fit into, or on the contrary contradict, the framework of the prophetic proclamation as derived from utterances whose "authenticity" can hardly be disputed? This question is important especially in evaluating the much debated

promises of salvation (e.g., Isa 2; 9; 11). Do these promises cancel out
the threats of judgment, or do they presuppose these threats and carry
matters a step further? Even when this criterion of coherence is applied,
uncertainties remain that make a variety of interpretations possible.

b) Main Categories of Prophetic Literature

The literary forms used in the prophetic books can be roughly organized
into three main categories: stories about the prophets, visions, and
words.

1. Stories about the Prophets
These narrate the experiences, actions, or sufferings of a prophet; but
their principal theme is not his overall destiny and certainly not the
data for a "life of a saint." For this reason the usual description "legend
about a prophet" is open to misunderstanding. The real emphasis is
on the words spoken; consequently, the stories about the prophets, at
least in the form in which we now have them, tell us of the
promulgation of a divine and prophetic utterance.

Traditions regarding the so-called prewriting or preclassical prophets
such as Nathan, Elijah, or Elisha, have come down to us only in third-
person or, properly, narrative form (2 Kgs 1). The words of these
prophets are thus reported only in the context of some action or event.
On the other hand, the transmission of the words of the so-called
classical writing prophets is only in exceptional cases set in a narrative
context that describes the circumstances in which the words were
spoken (Hos 1) or in regard to which they were spoken (e.g., Isa 7).
Especially when the utterance is directed to a particular individual (as
in Amos 7:10ff.; Isa 7), some description of the circumstances is
needed, along with an indication of the addressee, if the words are to
remain intelligible. But there is so little concern with biography that
the report need not tell us at all what happened to the prophet himself
(Amos 7:10ff.).

As a rule, the words of the writing prophets have been passed on in isolation,
without any detailed description of the circumstances, and can therefore more
easily have a meaning for the future. Precisely because no context is given,
later generations can relate directly to themselves what was not originally
said with them in mind.

The difference in the manner of transmission between the words of
the preclassical and those of the classical prophets is also based at the

very least on two profound differences in the ministry of the two types of prophets. First, the writing prophets address individuals such as the king (Isa 7) only in exceptional cases; their message is ordinarily directed to groups or rather to the people as a whole. Second, the writing prophets no longer "act" in the full sense of the term (they no longer play an active part in politics) but accomplish their purposes solely through their words.

The few actions still found in the writing prophets are "symbolic actions" or "sign actions," which may have a remote background in magic. Among these prophets, however, such actions do not produce with certainty a coming event but are simply signs (Isa 20:3; etc.) that announce the event and anticipate it in graphic form, thus supporting and confirming the prophetic word. Jeremiah wears an iron yoke in order to bring home to everyone the fact that Israel and its neighbors will be forced to wear the yoke of Babylonian domination (Jer 28:12ff.; cf. 1 Kgs 22:11). The command to perform a symbolic action, a report on its execution, and an interpretation of it are important but not indispensable elements (1 Kgs 19:19ff.; Hos 1; 3; Isa 8; 20; Jer 13; 16; 19; Ezek 4:f.; Zech 6:9ff.; etc.; see G. Fohrer).

The prophetic books contain not only stories in the third person, told by a disciple or a group of transmitters (e.g., Amos 7:10ff.; Hos 1; Isa 7; 20; the story of Baruch in the book of Jeremiah, or the entire book of Jonah), but also stories in the new form of an autobiographical or personal account (Hos 3; Jer 13; 24; etc.).

To this second category belong especially the accounts of a prophet's vocation (Isa 6; 40; Jer 1; Ezek 1ff.). These serve to establish, justify, and accredit the prophet, who can respond to doubters by pointing to the inner compulsion he has experienced (see Amos 7:15; Jer 26:12). Two basic types of vocation stories must be distinguished. In the one, the calling comes in a dialogue between God and the prophet in which the latter is able to object to the call on the grounds of his unworthiness and the difficulty of the task; but this objection is overcome by God's promise (so, in a more or less formulaic way, in the case of Moses, Exod 3f.; Gideon, Judg 6:11ff.; Saul, 1 Sam 9f.; and Jeremiah, Jer 1). In the other type, the call emerges more indirectly from a vision of the divine throne (Isa 6; 40; Ezek 1; cf. 1 Kgs 22:19ff.; Zech 1:7ff.; Job 1). In both types the commission may be summed up in the verbs "send" and "go" (Exod 3:10; Jer 1:7; Isa 6:8f.; Ezek 2:3f.; cf. Jer 14:14f.; etc.).

The stories about the prophets are generally contrasted with the "oracles" of the prophets. But since the term "oracle" is open to misunderstanding, we shall do better to distinguish stories, visions, and words or utterances.

2. Visions

While a priest gives an "instruction" and a wise man or elder a "counsel," a prophet is characterized by a "word" (Jer 18:18) or a "vision" (Ezek 7:26). Amos and probably Isaiah as well seem to have thought of themselves as "seers" (Amos 7:12, 14; Isa 30:9f.). The superscriptions of the books indicate that the prophets were the recipients not only of words (Amos 1:1; Hos 1:1; etc.) but of visions (Isa 1:1; 2:1; Nah 1:1; Hab 1:1; etc.). They themselves report, "I saw" (Amos 9:1; etc.).

In the prophetic tradition visions are admittedly much less common, but they do play a substantial part. In fact, one's understanding of prophecy depends in large measure on the importance one attributes to the visions; for nowhere does the primacy given to the future emerge so clearly as here, while the insight the visions give into the future can be gotten in only the smallest degree from an analysis of the present.

Do the visions come temporally as well as materially at the beginning of a prophet's activity? Amos's career seems to begin with a cycle of visions (Amos 7:1–8; 8:1–2); Isaiah (Isa 6), Ezekiel (Ezek 1–3), Second Isaiah (Isa 40), and perhaps Jeremiah too (Jer 1, especially vv. 13f.; cf. 24:1ff.) are commissioned in the course of inaugural or vocation visions. We are not told of any visions given to Hosea or Micah. On the other hand, in later prophecy, during the period of transition to apocalyptic, visions increase in number and importance in Ezekiel (1–3; 8–11; 37; 40–48). Thus a certain development and expansion of this category can be seen in the history of prophecy, until it acquires such a predominant place in apocalyptic (e.g., in the book of Enoch) that it becomes a literary genre of its own and its experiential background is hardly detectable any longer (but cf. Luke 10:18).

In visions the prophet may carry on a conversation with God. This means that his individual consciousness, far from being set aside, is fully awake and involved. Moreover, the content of the vision does not have to be subsequently transposed into clearly expressed ideas. Rather the visions lead of themselves to auditions, to knowledge that can be put into words and communicated; in fact, visions may simply turn into auditions or experiences of hearing (Isa 40:1–9)

In telling of his visions and passing them on the prophet is, in a way, already carrying out the assignment of proclamation that has been given to him directly (Zech 1:14) or perhaps only indirectly (see Amos 3:8). In addition, the insight given to the prophet in his visions influences his subsequent message.

The surviving visions can be distinguished on the basis of divergent formal structure or on the basis of content, especially the relationship between image and word. If what is seen matches directly the event being announced, we are dealing with an event-vision (e.g., Amos 7:1–6). If the content of the vision is connected with the reality only through the word that reproduces the content of the vision, then scholars speak of a word-play or assonantal vision (Amos 8:1f.). But the division into these and other types (e.g., presence vision, symbol vision, situation vision) is not completely satisfying; the assignment of a text to one or another type can often not be made with complete clarity, and the lines of division between the types remain fluid.

But there is one important difference that should not be overlooked. At times the prophet experiences a vision as an intervention by God, who brings a picture before his eyes: "Thus the Lord God showed me" (Amos 7:11; cf. Jer 24:1; Zech 3:1; also Ezek 37:1; etc.). At other times, God himself is the content of the vision, as he reveals himself: "I saw the Lord" (Amos 9:1; 1 Kgs 22:19; Isa 6:1). But even this distinction may be blurred, at least by subsequent editing (Amos 7:7).

Even in a vision, the transcendence of God is preserved; hearing takes priority over seeing (this is already clear in 1 Kgs 22:11ff.). The announcement "I saw the Lord" promises more than the actual vision offers; neither Amos nor Isaiah describes God. In Zechariah's vision a golden lampstand with seven lamps (4:2) symbolizes the omnipresence, the omniscience, or even the omnipotence of God on earth (4:10).

Greater freedom is shown by Ezekiel in describing the vicinity of God's throne (1:4ff.) and especially by Daniel in describing the "ancient of days" (7:9ff.). Ezekiel adds the qualification "There was the likeness of . . ." (1:22, 26f.) in order to call attention to the inadequacy of the description. True enough, despite the poverty of the description, the prophet dares to say in conclusion, "Such was the appearance of the likeness of the glory of the Lord" (1:28), but he seems deliberately to avoid the direct statement that "this was the form of Yahweh."

In the postexilic period there is a greater emphasis on the transcendence of God. As a result there appears, in an initial rudimentary way in Ezekiel's vision of the new temple (40:3f.; cf. Isa 40:6) and as a regular constitutive element in Zechariah's cycle of visions and in the book of Daniel (7:16; 8:15ff.; etc.), an angelic interpreter (*angelus interpres*) who acts as mediator between God and humanity, thus eliminating a direct encounter of God and the prophet.

3. Words

The largest category in the tradition of the writing prophets is made up of words or utterances. The concept of "audition," which is the counterpart of "vision," is less felicitous when applied across the board. It presupposes, does it not, that all the words a prophet utters are received, whereas in fact many of these are not presented as formally God's word but as coming from the prophet himself? But even the utterances introduced expressly as God's word raise a question. Did a prophet, in a concrete situation, have to wait until the word he was to communicate had been given to him (see Jer 28:6ff.; 42:7; Num 22:8, 19; etc.), or could he determine and speak the individual utterance on the basis of the insight into the future that had been given to him, especially through the visions?

The concept of "audition," then, is better reserved to that special form, or to that part of a vision, which tells not any longer what is seen but rather what is heard (see especially Isa 40:1–9).

Prophetic utterances are characterized by a surprising wealth of forms of discourse. The basic insight that these are for the most part only secondarily prophetic, that is, are borrowed by the prophet from other areas of life, helps us to reduce the multiplicity to a few basic forms. This not only makes a survey easier; it is also materially an advantage in that, when we look for "the genre of prophecy proper" (H. Gunkel, p. XLVI), the special character of the phenomenon we call prophecy stands out more clearly. The genre that is proper to prophecy must be considered the announcement of the future, whether in the form of threat or in the form of promise, together with the basis given for the announcement.

a) In the announcement of the future and the basis for it, even the utterances of the prewriting or preclassical prophets show the same characteristic two parts. They first specify a culpable condition as evidenced here and now; and then, often after the messenger formula, proceed to announce punishment: "Thus says the Lord, 'Have you killed, and also taken possession?' . . . Thus says the Lord: 'In the place where dogs licked up the blood of Naboth shall dogs lick your own blood'" (1 Kgs 21:19; cf. 2 Kgs 1:3f.; etc.).

Threats of disaster, but addressed now predominantly to groups or to the people as a whole, also make up most of the utterances of the writing prophets. Thus Amos uses these ironical, cutting words in reproaching the upper-class women of the capital of the northern kingdom:

> Hear this word, you cows of Bashan [i.e., fattened cattle],
>   who are in the mountain of Samaria,
> who oppress the poor, who crush the needy,
>   who say to their husbands, "Bring, that we may drink!"
> The Lord God has sworn by his holiness
>   that, behold, the days are coming upon you,
> when they shall take you away with hooks,
>   even the last of you with fishhooks
>
>   (Amos 4:1f.).

Although the future state corresponds to the present actions of those who will be thus sorely afflicted, only the announcement of the future that follows upon the opening accusation is presented as the word of God (see Amos 3:9–11; 8:4ff.; etc.). God's oath, which is a kind of intensified messenger formula, makes the threatened judgment irrevocable—brutal deportation at the hands of a foreign army. The grounds, which precede the announcement of punishment, are given as the prophet's own word. Consequently, the distinction between indictment and utterance about the future seems to some degree coextensive with the distinction between the human word and the word of God. Of course, the prophet has also formulated the very word of God, for the latter too shows clearly the linguistic peculiarities of Amos. But did he feel the statement about the future (which in the final analysis is inaccessible to human beings) to be to a greater extent a word coming from outside of himself? Or did God perhaps simply give the prophet a certainty about the obscure future (see Amos 8:2) and then leave it to him to recognize and describe the offenses of the people (G. von Rad)?

Insofar as the announcement of the future (often introduced by "See") has to do with disaster, it is given various names: threat or pronouncement of judgment, prediction of disaster, or announcement of punishment, judgment oracle, and so on. These various names have behind them in each case certain interpretations of the prophetic proclamation (e.g., it is viewed as a trial speech), which capture partial aspects of that proclamation but do not prove applicable throughout. For this reason, as long as scholars have not accepted a particular tradition-historical derivation of the structure of a prophetic utterance, the most formal description is also the most appropriate. At the very least, as far as possible a formalistic understanding of the usual concepts is to be recommended.

An announcement regarding the future must be substantiated if the prophet is to speak to a concrete situation, reach particular addressees, and have his pronouncement make sense to them. Only then will the hearers be able to see in the disaster a punishment for their sins; it will be seen not as the working of fate but as a judgment ordained by God. This justificatory part of the prophetic utterance (the reproach, the indictment, or the indication of situation, as it is variously called) contains an analysis of the situation, that is, a critique of the present, in regard to liturgy or society or politics. The announcement of the future, then, is one basic component of prophetic proclamation, and the analysis of a situation is the other. Either component may occasionally occur in isolation, but usually the two form a unit that is both reproach and threat, the two parts being often linked by a "therefore" or a "because," and so on.

The category "trial speech" is best reserved for texts that reflect a lawsuit (e.g., Isa 1:18ff.; Hos 2:2; Jer 2:5; see 21,2c). It is possible to distinguish further between pretrial discussion, indictments, defense speeches, and so on (see H. J. Boecker).

b) In prophetic woe cries the introductory "Woe!" (*hôy*) is followed by a substantive, often in the form of an active participle, which describes a person or group by their behavior and singles them out:

> Woe to you who desire the day of the Lord!
> (Amos 5:18).

> Woe to those who call evil good and good evil!
> (Isa 5:20; cf. Mic 2:1).

Such woe cries often occur in series (Isa 5:8ff.; Hab 2:6ff.), whether because they originally formed a single discourse, or because they were put together at the redactional stage, in which case they also functioned as a way of organizing the text (Isa 28:1; 29:1; 30:1; etc.). Where did the prophets get this "Woe!" from? The question has been the subject of lively discussion (most recently, C. Hardmeier). How are structural similarities with curses (Deut 27:15ff.) to be explained? There are thematic points of contact with the sapiential writings (Isa 5:20ff.; etc.). But the "Woe!" actually comes from the dirge (1 Kgs 13:30; Jer 22:18; 34:5; cf. Amos 5:16). The prophet addresses it to the living in order to bring home to his hearers "that the seeds of death are already present in certain kinds of human behavior" (G. Wanke). As evaluated from the standpoint of the distinction between the announcement of the future and the justification for it, the woe cry is a mixed genre in which evidence of guilt (in the description of the situation) and announcement of punishment are combined. The "Woe!" that mourns for the living as doomed to death already contains disaster as threatening or even already present. Nonetheless an explicit announcement of the future may follow (Isa 5:8f.; 30:1–3; etc.).

The *Qinah* or lament (dirge) is comparable to the woe cry in its intention. In form, the *Qinah* has the longer part of a verse followed by a shorter (e.g., Amos 5:2); in content it likes to contrast the "formerly" and the "now" (Isa 1:21; 14:12ff.; Ezek 27; etc.; see §26,2).

The opposite of the woe cry is the macarism (*'ašrê*, "happy"), which may express congratulations (1 Kgs 10:8; cf. Pss 127:5; 128) or praise a type of behavior (Pss 1:1; 2:12; 32:2f.; etc.; cf. Matt 5:3ff.).

c) Prophets gaze not only into the future but also into the past. In the so-called prophets of disaster, however, the historical retrospect, whether it be brief (Amos 2:9; 9:7; also Isa 28:21; etc.) or detailed (Hos 9:10ff.; especially 11:1f.; Isa 9:8ff.; §20,3c), serves essentially as proof of guilt, that is, as the basis for their announcement of the future. Therefore we must "recognize the onesidedness of this view of history, the purpose of which was to prove the constant sinfulness of Israel" (H. Gunkel; cf. J. Vollmer).

d) In the disputation (*Disputationswort, Diskussionswort, Streitgespräch*) the prophet gets into a discussion with his hearers in which he presupposes their doubts regarding his message and tries to lead them by means of questions to certain conclusions (Amos 3:3–6, 8; 6:12; 9:7; Jer 13:23; 23:23f.; Hab 1:2, 4ff.; etc.). The style of these disputations seems to have become more formalized in the course of time (Second Isaiah, §21,2b; Malachi, §22,4). Did the prophetic disputation have its origin in the differences of opinion that occur in everyday life or did it stem rather from the disputations held in the sapiential schools (see Job 6:5f.; 8:11)?

e) The exhortation or admonition (*Mahnwort*) contains a demand couched in the imperative form: "Rend your hearts and not your garments" (Joel 2:13; Jer 4:4). To this may be added either a consequence ("so that," "lest") or a reason ("for," "because"). The negative form (whether simply rhetorical or material as well), for example, "Do not seek Bethel" (Amos 5:5) or "Cease to do evil" (Isa 1:16), is called a "warning" (*Warnwort*), and one particular exhortation, "Return" (Jer 3:22; etc.), is given the name "call to repentance" (*Bussruf*). The themes and key words of exhortations differ, showing that these exhortations have varying origins and areas of application: wisdom (§27,3e), law (Hos 2:2ff.; cf. 1 Kgs 3:24ff.), war (Hos 5:8; Jer 6:1; 51:6, 27f.; Joel 2:1; 3:9; cf. Exod 14:13; Deut 20:3; Isa 7:4; etc.), and cult. It uses the imperative, for example, in hymns (§25,4a), in calls to community laments (Jer 36:9; 6:26; etc.; §25,4b), or in the priestly *torah* ("instruction" regarding pilgrimages or sacrifice, Amos 4:4f.; 5:4, 21ff.; Isa 1:10ff.; etc.), which the prophets take over for their own use.

f) The word of salvation or the promise, which is the opposite of the announcement of disaster, seems far less unified in its form (see, e.g., Hos 2:14ff.; Amos 9:11ff.; Isa 11; Jer 28:2f.; 30f.; or Ezek 27). Frequently used introductory formulas are "On/in that day/those days" (Hos 2:16ff.; Joel 3:1), "in the latter days" (or "in days to come," or "at the end of days") (Isa 2:1), "Behold, the days are coming" (Jer 31:31; cf. Amos 4:2), and so on. The most clearly recognizable is the (formerly priestly) "oracle of salvation," "which, in the name of God promises the praying person that his petition will be heard" (J. Begrich; see §21,2a). Should we distinguish between this promise of salvation and the announcement of salvation as well as the description of salvation (C. Westermann)? In any case, like the prediction of disaster the promise of salvation is often characterized by the introduction of the divine "I" and thus calls the hearer's attention to him who makes the future a possibility and a reality (Hos 14:4; Isa 1:26; etc.).

c) Questions in Contemporary Study of the Prophets

Since the prophets use a variety of literary forms, where is the essential and decisive element of their proclamation to be located: in the announcement of the future, in the analysis of the present situation (including criticism of society), or in the exhortation with the call to repentance as its climactic form? Let me at least call the reader's attention here to some basic questions in contemporary study of the prophets (the list might easily be extended).

1. To what extent may the message of the writing prophets be "derived" from Israel's earlier traditions, whether these have to do with cult or law or wisdom? The prophets certainly adopt various literary forms, themes, traditions, and representations, which they remodel in the context of their own message and use in order to address their hearers in the actual situation of the moment. But is it possible that in their announcement of the future, to the effect that God is cancelling his communion with his people (Amos 8:2; Hos 1:9; Isa 6:9ff.; Jer 1:13f.; 16:5; etc.), the writing prophets are likewise continuing an ancient idea? Or in this discernment of the future are they rather contradicting the very substance of the tradition, which professes this very communion of God and the people (Gen 15; Exod 3; etc.)?

2. Conversely, in their discernment of the future, in the literary forms they adopt (announcement of disaster with justification for it, woe cry, lament or dirge, etc.) and in their themes (criticism of cult, of society, and so on), the writing prophets have so much in common with one another that they can hardly have come on the scene in complete independence of one another. Despite individual traits and despite unmistakable differences even on major points, their messages are closely related. How, then, are we to account for these common characteristics? A direct dependence, and in particular a dependence on written sources, cannot be demonstrated. Is there, however, a link

through oral tradition (see the citation of Mic 3:12 in Jer 26:18), possibly one mediated by disciples of the prophets (Isa 8:16)?

In any case, the writing prophets only rarely associate themselves explicitly with other prophets (Hos 6:5; cf. Jer 28:8). Groups of prophets are more often critical of one another (Amos 7:14; Mic 3:5ff.; etc.).

3. Announcement of the future and analysis of the present usually go together. But there is disagreement on how the connection is to be interpreted. Does the premonition of the future arise out of profound insight into the present condition of the people, or is the demonstration of guilt rather a consequence of prophetic certainty about the future?

Latent here is also the problem of the connection between individual utterance and revelation. Are a prophet's individual utterances concrete applications, which he himself has worked out, of his general insight into the future, an insight gained in visions? Or is every utterance that is presented as God's word based on a new act of revelation?

4. The question of the relation between future and present arises anew when the attempt is made to understand utterances about the future. Are the prophetic announcements of disaster to be interpreted in the light of the exhortations, or, on the contrary, are the exhortations (which are rather infrequent, at least in the earlier period) in the service of the eschatological proclamation (see, e.g., Amos 5:5)? In fact, are even the announcements of judgment meant only as threats, that is, final warnings, the purpose of which is to have the people avert the judgment by their manner of life? Or is the prophetic message, whether of disaster or salvation, meant as the announcement of a future that will certainly come and is already at hand?

A more limited problem within this larger question is the following: Are such radical statements as the "obduration commission" of Isaiah (6:9f.) formulated only after the fact and on the basis of the hearers' reactions to the prophetic proclamation?

5. Apart from Amos, the "prophets of disaster" do not at all seem to have prophesied only disaster, but rather to have announced salvation as well. If it is not possible to explain the promises of salvation as by and large "inauthentic" (§13a3), then the questions arise, Is the prophetic message ultimately lacking in harmony? Is it even inconsistent, inasmuch as at different times and to different audiences a prophet could convey divergent and even contradictory messages? Or are the announcements of judgment and of salvation objectively coherent?

According to one view, the two types of messages are linked by hope of a "remnant" that will survive the judgment (1 Kgs 19:17f.).

But in prophetic words that are accepted by all as "authentic" the remnant can be a sign of the catastrophe: a vestige that is no longer pregnant with the future and may even itself be threatened and that bears witness to the extent of the destruction (Amos 3:12; 8:10; 9:4; Isa 17:5f.; 30:17; etc.; cf. Job 1:15ff.). Conversely, it is often in disputed oracles that the remnant appears as a "holy seed," that is, as ulterior goal of the judgment and as bearer of a new salvation (Isa 6:13; 4:3; earlier, Amos 5:15; 9:8; etc.).

Similarly, was it only in retrospect that later times looked upon the call to repentance as recapitulating the prophetic message (2 Kgs 17:3; Zech 1:3f.)? Not infrequently the prophets observe that repentance has not ensued (Amos 4:6f.; Isa 9:13; 30:15) or is even impossible (Hos 5:4; Jer 13:23). Correspondingly, they may promise a conversion effected by God himself (Hos 14:5; Ezek 37; etc.). There is room here even for a call to repentance within the context of promised salvation (Hos 14:2; Jer 3:12; cf. Isa 55:6; etc.). In the eyes of the prophets, then, can human beings not preserve salvation but only receive it as a constant new gift from God?

Such differences as these receive quite divergent answers in contemporary study of the prophets. Since every interpretation of prophecy presupposes decisions about the "authenticity" or "inauthenticity" of texts, each picture of the prophets differs widely from the others.

d) Precursors of the Writing Prophets

The writing prophets of the OT represent a relatively late form of the many-layered phenomenon we call prophecy, which goes back even to pre-Israelite times and is represented by (ecstatic) groups (1 Sam 10:5ff.; 19:22ff.) as well as by individual personalities.

Being a foreigner, Balaam really does not belong to the succession of Israelite prophets. In early times he supposedly pronounced a powerful magical-religious oracle (*Machtwort*) upon Israel. Was it a curse that Yahweh "turned into a blessing" (Deut 23:5), or was Balaam compelled by Yahweh to utter a blessing instead of the curse expected of him (Num 22–24)? In any case, this quite extensive tradition, which takes both a Yahwist (24) and an Elohist (23) form, shows a number of prophetic traits, such as the experience of divine compulsion (22:8, 18) or revelation in vision and word (23:3; 24:3f., 15ff.).

As in this case, so in regard to the traditions about individual Israelite personalities there is a good deal of disagreement about the extent of the part played by later times in the formation of the tradition. Narrative complexes, such as the cycles of sagas about Elijah or Elisha, grew out of individual stories, each of which must be studied for its historical background and its evolution. Given this situation, only a brief survey of the prewriting or preclassical prophets can be given here. But the very thing that makes a historical investigation so difficult may represent a gain for theological reflection. When the stories move into the realm of the miraculous and the legendary, they point beyond the world of brute facts and tell the reader that it is really not the prophet but God himself who is at work here. Ultimately all these more or less fabulous stories of the prophets are meant as "stories about Yahweh" (G. von Rad).

Is Samuel the first in the series of individual Israelite prophets? According to what is probably the earliest account, he appears as one of the "lesser" judges (1 Sam 7:15ff., 6). As "man of God" or "seer" (9:6ff.) and even as a shade among the dead (28:7ff.), he imparts information, appears as leader of a group of ecstatics (19:18ff.), and in the certainly later story of his childhood is even given the title of "prophet" (3:19ff.). On one occasion he is described as a charismatic military commander (7:7ff.). But above all, the tradition tells of the role Samuel played in the emergence of the monarchy (see §11c3). Whatever be the various functions the historical Samuel exercised, from his time on leadership and charism, which had been combined in the persons of the major judges, were separated. The prophets became corrective critics of the kings.

The time of David saw the appearance not only of Gad the "seer," who stands up to the king after the latter's census of the people (2 Sam 24, with the etiological explanation of an altar in Jerusalem; also 1 Sam 22:5), but also of Nathan the "prophet." After the Ark has been transferred to Jerusalem (2 Sam 6), Nathan tells David that he is not to build a temple but that on the other hand his house will abide for ever (2 Sam 7). This prophecy echoes repeatedly throughout the OT, but in the process, on the basis of a centuries-long history, it is increasingly made conditional (Pss 89; 132; 1 Kgs 2:4; 8:25; 9:4f.; cf. Zech 3:7; etc.), and the exilic prophets even transfer it to the people (Isa 55:3f.). On another occasion Nathan brings the king not a promise but a threat when after a criminal act on David's part (violation of the marriage of a non-Israelite) the prophet uses a parable about a violation of rights to force the king to pass judgment on himself (2 Sam 12). Finally, Nathan plays a decisive part in winning Solomon's succession amid the palace intrigues being carried on as David lies dying (1 Kgs 1).

The following noteworthy prophets carry on their ministry in the northern kingdom, beginning with Ahijah of Shiloh (1 Kgs 11; 14).

Elijah, who in the eyes at least of later ages is the most important of the prewriting prophets (cf. Mal 4:5f.; Mark 9:11), embodies his program—"I have been very jealous for the Lord" (1 Kgs 19:10, 14)— in his very name, which means "My God is Yahweh." At a time when syncretism is being promoted in the northern kingdom under Ahab, Jezebel, and Ahaziah and when the cult of Baal is even in the ascendancy, Elijah fights for the exclusiveness of the Yahwistic faith (2 Kgs 1, consultation of Baal as source of health) and confronts his contemporaries with the choice between Yahweh and Baal: "How long will you go limping with two different opinions?" (1 Kgs 18:21, divine judgment on Mt. Carmel). Like Nathan before him, Elijah stands up for justice in the face of a concrete crime of the king, namely, the murder of Naboth, owner of a vineyard. In the background of this story are two different conceptions of justice: the power, taken for granted in the Canaanite world, of a ruler to take what he wants, and the inviolability of an inheritance in Israelite tradition.

The ultimate significance of Elijah emerges in the tradition according to which, as Moses' successor, he returns to the mountain of God, the place where the Yahwistic faith originated, and experiences a theophany (1 Kgs 19; cf. Exod 19; 33). God is not (any longer) in nature's manifestations: storm, earthquake, and fire, but in tranquillity and stillness. Since Elijah is there told to anoint Hazael as king of Syria and Jehu as king of Israel (1 Kgs 19:15ff.), two decisive events of the coming time—the ferocious wars with the Arameans and the revolution of Jehu (2 Kgs 8; 9f.)—are connected with the man of God and understood as purifications of the people. Elijah threatens Israel with a judgment that only seven thousand, "all the knees that have not bowed to Baal, and every mouth that has not kissed him," will escape.

It is not only the general character of Elijah but his unique individuality that finds expression in the tradition of his ascent to heaven, his "being taken away" (see Gen 5:24; Ps 73:24), in a chariot drawn by fiery horses (2 Kgs 2). But this scene, in which Elisha takes part as spectator and successor, really belongs to the cycle of sagas about Elisha (2 Kgs 2–9; 13). Elisha had been called to an immediate and unconditional "following" by having the mantle of Elijah thrown over him (1 Kgs 19:19ff.); now he receives the firstborn's share of Elijah's spirit (2 Kgs 2:9; cf. Deut 21:17). Consequently, Elisha's charism is regarded not as coming directly from God but as being mediated by Elijah (just as the elders of Israel received a share in Moses' spirit according to Num 11:17, 25). Elisha himself is leader of a community of disciples who gather at least occasionally (2 Kgs 2:3ff.; 4:1, 38; 6:1; etc.).

Although conflicts with the religion of Baal recede into the background in the traditions about Elisha, he seems, together with the disciples just mentioned, to have fomented (2 Kgs 9) the "revolution" of Jehu (845 B.C.), a man zealous for Yahweh. As the honorary title "Israel's chariots and drivers!" (13:14; 2:12) indicates, Elisha's political activity included some role in war (with the Arameans) (6:8ff.). In addition, Elisha, like Elijah before him, was connected with the accession of Hazael the Aramean (2 Kgs 8). Even more than in the Elijah cycle, miracle stories predominate. Among these the story of Naaman the Aramean, who becomes a believer in Yahweh but must continue to do service in the temple of an alien god (2 Kgs 5), deserves special attention for its theological implications ("conversion" of a foreigner, but with a dispensation from the first commandment?).

Just as the king of Israel addresses Elijah as "my enemy" (1 Kgs 21:20; cf. 18:17), he passes a similar judgment on Micaiah the son of Imlah: "He never prophesies good concerning me, but evil" (1 Kgs 22:8, 18). The only story told of this final prophet to be mentioned before the coming of the writing prophets foreshadows the later oppositions within the prophetic movement, when professional prophets with their promises of salvation stand over against individuals who announce disaster. To what extent is the story of Micaiah influenced in its telling by the later situation? To what extent, that is, is it intended to be didactic and to bring home by an example the difference between true and false prophecy? To what extent, on the other hand, does it reflect what actually happened? Micaiah not only sees disaster coming on the people as a whole ("I saw all Israel scattered upon the mountains, as sheep that have no shepherd"), but, with the help of a further vision in which he is present at the heavenly council ("I saw the Lord sitting on his throne"; cf. Isa 6; Jer 23:22; Job 1), he is able also to explain the false message of salvation given by his opponents: "The Lord has put a lying spirit in the mouth of all these your prophets."

By such visions as these the way is prepared for the message of judgment to be proclaimed by the "great" prophets, or else the message is put by hindsight into the mouths of earlier prophets. Whatever be the historically obscure background of the stories about the prophets in the books of Samuel and Kings, there is no doubt that the prewriting prophets in their dedication to Yahweh were already uttering threats and promises to the kings. The writing prophets convey the same message to the people as a whole.

§14

AMOS

1. In the person of Amos there is a sudden and definitive transition to the "writing prophets," who, apart from some symbolic actions, "act" henceforward only through oral proclamation that is later put down in writing. The book in which the traditions regarding Amos are assembled contains almost exclusively utterances and visions; a single story about the prophet, told in the third person, is an exception (Amos 7:10–17). In addition to isolated sayings that consist of one (3:2, 8; 6:12; 9:7) or several verses, there are also more extensive units. Thus in a manner unusual in comparison with the other prophetic books, the book of Amos opens with a cycle of oracles against foreign nations (1:3–2:16). Apart from additions, the strophes of this spacious composition form a material whole that existed as such from the beginning. The cycle of visions (7:1–9; 8:1–3) is likewise a preexisting unit, the climax of which comes at the end, as it does in the series of oracles against the nations. The book of Amos is so structured that the superscription (1:1) is followed by:

Amos 1:2	Motto (for chaps. 1–2 or 1–9?): "The Lord roars from Zion"
I. Amos 1:3–2:16	Cycle of oracles against foreign nations, with the refrain: "For three transgressions . . . and for four, I will not revoke the punishment. . . . I will send a fire upon . . ."
	2:6–16 Against Israel Criticism of society, vv. 6–8; God's action in behalf of Israel, v. 9 (10–12); announcement of earthquake and war, vv. 13ff.
II. Amos 3–6	Individual sayings with announcements of judgment upon Israel, structured by the introductions used: a) "Hear this word" (3:1; 4:1; 5:1; cf. 8:4)
	3:2 Election means punishment of guilt
	3:3–6:8 Disputations
	3:9–4:3 Various sayings against the capital Samaria
	3:12 No deliverance
	4:1–3 Against the upper-class women (cf. Isa 3:16ff.)
	4:4f. (5:5) Warning against cult

2. The book of Amos contains all sorts of additions, but there is no full agreement on their identification:

(a) The doxologies (4:13; 5:8; 9:5f.), which originally may have formed a continuous hymn, were, like the motto, in all probability (1:2) scattered throughout the book of Amos at a later date, probably in the exilic or the postexilic period. In this praise of the creator the community acknowledges the judgment to be a just one (see Ps 51:4; F. Horst) or confesses the coming eschatological significance of the prophet's words (see K. Koch; W. Berg).

(b) It was probably the exilic and postexilic periods, which experienced the judgment, that added a conciliatory conclusion to the message of judgment, in the form of hope for the reestablishment of the booth of David and for the blessings of nature (9:11–15). Even though the elimination of these oracles of salvation represents a decision on how the prophet is to be understood on the whole, the majority of exegetes are nonetheless in agreement on the excision (for a different view, see, e.g., W. Rudolph).

(c) The following must probably be regarded as Deuteronomistic or in any case postexilic additions: first, the oracles against Tyre, Edom, and Judah (1:9f.; 11f.; 2:4f.), which are notable for what they have in common, namely, the omission of the concluding formula "says the Lord," the shortening of the announcement of punishment, and the expansion of the proof of guilt; second, such individual sayings as 2:10–12; 3:1b, 7; 5:25(f.); in part, 1:1. There is disagreement on 5:13; 8:11ff.; 9:8ff.; and others.

The book of Amos, then, reached its present form through a gradual process of growth, as the words and visions of Amos himself were supplemented by the third-person account (7:10–17), perhaps also by sayings from a circle of friends or disciples whose existence is a matter of inference ("the school of Amos"), and finally by later additions. This development of the book took place in the southern kingdom (see 1:1f.; 2:4f.; 7:10; etc.), from which Amos had come and to which he was sent back (7:12). But a specifically Judean redaction is more clearly recognizable in the book of Hosea.

3. Amos, whose home was in Tekoa in the southern kingdom (1:1), exercised a ministry (only) in the northern kingdom, around 760 B.C., under Jeroboam II in a period of tranquillity on the international scene and even of some military successes (compare Amos 6:13 with 2 Kgs 14:25ff.) and economic prosperity. The reason for the prophet's "ministry is therefore not to be found in the political or cultural conditions of the time; viewed from without, these gave little cause for offense" (A. Weiser, ATD, on Amos 1:1). Domestic political circumstances and social injustice (see §3d) are more likely to have occasioned lament, for only to those of farseeing political vision did the Assyrians appear even remotely as a threat. The Assyrians had indeed stripped the Arameans more or less completely of their power, but they themselves made no move farther south. Thus Amos simply alludes to them (5:27; 4:3; 6:2, 14); unlike Hosea or Isaiah later on he does not refer to them by name.

Amos's ministry lasted only a short time, perhaps a few months; it was exercised in the northern kingdom (see 1:1, "two years before the earthquake," which Amos himself threatened), specifically at Bethel (7:10ff.) and possibly in Samaria (see 3:9; 4:1; 6:1) and other places. He is familiar with the past and present of Israel and Israel's milieu (1:3ff.; 9:7; etc.) and shows poetic power in shaping his vivid sayings with their wealth of imagery (see 3:3ff., 12; 5:19; etc.). H. W. Wolff has noted connections between Amos and (clan) wisdom, for example, in his use of the numerical sequence (compare 1:3ff. with Prov 30:15ff.; for a critique, see H. H. Schmid). But in any case the prophet's message regarding the future cannot be explained against such a background.

Unlike Hosea, Amos only occasionally looks back to Israel's early history.

When he does he turns the basic traditions—the deliverance (9:7; cf. 3:1f.) and settlement (2:9)—against Israel, just as he turns the tradition of a war waged by Yahweh on Israel's behalf into an announcement of a war against Israel (2:13ff.). In addition—again unlike Hosea, it seems (4:2)—he does not cite the law of God verbatim, but simply communicates its intention.

By trade Amos was a "herdsman, and a dresser of sycamore trees," and perhaps owned flocks as well. In any case, he did not have to support himself by his prophetic activity; in fact, he did not even regard himself as a prophet or a disciple of prophets, but was conscious of having been called by God directly (7:14f.; cf. 1:1)—by means of his visions?

4. The visions probably belong to the beginning of his ministry, since in the first pair of visions, which see a harsh but perhaps not yet unavoidable judgment coming (destruction of the harvest by locusts and of the fields by fire), Amos still intercedes for the people: "O Lord God, forgive, I beseech thee! How can Jacob stand?" Only in the second pair of visions, which lead up to the divine saying that "the end has come upon my people Israel" (8:2), is Amos convinced that judgment on the people as a whole is unavoidable (see 8:7; 9:4). This basic insight sums up, as it were, what is new and special about the preexilic writing prophets (for the substance of the divine saying [i.e., in 8:2] see Hos 1:9, etc.; for the wording itself see Ezek 7; Gen 6:13 P). The form that the judgment will take seems initially to be left undetermined; Amos will later specify it sometimes as an earthquake (2:13; 9:1; cf. 3:14f.; 1:1) but usually as a war (2:14ff.; 3:11; 4:2f.; 5:3, 27; 6:7; 7:11, 17; 9:4), which God will wage against Israel through the agency of a foreign nation (6:14).

Not even a specific reason is given initially; it seems to come only subsequently in the preaching of the prophet with his criticism of cult and society. Prior to his vocation Amos need not, of course, have lived his days with eyes closed to the surrounding world; but did he not learn from his premonition of the future to see the present differently and to recognize its defects? In any case, from the outset there is no doubt that disaster awaits guilty Israel and that this disaster is not the result of blind, inexplicable fate but a punishment from God ("I will never again pass by them" [i.e., and spare them], 7:9; 8:2). This judgment, which threatens the entire people, is not to be looked for in the remote future; it is imminent and even "seems to be a fait accompli" (A. Weiser, ad loc.). To the extent that the announced future already determines the present, the prophetic message deserves the (disputed) name "eschatological."

5. In the prophet's proclamation to his hearers the insight just

mentioned affects his understanding of his age and the content of what
he says. Take, for example, the lament over a people who are outwardly
living in an age of prosperity:

> Fallen, no more to rise,
>   is the virgin Israel;
> forsaken on her land,
>   with none to raise her up (5:2).

What is here said of the people as a whole can be applied more
concretely in the woe cry with its announcement of graduated punishment that allows of no escape:

> Woe to you who desire the day of the Lord! . . .
> It is . . . as if a man fled from a lion,
>   and a bear met him;
> or went into his house and leaned with his
>   hand against the wall,
>   and a serpent bit him (5:19; cf. 9:2–4;
>   1 Kgs 19:17; Isa 5:5f.).

While Amos here makes use of images, he can also announce death
(5:3, 16f.; 6:9f.; 8:3; 9:4) and exile (5:5, 27; 6:7; 7:1) for Israel in so
many words. He includes in this general destiny the family of the
priest who denounced him at court as a "conspirator" and forbade
him to preach (7:17). Not even a remnant will survive (3:12; cf. 4:2;
6:10; etc.).

In response to objections from his hearers Amos refers first to the
compulsion he has experienced (3:8; 7:14f.; cf. 3:3–6). The oracles
against the nations, which are perhaps Amos's first public utterance
(1:3–2:16), put Israel more or less on the same level as the neighboring
peoples as far as guilt and punishment are concerned. From the election
of Israel, which was probably urged as an objection against his message,
Amos draws a different conclusion—Israel's responsibility, and the
vengeance to be exacted for its sins (3:2; cf. 6:12)—or else he simply
relativizes the favor shown to Israel:

> "Are you not like the Ethiopians to me,
>   O people of Israel?" says the Lord.
> "Did I not bring up Israel from the land of Egypt,
>   and the Philistines from Caphtor and the Syrians
>   from Kir" (9:7; cf. 6:2).

Such a saying also reveals something of the scope and universality
of this prophet's conception of God. Yahweh is not only the judge of

the nations (1:3ff.), who does not fail to avenge crimes even though not committed against Israel (2:1); he also has power far beyond Israel's immediate surroundings (9:7) even to the boundaries of the cosmos (9:2f.).

6. While Amos sees the guilt of the nations as arising primarily from their deeds in time of war (1:3ff.), he regards Israel as guilty of failures against justice (3:10; 5:7, 24; 6:12). His emphasis is thus on criticism of society: "They sell the righteous for silver" (2:6; cf. 2 Kgs 4:1). Along with oppression of the poor and luxurious living at the expense of the poor (4:1), the prophet mentions criminal economic activities such as the falsification of weights and measures (8:4f.), the warping of justice "in the gate" (5:10, 12, 15), and others (2:6–8; 3:9f., 15; 4:1f.; 5:7ff.; 6:4ff., 12; 8:4ff.; cf. 7:9, 11 against the royal house). In the process Amos does not seem to concentrate solely on the sins of the upper class (2:7, "A man and his father go in to the same maiden"), or at any rate he does not really show partiality to the lower classes. His social criticism is meant rather as a demonstration of guilt, so that it can turn into an announcement of judgment against all Israel (2:13ff. after 2:6ff.; cf. 3:11). Amos "does not go beyond a rejection of what he describes, but it is precisely this that makes his analysis and indictment so penetrating" (M. Fendler, p. 53).

When we describe Amos as a prophet of social justice, we put our finger on the principal but not the only theme of his arraignment. There is also an attack on false security or even arrogance (6:1f., 8, 13; 8:7)—a motif that will reappear especially in Isaiah—and a criticism of the cult. What Amos experiences in his fifth vision is communicated in his sayings—the destruction of the altar (3:14), that is, of the sanctuaries of the northern kingdom (5:5; 7:9). Was this condemnation subsequently interpreted as an argument in favor of a single sanctuary at Jerusalem (1:2), though this was certainly not what Amos intended? Unlike Hosea, who was almost his contemporary, Amos does not base his criticism of the cult on the defection to the cult of Baal. Rather, like the later prophets, he makes the special idiom of the priests his own for polemical purposes and attacks the sacrifices and feasts (4:4f.; 5:21ff.; 8:10; cf. 2:8). Like his criticism of society his criticism of the cult cannot be left in isolation; it is integrated into his message regarding the future (5:5, 27; 8:10) and thus into his prophetic understanding of God. For this reason we may ask whether the motto Justice and Ethics instead of Cult is not in the final analysis inadequate, even though it does capture part of his message (5:24, 14f.).

7. There is strong disagreement about whether Amos's indictment and announcement of punishment leave room for any ray of hope. It

is hardly Amos himself who utters the predictions of salvation at the end of the book. Yet it remains uncertain whether the exhortation allowing a conditional deliverance—"Seek me and live" (5:4f., 6, 14f.)—is to be disallowed as authentically Amos's (so H. W. Wolff). In any event, whether it is the prophet himself or a group of disciples who speak here, the possibility of survival for those who love God and do justice is restricted in two ways: clemency is only for a remnant, and even for them it is qualified by a "perhaps" (5:15). Is such a saying even intended to encourage people to adopt a different way of life? Could it have such an effect? Hosea will be the first to express a real hope of salvation, but the course of history and the destruction of the northern kingdom (722 B.C.) will show that Amos was more correct in his estimate of the situation.

§15

HOSEA

The book of the Twelve Prophets (the *Dodekapropheton*) begins with the book of Hosea either because it is the longest of the books of the minor prophets or because a later age thought Hosea to be the earliest in the series. As a matter of fact, he was Amos's younger contemporary and exercised his ministry about a decade later, during the reigns of Jeroboam II of Israel, whom Amos mentions (7:9, 11), and of King Uzziah of Judah, in the year of whose death Isaiah received his call (6:1). The Syro-Ephraimite War of 734/733 B.C. is reflected in Hosea's preaching (5:8ff.). On the other hand, it is not likely that he lived to see the fulfillment of his threats against Samaria (14:1) in the destruction of the northern kingdom by the Assyrians in 722 B.C. Thus, Hosea's prophetic ministry lasted approximately from 750 to 725 B.C. and was therefore much longer than that of Amos, even though the book of Hosea is only one and one-half times as long as the book of Amos.

Hosea was the only non-Judean writing prophet; the northern kingdom was not only the locale of his activity but in all likelihood his native place as well. This fact may explain many linguistic peculiarities of his preaching and even certain themes, such as the acceptance of the traditions regarding Jacob and the exodus (chaps. 11f.). The fact that the precursors of the writing prophets exercised their ministry chiefly in the northern kingdom makes it easier to understand why Hosea, unlike Amos, who came from the south, regarded the prophets as very important in the life of Israel (6:5; 12:10, 13). May we see a continuity of tradition at work here? Perhaps we may admit a chain of tradition running from Elijah and the Elohist by way of Hosea to the traditions in Deuteronomy and to Jeremiah, who in his youth may have been influenced by Hosea (§10a3). For example, it can hardly be accidental that Hosea, Jeremiah (7:9), and Deuteronomy all include the Decalogue or the traditions associated with it.

We know little of Hosea's life, not even (as we do for Amos) his place of birth and his profession. We do, however, know the names of his father (Beeri, 1:1), his wife (Gomer, 1:3), and his three children

(1:4ff.), who with their symbolic names play a part in Hosea's proclamation. Nor has a vocation story in the proper sense (as in Amos 7:14; Isa 6) come down to us (but see Hos 1:2). Hosea had to put up with hostility and mockery, as most of the prophets likely did: "The prophet is a fool, the man of the spirit is mad" (9:7f.). Thus was Hosea spoken of, at least ironically, as a "prophet."

2. In the book of Amos, the small units of oral speech can be easily distinguished from one another; in the book of Hosea, on the other hand, they have been combined into longer compositions, the unity of which is either thematic or historical. Since transitional formulas such as the messenger formula are almost completely lacking (but see 2:13, 16; etc.), it is difficult to isolate the original sayings. Only now and then is the beginning (4:1) or end (2:21; 11:11) of a collection indicated by a formula; the book concludes with a sapiential exhortation (14:10). Is this astonishing continuity of the book of Hosea to be explained as a reflection of its original oral delivery (H. W. Wolff suggests that the book contains "sketches of scenes") or rather as the result of the subsequent transmission process prior to and during the commitment of the tradition to writing? If Hosea did not himself write down his sayings, or if he did so only in exceptional cases, and if he did not himself shape these lengthy compositions, then it is necessary to assign the redactors a larger share in the formation of the book. In any case, it is hardly possible now to distinguish clearly between later revision and original material in the book of Hosea.

The book of Hosea has two main parts, each made up of smaller collections. The first part (chaps. 1–3), with its third-party account (1), its first-person account (3), and the threats and oracles of salvation in the connecting chapter (2), is intended to show "how the private life of Hosea was reflected in his preaching" (W. Rudolph). The second part of the book (chaps. 4–14) consists of two large units (4–11; 12–14) in which, as in 1–3, the message of disaster and the message of salvation follow on one another. In the book of Hosea, then, as in the book of Isaiah, threat and promise frequently alternate:

	Disaster	*Salvation*
I. Chaps. 1–3	1:2–9	1:10–2:1
	2:2–13	2:14–23
	3:1–4	3:5
II. Chaps. 4–14	4:1–11:7	11:8–11
	11:12–14:1	14:2–9

In the individual utterances of the second main part no clear structure is discernible; from 9:10ff. on there is a predominance of historical retrospects that are meant to demonstrate the guilt of Israel.

I. Hos 1–3
  1   Third-party account. Commission to marry a prostitute

                               Three children: Jezreel, Not-pitied, Not-my-people

  2   Individual sayings (there are divergent arrangements of verses)

                 1:10–2:1   Promise. Change of a name indicating disaster to a name indicating salvation: "The sons of the living God"

                 2:2–13   Threat. God takes away the gifts of the earth. Image of a marriage. Altercation with the cult of Baal

                 2:14–23   Promise. Return from the wilderness ("second exodus"). New community

  3   First-person account. "Give your love to an adulteress!"

                 V. 4   "Without a king . . . without sacrifice"

                 V. 5   Return to God and David (cf. Jer 30:9)

II. Hos 4–14
  4–11   4   Against the priests (vv. 1–10) and the cult (vv. 11–19)

                 V. 2   No knowledge of God in the land

               5:1–7   Against the leaders of the people

                 Vv. 4, 6   No possibility of return

               5:8ff.   Syro-Ephraimite War

                 6:1–3   Song of repentance (cf. 14:3f.). Revival after two, three days

                 6:4   Israel incorrigible

                 6:6   Knowledge of God instead of sacrifice

                 7:8   "Ephraim mixes himself with the peoples"

               8:4ff.   Against monarchy and cult

                 9:7ff.   "The prophet is a fool"

               9:10ff.   First historical retrospect (Baal-peor)

                           "Like grapes in the wilderness I found Israel"

               11   Israel as a rebellious son

                           "When Israel was a child, I loved him"

               11:8ff.   God's holy love: "I am God and not man"

  12–14   12   Israel is like its deceitful ancestor Jacob

                         (see Gen 27ff.; Jer 9:3; Isa 43:27)

               13   Israel's destruction

               14   Call for repentance (vv. 2–4) in consequence of God's healing action (vv. 5ff.)

                         Explanatory sapiential conclusion (v. 10): "The ways of the Lord are right"

Hosea's message, like that of Amos, was brought to the southern kingdom, although (it is probable) only at the time of the destruction of the northern kingdom. Does the fate of the book explain the poor condition of the text? Like the second section of the book of Amos (3:1), the second main part of the book of Hosea is introduced by a call for attention: "Hear the word of the Lord" (4:1; cf. 5:1). Doxologies are frequent in Amos; there is one in Hosea as well (12:6). May we conclude to a connection between the redactions of the two prophetical books, especially since sayings of Amos (5:5; 1:4; etc.) made their way in altered form, probably in a subsequent stage, into the book of Hosea (4:15; 8:14; cf. 7:10; 11:10)?

In any case a Judean redaction (probably in several stages) applied to the southern kingdom the sayings of Hosea against the northern kingdom and, in the process, expanded them (1:7; 4:15; 5:5; 6:11; also 1:1; 3:5; etc.). The redactors could justify themselves by the fact that Hosea himself occasionally included Judah in his message (5:10, 12; 6:4).

The chief difficulty with the book has to do with the oracles of salvation. Although a few of these can be clearly set aside as secondary (1:7; 3:5), similar proof is difficult with regard to numerous others (especially 1:10–2:1 or 2:20ff.), so that the question of "authentic" or "inauthentic" must be left open. The situation is different here from that in Amos: there can be no doubting that Hosea not only threatened disaster but also promised salvation.

3. Initially, indictment and announcement of disaster predominate, as the two accounts in third-person and first-person form (chaps. 1 and 3) show. These describe the relationship of Hosea with an (adulterous) wife and have always confronted exegetes with almost insoluble problems. Do the two chapters deal with one and the same event or two different events? With one and the same wife or with two? Did Hosea, at God's command, deliberately marry a prostitute, or did he learn only later on, during the marriage, of his wife's infidelity? Was the text (1:2) subsequently mutilated? And what is the meaning of the "harlotry"—marital infidelity, sacral prostitution, or participation in an alien cult, and in particular in a Canaanite sexual ritual (see 2:2ff.; 4:12ff.; 5:4)?

It is impossible to review here all the possible solutions. Despite all the uncertainties that remain, preference should perhaps be given to the interpretation of H. W. Wolff for chap. 1 and of W. Rudolph for chap. 3.

According to Wolff, Hosea at God's command marries a "young

woman ready for marriage . . . who had submitted to the bridal rites of initiation then current in Israel" (*Hosea*, p. 15), "in which young virgins offered themselves to the divinity and expected fertility in return" (p. 14).

Chap. 3, on the other hand (according to Rudolph) does not speak of the same wife or even of a marriage at all, but of the purchase and confinement of a prostitute: "Go again, love a woman who is beloved of a paramour."

Whatever the actual course of events may have been, the meaning of the two accounts is clear. They are intended neither as vision nor as allegory, but as symbolic actions by means of which the prophet illustrates and confirms what he proclaims. In a similar fashion Isaiah will later on introduce his family into his message (7:3; 8:3). The two events (in chaps. 1 and 3) have a twofold (symbolic) intention, in that they describe Israel's present condition and specify its future. The woman in both cases represents Israel in Hosea's time, which has apostatized from Yahweh and given itself to the worship of idols (1:2; 3:1). Once guilt has been shown, the course of the action then represents the future. The name of the first son, Jezreel (named after the place of Jehu's murders in 2 Kgs 9f.), announces the destruction not only of the dynasty but of the monarchy as such (Hos 1:4). The names of the prophet's daughter, Not-pitied, and of his second son, Not-my-people, foretell the end of the community of God and people: "You are not my people and I am not your God" (1:6, 9, contrary to Exod 3:14). In like manner, the solitariness of the prostitute (Hos 3:3) symbolizes neither the education nor the improvement of the woman or the people, but the end of the monarchy and of at least some liturgical practices. Israel will long remain without king and sacrifice (v. 4; v. 5, which in its entirety is probably an addition, looks for conversion only after judgment).

4. The intention expressed in these two symbolic actions emerges also in other parts of Hosea's message. In accord with Amos, Hosea cancels God's loving care of Israel (1:6; 2:4) and announces war (7:16; 8:3; 10:14; 11:6; 14:1; etc.), death (13:14f.), and dispersion: "They shall be wanderers among the nations" (9:16f.). Hosea even goes beyond Amos in the trenchancy of the images used for God's punishments: "I am like a moth . . . like dry rot . . . like a lion . . . like a bear" (5:12, 14; 13:7f.; cf. 7:12).

In their indictments, however, characteristic differences between the two prophets can be seen. In Amos social criticism dominates, in Hosea criticism of the cult. Hosea utters predictions of destruction

against the altars and sanctuaries of the northern kingdom (8:11; 10:2,
8; 12:11), threatens the end of festal joy (2:11; 9:5), and rejects the
sacrifices:

> For I desire steadfast love and not sacrifice,
>   the knowledge of God, rather than burnt offerings
>   (6:6; cf. 3:4; 8:13; 9:4).

Amos has one run-in with a priest (7:10ff.); Hosea, on the other
hand, pronounces a general harsh judgment on the priesthood (4:4ff.;
5:1; 6:9). Above all, he bases his criticism of the cult on reasons that
in Amos must be said to be in the background (despite 5:26; 8:14): he
censures the drift into the cult of Baal and into idolatry or, in other
words, the violation of the first and second commandments. To what
extent is he expressing here typical problems of the northern kingdom
(see 1 Kgs 12:28f.) and perhaps even specific themes of the prophets
of the northern kingdom (see 1 Kgs 18; 2 Kgs 1)? Zeal for the prohibition
of images is in any case still alien to the Elijah tradition.

Being the work of human beings, images of God cannot represent
him; they degrade both God and humanity:

> A workman made it;
>   it is not God. . . .
> Men kiss calves! (8:6; 13:2;
>   cf. 8:4ff.; 10:5; 11:2; 14:4).

Because prostitution (originally an earthly imitation of the heavenly
marriage of god and goddess) is connected with the foreign cult, Hosea
speaks of the entire business as "harlotry" (2:2f.; 4:10ff.; 5:3f.; 9:1;
picked up in Jer 2f.; Ezek 16; 23). The term expresses both a depreciation
of the Canaanite fertility cult and a confession of the exclusivity of
the Yahwistic faith. Hosea can condemn as "lechery" even the political
quest of aid from foreign peoples (8:9ff.; cf. 5:13; 7:8ff.; 10:4; 12:1).
When he nonetheless represents God's union with his people as a
relationship of husband to wife (2:2ff.; cf. Jer 2; etc.), he is taking over
from the Canaanite religion the familiar mythical notion of a marriage
between god and goddess, although he reinterprets it as an image of
Israel's adultery, the infidelity of the people to its God. Hosea thus
concretizes the demand made in the first commandment, which he
cites directly (13:4; 3:1), just as he uses the ethical part of the Decalogue
or at least of the Decalogue tradition in his demonstration of guilt
(4:2).

Is it because of his polemic against an alien religion that Hosea harks back to history to such an extent? The retrospects help him above all to show God's fidelity and Israel's apostasy and thus the constancy of guilt through changing times (chaps. 9–12). In this demonstration the traditions of the exodus ("Out of Egypt I called my son," 11:1; 12:9; 13:4) and of the sojourn in the wilderness (2:3, 14f.; 9:10; 13:5f.) play a dominant role. Hosea appeals also to the patriarchal tradition, which will not be important again until Second Isaiah (Jacob, Hos 12).

While Amos cites concrete offenses in the social contrasts of his day (e.g., 2:4–6), Hosea for his part is content with generalities in the area of social criticism:

> There is no faithfulness or kindness,
> and no knowledge of God in the land
> (4:1; cf. 6:6ff.; 12:6).

On the other hand, Hosea of all the prophets is probably the severest critic of the monarchy as such: "They made kings, but not through me" (8:4). He can therefore understand it as being a purely human institution or even a divine gift motivated by anger (13:11) and can utter the threat "I will put an end to the kingdom of the house of Israel" (1:4; 3:4). It is this that gives his criticism its radical character; later prophets of the southern kingdom, on the other hand, will reproach rulers or reigning dynasties but will hold fast to the messianic prophecies made with regard to the institution. Even the disputed prophecy about the union of Judah and Israel promises only a single "leader" (1:11; addition, 3:5). In his hope of salvation after judgment did Hosea expect the continuance neither of the monarchy nor of the cult, since he does not mention them among the gifts that God will grant anew (2:14ff.)?

5. The judgment will take the form of God's withdrawing from Israel the insidious blessings of the earth but also the monarchy and the cult (2:3, 9–12; 3:4). Hosea develops this basic idea in the light of Israel's entire history. Assyria will overrun the country and drag its inhabitants into exile, not however to Assyria but to the place whence Israel originally came: "They shall return to Egypt" (8:13; 9:3, 6; 11:5; cf. 7:16). Thus the exodus and the settlement, in fact the entire history of the people, will be reversed. The return to Egypt or (contrary to the tradition, concretized on the basis of the political situation as) the banishment to Assyria has a double meaning for Hosea. Inasmuch as

what now exists is removed, it represents a return to the origins, but by this very fact it also makes a new beginning possible:

> They shall come trembling like birds from Egypt,
>   and like doves from the land of Assyria;
>   and I will return them to their homes
>   (11:11; cf. 2:14f. on the wilderness).

This idea of a second exodus will be taken up later on by Jeremiah, Ezekiel, and Second Isaiah. The most important thing, as far as Hosea is concerned, is that his message does not break down into two independent parts. The promised salvation does not limit the judgment or eliminate it, but rather presupposes it. Only when "the nadir has been reached" (H. W. Wolff) will God grant a new, peaceful, and abiding communion and a restoration of what has been lost. "You will call me, 'My husband,' and no longer will you call me, 'My Baal' [i.e., Lord]" (2:16ff.; 14:6ff.).

Israel is to receive salvation once again, but it is unable to preserve this salvation by its own power. Whenever it receives that kind of offer, it rejects it (2:2ff.; cf. 4:16; 6:4; 7:14ff.; 10:12f.). Israel "forgot me" (2:13); "they have not hearkened" (9:17; cf. 11:5ff.). "The iniquity of Ephraim is bound up, his sin is kept in store" (13:12). Thus (despite 14:2ff.) God can hardly expect Israel to be ready to repent; he must himself create this response:

> I will heal their faithlessness;
>   I will love them freely (14:5).

In the final analysis God's mercy can have its basis only in his own holiness (see Isa 40:25); in his heart love must struggle against justified anger:

> How can I give you up, O Ephraim!
>   How can I hand you over, O Israel! . . .
> My heart recoils within me,
>   my compassion grows warm and tender.
> I will not execute my fierce anger,
>   I will not again destroy Ephraim;
> for I am God, and not man,
>   the Holy One in your midst
>   (11:8f.).

Hosea's promises to the northern kingdom were not fulfilled, but later prophets like Jeremiah (3:12, 22; 31:3, 20) continued the hope.

§16

ISAIAH

1. The lengthy book that tradition has attributed to the prophet Isaiah is a highly complex literary structure that developed through several centuries. After differences within the book of Isaiah had been noted as early as the Middle Ages, it gradually came to be accepted after 1780, as a result of the work of J. G. Eichhorn and J. Chr. Döderlein, that chaps. 1–39 and 40–66 must be dealt with separately and assigned to two different authors: Isaiah ("first" Isaiah) and a second, unknown writer who is usually called "Deutero-Isaiah" or "Second Isaiah." Several reasons compel us to accept that the book of Isaiah does not form a single unit:

(a) According to 6:1 and other passages Isaiah lived before 700 B.C., at a time when the Assyrians, of whom he speaks by name, were threatening Israel (10:5ff.). But chaps. 40ff. suppose that Jerusalem has already been destroyed by the Babylonians in 587 B.C. In keeping with this, in Isa 47 it is no longer Assyria but Babylon that is threatened with destruction; even the Persian king Cyrus is occasionally mentioned (44:28f.).

(b) Linguistic usage, idioms, intellectual background, and intention completely change beginning with chap. 40. Instead of threats of judgment, announcements of salvation predominate, and the author likes to add descriptions such as "the Holy One," "the Redeemer" to the name of God.

(c) The chapters in prose, Isa 36–39, which are an appendix taken from 2 Kgs 18–20, show that the book at one time ended with chap. 35.

Only since the still important commentary on Isaiah of B. Duhm (1892, 1922⁴) have scholars distinguished between Second Isaiah, chaps. 40–55, and Third Isaiah (Trito-Isaiah), chaps. 56-66.

As in the composition of the other prophetic books, so in the overall arrangement of the book of Isaiah there is an underlying meaning. The message of Isaiah (I), in which the announcement of disaster predominates, seems to lead up to the promise of salvation in Isa 40ff.

2. Within Isaiah I, we find a new superscription as early as the

beginning of chap. 2 (compare 2:1 with 13:1). This book too, therefore, is made up of more or less clearly distinguishable smaller collections, such as 1; 6–8; 28–32; and others. It is true that because of the future importance of his message Isaiah wrote things down or dictated them (8:1f.; 30:8; see the first-person accounts in chaps. 6 and 8), but the collections as such originated rather in a group of disciples (8:16; see the third-person account in Isa 7; also 20)—although allowance must also be made for expansion at a later time.

As in the book of Hosea, oracles of salvation are appended to existing collections; for example, the promise of the pilgrimage of the nations to Zion (2:1–5) after chap. 1, or the messianic prophecy (9:1–6) after chaps. 6–8; see also 4:2–6 after 2:6–4:1 and, in later chapters, 32:15ff., etc.

Even though expectations of salvation become more frequent in the concluding part of Isaiah I (24ff.; 33ff.), the chief organizing principle of the book is not the sequence disaster–salvation. Rather, sayings against Isaiah's own people are gathered together (1–12; 28–32) as are sayings against foreign nations (13–23), so that First Isaiah falls into three main parts (I–III below). In addition, three extensive supplements are introduced (A–C below: 24–27; 33–35; 36–39).

I. Isa 1–11(12)		Primarily threats against Judah and Jerusalem	
	1	"Summary of the message of Isaiah" (G. Fohrer)	
		Vv. 2–3	Rebellious sons
		Vv. 4–8(9)	Jerusalem like Sodom (701 B.C.)
		Vv. 10–17	Cult-criticism and justice. "Your hands are full of blood"
		Vv. 18–20	Summons to a legal proceeding
		Vv. 21–26(27f.)	Purification of Jerusalem "I will restore your judges as at first"
		Vv. 29ff.	Tree worship (cf. 17:9–11; 57:5; 65:3; etc.)
	2–4	2:1, 2–4:5	(= Mic 4:1–3, 4f.) Pilgrimage of the nations to Zion
		2:12–17	Day of the Lord (in a frame provided by 2:6–22)
		3:1–7, 8f.	Against "stay and staff," i.e., current functionaries
		3:16f., 24(18–23)	Against the upper-class women (cf. 3:25f.; 4:1; 32:9ff.)
		4:2–6	Glorification of Zion
	6–8	The "original Isaiah" or the "memorial" of Isaiah (6:1–8:18, expanded to 9:7)	
		6	Call vision in the form of a first-person account ("I saw the Lord"), with commission to harden the hearts of the people

A) Isa 24–27	"Apocalypse of Isaiah" from the postexilic period (cf. §24,2)

III. Isa 28–32		Threats against Jerusalem from Isaiah's late period (before 701)
		The "Assyrian cycle." Numerous "woes"
28f.	28:1–4(5f.)	Woe upon Samaria (before 722 B.C.)
	28:7–13	Against priests and prophets
	28:14–22	Covenant with death
		God's strange work (28:21; 29:14)
	v. 16	"Behold, I am laying in Zion ... a ... cornerstone"
	28:23–29	Didactic poem (or parable?) on the farmer
	29:1–4, 5–8	Woe upon Ariel-Jerusalem
	29:9f., 11f.	Blindness (cf. 6:9f.)
30f.		Against protection from Egypt (especially 30:1–3; 31:1–3)
	31:3	The Egyptians are humans and not God
	32:9–14	Against the idle women of Jerusalem (cf. 3:16ff.)

B) Isa 33–35		Appendix on hope
	33	Imitation of a liturgy with an indictment and an oracle of salvation (cf. Mic 7:8ff.)
	34	Judgment upon Edom (cf. Obadiah; Ezek 35; etc.)
	35	Liberation and return to Zion (as in Second Isaiah)

C) Isa 36–39	Historical appendix from 2 Kgs 18–20
	Account of the siege of Jerusalem by Sennacherib (701)
	Hezekiah's psalm of thanksgiving (38:9ff.)
	Cf. the appendix in Jer 52 from 2 Kgs 24f.

Authentic Isaian sayings are most likely to be found in chaps. 1–4:1; 5–11; 14; 17f.; 20; 22; 28–32.

Amos and Hosea exercised their ministry in the northern kingdom; Isaiah is the first writing prophet in the southern kingdom. But he addresses "both houses of Israel" (8:14). A series of threats from the period before 722 B.C. are addressed to the northern kingdom (9:8ff.; 28:1ff.; etc.). But as a rule Isaiah speaks to "Jerusalem and Judah," that is, the city of David and the country (3:1, 8; 5:3; 22:21), and ultimately, like Amos before him, to foreign peoples as well (e.g., 18:1ff.).

The name of the prophet's father was Amoz—not to be confused with the prophet Amos (whose name in Hebrew has a different first and final sound). Isaiah's wife is called a "prophetess" (*nĕbîʾâ*, 8:3) or possibly "wife of the prophet," while Isaiah himself avoids the title "prophet" (see 28:7) and, like Amos, thinks of himself rather as a "seer" (see 1:1; 30:10; 2:1). Like Hosea with his children, Isaiah relates his two sons (7:3; 8:3), as "signs and portents" (8:18), with his preaching by giving them offensive symbolic names. "Immanuel" (7:14) is hardly to be taken as another son of Isaiah.

Since Isaiah has access to the king and to the leading official circles (7:3; 8:2; 22:15ff.) and has a good knowledge of the political, social, and cultic situation in the capital, he may have been from an eminent family and have grown up in Jerusalem. This would explain his surprising closeness to the world of the sapiential writers (1:2; 11:2; cf. 10:15; etc.); this does not mean that he is in any sense uncritical of them (5:20f.; 10:13; 29:14ff.; 31:2; cf. 2:17; 3:3; etc.). Furthermore, he is strongly influenced by the Zion (1:21ff.; 6; 8:18; 28:16f.; etc.) and David traditions (29:1; 11:1ff.; etc.), whereas the exodus and patriarchal traditions so important for Amos and Hosea are absent. In addition, the Jerusalem temple, in which he probably received his call, may have made him familiar with the language of the psalms, which, again, he critically reinterprets (8:14, 17; 28:15; 30:2f.; 31:2f.; etc.).

A late, apocryphal legend, the "Martyrdom of Isaiah," tells of the prophet's being sawed to death in the time of Manasseh (see 2 Kgs 21:16), because he said he had seen God (Isa 6:1), because he called Jerusalem "Sodom" (1:10*), and because he foretold the devastation of city and country (6:11; etc.). The legend indicates that important utterances of Isaiah continued to scandalize people down to a late period.

4. The period of Isaiah's ministry, from about 740 B.C. (the year of Uzziah's death, 6:1, cannot be dated with complete certainty) to about 701 B.C., is a time of political unrest due to the growing threat from Assyria, and Isaiah increasingly takes a position on contemporary politics. On the basis of the principal events of the times scholars usually divide Isaiah's ministry into various periods, although the temporal sequence of not a few texts remains disputed.

(a) In the "early proclamation" of Isaiah, which is recorded, roughly, in chaps. 1–5, the later important interest in foreign politics (Isa 7f.; 20; 30f.) is still dormant. The demonstration of Israel's guilt is based chiefly on criticism of society.

The early proclamation cannot be located prior to the call of Isaiah, because 6:1 contains the earliest factual information supplied in the book of Isaiah and because the radicality of Isaiah's message of judgment in chap. 6 is reflected in this early textual complex (1:10, 15; 3:8f., 25ff.; 5:5–7, 13f.; etc.). An exhortation such as the one in 1:16f. should not be interpreted in isolation, without regard for its context. As a rule the early proclamation of Isaiah is located by scholars in the

period between the call of Isaiah and the Syro-Ephraimite War;
occasionally, however, it is dated after the latter event.

(b) The lively scenes in Isa 7f. take place in the time of the Syro-
Ephraimite War, around 733 B.C., in which an attempt was made to
force Judah to join the anti-Assyrian coalition. A period of silence
follows, in which Isaiah "seals" his message among his disciples and
leaves to God the fulfillment of what has been announced (8:16–18).

In both of these first two periods—or even after them—but in any
case in the years before 722 B.C., there are also announcements of the
fall of the northern kingdom (Isa 9:8ff.; 5:25ff.; 17:3ff.; 28:1–4; cf.
7:4ff.; 8:4).

(c) The symbolic action in Isa 20 and such utterances as 18:1ff. and
perhaps 22:15ff., etc., belong to the period of quickly suppressed
rebellions against Assyrian rule, especially the revolt of the Philistine
city of Ashdod in about 711 B.C. (cf. Isa 20:1).

(d) Important parts of the "Assyrian cycle" in chaps. 28–32 were
spoken during or after the devastation of the country by the invasion
of Sennacherib the Assyrian (siege of Jerusalem, 701 B.C.). Isaiah's
activity ends in 701 or 700 B.C.; his last three utterances are probably
1:4–8; 22:1–14; 32:9–14.

5. Isaiah shares Amos's criticism of cult and society, the expectation
of the "day of Yahweh," the woe cries, the attack on human arrogance,
and so on. But Isaiah goes beyond Amos in the variety of his themes;
for example, he extends his message to Jerusalem itself, includes
foreign politics, and closely links announcements of disaster and
salvation (1:21ff.). Isaiah's language, too, is rich in images; on one
occasion he develops an image into a parable (5:1ff.).

"The preaching of Isaiah represents the theological high water mark of the
whole Old Testament" (G. von Rad, *Old Testament Theology*, vol. 2, p. 147);
unfortunately it is also the subject of the greatest disagreements. So divergent
are the interpretations given on decisive questions of content and so varying
are the applications of the distinction between "authentic" and later redactional
texts—a distinction that is extremely important for any overall interpretation—
that it is difficult to find in scholarly research basic lines that are generally
accepted.

The vision of the holy God surrounded by his royal council (Isa 6;
see §13b2) develops into an expiatory rite in which Isaiah is freed of
guilt and rendered capable of serving: "Whom shall I send? . . . Send
me!" Thus, the call vision at the same time provides an etiological
explanation of the prophet's message of disaster. The comparable
vision of Micaiah son of Imlah (1 Kgs 22:19ff.) explains the deluding
of the king, and Isaiah's commission is to harden the hearts of the

people: "Hear and hear, but do not understand; see and see, but do not perceive." To the question "How long?" comes the harsh answer "Until cities lie waste without inhabitant" (v. 11; vv. 12f. are probably an addition). As in the vision of Amos, no more details are given on the when and the how, and the why is only intimated (v. 5). The extent to which Isaiah's call is accurately reflected in this account and the extent to which it already reflects his later prophetic experience are subjects on which there are widely differing views. But does not an interpretation of the text in the light of later events lessen its shocking character?

Isaiah experiences less the fulfillment of his own proclamation than he does the effects of his preaching activity on himself; lack of success is accepted as willed by God and therefore as part of his commission. The way in which Isaiah's exhortation to discernment is rejected and thus helps to bring about the judgment is illustrated by the meeting of the prophet and the king (Isa 7). At a time when Damascus and Israel are trying to force Jerusalem into an anti-Assyrian coalition and to replace the ruling Davidic king, Ahaz, with a certain Tabeel, Isaiah continues the tradition of the holy war (Exod 14:13f.; Deut 20:2–4) and calls for fearlessness and coolness and thus to trust in Yahweh (Isa 30:15). In the prophet's anticipatory understanding of the future the two hostile states of Syria and the northern kingdom are simply "two smoldering stumps of firebrands"; the forces of Assyria, which Isaiah expressly names only later (8:4ff.; 7:18ff.), are drawing closer. But even the royal house of Jerusalem is not given a promise, but only a conditional announcement of disaster: "If you will not believe, surely you shall not be established" (7:9; cf. 28:16). In the following scene, in which Ahaz rejects the offer, this conditional announcement turns into an unconditional declaration of judgment upon king and people— this in the much disputed Immanuel prophecy, which is really concerned not with the birth and naming of a child but with a chronological indication, namely, the partitioning of the country (7:14, 16f.).

Was the correspondence of Isa 6 and Isa 7 felt only in retrospect? Is it only in the course of the conversation that Isaiah becomes convinced of the disaster that threatens even Judah (immediately from the Assyrians but in the final analysis from Yahweh himself, 8:12ff.), or does he begin the scene with a premonition of the way things will turn out?

Isaiah takes his son Shear-jashub with him to the meeting with the king. The boy's name, "(Only) a remnant will return" (i.e., from battle; the meaning is hardly that "a remnant will be converted"), is probably intended as a threat against Judah, just as the name of Isaiah's second son, Maher-shalal-hash-baz, "Speedy-spoil-quick-booty," announces disaster for the northern kingdom. As for Amos (3:12), so for Isaiah the remnant means the survivors of the catastrophe (1:8; 17:3, 5f.; 30:14, 17) rather than a group that is the ultimate object of the judgment and consists of the sharers in a new salvation (the situation is different in a number of texts suspected of being additions: 1:9; 4:3; 6:13; 10:20f.; 11:11, 16; 28:5; etc.). In addition, a series of announcements of judgment (5:6, 24, 29, 6:11; 28:2–4, 18–20; also 8:8; etc.) hardly leaves room for the hope of a remnant.

6. In the various periods of his activity, then, Isaiah returns to foundational statements made in Isa 6. Not only individuals, such as the king or a royal official (22:15ff.), and not only groups (3:16ff.; 5:8ff.), but the entire people are guilty (6:5; 9:13; 10:6; 30:9; 31:2) and on the road to judgment (6:11f.; 3:8; 5:13, 29; 8:5ff.; 28:18ff.; etc.). Yahweh himself will become "a rock of stumbling to both houses of Israel" (8:14). Isaiah laments Israel's ingratitude and disobedience, which create a barrier against God's fatherly concern (1:2f.; 5:1–7). What is described as God's own action in Isaiah's commission to harden hearts (6:9f.; 29:9f.) is seen here to be the guilty, responsible action of the people; inability and unwillingness are intertwined.

> "In returning and rest you shall be saved;
> in quietness and in trust shall be your strength."
> And you would not (30:15).

The people of Israel are willing neither to see (5:12) nor to hear (28:12; 30:9, 12; cf. 1:5; 8:6; 29:13; etc.); even conversion can be seen as an opportunity that has been wasted (9:13, on the northern kingdom; cf. 6:10). The Israelites are God's children, but children who have gone astray (1:4; 30:1, 9). Therefore God can speak not only of "my people" (1:3; etc.) but also, with contempt, of "this people" (6:9f.; 8:6, 11f.; 29:14f.; etc.).

Like Amos or Hosea before him, Isaiah as a rule sees judgment taking the form of an invasion by a hostile army (5:25ff.; 7f.; and often); occasionally, however, he sees it as a direct intervention of God (1:24ff.; 8:13f.; 29:1–3) and even, exceptionally, as a natural catastrophe (2:12–17; cf. 5:14, 24; 32:12–14). Is not the prophet thinking, in the final analysis, of an event that can be presented in various concrete ways?

In any case, it is consistently understood as an event that is imminent or is even already reaching into the present (1:15; 7:4; 29:10; etc.). On numerous occasions, however, Isaiah seems to be thinking of a slightly longer period of two or three years (7:16; 8:4).

7. Isaiah continues Amos's indictment of injustice and oppression, but in addition to the poor and the weak, who are subjected to discrimination (3:14f.; 10:2), he speaks of a group that Amos does not mention but that has no spokesman in the legal assembly:

Defend the fatherless,
plead for the widow (1:17, 23; 10:2;
earlier, Exod 22:21; etc.).

Isaiah's "woe" against the large landowners "who join house to house, who add field to field" (5:8) first appears elsewhere in his contemporary, Micah (2:2). Even more characteristic is the threat against "stay and staff," the higher circles of officialdom (Isa 3:1ff.). Thus, the theme of "justice" dominates the early preaching (1:16f., 21–26; 5:7ff.; etc.), but it is not forgotten in the late period (28:17). It determines both indictment and expectation of salvation: "I will restore your judges as at first" (1:26; 9:7; 11:3ff.; 28:17).

Far less space is given to criticism of the cult, and what there is is interwoven with social criticism. This criticism too brings guilt to light: "Your hands are full of blood," and the guilt belongs not only to the ruling classes but to the people as a whole, who are addressed as "you rulers of Sodom" and "you people of Gomorrah" (1:10–17; cf. 22:12f.; 29:1, 13f.; against the priests, 28:7).

Is Isaiah also linking himself to Amos when he sets himself against human arrogance? He senses the presence of this arrogance in all whom he addresses—in Assyria (10:5ff.), in the northern (9:9; 28:1ff.) and southern kingdoms, and especially in Jerusalem (5:14), in the upper-class women of the capital (3:16f.; 32:9ff.), and in a royal official (22:15ff.). Pride and haughtiness are ultimately offenses against the God whom Isaiah saw "upon a throne, high and lifted up" (6:1), against the "Holy One of Israel" (1:4; 30:15; 31:1; etc.). On his "day" God will secure the exclusiveness that the first commandment calls for:

The haughtiness of man shall be humbled,
and the pride of men shall be brought low;
and the Lord alone will be exalted in that day (2:17).

8. Another principal theme in Isaiah's preaching is his position on contemporary events in the area of foreign politics. In his early period he takes a stand on the Syro-Ephraimite War and proclaims Assyria to be the power which at God's bidding is executing judgment on the northern (5:25ff.; etc.) and southern kingdoms: "Behold, the Lord is bringing up against them the waters of the River, mighty and many" (8:7); "the Lord will whistle . . . for the bee that is in the land of Assyria" (7:18). Because this foreign power is acting under commission, it can be referred to indirectly in such terms as these: "The Lord has one who is mighty and strong" (28:2). But when Assyria becomes

presumptuous and arrogant and goes beyond its role as instrument of judgment, Isaiah calls down "woe" upon it (10:5ff.; also 14:24ff.?). In his late period, nonetheless, he passionately resists all temptations to shake off the Assyrian yoke through alliances with Egypt (20; 30:1ff.; 31:1ff.). What do such alliances represent but human self-assertion against Yahweh (30:2)?

> And yet he is wise and brings disaster. . . .
> The Egyptians are men, and not God;
>   and their horses are flesh, and not spirit.
> When the Lord stretches out his hand,
>   the helper will stumble, and he who is helped will fall,
>   and they will all perish together (31:2f.).

God's "plan" or "counsel" and "work" are, like his word (9:8), active in history. But Israel has no eye for the future: "They do not . . . see the work of his hands" (5:12, 19; 9:13; 22:11; cf. 14:26; 28:21; etc.). In this linguistic usage, which is shaped with surprising sureness and firmness, we can see the beginnings of the formation of a concept. It allows Isaiah to understand God's coming for judgment or even the hardening of hearts as God's *opus alienum:* "Strange is his deed . . . alien is his work!" (28:21; cf. 29:14; 31:2).

9. If we prescind from the messianic prophecies, the element in Isaiah's work that is the subject of the greatest dispute is his message regarding Zion. The interpretation of it depends to a great extent on the decision taken with regard to the "authenticity" of texts which in a more or less unconditional way promise Jerusalem the coming of salvation in the midst of affliction. Is Isaiah promising Zion a miraculous rescue at the last moment? Or are we to regard as later additions (8:9f.; 17:12ff.; 29:5ff.; cf. 14:30a, 32b) promises that in a quite general way expect protection against the attacks of "nations" and thus do not suggest any contemporary situation and which recall the motif of the assault by the nations in the psalms of Zion (46; 48; 76)? Especially suspect as being later additions are sayings in which a threat against Jerusalem is immediately followed by an oracle of salvation and which thus more or less expressly look for a reversal (29:5ff.; 31:5ff.; 32:15ff.; cf. 18:7; 28:5f.; etc.). If texts that have long been the subject of dispute are excised, the preaching of Isaiah gives an impression of greater unity and coherence. Since toward the end of his ministry (22:14; 28:22; 29:9f.; 32:14; etc.) he returns to the announcements of disaster connected with his call (6:11), he can only temporarily have adopted a different outlook. On the other hand, the basis required for assuming

two successive changes in Isaiah's thought is lacking. Does not Isaiah, like Micah (3:11) or Jeremiah (7:8ff.), attack the Jerusalemites' sense of security (28:15, 18ff.), as this is expressed in the Zion tradition (Ps 46; etc.)? At any rate he is able to threaten the inhabitants of the capital with death (22:14; cf. 29:4; etc.) and the city itself with destruction (3:8; 5:14, 17; 32:14).

10. Does Isaiah "hope" in the God who "is hiding his face" (8:17)? Disaster and salvation are undoubtedly intertwined. When purified, the ruined capital will once again bear the name "city of righteousness, the faithful city," which it earned for itself of old (1:21–26).

Except for this text, in which the future newness emerges from the judgment on present reality, the "authenticity" of texts expressing an expectation of salvation is disputed. This is true not only of the concluding words of the call vision (the stump of the tree is a "holy seed," 6:13) but also of the three great promises in chaps. 2, 9, and 11. It is difficult to relate these clearly to a historical situation—but this is often true of oracles of salvation. Since it is difficult in general to find objective grounds that are independent of one's personal understanding of the prophets for excluding texts—especially grounds of a linguistic kind—one must admit "authenticity" to be possible—at least for Isa 11, and for Isa 9, which is closely associated with Isa 11. As a matter of fact, the prophecies of salvation, with, for example, their strong concentration on the accomplishment of justice, are a counterpart of Isaiah's indictments and are by this fact linked both with the rest of Isaiah's message and with one another.

Isa 9:2–7 (probably without 9:16) only promises "a great light" to the "people who walked in darkness" and dwelt in a world where death reigns (9:2; cf. 29:4). This "light" is liberation by God himself, the birth of a ruler, and unending peace. In Isa 11 (vv. 1–5, with supplementary details in vv. 6–8, 9f.), on the contrary, the messianic prophecy has become an entity in its own right; the endowment with the spirit (11:2) corresponds to the honorary titles in 9:6. The future ruler is to bring what the people lack: discernment, justice, and concern for the poor (1:3, 17; etc.). The image of a branch growing from a stump tells us that this ruler will not come from the reigning Davidic dynasty, which is rather faced with judgment (7:16f.).

Just as Isaiah here looks for the continuation of the institution and not the preservation of those who fill the office, so in the case of Jerusalem he seems to see only the identity of the place being maintained. Isa 28:16f. announces a new foundation in or on Zion: "Behold, I am laying in Zion for a foundation a stone . . . ." The promise of the pilgrimage of the peoples (2:2–4; also transmitted in

Mic 4:1–3) even speaks of the establishment and exaltation of Zion. The prophet says nothing of Israel's national greatness and dominion but speaks only of justice established and war ended among all peoples through encounter with the one exalted God (see Isa 6:1; 2:17).

§17

MICAH

1. Micah is a younger contemporary of Isaiah; both exercise their ministry in the same area—the southern kingdom—and in the same period. The year of Uzziah's death (Isa 6:1) is not mentioned in Micah, but the superscriptions of both books (Isa 1:1; Mic 1:1) name the same three kings: Jotham, Ahaz, and Hezekiah. Only one utterance of Micah (1:2–7) is addressed to the northern kingdom: "I will make Samaria a heap in an open country." This announcement of judgment must have been delivered before it was fulfilled in 722 B.C. in the fall of the city. The profound break that the collapse of the northern kingdom effected is noticeable in a linguistic shift; the honorific name "Israel" passes from the northern kingdom (1:5) to the southern (3:1, 9; etc.). At the other end, the expedition of the Assyrians against Jerusalem in 701 B.C. seems to be reflected in Micah's message (1:8ff.). His ministry, then, extended from about 740 (?) to about 700 B.C.

Micah probably entered public life in the capital (3:9ff.), but unlike Isaiah, a native of Jerusalem, he came from the countryside, from Moresheth-gath (1:1, 14; Jer 26:17f.) in the hill country of Judah not too far from Amos's native place. Does his origin explain why Micah threatens Jerusalem, the capital, with the same fate as Samaria (3:12; cf. 1:12, 16; 2:4), but holds fast to hope in the Davidic dynasty, which came originally not from Jerusalem but from Bethlehem (5:2ff.)? Did the prophet belong to the landowning rural population ('am hā'āreṣ), which through all the coups at the court remained faithful to the Davidic dynasty (2 Kgs 11:14; 14:21; etc.)? Did Micah fill the office of a village elder, who takes care of "my people" (1:9; 2:8f.; 3:3, 5; H. W. Wolff)? Only occasionally does Micah speak of himself, as for example in his lament over the fate of his people (1:8; cf. 7:1, 7) or in the self-confident reference to his own commission (3:8).

2. Just as oracles of disaster and of salvation follow upon one another in the book of Hosea, so in Micah promises on three occasions terminate collections of threats (W. Rudolph):

221

	Disaster	*Salvation*
I. Chaps. 1–2	1:2–2:11	2:12–13
II. Chaps. 3–5	3:1–12	4:1–5:15
III. Chaps. 6–7	6:1–7:7	7:8–20

Each of the three collections—again as in the book of Amos (3:1; and often) or the book of Hosea (4:1)—opens with a call for attention: "Hear!" (Mic 1:2; 3:1; 6:1; cf. also 3:2; 6:2, 9).

I. Mic 1–2

1   Fall of Samaria (vv. 2–6). Threats to towns of Judah and to Jerusalem (vv. 8f., 10ff.)

      Vv. 2–4   Call to the peoples to pay heed (cf. Isa 1:2) Theophany

2   Woe to the large landowners (vv. 1–5). A preacher for the people. In response to objections from the hearers (vv. 6f.) new indictments (vv. 8ff).

      Vv. 12f.   (Exilic-postexilic) promise that Israel will be gathered under the leadership of Yahweh's king (cf. 4:7)

II. Mic 3–5

3   Preaching to various classes. Against the "heads and rulers" (vv. 1–4, 9), the prophets (vv. 5–8), the judges, priests, and prophets (vv. 9–12)

      V. 12   Destruction of the temple (Jer 26:18)

4f.   Promises

      4:1–4, 5   = Isa 2:2–4, pilgrimage of the peoples to Zion

      4:6–8   Return of the Diaspora (cf. 2:12f.) from exile (4:9f.)

      4:11ff.   Conquest of the peoples (cf. Isa 8:9f.; etc.)

      5:2–6   The future ruler from Bethlehem

      5:10–15   Acceptance of the first commandment–against the weapons of war and foreign cults

III. Mic 6–7

6:1–7:7   God puts his people on trial (vv. 1–8; vv. 4f. an addition?) The following sayings deplore the nonfulfillment of God's requirement (6:8):

      6:9ff.   Against Jerusalem's avarice. False measures

      7:1ff.   No more upright people in the land (cf. Jer 5:1)

      Vv. 5f.   Put no trust in a neighbor!

      V. 7   Profession of trust (cf. Isa 8:17)

7:8–20   Prophetic liturgy from the postexilic period: Pledge of God's favor to Jerusalem, the walls of which are still in ruins (in the oracle of salvation, vv. 11f.)

      V. 18   "Who is a God like thee?" (allusion to the name Michael?)

There is agreement only that the main part of chaps. 1–3 (without 2:12f., among others; cf. J. Jeremias) is to be attributed to Micah. There is disagreement about the "authenticity" of the judgment oracles (6:1–7:7) and especially about that of the oracles of salvation. Did this prophet simply threaten disaster (from Yahweh, 1:9, 12)? But even if most of the promises (especially 4:1ff.) are not from Micah, at least the substance of the messianic prophecy (5:2ff.) fits well into his preaching. It seems, then, that Micah—like Isaiah?—combines the announcement of inevitable judgment and even of total destruction (1:6; 3:12), with the promise of a new turning after the judgment; but this is disputed.

3. On essential points of social criticism Micah is in agreement with Amos and especially with Isaiah (Isa 5:8ff.); the criticism, so predominant in Hosea, of foreign cults and image worship becomes secondary here. When Micah criticizes the economy based on large estates and the greed of the upper classes for houses and property, he seems to be giving concrete form to the tenth commandment (Exod 20:17):

> Woe to those who devise wickedness. . . .
> They covet fields, and seize them;
>   and houses, and take them away;
> they oppress a man and his house,
>   a man and his inheritance
>   (2:1f.; cf. 2:8ff.; 3:2f., 10).

In general, Micah laments the oppressive actions of the upper classes of society, and especially their violations of justice: they "hate the good and love the evil" (3:1ff., 9ff.; cf. 6:10ff.; 7:2f.). Like the prophets before him (Amos 5:21ff.; Hos 6:6; Isa 1:10ff.) Micah can—if the saying indeed is his—oppose righteousness and (sacrificial) cult:

> With what shall I come before the Lord,
>   and bow myself before God on high?
> Shall I come before him with burnt offerings,
>   with calves a year old? . . .
> He [Yahweh; or: "they"] has showed you, O man, what is good;
>   and what does the Lord require of you
> but to do justice, and to love kindness,
>   and to walk humbly with your God? (6:6–8).

Just as a pilgrim is told the conditions for entering into the sanctuary (Pss 15; 24), so too the prophet shows "man" what he ought to make his own as God's will for him. In choosing these three demands is Micah repeating the three main concerns of the three earlier writing prophets: to do justice (Amos), to love kindness (Hosea) and to walk humbly before God (Isaiah)?

In addition to criticizing the priesthood (3:11), Micah tackles a theme to which Isaiah only alludes (28:7) and which will become decisive only in Jeremiah: he comes to grips with the problem of prophecy itself:

> Thus says the Lord concerning the prophets
> who lead my people astray,
> who cry "Peace"
> when they have something to eat,
> but declare war against him
> who puts nothing into their mouths.
> Therefore it shall be night to you, without vision,
> and darkness to you, without divination (3:5f.).

Micah finds fault with his enemies among the prophets, because they make their responses—predictions of salvation or disaster—depend on their being paid. Micah claims to have superior knowledge of the future, for he dares announce to them the termination of their effectiveness. They may have received revelations in the past, but in the future God will be silent (3:4, 7)! Micah understands his own power to be something he has received as a gift, but it gives him the authority to bring to light the guilt of the entire people; the demonstration of guilt and not the call to repentance defines his task:

> But as for me, I am filled with power,
> with the Spirit of the Lord,
> and with justice and might,
> to declare to Jacob his transgression
> and to Israel his sin (3:8; cf. 1:5).

4. What Isaiah mentions only in passing (28:15ff.), Micah attacks directly—the feeling of security and the hope of the city's being unharmed, which are part of the Zion tradition (Pss 46; 48):

> "Is not the Lord in the midst of us?
> No evil shall come upon us."
> Therefore because of you
> Zion shall be plowed as a field;
> Jerusalem shall become a heap of ruins,
> and the mountain of the house a wooded height
> (3:11f.; cf. 1:6; Isa 32:14; retrospectively, Lam 5:18).

Micah's oracle against the temple was still in circulation a hundred years later (freely cited in Jer 26:18), when Jeremiah renewed this prediction of disaster.

Since there are many connections between the preaching of Isaiah and that of Micah in regard to indictments and announcements of judgment, the tradition is probably correct in attributing to Micah, as to Isaiah, the acceptance of the David tradition in regard to messianic predictions:

> But you, O Bethlehem Ephrathah,
>   who are little to be among the clans of Judah,
> from you shall come forth for me
>   one who is to be ruler in Israel (5:2, 4a, 5a;
>   vv. 3, 4b, 5b–6a and perhaps 6b are probably additions).

Like Isa 11:1 Micah harks back to the origin of the Davidic dynasty and hopes not for continuity but for a new beginning—for a ruler who will come from David's birthplace (1 Sam 17:12; Ruth 1:2). Does this expectation of salvation presuppose the destruction of Jerusalem and the royal house that dwells there? In any case, God chooses one who is small and insignificant (see 1 Sam 9:21; etc.) to be his viceroy; this ruler will reign by God's power and in his person will embody peace (Mic 5:4a, 5a).

§18

NAHUM, HABAKKUK, ZEPHANIAH, OBADIAH

When the ministry of Isaiah had ended, the prophets were silent for a half century, ca. 700–650 B.C., during the period of oppressive Assyrian domination. Then in succession came Nahum, Zephaniah, Habakkuk, and above all Jeremiah.

1. As the superscription, "An oracle concerning Nineveh," already indicates, the message of the prophet Nahum from Elkosh (a place unknown) focuses on a single theme: the destruction of Nineveh, the capital of Assyria (since the time of Sennacherib, ca. 700 B.C.). The vivid picture of the capture of the city in a series of graphic scenes (2:3ff.) hardly presupposes that Nineveh has already been destroyed (612 B.C.), but rather flows from a prophetic "vision" (1:1) of the future, at a time when Assyrian power was still at its height. The only historical event presupposed is the capture of the Egyptian capital, Thebes, by the Assyrians in 663 B.C. (3:8). It is likely, then, that around 650 B.C. or a little later Nahum looked ahead longingly to the fall of the mighty power that was universally hated throughout the ancient Near East: "Wasted is Nineveh; who will bemoan her?" (3:7).

The first part of the book takes its tone from a hymn (the "authenticity" of which is much disputed) to the power of God who is able to alter nature and protect those who belong to him. This introductory psalm gives the theological basis for the subsequent announcement of the future: God can and will bring about a reversal of the political situation. In the main part of the book (2:3ff.), which follows upon a few intermediate sayings (1:11–2:2), there are three sets of threats against Nineveh, each followed by laments or taunt-songs over the fallen city.

1:2–8;9f. Hymn to the power of Yahweh
           The psalm is alphabetic (a–k), like Pss 9f.; etc.
           "The Lord is a jealous God and avenging"
           Theophany (vv. 3b–6; cf. Ps 18:7ff.; Hab 3; etc.)
1:11–2:2   Individual sayings (difficult to understand)

226

<table>
<tr><td>1:12f.</td><td>Promise of salvation for Judah: "I will break his yoke from off you"</td></tr>
<tr><td>1:15</td><td>(Eschatological?) summons to festive celebration (cf. Isa 52:7)</td></tr>
</table>

2:3–3:19	The fall of Nineveh
2:3–13	Threat (vv. 3–10), lament or taunt-song (vv. 11f.)
	The "challenge" formula: "Behold, I am against you" (2:13; 3:5)
3:1–7	Threat (vv. 1–4, 5f.), lament or taunt-song (v. 7)
3:8–19	Threat (vv. 8–17), lament or taunt-song (vv. 18f.)
	Comparison of Nineveh with conquered No-amon = Thebes in Egypt (v. 8)

Does the composition of the book, with its use of psalm and announcement of salvation for Israel, reflect liturgical practice? The structure of the book of Habakkuk provides a better basis for such a hypothesis.

The threats against Nineveh show, in part, such close connections with other prophets' announcements of judgment against Israel/Jerusalem that J. Jeremias draws the conclusion that sayings of Nahum (e.g., 3:1ff.) were originally addressed to Jerusalem and only subsequently transferred to Nineveh. Was Nahum therefore not simply a prophet of salvation (cf. 1:12)?

The prediction of disaster for Nineveh was fulfilled. However one-sided the message of Nahum may have been, directed as it was against an outside foe, in any event it contained a profession of faith that was to be decisive for later prophets (Zech 2) down into the age of apocalyptic (Dan 2; 7)—that God can put an end to even the greatest power in this world. On the basis of this insight the book of Nahum urges confidence in the power of the Lord; it was probably in this light that it was read in later ages.

2. Prediction of the fall of the conquering power also provides the principal content of the message of Habakkuk. He came on the scene shortly before 600 B.C., a few decades after Nahum, during the period of unrest that followed the collapse of the Assyrian and the rise of the Babylonian empire. The Chaldeans or Neo-Babylonians are expressly named (1:6, which is probably in the original text) and Israel still has a king ("thy anointed," 3:13), but there is no hint yet that the first conquest of Jerusalem in 598 B.C. has taken place.

The book of Habakkuk has three main sections, each of which, as in Nah 2:3ff., is a small composition. In the first unit (1:2–2:5) there are two complaints of the prophet, each followed by an answer from God. The second divine oracle (2:1–5) is actually the heart of the book since the discernment of the future that it gives is taken up in the woe cries (2:6ff.) and given broad development in the "prayer" of chap. 3.

1:2–2:5 Dialogue between the prophet and God
    1:2–4   Complaint of the prophet about lawlessness and violence
    1:5–11   God's response: an announcement of judgment: "Lo, I am rousing the Chaldeans, that bitter and hasty nation" (v. 6)
    1:12f., 14–17 Objection (cf. 2:1) or new complaint of the prophet
    2:1–5   Concluding answer from God
        V.1   The prophet as a watchman (cf. Jer 6:17; Ezek 3:17; etc.)
        Vv. 2f. Writing down of the revelation (cf. Isa 8:16)
        Vv. 4f. Content of the revelation. End of the wicked, survival of the just
2:6–20 Five woe cries (cf. Isa 5:8ff.) against Babylon
    "The Lord is in his holy temple; let all the earth keep silence before him" (v. 20; cf. Zeph 1:7; Zech 2:17)
3 Prayer of Habakkuk
    Supplications (vv. 2, 16, 18) set around a description of a theophany (vv. 3–12, 13–15)

When, in time of temptation, Habakkuk turns to God with his complaints (1:2ff., 12ff.) and with expectant longing for a divine response (2:1), the initiative seems to be with the prophet rather than with the God who reveals himself. Was Habakkuk a cult prophet, as scholars like to think? Certain indications, such as the title "prophet" (1:1), the manner in which the revelation is received (2:1; 3:2, 16), and the similarity to the language of the psalms (1:2ff., 12f.; 3:2, 18f.), do allow such a hypothesis but hardly a sure decision on this point. Does the entire book—which was hardly put together by Habakkuk himself—form a liturgy (P. Humbert)? In any case, there are traces in chap. 3 of its use in the liturgy (see below).

In the first prayer (1:2–4) the prophet complains about injustice and violence; concretely, his complaint is more about legal and economic oppression within Israel itself than about oppression by the Assyrians. God answers by announcing an incredible "work" (1:5; cf. Isa 28:21). He will inflict punishment through the agency of a hasty enemy possessing overwhelming power—the Babylonians (1:5–11, 14ff.). But suppose they go beyond their task of purifying Israel? In any case, the cruelty and arrogance (1:11, 16) of the great power causes the prophet to object: How can the holy, immortal God see their wicked, unpitying rage and remain silent (1:12f.)? Like a watchman on a tower—a real place (for a cult prophet in the temple?) or simply an image?—the prophet is on the lookout for God's answer (2:1). In responding, God first tells him to write down the revelation, which has to do with the "end" (2:2f.). In its content the answer reasserts the connection between action and consequence and thus the distinction between the wicked and the just: "(Only) the righteous shall live by his faith (i.e., his faithfulness to God)" (2:4; made more pointed in Rom 1:17; Gal 3:11).

The divine oracle (2:4f.) is developed in the second part of the book (2:6ff.) in the form of five woes uttered by the prophet against Babylon the conqueror. The text, however, has undergone a later revision (see the interpretation of the woes as a riddle in the superscription, 2:6a, or the attack on images in 2:18ff.), so that some have even asked whether the woe cries had always been directed against the great outside power (J. Jeremias, E. Otto). The concluding sayings of this section (2:19f.), which contrast the dead idols with the living God, form a transition to Habakkuk's prayer, which again picks up the announcement of the future in 2:4f.

Laments and expressions of confidence by the prophet ("I," 3:2, 16, 18f.) frame a visionary description of a theophany. God's majestic appearance on Sinai (v. 3; cf. Judg 5:4f.; Deut 33:2), accompanied by the trembling of nature, has for its purpose the punishment of the "wicked" (vv. 13–15; cf. 1:13; 2:5), that is, the destruction of the power of Babylon. The coming of the revelation causes the prophet's own body to tremble (3:16; cf. Isa 21:3f.; Job 4:12ff.).

Although the prophet looks longingly for the quick execution of what he has seen (3:2; 2:3) and thus for God's aid to his people (3:13), he already rejoices now because he trusts in the power of "the God of my salvation"—if indeed the concluding words (3:18f.) are from Habakkuk and not from some one praying at a later time. For, as superscription and subscription (3:1, 19b) and the *Selahs* scattered throughout (vv. 3, 9, 13) show, the prophet's vision (3:2ff.) was, like other psalms, later used in Israel's liturgy as a prayer for God's intervention in time of distress.

3. Zephaniah's message is narrow in its scope, but the radical character of his demonstration of guilt and his announcement of punishment cause him to be ranked with the "great" prophets; in his themes he is close to Isaiah and to his own contemporary, Jeremiah. Above all, Zephaniah "actualizes" his announcement of the impending judgment or "day of Yahweh" (Amos 5:18ff.; Isa 2:12ff.), so that the element of imminency that characterizes prophetic announcements

of disaster stands out sharply: "The day of the Lord is at hand" (1:7, 14ff.; 2:2; picked up in Joel 1:15; etc.). In this form (Zeph 1:14ff.) it becomes a model for the medieval sequence *Dies irae, dies illa.*

Like the young Jeremiah (chap. 2), Zephaniah (1:4ff.) attacks the idolatry, and especially the cult of Baal and the stars, that spread during the period of Assyrian domination in the seventh century and would shortly be eliminated, at least for a while, by the Josianic reform of 622 B.C. (see §10a5). Since Josiah had been crowned while still a child (1 Kgs 22:1), it is understandable that in criticizing the royal officials and the royal house (1:8) Zephaniah should not name the king himself. There is thus confirmation of the superscription of the book (1:1) with its statement that Zephaniah exercised his ministry in the time of Josiah—more precisely, around 630 B.C., before the reform, and probably in Jerusalem (1:10f.). The rapid collapse of Assyrian power is not yet reflected in Zephaniah's threat (2:13ff.).

The superscription gives the name not only of Zephaniah's father but also of the three preceding generations. This is so unusual for a prophetic book as to cause speculation about the prophet's possibly being of foreign (Cushi = the Ethiopian?) or Davidic origin (Hezekiah being the king of that name?).

In the course of the book oracles of disaster (1:2–3:8) are followed by oracles of salvation (3:9–20), but the usual threefold division is present only in an imperfect form. After threats against foreign peoples (2:4–15) there are further announcements of judgment against Jerusalem (1:2–18; 3:1–8), while prophecies of salvation are subdivided into promises for the nations (3:9f.) and promises for Israel (3:11ff.).

1:1	Superscription
1:2–18	Threats against Judah/Jerusalem
	Vv. 2f., 17f.　General contextual sayings (an addition? Cf. 3:8)
	Vv. 7, 14ff.　The day of the Lord. *Dies irae*
2:1–3	Exhortation to humility and justice—"perhaps" protection against the day of the Lord
2:14–15	Threats against foreign peoples: Philistines—Moab/Ammon—Cush (Ethiopia)—Assyria
	V. 11　(Addition expressing universal hope): to Yahweh "shall bow down, each in its place, all the lands of the nations" (cf. Mal 1:11)
	V. 15　Lament over the fall of the self-confident Nineveh
3:1–8	Threats against Jerusalem
	Vv. 1–5　Woe cry of the prophet, with preaching about various classes, vv. 3f. (cf. Isa 3; Mic 3; etc.)
	Vv. 6–8　Oracle of Yahweh: I am gathering nations against you
	The threat against Jerusalem in 3:8 seems to have been subsequently turned, by alteration of the text

		("them" for "you") into an announcement of judgment against the nations and thus into a promise for Jerusalem
3:9f.	Oracle of salvation for Israel	
		Transformation of the peoples into worshipers of Yahweh (cf. 2:11)
3:11-20	Promises of salvation for Israel	
	Vv. 14f.	Eschatological summons to joy (cf. Zech 2:10; 9:9f.) at God's royal reign
	Vv. 16f., 18f., 20	From the (post)exilic period: God is "a warrior who gives victory"
		"I will . . . gather the outcast" (the Diaspora)

The announcement of judgment, "I will stretch out my hand against Judah, and against the inhabitants of Jerusalem," is set in a universalist context. But while the expectation of a universal judgment and the eradication of humans and beasts from everywhere on earth (1:2f., 18) is not given any justification, reasons are supplied for the punishment of Jerusalem in the form of a detailed demonstration of guilt: foreign cults (1:4ff.), the violence and deception practiced by the upper classes (1:8f., 3:3) and the tradesmen (1:11), the faithlessness of the prophets and priests (3:4), along with self-confidence and lack of trust in God's power, as expressed in the cited words: "The Lord will not do good, nor will he do ill" (1:12; cf. Isa 5:19; Mal 3:14f.). The criticism (types are chosen) of classes and groups is integrated into the announcement of judgment against the people as a whole (1:4) so that Zephaniah (3:1f.; cf. 1:12) can renew the "woe" directed at the city of Jerusalem with its violence and its contempt of God (Isa 29:1; cf. Ezek 22). And yet in the face of the imminent day of judgment Zephaniah can cry out:

> Seek righteousness, seek humility;
>   perhaps you may be hidden
> on the day of the wrath of the Lord (2:3; cf.
>   Amos 5:14f.; Isa 2:10ff.).

In this saying Zephaniah offers the possibility of rescue from the judgment, but he asserts a condition (only for those who humble themselves before God) and at the same time maintains God's freedom (only "perhaps"). To what extent, then, does the prophet count on his hearers' acting as they should? In the final analysis, he hopes that the transformation of humanity will be effected by God himself: "I will change . . ." (3:9).

> I will leave in the midst of you
>   a people humble and lowly.
> They shall seek refuge in the name of the Lord,

those who are left in Israel;
they shall do no wrong
and utter no lies (3:12f.).

This hope, which seems to adopt Isaiah's expectation of a divine victory over human arrogance, is surpassed—if not in the prophet's own preaching, then at least in the contextual framework added to the book of Zephaniah—by the hope of a turning of all nations to Yahweh (3:9f.; 2:11).

4. Habakkuk exercised his ministry just before the first siege of Jerusalem; Obadiah, on the other hand, presupposes the events that took place in the disastrous years 597–587 B.C. He seems to show close acquaintance, perhaps even direct experience, with some of the phenomena attendant on the catastrophe. The Edomites, who had earlier taken part in an anti-Babylonian coalition, turned into gloating enemies once Jerusalem fell; they persecuted or betrayed Judean refugees (Obad 14). Edom's hostile actions and Israel's own enmity toward Edom are reflected in a series of postexilic texts (Ezek 25:12ff.; 35; Lam 4:21f.; Ps 137:7; Isa 34; etc.).

As a "messenger from the Lord" Obadiah pronounces God's judgment on Edom: "Behold, I will make you small among the nations" (vv. 1f.). Esau/Edom has done violence to his "brother" Jacob/Israel (see Gen 25ff.; Deut 23:8f.) (Obad 10ff.). While the nations serve initially as Yahweh's instrument of punishment (vv. 5ff.), they themselves are later threatened: "The day of the Lord is near upon all the nations" (vv. 15a, 16ff.). The basic principle that action brings about certain results is applied not only to Edom (v. 15b) but also to the nations (vv. 16f.) as well:

As you have done, it shall be done to you,
your deeds shall return on your own head (v. 15b;
cf. Prov 12:14; 26:27; etc.).

Obad 1–14, 15b   Threats against Edom, which is directly addressed, with reason for them:
     Arrogance of the mountaineers (vv. 3f.), violence done to their brother-nation Jacob/Israel (vv. 10ff.)
     Summons of Yahweh to the nations to do battle against Edom (v. 1)
     Vv. 1–4, 5 correspond to Jer 49:14–16, 9
     Edom's famed wisdom (Jer 49:7; Job 1:1; etc.) will be destroyed (Obad 8)
Obad 15a, 16–18   Judgment on the nations (cf. Joel 4; Isa 34)

	The nations drink the cup of Yahweh's wrath (cf. Jer 25:15ff.; etc.)
Obad 19–21	Three additions in prose (?)
	Vv. 19 and 20 link up with v. 17b, v. 21 with v. 17a

The very short book of Obadiah falls into two or three parts. The main line of division runs through v. 15, the second half of which, v. 15b, states the principle and purpose of the first part of the book (vv. 1–14). V. 15a acts as a superscription stating the theme of the second part (vv. 16–18). Vv. 1–14 contain several groups of sayings, so that scholars have attributed this little book of only twenty-one verses to different authors. Is it possible that the name given to this otherwise unknown prophet, namely, Obadiah, "Servant of Yahweh" (compare Malachi, "my messenger"), is in fact a symbolic name (cf. Amos 3:7)? It is more likely, however, that the book contains the message of a prophet who in a time of disaster announced a revealed judgment upon Edom and the nations. Was Obadiah a cult prophet who uttered his oracle of salvation during liturgies of lamentation (H. W. Wolff)? In any case, there are close connections with the sayings of other prophets (especially Jer 49); the accords with Joel 4 (Amos 9:12) may explain why the book comes after Joel and Amos in the book of the Twelve Prophets.

Only the concluding verses are likely to be a later addition. They describe the extent of Israel's future possessions (vv. 19f. link up with 17b), but they surpass all expectations in regard to the hope of Yahweh's kingly rule. Despite all the retribution that has been announced, it is to him and not to Israel that dominion belongs (v. 21; cf. Zech 14:9; Zeph 3:15; etc.).

§19

JEREMIAH

1. The book of Isaiah tells us on occasion that Isaiah wrote down, or had others write down, individual sayings, perhaps even short collections of sayings (8:1, 16; 30:8), but an actual account of the writing down of prophetic preaching comes for the first time in the book of Jeremiah. At Jeremiah's dictation Baruch writes down the prophet's utterances on a scroll and reads it, first to the people in the temple, later to the royal officials in the palace. When the scroll is cut up and burned by King Jehoiakim after he has listened to a third reading of it, Jeremiah dictates it anew and adds further material (Jer 36). This account, the historicity of which has not infrequently been doubted, has long compelled exegetes to ask which texts of Jeremiah were written down in the original scroll. An unqualified answer is no longer possible. Since the scroll seems to have contained only threats, oracles of salvation must be excluded, as must stories about Jeremiah in the third person and, of course, all later redactional sayings. But how are we to separate out all of these?

As a matter of fact, the book of Jeremiah poses difficult problems of redaction history. On the one hand, like the message of the earlier prophets in the eighth century, the book contains poetical and rhythmical sayings in metrical form, but on the other it also contains sermonlike discourses in prose (e.g., Jer 7). The latter immediately catch the eye on several counts: (a) their prose form; (b) their links in expression and ideas with the Deuteronomic-Deuteronomistic literature; and (c) the alternative set before the hearers, namely, the choice between salvation and disaster. Could the same Jeremiah have used two modes of expression so different in style and intention?

If the prose texts be accepted as authentic parts of Jeremiah's preaching, the connection between the prophet's sayings and the Deuteronomic-Deuteronomistic literature can be explained in various ways. After the Josianic reform, Jeremiah came under the influence of Deuteronomy; the language in question reflects the elevated style in use at the end of the seventh century and was typical of the cult. But why is this style not used in the metrical sayings to which we must look first for the authentic preaching of Jeremiah? And should not the "elevated style" of the seventh century, whether it be literary prose or sermonic discourse, be also identifiable outside the circles that adopted Deuteronomistic language?

Every position taken in this complex literary question has profound consequences for the overall understanding of the prophet. He will be integrated into the series begun by his predecessors, or else we must assume that prophecy underwent a perceptible change toward the end of the seventh century, so that there was a notable increase in exhortations and warnings and that the message of Jeremiah (36:3, 7), like that of all the prophets (25:4f.; 35:15), can be summed up as a call to repentance.

Following the lead of B. Duhm's commentary (1901), which marks the beginning of the modern study of Jeremiah, S. Mowinckel (1914) assigned three or possibly four sources for the book of Jeremiah, and this division has been largely accepted, although with modifications:

a) Sayings of the prophet and first-person accounts

As in the other prophetic books so here there is a large number of rhythmic individual sayings. These have been assembled into various collections, the bond of which may be a common theme (e.g., 2; 4–6; or the sayings on kings and prophets in 21–23; cf. Deut 17f.).

A number of first-person accounts (comparable to Hos 3 or Isa 6) are scattered throughout (Jer 1; 13; 18; 24; 25:15ff.; cf. 3:6, 11; 14:11, 14; etc.).

b) Third person stories about Jeremiah, the "biography by Baruch"

Jer 19–20:6; 26–29; 36–44; 45 (51:59–64) are primarily third-person reports that consistently tell of the sufferings of Jeremiah. They begin in the time of Jehoiakim and carry the story down to the flight into Egypt. Since they give details that could only have come from sources close to Jeremiah, scholars prefer to attribute these third-person accounts to Baruch, the confidant of Jeremiah (see chaps. 36; 43; especially 45 with its prophecy addressed to Baruch). In any case, as a result of these accounts we are better informed about the life and experience of Jeremiah than we are about those of the other prophets.

c) Prose discourses with Deuteronomistic revision

These share a common style, choice of words, and theme (the guilt of the people because of disobedience to prophetic warnings; announcement of punishment) and thus interpret the exile in the light of the words of Yahweh or the prophets. Does the structural pattern reflect the style of preaching in the exilic-postexilic period?

No clear delimitation of this material has thus far been made successfully, but scholars usually locate under this heading 7–8:3; 11:1–14; 18:1–12; 21:1–10; 22:1–5; 25:1–11(14); 34:8–22; 35; etc.).

d) The oracles of salvation in 30f.

These two chapters certainly form a separate collection. But since they are Jeremian in substance, they can be put in group (a) (so W. Rudolph) and linked especially with Jer 3.

As an approximation, this explanation of the literary relationships has its advantages, for it can explain certain duplications (e.g., Jer 7; 26) and linguistic differences. But in fact the situation is far more involved than Duhm makes it appear. The biography by Baruch is not a unity; it is likely that originally only chaps. 37ff. belonged together (see G. Wanke). Above all, Deuteronomistic language is found not only in (c) but in (b) and (a) as well, and therefore not only in passages marked by a broad leisurely style but also in brief additions to poetic texts (basic study in W. Thiel, with history of the scholarship on the subject). We must therefore reckon rather on levels of tradition than on sources (a view already adopted by S. Mowinckel, 1946). In the oral tradition the sayings of Jeremiah underwent revision, some less, some more, and were applied to the situation of the exilic or even the postexilic period or simply given a new form. Consequently the transitions between (a), (b), and (c) are blurred.

All this means that we must reckon with a lengthy process of redaction and with several redactional strata for the book of Jeremiah. Even the Deuteronomistic parts do not form a unity but show rather profound differences of intention. Attention is paid not only to Israel or to individual Israelites but also to the nations (18:7ff.; cf. 12:14ff.). There are demonstrations of guilt and threats but also oracles of salvation, which are likewise couched in the Deuteronomistic style (e.g., Jer 30f.; especially 31:31ff.). The hope of God's turning back to Israel after the judgment, a hope already inchoately present in additions to the Deuteronomistic history (§11b4), is further developed in the book of Jeremiah (12:14ff.; etc.). If the Deuteronomistic revision is understood as the work of a changing and at the same time expanding school (§11a2), the complicated situation can be explained: agreements with and differences from the language, itself not fully unified, of the Deuteronomistic history; acceptance and modification of Jeremiah's preaching; and, finally, unevennesses within the Deuteronomistically influenced texts of the book of Jeremiah itself.

For methodological purposes we may distinguish: (a) sayings of Jeremiah with Deuteronomistic additions; (b) sayings in Deuteronomistic language that take an "authentic" saying of Jeremiah for their starting point but develop it; (c) sayings of the Deuteronomistic redactors, without any basis in Jeremiah.

A clear differentiation of these three groups is difficult, however. The result is, first, that the investigation of the redaction history of the book of Jeremiah is to a unique degree incomplete, and, second, that the identification of authentic Jeremian material has by no means been accomplished to the general satisfaction of scholars. An accurate investigation must analyze the text verse by verse and deal even with each part of each verse. All the indications are that the process of revision has affected the book of Jeremiah more deeply than is the case with the earlier prophetic books. The exile was a decisive turning point that influenced the further transmission of the prophetic message.

2. Several criteria come into play in an analysis of the structure of the book of Jeremiah. To begin with, sayings predominate in the first part (chaps. 1–25), prose accounts in the second (26–45; 52). Second, as in the book of Isaiah, so here there is to some extent a chronological framework inasmuch as the sayings of Jeremiah's early period (1–6) are placed before those of the second (7ff.), while 1–39 relate to the period before the exile and 40–45 to the period after the fall of Jerusalem. Finally, the book of Jeremiah is organized according to the usual (probably eschatological) pattern—first disaster, then salvation (29; 30ff.)—and the predictions of disaster are divided into sayings against the prophet's own people (1–25) and sayings against foreign people (25:15–38; 46–51).

I. Jer 1–25:13(14)		Chiefly threats against Jerusalem and Judah
1		Account of Jeremiah's call (vv. 4–10) with the symbolic touching of his mouth (v. 9)
		Election "in the womb . . . as prophet to the nations" (v. 5; cf. v. 10)
		Vision of the almond tree (or "Watchful Tree") (vv. 11f.) and of the boiling pot (vv. 13f. [15f.])
		Sending, vv. 17–19 (cf. 15:19ff.): "I will make you a wall of bronze"
2		Complaint about worship of natural forces. Israel a faithless wife
	Vv. 2f.	"I remember the affection of your youth" in the wilderness
	Vv. 10f.	Summons to compare religions
	Vv. 13, 32	Unnatural apostasy (cf. 8:7; etc.)
3–4(:4)		Theme: Return to Yahweh
	3:1–5	Return to first husband impossible (cf. Deut 24)
	3:6ff.	Two faithless sisters, Israel and Judah (cf. Ezek 22)
	3:12f.	Appeal to the northern kingdom (cf. 31:2ff.)
	4:1f., 3f.	Return on one condition: Circumcise your hearts! (cf. 9:24f.)
4(:5)–6		The enemy from the north. The "Scythian Songs"

	I have heard the cry of war (4:19), I see a formless waste (4:23)
	5:1 — Roam Jerusalem's streets and see if anyone does right!
	6:27–30 — Assaying of Israel: "refuse silver" (cf. 13:10f.)
7; 26	Discourse on the temple. Jerusalem is like Shiloh
	V. 9 — Decalogue (cf. Hos 4:2)
	Vv. 16ff. — Against the worship of the queen of heaven (cf. 44:17ff.)
	Vv. 21ff. — Against sacrifice (cf. 6:20)
8–9	Individual sayings
	8:8f. — A torah of lies
	9:23f. — No boasting (cf. 1 Cor 1:31)
10(:1–16)	Addition: Polemic against idols (cf. Isa 40:19f.; 44:9ff.: etc.)
11	The words of the covenant
In 11–20	Jeremiah's confessions (11; 15; 17f.; 20)
	11:18–12:6 — Persecution in Anathoth by relatives
	17:14ff.; 18:18ff. — Complaint about enemies (cf. 11:20–12:3; 20:11f.)
	15:10ff. — "Woe is me, my mother, that you bore me!" (cf. 20:14ff.)
	20:7ff. — "Thou has deceived me, and I was deceived"
13	Allegorical action or vision (?) of the waistcloth at the Euphrates
	13:23 — Inability to do good (cf. 2:21f.; etc.)
14(–15:4)	Liturgy with lament of the people (vv. 7–9; 19–22) and God's response
	14:11 — Prohibition against intercession (cf. 7:16; 11:14; 15:1)
16	Celibacy as a sign
	17:5ff. — Wisdom sayings (cf. Ps 1)
	17:19ff. — Zeal for observance of the sabbath
18	Jeremiah at the potter's
	Vv. 7ff. — Disaster and salvation for the nations. God's repentance
19f.	Symbolic actions: breaking of the jug; first beating (20:1–6)
21:11–23:8	Sayings "to the royal house" Shallum/Jehoahaz–Jehoiakim–Jehoiachin
	22:15 — Josiah did what is right
	23:1–4 — "Woe to the shepherds" (cf. Ezek 34)
	23:5f. — Messianic prophecy (cf. 33:14ff.)
	23:7f. — A new credo
23:9–20	Sayings "concerning the prophets"
	V. 29 — "Is not my word like fire?"
24	Vision of two baskets of figs
II. Jer 25(:15–38)	Vision of the cup (as introduction to:)
46–51	Threats against the nations
	The oracles against the nations, chaps. 46–51, are only in part "authentic" (especially 46:3–12) and in the

Greek textual tradition (LXX) have been transposed and inserted before 25:15ff. This gives them a clearer—and more original?—place in the overall structure of the book

III. Jer (29)30–33   Oracles of salvation for Israel

30f.   "Booklet of consolation" (cf. 30:2) for Ephraim (the north-
                     ern kingdom)

"I will restore the fortunes of my people" (30:4)

The core of the material (especially 31:2ff., 15ff.) is addressed to the inhabitants of the former northern kingdom. Has the text been subsequently revised here and there in favor of Judah by the addition of "and Judah" (30:3f.; 31:27, 31)?

31:15   Rachel (ancestor of northern Israel) weeps for her children

31:31ff.   A new covenant

32   Jeremiah buys a field at Anathoth during the siege of Jerusalem

V. 15   "Houses and fields and vineyards shall again be bought in this land"

33   Various promises

34   Beginning of the siege of Jerusalem. Fate of Zedekiah

Emancipation and resubjection of Hebrew slaves

35   Example of the Rechabites

IV. Jer (19f.)26–29;

36–45   The biography by Baruch

26   Jeremiah's experience after the discourse against the temple

Citation of Mic 3:12. Death of the prophet Uriah

27–29   Against false prophets

27   Symbolic action: wearing of the yoke as a sign of subjec-
                     tion to Nebuchadnezzar

28   Jeremiah and Hananiah

Vv. 8ff.   The true prophet predicts disaster (cf. Deut 18:21f.)

29   Letter to those deported (597) to Babylon

"Build houses, pray for the good of the city/the country"

36   The scroll: origin, reading, fate

37–39   Siege and destruction of Jerusalem

Consultation by Zedekiah, Jeremiah's warnings, and the outcome

40–43   Assassination of Gedaliah the governor (40–41) and flight to Egypt against Jeremiah's advice (42f.)

44   Against the worship of the queen of heaven (cf. 7:16ff.)

45   A prophecy for Baruch

"I will give you your life as a prize of war"

V. Jer 52   After the concluding remark (51:64) at the end of the oracles against the nations, an appendix from 2 Kgs 24f.: capture of Jerusalem, deportation, reprieve of Jehoiachin

Cf. Isa 36–39 from 2 Kgs 18–20

According to the information given in the book (1:2f.; 3:6; 25:3; 36:2) Jeremiah was called in the thirteenth year of King Josiah's reign, that is, in 627/626, and thus was probably born ca. 650; his ministry lasted until about 585 B.C.

Unlike Ezekiel (1:3), he was hardly a priest himself but he did come from a priestly family; his father's name was Hilkiah (1:1). His home was Anathoth (see 1 Kgs 2:26), a short distance northeast of Jerusalem. He did not come from the capital, as Isaiah did, but from the countryside, like Amos and Micah. Does this explain Jeremiah's critical attitude to the capital and the temple (5:1; 7; 26)? Perhaps it is not an accident that the David and Zion traditions play little or no part in Jeremiah's hopes for salvation (23:5f.); for those who have been exiled "salvation" (*shalom*) is to be won even outside of Jerusalem.

Hosea received a divine command to marry, and his children became witnesses to his message of judgment (Hos 1; cf. Ezek 24:16ff.); Jeremiah, on the other hand, was to remain without a wife and children as a sign of coming disaster (16:1ff.). His mission of preaching determined the course of his life (15:17; 20:10) and even brought him treachery from his own family (11:8ff.), persecution, mistreatment, imprisonment, and abduction to Egypt. On the other hand, Jeremiah found in Baruch a helper, friend, and companion in suffering (32; 36; 43:3; 45).

In these four decades, from ca. 625 to ca. 585, Jeremiah experienced such decisive events as Josiah's centralization of the cult, the decline of Assyrian power and the rise of the Babylonians, the attempt of the Egyptians to halt this course of events, the first capture and the final destruction of Jerusalem in 587 B.C. (see §2c). In the confusion at the beginning of the exilic period Jeremiah was abducted to Egypt, where he vanished from the scene.

On the basis of the principal events it is possible to divide the ministry of Jeremiah, like that of Isaiah, into three or four period:

a) The early preaching during the reign of Josiah, from Jeremiah's call to Josiah's reform (approximately 626–622 B.C.), is contained roughly in chaps. 1–6 and ends with disheartening results (6:27ff.). The cultic abuses attacked in chap. 2 were apparently eliminated by Josiah's reform.

After this, Jeremiah, like Isaiah, is silent for more than a decade. Is it that after the reform he no longer sees any occasion for a ministry as a prophet, or is it rather that he remains aloof, either because he is waiting for the right moment or perhaps even because he rejects such a ministry? (Because of the problem at this point, Jeremiah's call has been dated by some, despite the information given in the book itself, to the time after the death of Josiah.)

Jeremiah has good relations with the supporters of the reform (compare 26:24; 36:10 with 2 Kgs 22:12), but at no point does he take an explicit position on it. King Josiah is praised not for his reform but for his dedication to social justice (22:15f.). Does the critical utterance with regard to the law of Yahweh (8:8f.) include Deuteronomy or its application (see §10a5)?

As Isaiah in his first period uttered threats against the northern kingdom, Jeremiah in his early period—when Josiah's policy of expansion turned northward?—also addressed the inhabitants of the former northern kingdom, which had been destroyed a century earlier, and promised them repentance or, in another oracle, a return to their homes and a restoration (3:12ff.; 31:2ff., 15ff.). In his announcement of salvation for the northern kingdom as well as in his criticism of the cult Jeremiah may have been influenced by Amos in his early period.

b) A large part of chaps. 7–20; 26; 35f. has its place in the reign of Jehoiakim down to the first capture of Jerusalem (ca. 608–597 B.C.).

After the short, three-month reign of Jehoahaz/Shallum (Jer 22:10ff.; 2 Kgs 23:31ff.) Jeremiah speaks out at the very beginning of Jehoiakim's reign in his discourse against the temple, in which he is probably confronting certain effects of the Josianic reform on the self-awareness of the citizens of Jerusalem. On other occasions, too, he is compelled to enter the lists against the priesthood (Jer 20; 36:5; cf., early on, 6:13; 8:8f.) as well as against the king himself (22:1f., 13ff.). The latter's attitude to the prophet can be seen in his response to the reading of Jeremiah's scroll (Jer 36) in the year 604 B.C.

The reign of Jehoiakim's successor Jehoiachin, also known as Coniah (Jer 22:24ff.), is again short, and his fate an unhappy one (2 Kgs 24:8ff.).

c) Chaps. 21–24*; 27–29; 32; 34; 37–39 relate to the reign of Zedekiah between the first and second captures of Jerusalem (ca. 597–587 B.C.).

This third period of Jeremiah's ministry is a time of serious conflicts with "false" prophets (Jer 27–29) and of persecution that reaches the point of imprisonment (37–39). But Jeremiah's relationship with the reigning king is a friendlier one; Zedekiah would like to heed the prophet's advice—to submit to the Babylonians—but has not the courage to do so (Jer 21; 27; 37f.).

d) The final brief time from the fall of Jerusalem down to the forced sojourn in Egypt (after 587 B.C.) is a distinct period in the prophet's ministry only in the sense that the circumstances are entirely new and not in the sense that there is any change in the content of his preaching (Jer 40–44).

After the Israelites dismiss Jeremiah's warning and flee to Egypt after the assassination of Gedaliah the governor, Jeremiah is bidden to tell them, on reaching Egypt, that even in the land of the Nile they are not safe from Nebuchadnezzar (43:8ff.); he is also compelled to renew his rebukes of Israel's idolatry (44).

4. Although presented as a first-person account, the story of Jeremiah's call, now part of the larger unit that is chap. 1, has undergone redactional revision at least, if indeed it has not in its entirety been given its form at a later date. How else can we explain the fact that the structure, with its objection "I am only a youth," corresponds to that of the "vocation formulary" (in Exod 3f.; Judg 6) and reminds us of what is said in Deuteronomy about a future prophet (Deut 18:18)? Jeremiah is already "known" before his birth (cf. Isa 49:1, 5; Gal 1:15) and appointed to be "a prophet to the nations"; but when he talks of himself, he, like Amos and Isaiah, does not seem to call himself a prophet but rather leaves this title for his adversaries (23:9ff.). Furthermore, his commission with regard to the nations and the description of his task as one of "tearing down and building up," which defines his preaching as a whole as a message of disaster and salvation, belong rather to his late period. His early ministry was confined to Judah and Jerusalem and probably consisted only of laments, indictments, and threats. Chap. 1, then, indicates in advance the future threats, promises, and sufferings of Jeremiah, his struggles and the strength that will be given to him.

While the first vision with its divine pledge "I am watching over my word to perform it" embraces the entire preaching of the prophet (1:11f.), the second vision, that of the boiling pot, contains the announcement of disaster for the southern kingdom: "Out of the north evil shall break forth upon all the inhabitants of the land." Here it is the "authentic" Jeremiah who speaks. In its structure, radicality, and generality this vision recalls Amos (8:1f.) and introduces a theme that Jeremiah develops with increasing fullness. The destruction from the north comes in military form (1:15) by the agency of an enemy from the north who is not named at first (Jer 4–6; especially 6:22) but who is later identified with the Babylonians (20:4ff.; etc.)—and Nebuchadnezzar is finally named. As in the earlier prophets, the foreign world power is presented as Yahweh's helper (20:4ff.; cf. 1:15; etc.), and Nebuchadnezzar is even called Yahweh's "servant" and his viceroy in the government of the world (27:6ff.; 28:14). But in the final analysis the judgment remains Yahweh's own work (9:11; 10:18; 13:26; etc.).

Accusations of social evils are not lacking in Jeremiah (5:1f., 26ff.; 6:6; 22:13ff.; cf. the citation of the Decalogue, 7:9; etc.), but at least in the prophet's early phase the charge of violation of the first and second commandments predominates (Jer 2; cf. 7:16ff.; 44; Zeph 1:4ff.;

etc.). In fact, as far as the themes of his preaching are concerned—the relationship of God and people as a marriage; the wilderness as a time of harmony before the apostasy that occurred after entry into the arable land; or the reproach of worship of foreign gods and idols, and especially the cult of Baal with its rites—Jeremiah seems to have been influenced by Hosea in the concepts he uses (to be faithless, to go whoring; to abandon or forget God), even when his formulations are independent:

> My people have committed two evils:
>   they have forsaken me,
> the fountain of living waters,
>   and hewed out cisterns for themselves,
> broken cisterns,
>   that can hold no water (2:13).

Admittedly it is not easy in regard to these themes to distinguish what is "authentically" Jeremian and what comes from the redactors. The Deuteronomic school takes over these themes and ideas, although it seems simply to be developing Jeremiah's message and to be standardizing it and applying it universally (e.g., 2:20b). Even the radicality of his insight into human guilt is something Jeremiah shares with Hosea (Hos 5:4l etc.):

> Though you wash yourself with lye
>   and use much soap,
> the stain of your guilt is still before me
>   (2:22; cf. 3:1–5; 17:1, 9; 30:12f.).

Evil has become as it were humanity's "second nature" (W. Rudolph), of which people are neither able (13:23; cf. 4:22; etc.) nor willing (6:16; 8:5; etc.) to divest themselves. Once again, inner compulsion and subjective intention, character and behavior, inability and unwillingness are interwoven. Israel's "ears are closed, they cannot listen" (6:10). This self-assertiveness seems as unnatural and absurd to Jeremiah as it did to Isaiah (1:2f.; 5:1-7):

> Can a maiden forget her ornaments,
>   or a bride her attire?
> Yet my people have forgotten me
>   days without number (2:32; cf. 2:10ff.;
>   6:10; 8:4ff.; 12:8; etc).

In vain will one look in the streets and squares of Jerusalem for "one who does justice" (5:1); not even a purification of the people would yield good results (6:27–30; cf. 9:7).

In the face of such explicit testimony, it is improbable, on the grounds of content as well as language, that the redactors are correct when in the third-person account they sum up Jeremiah's message in a call to conversion (36:3, 7; 26:3).

In the message concerning judgment the intention of leading the people to repentance is expressed only once in the metrical texts, and this particular passage (23:22b) is probably an addition (W. L. Holladay, G. Münderlein, etc.). As is already true of the earlier prophets (Isa 9:12; Hos 7:10; etc.), the call to repentance does not envisage the possibility of salvation but is meant to highlight the accusation that Israel refuses to be converted (8:4ff.; cf. 3:1; also 23:20; etc.).

This critical judgment may probably be extended to warnings generally (cf. 2:10ff., 25; 6:16; etc.); this generalization allows, of course, for the fact that there are already reservations regarding particular utterances that are probably redactional (e.g., 4:3f.). Warnings and the calls to repentance have an entirely different function when they are part of the message of salvation (see below).

In making a distinction between prophetic utterances and redaction of a prophetic book we must not forget that the redactors too can emphasize the people's lack of repentance (7:23f.; 11:8ff.; 18:11f.; 44:5, 16; etc.). To what extent, then, is the call to repentance still valid in the situation of exile? See §11b4.

5. After a period of silence and at the moment when Jehoiakim accedes to the throne, Jeremiah speaks out against the sense of security that the temple was providing, probably as a direct result of Josiah's reform (Jer 7; 26), and in the final two decades before the destruction he calls both by word and by the symbolic action of wearing a yoke (27f.) for submission to Babylonian domination. Yahweh has given the Babylonians dominion over the world, even over Egypt (43:8ff.). The criticism that Jeremiah levels at the last Judean kings (21:11ff.; 36:30f.) down to and including Zedekiah (34; 37f.) is at bottom an aspect of his message for the people as a whole (8:14ff.; 10:18ff.; 13:12ff.; 15:1ff.; 16:3ff.; 17:1ff.).

The same observation holds for Jeremiah's conflict with his enemies among the prophets, a conflict that is more intense now than it had been in an earlier time (Mic 3:5ff.). To the so-called prophets of salvation or, as they appear in retrospective judgment (in the Greek text but not yet in the Hebrew), the false prophets, Jeremiah responds with his own insight. The time for salvation and peace (8:11ff.), for favor and mercy (16:5; cf. 12:12; 30:5), and even for intercession (14:11ff.; 15:1ff.) is now past. Given this situation, a message of salvation can originate in wishful thinking, in a lie (6:13f.; 23:16ff.; 28:15f.; etc.) or in an individual's dreams, but not in the word of God (23:25ff.). "Is not my word like fire, says the Lord, and like a hammer which breaks the rock in pieces?" (23:29). While Jeremiah's opponents reject his announcement of disaster (23:17; cf. 28:2f.), he in turn challenges their authority: "I have not sent these prophets, yet they are running" (23:21 JB; cf. v. 16). The real difference between Jeremiah and his opponents is not in their ethical behavior (23:11ff.) but in their proclamation of the future. In the radicality of the threat of judgment upon the people as a whole is to be seen not indeed a criterion of truth, but at least a criterion for distinguishing between "true" and "false" prophecy. The fulfillment of the prediction about the future can only be a retrospective confirmation (to what extent is it a convincing one?).

6. A form of discourse that occurs only exceptionally in the older prophetic books holds a large place in the book of Jeremiah. Alongside the prophetic utterance to the prophet's contemporaries stands his discourse with God—in the form of a lament or complaint. Even Jeremiah's indictment and announcement of judgment can take this rhetorical form:

> My anguish, my anguish! I writhe in pain! . . .
> How long must I . . . hear the sound of the trumpet?
> (4:19ff.; 8:18ff.; 10:19ff.; 13:17; 14:17f.).

Did Jeremiah take over this genre in order to find self-expression in it? The confessions, whose genuineness is disputed, attest in austere, almost formal, language to the effect of the message on the man who is to transmit it: "I did not sit in the company of merrymakers" (15:17). External persecutions are matched by interior sufferings that lead the prophet to dispute with God and even to complain against him:

> O Lord, thou hast deceived me,
>   and I was deceived;
> thou art stronger than I,
>   and thou hast prevailed (20:7ff.).

Like his enemies (23:29; 5:14), Jeremiah must (20:9) experience the word as a "burning fire" within him. True enough, the way of conversion is offered to him (15:19ff.; cf. 4:1), but the cycle ends in darkness, as Jeremiah curses the day of his birth (20:14ff.; cf. 15:10; Job 3).

7. Admittedly, the "authenticity" of the majority of the prophecies of salvation in the book of Jeremiah (23:3ff.; 30f.; etc.) is disputed, but there is also a firm basis (29; 32) for saying that this prophet too, like Hosea, for example, or Isaiah, knew a hope of salvation. Probably while still in his early period, the age of Josiah, Jeremiah turned to

the inhabitants of the northern kingdom that had been destroyed about a hundred years before:

> Return (or: return home), faithless Israel. . . .
> I will not (any longer) look on you in anger,
> for I am merciful, says the Lord (3:12f.;
> at greater length in 31:2ff., 15ff.).

This new salvation is unconditional and has its basis in the nature of God or even in a change in God (cf. Hos 11:8f.; Jer 3:22; 31:3, 18–20). In the context of this promise the call to repentance acquires a new meaning. It does not confront human beings with a choice between good and evil but calls upon them to accept the gracious love of God.

Just as in his message for the northern kingdom Jeremiah promises salvation to those who have experienced disaster, so too he announces salvation for Judah/Jerusalem only in and after their passing through judgment. Yahweh looks with kindness on those who have been dragged off to Babylon and not on those who (in 597) remained behind in Jerusalem (Jer 24). But the exiles must remain far from home for two or three generations, or about seventy years; Jeremiah urges them to settle down with this in mind and to pray for the welfare of the great foreign power that now controls them. Those now alive will not see their homeland again, but they do have "a future and a hope" that is, as it were, a glimpse of what will come to pass (29:5–7, 10f.; cf. 27:7). In the same quiet way Jeremiah's purchase of a field at Anathoth during the siege of Jerusalem by the Babylonians serves as a promise of new life after the destruction: "Houses and fields and vineyards shall again be bought in this land" (32:15; cf. 31:5; 33:12f.; also the promises to individuals, 39:17f.; 45:5; 35:19).

In contrast, the messianic promise of a "righteous Branch" (23:5f.) is colorless, even in comparison with the promises in the book of Isaiah with which Jeremiah's is connected. In any case, the Davidic tradition was not of decisive importance for Jeremiah.

The saying about the "new covenant" (31:31ff.; cf. 32:27ff.), which was to have such an important subsequent history (1 Cor 11:25; etc.; see §1a), is hardly from Jeremiah himself, but its contrast between Israel's sinful violation of the covenant and God's new institution of one does reflect a preaching that is at bottom that of the prophet. The realization of unalterable human wickedness (Jer 13:23; etc.) leads to a hope that God will infuse his will into the human heart and thus make it possible for all to obey freely and in this way come to knowledge of God (cf. 24:7).

§20

EZEKIEL

1. Redaction-historical problems no less serious than those in the book of Jeremiah are also to be found in the book of the prophet Ezekiel, although they are of a different character. All sorts of evidence—the breadth of the presentation, the reprise of themes, certain unevennesses despite similarities in language, and recognizable stages of growth— all suggest that an (anonymous) "school" not only gathered and combined existing utterances of the prophet but also interpreted them, developed them, gave them a new form, or, in short, "continued to write" Ezekiel.

Any interpretation "must come to grips with the realization that the utterances of the prophet have been distilled into a prophetic book through the mediation of a school which transmitted them. The work of the school is not to be seen solely in the formal redaction and fitting together of the transmitted material. Rather it reshaped the existing utterances, although in degrees that varied from saying to saying" (W. Zimmerli, *Ezechiel*, 1972, p. 21).

The strikingly uniform style of the book makes it difficult to distinguish between traditional material and secondary revision. Ezekiel was, of course, not (only) a writer but also a man who like his predecessors played a public role with his sayings and his symbolic actions (Ezek 4f.; 12; 21; 24; 37). But to what extent was his message preserved and simply clarified in its content, and to what extent was it altered? Where is the authentic preaching of the prophet really to be seen? Are we to ascribe to Ezekiel only such utterances as take a more or less rhythmical form, or did he speak in prose as well? How far can we trust the first-person form the book takes almost throughout, which had not been used to such an extent in the earlier writing prophets? How far can we give credence to the precise dates interspersed through the book (from 1:2 to 40:1), which anticipate the datings in the books of Haggai and Zechariah?

Scholars have been torn between trust and skepticism. The latter has once again become common as a result of the criticism of G. Hölscher. Hölscher understood this prophetic book—essentially on

247

the basis of the difference between the poetic texts and the prose texts—to be "a work created by many levels of redaction, with the visions and poems of the prophet Ezekiel providing only a nucleus" (1924, p. 26).

2. According to the information given in the book, Ezekiel, the son of Buzi, was among those deported to Babylon by Nebuchadnezzar in 597 B.C. Those deported included not only King Johoiachin and his entourage but also members of the upper class and of the artisan class (2 Kgs 24:10ff.). Ezekiel was part of a group that settled at Tel Abib (Hebrew: "Hill of the ear [of grain]"; Babylonian: "Hill of the flood") by the river or canal named Chebar, which was probably near Nippur. There, in the fifth year after the banishment of King Johoiachin (593 B.C.), the prophet received his call (1:1–3; 3:15). The substance of the oracles of judgment against the capital, Jerusalem, and the land of Israel (chaps. 4–24; cf. 8:1; 20:1; 24:1) belongs to the few years between this call and the destruction of Jerusalem in 587/586, of which Ezekiel in his distant exile learns from one of those who had "escaped" from the catastrophe (33:21f.). The final part of this short period is given as the date also for most of the oracles against the foreign nations (chaps. 26–32), and the vision of the new temple is said to have come to the prophet a decade later, in 573 B.C. (40:1; cf. 29:17). The chronology given allows us to assume at least that the threats have their origin in the period before the fall of the city in 587 B.C., and the oracles of salvation probably originated only after that date.

The vision of the temple in Jerusalem (chaps. 8–11) has given rise to the question whether Ezekiel may not also have exercised a ministry in Palestine. But the vision (according to 8:3; 11:24) comes in a rapture caused by the spirit of God, and insofar as the information about the situation in Jerusalem did not come from an earlier period (with a blurring of the time span?), it may have reached the prophet through the reports of messengers (see Jer 29).

As celibacy had a symbolic significance for Jeremiah (16:2ff.), so too the sudden death of Ezekiel's wife seems to have taken on symbolic meaning for him (24:15ff.), as a representation of the reaction of Israel to the destruction of Jerusalem: "You shall not mourn or weep!" Elsewhere too Ezekiel's personal experience, which even takes at times a physical form—trembling, being stunned, being rendered dumb, and being bound (3:15, 22ff.; 4:4ff.; 6:11; 12:17ff.; 21:6f.; 33:21f.; etc.)— plays a part in the form and intention of his preaching, and especially in the announcement of judgment, so that these striking phenomena can hardly be taken as symptoms of illness.

3. The book of Ezekiel is different in a number of ways from the earlier prophetic books. It is made up less of collections of short, independent sayings than of more extended compositions, each of

which gives broad development to a theme. Some of the characteristics are the following:

a) In comparison with earlier prophecy the visions are so voluminous (1–3; 8–11; 37; 40–48) that they give us a foretaste of the importance visions will have in apocalyptic literature. Ezekiel can play a part in the visionary event not only as an intercessor (9:8; 11:13) but also as one who prophesies and acts (11:4; 37:4ff.; cf. 4:14; 20:49).

b) The extended figurative discourses (allegories) may describe the same material but with different nuances and intentions: the image of the one unfaithful wife or the two unfaithful wives (16; 23), of the vine (15; 17; 19:10ff.), of the fire (22:17ff.; 24). The various images (e.g., the vine and the eagle in 17) may be combined, as may image and interpretation.

c) The detailed historical retrospects, using representative figures (16, Jerusalem; 23, the two kingdoms) or dispensing with them (20), embrace the whole of Israel's history from its disreputable beginnings (16:2; 20:7f.; 23:3) onward. These retrospects with their complaints and threats show uncommon critical acumen as they bring the past before the eyes of the prophet's contemporaries.

d) There are certain more or less typical phrases, such as the recognition formula "(You—sing. or pl.—shall . . .) know that I am the Lord" (6:7, 13; etc.), which the prophet likes to use in concluding an announcement of an action of Yahweh (W. Zimmerli: a proof-saying); the instruction that introduces an "expressive action," "Set your face toward . . ." (6:2; 20:46; 21:2; 38:2; etc.); the divine self-assertion that consistently comes toward the end of a speech to emphasize the validation or realization of what is said, "I, the Lord, have spoken—and I will do it" (5:15, 17; 17:24; 37:14; etc.; cf. 12:25ff.); or, above all, God's manner of addressing the prophet as "son of man," in the sense of man, "individual person," "creature" (2:1; and frequently).

e) Ezekiel likes to take prophetic traditions and inflect them in a new way. On the one hand, he revives ideas that are known to us from the traditions of the prewriting prophets but play an unimportant role in the writing prophets—for example, the idea of being seized by the "hand" of Yahweh (Ezek 1:3; 8:1; 37:1; 40:1; etc.; cf. 1 Kgs 18:46) or by the "spirit" who transports the prophet (3:12ff.; 8:3; etc.; cf. 2 Kgs 2:16; 5:26); or the custom whereby the elders sit with Ezekiel in his home (8:1; 14:1; 20:1; cf. 2 Kgs 6:32). On the other hand, the preaching (compare Ezek 7 with Amos 8:2) and images (compare Ezek 16 and 23 with Hos 2 and Jer 3) are in continuity with the themes of the earlier writing prophets, especially Jeremiah.

f) The fact that Ezekiel himself was a priest or at least the son of a priest (1:3) explains not only his interest in the temple and its layout (especially 8; cf. 40ff.) but also the similarity, surprising when compared with the earlier writing prophets, between his language and that of the Priestly document, especially the Law of Holiness (Lev 17–26).

4. In the composition of the book of Ezekiel the tripartite division—disaster for the prophet's own people (1–24), for foreign nations (25–32), and salvation (33–48)—is maintained with uncommon strictness, although there are some exceptions. Oracles of salvation are occasionally attached to, or introduced into, announcements of judgment (11:14ff.; 17:22ff.; 20:32ff.; etc.), and conversely the promise of a true shepherd begins with a "Woe!" (34; cf. Jer 23). More particularly, it is characteristic of the book's structure that symbolic actions (4f.; 12; 37:15ff.) often follow upon reports of visions (1–3; 8–11; 37), and that a chronological order is followed throughout chaps. 1–24, 29–32.

I. Ezek 1–24		Oracles of judgment against Judah and Jerusalem
1–3		Vision of the "throne-chariot" or "chariot of Yahweh" (1) with an audition and a symbolic reception of the word (eating of a scroll) (2f.)
	3:16ff.	Appointment as a sentry (cf. 33:1ff.; Jer 6:17)
4f.		Three symbolic actions (introduced by 3:22ff.) meant to depict the siege of Jerusalem
	4:1f., 3	Siege of a brick on which a picture of the city is scratched
	4:9ff.	Rationing of bread (made of several ingredients) and water as a sign of the scarcity of food (cf. Jer 37:21)
	5:1f., 3f.	Cutting off of the prophet's hair: a third is to be burnt, a third cut to pieces, a third scattered (cf. Isa 7:20)
	4:4–8, 12ff.	Insertion: further symbolic actions—carrying of guilt and baking of bread—as a representation of the situation in exile
	5:5ff.	Judgment upon Jerusalem as center of the nations (cf. 38:12)
6		Against the mountains (and valleys) of Israel Destruction and pollution of the altars (cultic high places)
7		The day of the end (cf. Amos 8:2)
8–11		Vision of Jerusalem's sin and judgment
	8	The prophet taken in a rapture to Jerusalem. Four abominations: unclean or alien cults, such as idolatry, cult of Tammuz, cult of the sun
	9–11	Judgment
	9	Six angels to punish, one to write
	10	Burning of the city. The chariot of the cherubs (cf. chap. 1)

II. Ezek 25–32   Sayings about (seven) foreign nations (cf. Amos 1f.; Jer 46ff.; etc.)

      25   Against Ammon, Moab, Edom (cf. chap. 35), the Philistines

     26–28   Against Tyre (which, however, was not conquered by Nebuchadnezzar; cf. 29:18)

As earlier in 19, the text in 26:15ff.; 27; 28:11ff.; 32 takes the form of a lament. Mythical traditions echo in 28–32; 47

      27   Lament over Tyre, which is depicted as a ship

      28:1ff.   Fall of a heavenly being into hell (cf. Isa 14; Ezek 31:14ff.; 32:17ff.)

      28:11ff.   Lament. The king as primal human ejected from the garden of God (cf. Gen 3)

      28:20ff.   Against Sidon; promise to Israel

     29–32   Against Egypt (cf. 17:7ff., 15ff.)

Pharaoh as a crocodile (29; 32) and as a world-spanning cedar (31; cf. Dan 4)

III. Ezek 33–39   Oracles of salvation

Chap. 33, with its correspondences to chap. 1–24, marks the turn from a message of disaster to a message of salvation

     33   Appointment as a sentry (cf. 3:16ff.)

      Vv. 10ff.   Preaching of conversion: the just and the unjust (cf. chap. 18)

      Vv. 21f.   News of the fall of Jerusalem (cf. 3:26f.; 24:25ff.)

      Vv. 23ff.   Against the sense of confidence of those who have remained behind in the homeland and of the exiles (vv. 30ff.)

     34   The evil shepherds of Israel (vv. 1–10) and the true shepherd, namely, God (vv. 11ff.) and his servant David (vv. 23f.; 37:22ff.; cf. Jer 23)

      Vv. 25ff.   A covenant of peace

   35–36:15 Judgment on Seir/Edom (because of its behavior during and after the fall of Jerusalem; cf. Obadiah; Isa 34; 63), and salvation for the mountains of Israel (cf. chap. 6). Against enemy claims to the country

    36:16ff. Purification of Israel. A new heart, a new spirit (vv. 26f.; 11:16ff.)

     37   Vision of the restoration of life to the bones: new life and the homecoming of the people

      Vv. 15ff.   Symbolic action: joining of two sticks with "Judah" written on the one and "Joseph" on the other as a figure of the reunification of the northern and southern kingdoms

     38f.   Attack from the north (cf. Jer 4–6) under Gog of Magog, prince of Meshech and Tubal. His utter destruction. Securing of the country

5. In his call vision Ezekiel sees a fiery cloud coming from the north and, emerging from it, four four-winged creatures (each with four faces—a man, a lion, an ox, and an eagle), who carry a crystal-like vault above their heads. Upon the vault there is a gleaming figure, "a likeness as it were of a human form," upon a throne. This was "the appearance of the likeness of the glory of the Lord" (1:5ff., 22ff., especially 28; see §13b2). God's throne, which since the time of David and Solomon had been firmly fixed on Zion, becomes mobile, having wheels, as it were (1:15ff., in a more recent stratum; cf. 10:9ff.), and makes its appearance in a distant, unclean land (4:13; 11:15). The vision leads to a commission: "Son of man, I send you to the people of Israel" (2:3). Like the earlier prophets, Ezekiel is sent to Israel as a whole, and the reaction of the latter to the message is anticipated to be no more favorable than that of their predecessors: "Whether they hear or refuse to hear (for they are a rebellious house) they will know that there has been a prophet among them" (2:5; cf. 33:33). Thus the "house of Israel" is regarded as fully responsible for its being a "rebellious house," but the prediction is already made that only in retrospect will it recognize the fact. In order that he may resist the opposition of those who "are not willing to listen" Ezekiel's forehead is made like adamant (3:5ff.; cf. 2:6ff.; 12:2ff.; etc.). The inaugural vision is reminiscent of Isaiah's (Isa 6), but the promise of steadfastness amid all attacks goes beyond even Jer 1 (vv. 17ff.). In addition, the symbolic reception of the word turns an image of Jeremiah (15:16; cf. 1:9) into a visionary experience. Ezekiel must eat a scroll that on both sides has "written on it words of lamentation and mourning and woe," and it tastes as sweet as honey to him (2:8–3:3).

6. The writing on the scroll anticipates indirectly the theme of chaps. 4–24 and directly the effect which the future that is to be announced will have on the hearers. Thus in the final years before the catastrophe Ezekiel harks back to the harsh message of judgment that the earlier writing prophets had proclaimed; he gives it a more critical

form and at times even exaggerates it. In ever new variations—in vision (8–11), symbolic actions (4f.; 12; 21:19ff.; 24:15ff.), and sayings— Ezekiel gives notice of the "end" to the country and to the city of Jerusalem (chap. 7):

> Woe to the bloody city! (24:9).
> Like the wood of the vine among the trees of the forest,
> which I have given to the fire for fuel,
> so will I give up the inhabitants of Jerusalem (15:6).

The temple, from which the glory of God departs (10:18f.; 11:23f.), is not spared: "Behold, I will profane my sanctuary" (24:21). Like Jeremiah and like Isaiah even earlier, Ezekiel takes a firm position (17; 23; 29ff.) against the temptation of entering into a treaty with Egypt in order to escape the judgment that will be executed by the Babylonians (especially 21:18ff.).

The indictment against Israel lists cultic (6; 8; 13f.; 43:7ff.) and social accusations (22; 34) but also accusations in the area of foreign policy (17). Israel in its entirety is guilty (16; 23; 22:23ff.; etc.); the coming judgment of God comes upon all:

> Shame is upon all faces,
> and baldness on all their heads (7:18).
>
> I will cut off from you both righteous and wicked (21:3).

Though the irrevocability of the judgment and the fact that no remnant is spared are consistently preached (9:8ff.; 11:13; 15; 20:47; 21:1; 22; 24; etc.), there are also contradictions, especially in the vision of chap. 9. Here it is said that anyone who receives from a (priestly) scribe a mark (in the form of a cross?) on the forehead is protected against being killed by the six destroying angels and thus is protected against judgment (see also 5:3; etc.). Is not this scene reminiscent of the apotropaic rite of the Passover blood (Exod 12:23ff.) and also of the baptismal action performed centuries later by John the Baptist, with its promise of salvation from judgment? In any case, such a scene implies an individualization, inasmuch as individuals are exempted from the judgment that threatens the group as a whole.

Judgment is to follow shortly: "The time has come, the day is near" (7:7). As in the book of Isaiah (5:19), so here in the book of Ezekiel there is a hint of the mockery that this expectation elicited from the prophet's hearers (12:21ff.).

7. According to the description given in the book and deliberately emphasized by the redactors, the news of the fall of Jerusalem, "The city has fallen" (33:21f.; cf. 3:25ff.; 24:25ff.), not only confirms Ezekiel's message of judgment but also leads to a complete change in his

preaching. On the other hand, the "authenticity" of the message of salvation is even more disputed than that of other sayings; authentic oracles of salvation are most likely to be found in the visionary and symbolic actions of chap. 37.

In the overall structure of the book announcements of disaster and announcements of salvation correspond. To the departure of God from his sanctuary (8–11) corresponds his return to it (40–48; and compare 6 with 36). Since the indictment emphasizes the deep-rooted guilt of Israel, the promise of salvation cannot be based on the behavior and character of the people; instead, the prophet expects new life from a new creative act of God (see 36:21).

The hopelessness of the exiles—"Our bones are dried up, and our hope is lost" (37:11; cf. 33:10; Isa 49:14)—is countered by the vision of the revitalization of the bones: "Behold, I will cause breath to enter you" (Ezek 37; cf. Gen 2:7). This new creation, restoration of life to the field of bones, and opening of the graves symbolize rebirth and liberation or, more specifically, the return of the people to their homeland. In the immediately ensuing symbolic action of joining of the two sticks, there is added the hope of a reunion of Judah and Israel (37:15ff.; cf. Hos 1:10–2:1).

The exodus (20; 23) and Jerusalem traditions, which in (for example) Hosea and Isaiah respectively live on in separation, are reunited in the book of Ezekiel. But the expectation of a new David as the just "prince" (34:23f.; 37:24f.; cf. 17:22ff.) probably occurs first in the more recent strata of the book. This person takes over God's role (34:10ff.) as the one true shepherd. Just as God himself appoints his servant David and makes the covenant of peace (34:25ff.; 37:26), so too he makes people obedient, renews them interiorly, and turns them into truly human beings:

> A new heart I will give you,
> and a new spirit I will put within you;
> and I will take out of your flesh the heart of stone
> and give you a heart of flesh (36:26;
>   cf. 11:19; 18:31; Jer 24:7; 31:33).

The understanding that God himself dwells among his people (37:26f.; cf. Zech 2:10) is developed in this ever-broadening vision of the new sanctuary and of its layout and buildings (40–48; especially 43).

8. Chaps. 3:17–21; 18; 33:1–20, and 14:1–20, with their orientation toward the individual, their offer of conversion, and their inclusion of

legal aspects, are notably alike in a way that more or less binds them together and isolates them from their context. Is their origin in Ezekiel to be simply denied (H. Schulz), or on the contrary do they belong to the later phase of his preaching, after 587 B.C.?

The book of Ezekiel introduces the announcement of salvation with a kind of second call to the prophet (33:1–9; anticipated in 3:17ff.). The office of prophet is expanded to include that of sentry or lookout (cf. Jer 6:17), whose duty it is to warn of danger so that the wicked may change their ways and be saved. The responsibility of a prophet who wishes to be true to his calling for the actions and destiny of his hearers is thus limited and transferred to the hearers themselves. The message of disaster (see Ezek 15; 2:5ff.; etc.) hardly leaves room for such a conversion of the individual. Does the possibility of conversion, which is so fully developed in chap. 18, derive only from the promise of salvation?

The bitter proverb "The fathers have eaten sour grapes, and the children's teeth are set on edge" (18:2; cf. Jer 31:29) captures the frame of mind of those whom disaster has already struck: "The way of the Lord is not just" (Ezek 18:25ff.; 33:17ff.). The citation seems not only to sum up Israel's historical experience but at the same time to reflect the prophet's (earlier) message of judgment, which binds the generations together in guilt and saddles them with it. Now Ezek 18 takes a different view. Accepting legal traditions that are reflected in the liturgy for entry into the temple (Pss 15; 24:3ff.), it emphasizes the responsibility of each new generation and even of each individual and thus opens up the possibility of new life: "Have I any pleasure in the death of the wicked, says the Lord God, and not rather that he should turn from his way and live?" (18:23; cf. 33:10ff.; 14:6).

The responsibility of each individual for his or her own life is here made possible in a measure still unknown to the earlier prophets; it is accepted, however, by the later prophets of salvation (Isa 55:7; 44:5; etc.).

§21

SECOND ISAIAH AND THIRD ISAIAH

1. In Isa 40–55 a different author speaks in a situation completely changed by comparison with that of chaps. 1–39, although the time is barely two centuries later (see §16,1). This author does not announce judgment; for him judgment is an accomplished fact. Jerusalem has been destroyed (44:26; 51:3; etc.); the people he addresses live under oppression (42:22; etc.) and in exile. He looks for the fall of Babylon (43:14; 46f.) and the rise to power of Cyrus the Persian (44:26f.; etc.).

Since Isa 40–55 contains no superscriptions with indications of place and time, we can only infer the place (Babylon, hardly Palestine) and the period of Second Isaiah's ministry. Whether accidentally or—as is more likely—deliberately, these chapters, like other documents from the final period of prophetic activity (Isa 56–66; 24–27), remain anonymous.

Within the overall structure of the book of Isaiah, chaps. 40ff. promise forgiveness after the indictment and announcement of judgment recorded in chaps. 1ff. Is there an antecedent connection between the two parts insofar as Second Isaiah links his message to that of Isaiah? In any case, Isa 40 is reminiscent of Isa 6 (or 43:8ff. of 6:9f.), and both prophets have in common the use of "Holy One of Israel" as a description of God (41:14, 16; etc.), the criticism of the sacrificial cult (43:22ff.), the Zion tradition, and other points.

Ezekiel's ministry was exercised in the early part of the exilic period; that of Second Isaiah in the final part, approximately 550–540 B.C. Cyrus's swift victory over Croesus, the king of Lydia (546) may be reflected in the texts (41:2f., 25; 45:1ff.), but not the capture of Babylon in 539 B.C. The prophet predicts the destruction of Babylon and the destruction of its gods (46f.; cf. 21:9), but as a matter of fact Cyrus entered in triumph and, as part of his policy of religious toleration in dealing with subject peoples, he preserved or restored the cult practiced in Babylon.

2. Second Isaiah speaks to the victims of the catastrophe, "all the

257

remnant of the house of Israel" (46:3), and opposes the hopelessness and despair of his contemporaries, who complain, "The Lord has forsaken me" (49:14; 40:27; cf. 45:15, "a God who hides thyself"). In this situation, Second Isaiah understandably does not use the pattern of discourse that was so important for the preexilic prophets of judgment, namely, the announcement of disaster with a justificatory proof of guilt, although Second Isaiah may in fact take over and repeat certain complaints of his predecessors. The criticism of the sacrificial cult (43:22ff.) shows that it is the people, and not Yahweh, who are responsible. But the people remain "blind" and "deaf" (42:18ff.; 43:8; cf. 6:9f.; Jer 5:21; Ezek 12:2) and are no more open to Second Isaiah's message of consolation than they had been to his predecessors' announcements of judgment. Thus, the contradiction between prophetic word and present reality is no less than it had been in the time of the prophets of judgment. And if the Servant songs (especially Isa 53) are to be interpreted as autobiography, Second Isaiah even suffered persecution and death.

Second Isaiah does occasionally use forms of discourse found in the earlier writing prophets, for example, the report of a vision or audition (40) or the exhortation, but even then the emphasis has been radically altered. The decisive genres used are "nonprophetic in origin" (J. Begrich).

a) The "oracle of salvation," which originally was a word of encouragement from a priest to an individual in distress and a promise that his prayer would be heard (see 1 Sam 1:17; Gen 21:17; Lam 3:57; see §25,4b), is transferred by Second Isaiah to the people as a whole: "Now, Israel, fear not!" God, speaking in the first person, addresses the recipient by name and calls for fearlessness. Then, in the perfect tense, comes the announcement of salvation proper, "I have redeemed you," which is spelled out in a set of consequences: "When you pass through the waters I will be with you." The preferred ending for a given unit consists in a statement of the purpose and goal of the divine intervention (Isa 43:1–7; 41:8–13; 14–16; also 44:1–5; etc.). Usually through indirect allusions but occasionally in an explicit way (cf. 49:14; 51:9ff.) the oracle of salvation is related to a preceding complaint of the people. Did Second Isaiah even pronounce his oracles during the liturgy, in the midst of communal lamentations (Zech 7; 8:19) (H. E. von Waldow)? But the freedom shown in the forms of discourse is an argument against the view that the prophetic proclamation was connected with the liturgy.

C. Westermann gives the name "announcement of salvation" to such texts as Isa 41:17–20; 42:14–17; and 43:16–21, and he distinguishes them from oracles of salvation (or promises of salvation). The texts in question lack the direct personal address and the exhortation to fearlessness, and they use the future, not the perfect tense. But since only the oracle of salvation has a complete structure and originally, a special life setting of its own (the liturgy), we must consider the texts in question to be prophetic variants and modifications of the basic form, which is the oracle of salvation.

b) In the "disputation," which had been used by the earlier writing prophets (Amos 3:3–6, 8; Jer 13:23; see §13b3d) but is now extensively developed, Second Isaiah endeavors to defend himself against reproaches—which are usually not stated and must be inferred. This exilic prophet defends the legitimacy and necessity of his preaching on the grounds that he is giving relevance to neglected or forgotten truths of faith and interpreting and developing the basic truth in the form of consequences: "They who wait for the Lord shall renew their strength" (Isa 40:27–31, 12–17, 21–24; 46:5ff.; etc.). Characteristic of this genre are questions (simply rhetorical and imaginary, or real and actual?), linguistic components of a wisdom kind, as well as hymnic participles that focus on praise of Yahweh's creative power, his uniqueness, and the trustworthiness of his word.

c) In the "judgment-speeches" Second Isaiah imitates the secular (rather than cultic) legal proceedings conducted at the gate by the elders of the village. The numerous forms of discourse in use there, such as the call for judgment (43:22ff.) or the speech to the court (44:6ff.), are reflected in the preaching of Second Isaiah. As far as content is concerned, we must distinguish between Yahweh's defense against accusations by Israel (43:22–28; cf. 50:1–3) and the more frequent dispute between Yahweh and the nations or their gods (41:1–5, 21–29; 43:8–13; 44:6-8), which is specific to Second Isaiah. In this second case is the prophet giving historical actualization to mythical representations of a court attended by the gods?

d) Finally, there are "eschatological hymns" (see §25,4a) that summon the entire world to join even now in joyous praise of God's future salvation, which is already becoming a reality (42:10–13; 44:23; 45:8; 48:20f.; 52:9f.). These short hymns of praise sometimes seem to play a role in the structuring of the book (C. Westermann), since they may serve to bring a lengthier composition to an end (this is obvious in 44:23).

If the combination of smaller units into larger ones (as can already be seen in Isa 40:12–31) is the work of Second Isaiah himself, we may ask whether he intended from the outset to create rather lengthy literary compositions and whether he also (or perhaps even exclusively) exercised his ministry in writing? Or was it rather the case that when the prophet's words were written down redactors played a part in shaping the message? A profession of faith in the efficacy of God's word (40:8; 55:10f., along with a promise of a return of the exiles, 40:10f.; 55:12f.) serves to frame the book. Scholars also like to contrast chaps. 40–48, in which Cyrus plays a role, with chaps. 49–55, which announce the coming of salvation in a more general form; but the two parts are connected by the Servant songs, the hope of a return to Zion, and other elements. The command "Cry!" (40:6), the citations of the hearers' words (40:27; etc.), the units that are more or less clearly distinguishable both formally and materially, and the strict poetic and rhythmic structure that once again catches the eye in comparison with the book of Ezekiel—all these are indications that even Isa 40–55 is based on oral individual sayings that were subsequently organized and formed into thematically distinct and kerygmatically oriented units. In addition, we must take into account various additions among which all the attacks on idols (see below) must be numbered.

As we survey 40–55 only a few focal points catch our attention:

40	Prologue. Call "vision" (vv. 1–8, 9–11)
	God's uniqueness. Disputation sayings (vv. 12–31)
41:8ff.; 51	Abraham
44	Outpouring of the Spirit (vv. 1–5). Attack on idols (vv. 9ff.)
41; 44:24ff.; 45:1–7	Cyrus
46f.	Fall of Babylon. 47: taunt-song
42; 49; 50; 53	Servant songs
51:9ff.	"Awake . . . O arm of the Lord." Complaint and God's answer
52:7–10	Eschatological enthronement song (cf. Pss 47; 93; 96–99)
54	Covenant with Noah (vv. 9f.)
55	Promise to David (vv. 3ff.). Epilogue
	"My thoughts are not your thoughts"

3. The book begins with a vision that is surprisingly like the one in Isa 6, and probably has a corresponding function—the call of the prophet to his office—but a very different intention. In any case, the "vision" takes the form solely of hearing; nothing is seen, but the prophet hears what on earth is still unknowable. Like Isaiah, Second Isaiah is allowed to be present at the council of God; he hears voices calling to one another and learns how God commissions his heavenly messengers:

> Comfort, comfort my people,
>   says your God.
> Speak tenderly to Jerusalem,
>   and cry to her
> that her warfare is ended,
>   that her iniquity is pardoned (40:1f.).

God himself announces a new age, the end of the time of service and suffering. The turning point for the exiles, the shift from judgment to salvation, is made clear even in details of language: "Your God" speaks (again) to "my people." The repeated exhortation ("comfort, comfort") is intended to attract, encourage, and console (see 49:13; 51:12; etc.). The weary are given a new hope—hope in a future—and the form of that hope seems to take into account from the start that the hearers will remain skeptical and be reluctant to accept it. For it is not humans but the inhabitants of heaven who are exhorted: "In the wilderness prepare the way of the Lord." And the highway for which the uneven ground is to become level is meant in the first instance for God himself. On it he will reveal his glory, and he will draw the exiles after him as his retinue.

The conversation in heaven leads to an act of commissioning: "Cry!" When the prophet asks "What shall I cry?" he is given the answer "All flesh is grass." The insight into human transiency (which was later applied in v. 7 to the people as such) is certainly to be taken not as an objection by the prophet but as the answer to his question. Only then does this third individual scene (40:6–8) have a concrete reference instead of being universal and timeless. It refers to the limitations and termination of the power of the oppressor (51:12f.; 40:24; 41:11f.), just as the pledge that "the word of our God will stand for ever" (see 44:26; 45:19; earlier, Jer 1:11f.; Isa 9:8; etc.) confirms the permanence and purposefulness of the consoling words just spoken. There could be no clearer way than this scene in heaven of showing that the promise of salvation is based not on the behavior of its recipients but on a change in God himself (43:25; 48:9ff.).

4. The themes introduced in the audition in Isa 40 are continued by the prophet in his message concerning the "redemption" of Israel (43:1, 14; etc.). "The Lord has redeemed his servant Jacob!" sounds almost like a new profession of faith (48:20; 44:23). The deliverance from Babylon takes the form of an exodus that proceeds unhindered and amidst the rejoicing of nature (41:17ff.; 42:16; 43:19f.; 49:9ff.; 55:12f.; etc.). This "second exodus"—to which Hosea (2) and Ezekiel (20) also looked forward, though in a more restrained way—will far surpass the first exodus (compare Isa 52:12; 48:21 with Exod 12:11; 17:5f.; etc.). Yahweh himself will conduct Israel (Isa 52:12; 40:10f.) and bring it to Zion. The prophet sees this event so palpably close that he has the messenger already announcing God's arrival—"Behold your God!"—and proclaiming his kingship, "Your God reigns" (52:7, in dependence on the tradition embodied in the enthronement psalms 47:8; 93:1).

The purpose of the exodus, then, is the return to Jerusalem and the

rebuilding of the destroyed city (49:16f.; 51:3, 11; 54:11ff.; etc.) but
also of the temple (44:26, 28; cf. 52:11). Here, in the place of God's
rule, is the dwelling of his community (cf. 52:1). But the city will no
longer be big enough (54:1ff.; cf. Zech 2), for the throng of returnees
is joined by all the "offspring" who are gathered together from the
four corners of the earth (43:5f.) and are even brought by the nations
themselves (49:22f.; in harsher terms, 45:14; 49:26).

By and large the patriarchal tradition had no importance for the writing
prophets. Hosea (12) appeals to the Jacob tradition only for polemical purposes,
as a proof of guilt; this is echoed in Second Isaiah (43:27). On the other hand,
Second Isaiah can console his hearers by reminding them of the promise to
Abraham (41:8f.; 51:1f.) and can address the exiles themselves not only as
Zion-Jerusalem (40:2; 49:14; etc.) but as Jacob-Israel (44:1–5; etc.). Reference
is even made to the tradition of God's "covenant of peace" with Noah after
the flood as a way of rendering vivid the extent of the change: "My steadfast
love shall not (again) depart from you" (54:9).

In this notion of the "everlasting covenant" with Noah (Gen 9) or in that
of the manifestation of the "glory of Yahweh" in the wilderness (Exod 16), as
well as in statements about creation and in other points, there are links
between the exilic prophets and the Priestly document, which is approximately
contemporary as a document although it deals with the distant past (see A.
Eitz).

The inclusion of this concept of "glory," the expectation of a second exodus
and of Yahweh's return to Jerusalem are some of the points of contact between
Second Isaiah and the somewhat earlier prophet Ezekiel (cf. D. Baltzer).

While Second Isaiah's message of consolation is already made
concrete in the expectation of the return, the gathering of the people,
and the rebuilding of Jerusalem, it is also repeatedly actualized. Just
as the earlier prophets saw the Assyrians or the Babylonians as
Yahweh's instruments of judgment, and as Jeremiah could even
describe Nebuchadnezzar as Yahweh's "servant" (Jer 25:9; etc.), so too
Second Isaiah regards the Persian king Cyrus as Yahweh's "shepherd"
(44:28) and even as his "anointed" (messiah, 45:1; cf. 48:14). It is no
longer Israel's own kings but Cyrus who exercises dominion at
Yahweh's bidding (41:25). Accordingly, Cyrus does not have independent significance in the strict sense, but receives his mission of
conquering Babylon and liberating the exiles only as part of Yahweh's
larger work of salvation, "He shall fulfill my purpose (44:28, in a self-
description of Yahweh, vv. 24ff.; cf. 41:2ff., 25ff.; 45:13; 46:11; etc.).
The "political" is, as it were, one sector within the "theological,"
within a faith and hope that are related to history. In the final analysis,
it is Yahweh himself who wins the victory (42:13; 49:24f.; etc.).

5. Second Isaiah also comes to grips with alien faiths in his defense
of the promise of salvation that he proclaims even amid an exile in

which the power and splendor of the Babylonian divinities (see 46:1) are so impressively manifested. Most of the judgment speeches are concerned with the challenge, Who is truly God? The criterion of truth—and here we perceive the influence of the preexilic prophets and of the fulfillment of their announcements of judgment—is the efficacious word, the correct announcement of times, of what is already past and what is still to come:

> Let them [the gods] bring them [their proofs]
>   and tell us what is to happen.
> Tell us the former things, what they are,
>   that we may consider them,
> that we may know their outcome;
>   or declare to us the things to come.
> Tell us what is to come hereafter,
>   that we know that you are gods (41:22f.; cf. v. 26).

The gods are silent, they do nothing, they are nothing (41:24, 29; etc.). The meaning here is hardly that in virtue of a consistent "monotheism" the existence of the gods is simply being denied. There is rather a denial of their power and ability to direct and predetermine the course of history. Prophecy (cf. 44:25f.) thus becomes a kind of proof for Yahweh as true God.

In this kind of polemic Second Isaiah is actualizing the first commandment ("My glory I give to no other," 42:8; 48:11). The second commandment comes into play in the prophet's mockery of idols made by human hands (40:19f.; 41:6f.; 44:9ff.; etc.). But these descriptions of the making of idols, like the similar polemical passages in the earlier prophetic books (Isa 2:8; 17:8; Jer 10; etc.), are probably to be regarded as later insertions. In them the Yahwistic faith uses a contrasting alien religion, which is even reduced to a caricature, in order to bring out its own special character and superiority and to profess its belief in a living God who is incomparable and cannot be imaged (see Pss 115; 135).

6. At a time when promised blessings such as land and temple have been lost, Second Isaiah makes only occasional use of the exodus tradition in his argument (43:16f.; 51:9f., with elements from the mythical struggle with the dragon). More often—and this represents a surprising novelty in comparison with the earlier prophets—in justifying his promises he appeals to creation as proof of the power of Yahweh. In the process Second Isaiah uses various cosmological representations; he can express his thought in hymnic participles and in first-person speeches by God (40:22, 26, 28; 42:5; 45:12, 18; etc.);

or in oracles of salvation he can equate Israel's creation and election
(43:1; 44:2; etc.). Thus, for Second Isaiah creation is not really an
independent theme that speaks of a primal event "in the beginning,"
but rather it is connected with history and thus with present and
future. The creator is the redeemer (44:24). Like the world as a whole
with its light and darkness (45:7), so the coming salvation is a creation
of God (41:20; 45:8; 44:3f.; cf. 65:17f.):

> Remember not the former things
> nor consider the things of old.
> Behold, I am doing a new thing;
> now it springs forth, do you not perceive it?
> (43:18f.).

"Former" and "new," or "past" and "future," can turn into real
opposites. This pair of concepts, which recurs often in variant forms
but is not easy to understand, contrasts the prophetic word that has
already been fulfilled with the prophetic word that has yet to be
fulfilled (see 42:9; 48:3, 6f.; also 41:22f.; 43:9), and therefore past
history and the salvation now announced. It is likely that "former"
looks beyond the judgment that has been experienced and includes
the whole of salvation history from the exodus on (43:16f.; 46:9), so
that the new salvation not only surpasses the old (as in the expectation
of a new exodus) but also suppresses it (see Jer 23:7f.). Such an extreme
statement serves to exhort the hearers not to look back any longer
but to give themselves wholly to the future God has in store (see
42:10ff.; 44:23; 52:9, 11; etc.). Like the announcement of disaster in
the earlier prophets of judgment, Second Isaiah's message of consolation
proclaims a future that is close at hand and already dawning, a future
that is in fact already present in the prophetic word and is to this
extent eschatological: "Now it springs forth!"

This salvation is by no means limited to those directly affected by
it. It is a reality visible to the entire world (40:5; 52:10), and in fact
includes the nations. While Second Isaiah gives penetrating expression
to his understanding of God's exclusive action in creation and history
in God's self-descriptions—I form light and darkness, weal and woe
(45:7), "I am the first and I am the last; besides me there is no god"
(44:6; 48:12; etc.)—he expects that in the future the nations too will
acknowledge this truth.

> To me every knee shall bow,
> every tongue shall swear.
> Only in the Lord, it shall be said of me,
> are righteousness and strength (45:23f.;
> cf. 45:3, 6, 14f.; 49:26; 43:10).

Not only, then, does Second Isaiah bring the first commandment to bear on the contemporary situation; he also hopes that the future will see the commandment obeyed throughout the world. For the attainment of this goal the people of God itself is commissioned as "messenger" (42:19) and "witness" (43:10, 12; 44:8): "Behold, you shall call nations that you know not" (55:5). There is really no question here of a "mission" to be carried out by Israel; the sense is more likely that the people of God will increase through the addition of foreigners (see 56:3ff.; Zech 8:20ff.).

7. The traditions of the Davidic rule and monarchy are divided up and reapplied by Second Isaiah. Yahweh alone is "king" (52:7) and in the form of world ruler; insofar as he devotes himself to Israel he is "your king" (43:15; 41:21; 44:6). The title "anointed" is reserved for the Persian king Cyrus (45:1). The "favor shown to David" in the form of Nathan's promise (2 Sam 7) is now transferred to the people (55:3). Does this mean that in the message of this exilic prophet—unlike his predecessors (most recently Jer 23:5f.; Ezek 34; 37) and his successors (Haggai, Zechariah)—there is no more place for a messianic prophecy? Is the enigmatic figure of the Servant of God to be located rather in the theological context just described, that is, is he to be understood as "the king's minister" (see 2 Kgs 22:12) or, in other words, as the representative of Yahweh the king?

The "songs" of the 'ebed Yahweh or Servant of God form an independent stratum that is self-contained and can be removed from the book. They describe the fate of the Servant from the time of his appointment (42) to his death (53). However, the demarcation of the texts—something that makes an important difference in their interpretation—is a matter of some disagreement: 42:1–4 (5–9); 49:1–6 (7–13); 50:4–9 (10f.); 52:13–53:12. The sections in parentheses are probably later expansions in which a different understanding of the Servant is already at work, one that differs from that of the original stratum.

In Isa 42:1–4 he is presented, probably to a royal household in heaven, as a "chosen" person, endowed with God's Spirit, who is to make known to the entire world the law, the gracious decrees, the justice, the "Torah" of God. The promise of success despite the future opposition here suggested ("he will not waver") is developed along both lines—effectiveness and suffering—in the subsequent songs. In the form of a first-person speech, which recalls the vocation formulary of Jer 1, the Servant himself in Isa 49:1–6 tells the nations of his being appointed before his birth. He must not only "raise up and restore" Israel but also be "a light to the nations" so that the salvation of Yahweh may reach the ends of the earth.

The third song, Isa 50:4–9, which is also cast in the first-person form, gives the impression of being a transitional song, with its two themes: the Servant's mission of proclamation, for which his tongue and ear are prepared and for which he has God's assistance, and the Servant's constancy in suffering. The conclusion and climax come in the fourth song, in which two speeches of God (52:13–15; 53:11b–12)—are these again spoken in a scene that takes place in heaven?—frame a report and a confession by a group that speaks as "we" (53:1–11a): "Ours were the sufferings he bore" (53:4 JB). The divine words confirm the success and exaltation of the scorned Servant, the one who suffered vicariously. This righteous one will justify the "many" (probably all nations) and carry their guilt, and kings shall shut their mouths before him (53:11f.; 52:15). The central statements made here about the death and burial of the Servant, his new life (indicated in an indirect way), his bringing of righteousness to all, and his worldwide acknowledgment after his humiliation—all these transcend any historically possible experience.

As in the book of Second Isaiah as a whole, so in the songs of the Servant of God there are elements from the psalms, especially the laments and psalms of confidence, and from the wisdom literature. Above all, however, there are two traditions that combine to yield something startlingly new (see 52:15).

From the royal-messianic tradition come, for example, in Isa 42, the courtly ceremonial, the addressing of the Servant as "my chosen," whom God upholds (Ps 89:3, 19ff.), the linking of the gift of the spirit with the administration of justice and with care for others (2 Sam 23:2f.; Isa 11:2ff.); or, in Isa 49, the call-saying with the assignment of a title (Ps 2:7) and the equipping of the Servant with the sharp or penetrating word (Isa 11:4).

In Isa 42; 49 this strand of tradition is developed and given a new interpretation with the aid of the prophetic tradition, which was, of course, thoroughly familiar with the office of the word and with suffering. In Isa 50 this tradition becomes the dominant one. Notable here are contacts with the book of Jeremiah and especially with the confessions of Jeremiah (12:5f.; 11:19; etc.).

Isa 53, however, with its universalist emphasis, which recalls Isa 42, returns to the royal tradition. It corrects this, however (53:2), and transcends it, as it does all the statements about suffering in the prophets and the psalter.

"Servant (of God)," a title expressing great esteem, is given in the OT to Moses, to prophets (44:26), and kings, and even to the messiah (Ezek 34:23f.; Zech 3:8; etc.). Consequently, the concept is really of no exegetical help in answering the difficult question Who is the Servant? The answers that have been given are very different in kind. There is (a) the collective interpretation, which sees Israel itself, either the entire people or the community in exile, as the "Servant." This interpretation can appeal to the context (Israel as servant, 44:1f., and elsewhere) and to Isa 49:3. But in 49:3 "Israel" is an insertion, since the Servant has a mission to Israel (49:5f.) and, unlike the "blind and deaf" people, willingly accepts his lot (50:5f.).

There is (b) the individual interpretation, which can select individuals in past, present, or future. The possibilities are quite varied: (1) the traditional eschatological-messianic view—but against this is the fact that the Servant is not a Davidic figure and has the task here and now of bringing Israel home. The "songs" certainly are not intended as predictions of the future; like Second Isaiah's eschatological preaching as a whole, they speak rather to the present situation. (2) The Servant has been identified with various individuals of the past, whether kings or prophets. But the only ones with any claim to consideration are Moses, as he appears in more recent tradition (Num 12:3; Exod 32:31f.; etc.), and Jeremiah, with whose literary legacy there are in fact many connections in Second Isaiah. (3) The autobiographical interpretation of the Servant as being Second Isaiah himself is today the most widely accepted (cf. Acts 8:34, long ago). It can appeal to the Servant's task of preaching and to the first-person form of the second and third songs; on the other hand, the fourth song, which shows certain special characteristics, even from a linguistic standpoint, must be ascribed to a different author, most likely from among Second Isaiah's disciples ("we").

The difficulties of the autobiographical interpretation can be summed up in two basic questions. (1) Why is the presentation of the Servant of God in Isa 42 not integrated with the audition report in Isa 40? Was there need of a second calling, as it were, because Second Isaiah's mission to Israel was being extended to the nations? But to what extent does the prophet really take up this worldwide mission of preaching (see 42:10; 43:10; 52:10; etc.)? (2) Are not the first three songs directed from the outset toward Isa 53, so that the four texts are to be understood as a unit? But how can the group of disciples say of their teacher that he received life after death and bore the guilt of the "many"?

Are not the statements in Isa 53, which transcend all historical experience, more intelligible as announcements of the future? At the very least, the songs of the Servant of God may have influenced the form taken by later messianic expectations, as when Zech 9:9f. looks for a "righteous humble" king who proclaims salvation to the nations (see also the obscure reference to "him whom they have pierced," Zech 12:10).

Second Isaiah's expectation of something imminent was not fulfilled in the manner in which he describes the reality: destruction of Babylon, glorious return of the people, acknowledgment of Yahweh by Cyrus (45:3), and so on. Nonetheless, the hope in God's future manifestation and in the coming of his royal rule was carried on by one who perhaps had been a disciple of Second Isaiah, the prophet known as Third Isaiah.

8. As B. Duhm (1892) realized, chaps. 56–66 of the book of Isaiah form an independent literary entity. There is disagreement, however, about whether these chapters are a unit or whether they are made up of small collections of sayings from different periods. There is agreement, on the other hand, that at least the prophecies of salvation in chaps. 60–62, which are the kernel of the book, go back to a prophet of the early postexilic, and therefore, the Persian, period. This prophet came on the scene (in Jerusalem) after 538, but perhaps before the rebuilding of the temple in 520–515 B.C.

The book is structured of various strata like layers around the kernel just mentioned. The innermost circle around this kernel is made up of a loosely structured communal lament (59) and one that is more compact (63:15ff.). The pledge of salvation at the center (the kernel) is the response to these laments. The next circle from the center contains accusations (56–58; 65f.), with announcements of salvation added to these as an insertion (57:14ff.; 65:17ff.) or an appendix (66:6ff.). The outermost frame sayings meditate in a relatively restricted (56:1–8) or a more comprehensive and almost apocalyptic (66:18ff.) way on the expansion of the community beyond the boundaries proper to it in preexilic times.

56:1–8	"Law for the community." Admission of foreigners and eunuchs, contrary to Deut 23
	"My house shall be called a house of prayer for all peoples" (v. 7)
56:9–57:13	A series of accusations
	(actualized from preexilic times?)
	56:9ff. Against shepherds (cf. Jer 23; Ezek 34)
	57:3ff. Against idolatry, whoredom
	57:14ff. Words of consolation for the humble and contrite
58	Sermon on fasting (cf. Zech 7). Exhortation to true fasting
	"Why have we fasted, and thou seest it not?" (v. 3)
	Feed the hungry, clothe the naked (v. 7)
59	"Prophetic liturgy" with elements of lament, accusation, confession of guilt (v. 12), and God's promise
	"Behold, the Lord's hand is not shortened" (v. 1)
60–62	Salvation sayings for Jerusalem. Glorification of Zion
60	Pilgrimage of the nations to Zion (cf. Isa 2; Hag 2)
	61:1–3 The prophet's role as consoler
	61:6 "You shall be called the priests of the Lord" (cf. Exod 19:6)

63	God's return from judging the people, especially Edom (vv. 1–6)
	Lamentational historical retrospect, especially to the time of Moses (vv. 7–14)
63:15–64:12	Communal lament with petitions, questions (cf. the book of Lamentations)
	Not Abraham but God is our father (63:16; 64:8)
	"O that thou wouldst rend the heavens and come down!" (63:19, 15)
65	The just and the wicked (vv. 1–16)
	"Sum total" of expectations of eschatological salvation (vv. 17ff.)
	"Behold, I create new heavens and a new earth" (65:17; 66:22)
66	Criticism of the temple: "Heaven is my throne" (cf. 1 Kgs 8:27)
	Joy at the riches of Jerusalem (vv. 7ff.)

Third Isaiah, speaker of these prophecies of salvation, a man whose name we do not know, himself describes his authority and commission:

> The Spirit of the Lord God is upon me,
>   because the Lord has anointed me
> to bring good tidings to the afflicted [or: poor];
>   he has sent me to bind up the brokenhearted,
> to proclaim liberty to the captives . . .
>   (61:1–3; cf., for the "me"
>   62:1, 6; for the content 57:14; 66:2).

This prophet seems to consider himself a disciple of Second Isaiah, for he takes over even the wording of the latter's message of salvation and renews it in the changed conditions of his own situation. In the process, Second Isaiah's announcement to a particular time takes on a more general tone or even a transferred meaning (compare especially 40:3ff. with 57:14f.). Yet, in the economically impoverished circumstances of his own day, when the nonfulfillment of Second Isaiah's promise of salvation has become disappointingly clear, Third Isaiah continues to announce the coming of salvation and to proffer the hope of the glorification of Zion. Consequently, the focus on the future that God is bringing will determine how the people are to act:

> Arise, shine; for your light has come,
>   and the glory of the Lord has risen upon you (60:1f.; cf. 56:1).

The circumstances and problems of the postexilic period find expression in the lament over the destruction of the temple (64:10f.), in the hope that the city (61:4; 60:10f., 18) and sanctuary (60:13, despite the criticism in 66:1) will be rebuilt, in the liturgy of fasting (58) and the laments (63:15ff.; 59), and in the longing for more favorable economic conditions (62:8f.; 60:17; cf. Hag 1), or in the significance attributed to the sanctification of the sabbath (56:1f.; 58:13f.).

The principal noteworthy difference from Second Isaiah's message of salvation is that chaps. 56–66 contain accusations that recall the preaching of the earlier prophets of judgment. "Your iniquities have made a separation between you and your God" (59:2). We find here once again, in addition to criticism of society, the rejection of alien cults, especially cults of vegetation divinities (57:3ff.; 65:3ff.; 66:17). Are we to remove all the accusations from among the authentic sayings of Third Isaiah and regard as his only the continuation of a proclamation that is derived from Second Isaiah (60–62; cf. 57:14ff.; 65:17ff.; 66:6ff.)? Even the sayings in which the community is divided into two groups, the wicked and the devout (57:19ff.; 65; 66:5), seem to take us on into a more recent age. On the other hand, the conditions of the postexilic period provided occasion for reviving the demonstrations of guilt and the announcements of punishment that had been current in the earlier prophets, although they are directed against groups and not against the people as a whole.

Futhermore, Third Isaiah expects that the nations will serve Israel and participate in the coming salvation (60:3f., 9; 61:9; 66:12, 20; earlier, 49:22f.) rather than that they will experience the judgment of God (63:1ff.; 60:12; 66:15f., 24). But in the book's concluding sayings (which are from a later time) every particularism is transcended in the universalist expectation that God will gather all peoples, allow them to see his glory, and even choose "priests and Levites" from among them without the legitimation of priestly descent (66:18, 12; cf. Mal 1:11; Zeph 2:11).

§22

HAGGAI, ZECHARIAH, SECOND ZECHARIAH, MALACHI

1. Probably only a few years after Third Isaiah, the prophet Haggai took up the message of salvation as imminent in the present darkness (Isa 60:1f.; 56:1) and connected it with events going on at that very time, just as Second Isaiah had connected his predictions with the victory of Cyrus the Persian. In keeping with the edict of Cyrus (Ezra 6:3ff.), Sheshbazzar, the governor appointed by the Persians, probably brought back, soon after 539 B.C., the temple furnishings that had been taken off to Babylon. Perhaps he also laid the cornerstone for the new temple (Ezra 5:14ff.; but cf. Hag 2:18; Zech 4:9). As a result of the poor economic situation (Isa 62:8f.; Hag 1:6, 9f.; 2:16f.) the work of rebuilding did not prosper. Then, in 520 B.C., the second year of the reign of the Persian king Darius I, Haggai exercised a ministry in Jerusalem for a few short months. He addressed himself both to the Judeans who had remained in the country and to the newly returned exiles (Ezra 2) and reversed the estimate of the situation that was being made by his contemporaries. He claimed that the economic situation was not the cause but the result of the fact that the temple was still in ruins.

> Go up to the hills and bring wood and build the house,
> that I may take pleasure in it
> and that I may appear in my glory (Hag 1:8).

The few utterances of Haggai are consistently given a precise date; in this they are comparable to the preaching of Ezekiel before him and of Zechariah, who comes immediately after him (see Hag 1:1–2:20). In the two chapters that make up the book of Haggai there is an alternation of narrative framework (1:1, 3, 12–15; 2:1f., 10, 20) and more or less rhythmical individual sayings. This raises, once again, the question of how far we are to trust the dates given (August–December, 520), but also the question of the original delimitation of the spoken units and (especially in 2:10ff.) of their addressee. The preaching of Haggai can be broken down into roughly four themes.

I. Summons to rebuild the temple

1–2:5   Disputation sayings (1:2, 4ff., 9ff.) and exhortations with a conditional promise (1:7; 2:3ff.; cf. 2:15–19)

II. Convulsion of the world

2:6–9   Unconditional promise: pilgrimage of the nations to Zion (cf. Isa 2; 60; 66:20)

III. An unclean people

2:10–14   Priestly torah regarding clean and unclean (cf. Lev 10:10f.), which is applied by the prophet

IV. Expectation of the messiah

2:20–23   Unconditional promise: convulsion and pacification of the world. Zerubbabel as Yahweh's signet ring

Haggai gives a sober estimate of the general situation, but then with the help of questions and exhortations, he brings his hearers to see that the rebuilding of God's house must take precedence over the improvement of their own housing situation (1:4, 9; cf. 2 Sam 7:2). In addition, God's spirit is with the work (Hag 2:5; 1:13), so that it will succeed. The present distress, which is caused by heaven (1:10f.), will turn into salvation. "From this day on I will bless you" (2:19; Zech 8:9ff.). In fact, God will soon shake heaven and earth, in order that the nations may bring their treasures and the new house may surpass in splendor the one that had been destroyed. "The silver is mine [Yahweh's, not Israel's], and the gold is mine" (Hag 2:6–9). The salvation looked for by earlier prophets—for example, Second and Third Isaiah—is thus still in the future, but it is dawning with the new temple (2:9).

As a matter of fact, Haggai's appeal is successful; the work begins immediately (1:12ff.) and is continued (2:1ff.; Ezra 5:1.; 6:14). But does Haggai dispute the right of (a part of) the people to take part in the work and thus to have access to the temple? The priestly instruction about clean and unclean leads to the prophetic insight that "this nation" with all the works of its hands and all its sacrifices is unclean (2:10–14). "This nation," which is not further defined, has usually (since J. W. Rothstein) been interpreted as referring to the population of the former northern kingdom or, in other words, to the later Samaritans (Ezra 4), who ever since the forced resettlements under the Assyrians had been compelled to accept groups of foreigners with their religions (2 Kgs 17). Is Haggai already distinguishing his community from the Samaritans, in order to prevent from the outset any possible corruption of the Yahwistic faith? Or is it rather that Haggai, like the prophets before him (see, e.g., Isa 6:4; Ezek 36:25; 37:23), can call his own people "unclean" (K. Koch)? In the second interpretation the contrast between God's promise of salvation and the situation of the people becomes all the more striking.

Haggai urges the rebuilding of the temple on Zerubbabel, the Persian commissioner for Judah and a grandson of King Jehoiachin who had been deported to Babylon in 598 B.C., and on Joshua the high priest (in the postexilic period the political and priestly offices exist side by side). In the final saying of the book Haggai promises messianic dignity to Zerubbabel, a descendant of David. In the course of the world upheaval (2:6, 21) God himself will shatter the weapons of the nations and appoint his own representative over his kingdom of peace (2:22f.). In content, therefore, Haggai seems to renew and universalize Isaiah's expectations of the future (Isa 9:4ff.); he also combines at least the traditions of Zion and David. As Yahweh's "servant" (Ezek 34:23f.; etc.) Zerubbabel is "chosen" to be the signet ring on God's hand (contrast with Jer 22:24).

Haggai too was mistaken in his expectations for the immediate future (2:6ff., 20ff.). Nonetheless, by giving the impulse to the rebuilding of the temple he helped determine the course of events and thus for a long period the history of postexilic Israel's faith. Above all, in his particular situation he kept alive the hope of the future planned by God.

2. Shortly after Haggai, perhaps as soon as two months later, Zechariah appeared on the scene and exercised a ministry for at least two years, 520–518 B.C. (compare Hag 1:1 with Zech 1:1; 7:1). The new prophet continued the earlier one's preaching of salvation but went further in breadth of vision (1:7ff.; 6:1ff.) and in the depth of realization of guilt (5:5ff.). In general, Zechariah renews the themes of his prophetic predecessors: God's restoration of favor to Jerusalem, the purification of the community from guilt, the return of the Diaspora, Israel's burgeoning population, the stripping of power from the nations but also their participation in salvation, the completion of the temple, and the messianic expectation. But the traditional motifs are independently developed and rendered actual with the help of new images. Within the message of salvation are to be found, as in Third Isaiah, accusations and the announcement of judgment (5; 7).

The first main section of the book of Zechariah (1–8) is divided into three parts, the demarcation coming from successive exact datings and from the use of the formula "the word of the Lord came . . . " (1:1, 7; 7:1). On the other hand, the opening section (1:1–6) with its short call to repentance and the concluding section (7f.) with its more fully developed sermon on fasting have a different character from that of the commanding central section, which is made up of visions and sayings (1:7–6:15). In the first and third sections, which frame the second, there are explicit references to the sayings of the "former prophets" (1:4ff.; 7:7ff.; 8:9ff.); the references to tradition become more frequent in the late age of prophecy and point from afar to the canonical status that the prophetic books later received.

The first part of the book of Zechariah (1–8) consists essentially of a cycle of seven visions in the night; these are reported in the first person and may have come to the prophet in a single night (1:8; 4:1; according to 1:7, in February, 519). In their structure—description and interpretation of the vision, the use of question and answer—they recall such visions as Amos 8:1f. or Jer 1:13f., but they are much more fully developed. Whereas Amos can say, "Thus the Lord showed me," in Zechariah's visions God is represented by an angelic interpreter or expounder (*angelus interpres*) who gives explanations, asks and answers questions, and may even provide the vision (4:1f., 5; 5:3ff.; etc.). He thus acts as a mediator between "the Lord of the whole earth" (4:14; 6:5) and the prophet (see earlier, Ezek 40:3f.; later, Dan 8; 10).

Into the cycle of seven visions (1:8–15; 1:18–21; 2:1–5; 4:1–6a, 10b–14; 5:1–4, 5–11; 6:1–8) a further vision (3:1–7) has been introduced, which is different both in form and in content. The angelic interpreter plays no part, and, unlike the seven, this one is directed to a concrete person, the high priest Joshua. This vision is inserted in fourth place, before the central, messianic vision of the cycle, to which it is related in content. (For this reason, scholars number the visions (I–VII or I–VIII, depending on whether or not they count the separate vision in chap. 3.)

As is the case, for example, with the visions in the book of Amos (7:9, 10–17; 8:3), explanatory but originally independent individual sayings have been added to the visions of Zechariah (1:16f.; 2:6–13; 3:8–10; 4:6b–10; 6:9–15). In these sayings the prophet seems to communicate the insights into the future that have been granted to him. In their substance, then, the sayings are from Zechariah, but it is hardly likely that he himself introduced them into the composition since they interrupt its flow.

The redaction of the book rather than the prophet's preaching is more likely to be responsible for a formula that occurs here and there (2:9, 11; 4:9; 6:15) and is reminiscent of Ezekiel: "You [sing. or pl.] will know that the Lord of hosts has sent me to you." The formula confirms the truth of the prophetic promise of salvation, perhaps in order to counter the present nonfulfillment of it.

As the closely related datings in the books of Haggai and Zechariah, as well as the echoes of Hag 1f. in Zech 8:9ff., suggest, there is a connection between the redactions of the two books, a redaction that may in turn indicate connections with the Chronicler's history.

The redactors of the book of Zechariah see not only the call to repentance (1:1–6) and the sermon on fasting (7f.) but also the extensive central section (1:7–6:15) as units received each on a single day, but there is little reason to trust this chronology. In fact, in 1:3–6; 7:7–14; and in 8:14ff. are we not really listening to a later voice, the voice of someone who is closely associated with the Deuteronomistic school (see W. A. M. Beuken)? That conversion should be a condition for the coming of salvation (and that is probably how the prefixing of 1:3ff. is to be understood) contradicts the intention of the visions (1:7ff.). "The visions of the night amount to an unconditional promise of salvation"; they proclaim "salvation as something new and absolute" (Beuken, p. 112).

A) 1:1–6	Preaching of repentance (October/November, 520)	
B) 1:7–6:15	A composition comprising visions and sayings (February, 519)	
1	Vision I (vv. 8–13, 14f.): a man on a red horse, among myrtle trees; behind him riders on horses of various colors	
	Individual saying (vv. 16f.)	
	Vision II (vv. 18–21): four horns, laid low by four smiths	
2	Vision III (vv. 1–5): a man with a measuring line to measure Jerusalem	
	Individual sayings (vv. 6–13)	
3	Interpolated vision (vv. 1–7): acquittal and investiture of Joshua as high priest	
	Individual sayings (vv. 8–10); the stone before Joshua	
4	Vision IV (vv. 1–6a, 10b–14): lampstands, with an olive tree on either side	
	Promises to Zerubbabel (vv. 6b–10)	
5	Vision V (vv. 1–4): a flying, curse-laden scroll	
	Vision VI (vv. 5–11): the woman in the bushel	
6	Vision VII (vv. 1–8): four chariots going to the four winds	
	Symbolic coronation (vv. 9–15)	
C) 7f.	Sermon on fasting (December, 518; cf. Isa 58) with accusation and various (in part, later) prophecies of salvation (8:1ff.)	

The purport of the images in the visions of Zechariah is sometimes hard to understand. But the entire emphasis here, as in the visions of the earlier prophets, is on the intention of what is said, and this consistently finds clear and unequivocal expression. In the first vision the prophet sees heavenly riders who are sent by God to investigate the situation on earth (see Job 1:7; 2:2). The report that the earth is peaceful and at rest elicits the lament. After seventy years still no end to the divine wrath at Judah and Jerusalem? But God answers with words of consolation. Here Zechariah is renewing and giving actuality to the eschatological message (see Isa 40:1; 66:13; Jer 29:10; etc.) in contrast to the present situation. Yes, the time of salvation is dawning, even though reality looks far different! God is "jealous" for Jerusalem and angry at the nations (Zech 1:15; 8:2). Time is running out for the nations.

The four horns of the second vision symbolize the power of the (oppressor) nations that have "scattered" Israel; their power is now being broken (by the four smiths). Since here as in the final vision the number four stands for the world in its entirety, the image used anticipates the apocalyptic hope that God will cast down the great empires (Dan 2; 7; cf. Hag 2:22).

In the third vision a man is seen measuring the extent of Jerusalem, but his activity is stopped. The promise of an increase in Jerusalem's population (Isa 49:19f.) is so richly fulfilled that the city will grow beyond its walls and can be protected only by the "glory" of God (Ezek 43:5; Hag 1:8):

> Jerusalem shall be inhabited as villages without walls,
> because of the multitude of men and cattle in it.
> For I will be to her
> a wall of fire round about, says the Lord,
> and I will be the glory within her (2:4f.).

Interpretative additions simply draw the conclusions contained in this expectation, since they exhort people to flee from Babylon (2:10ff.; cf. Isa 48:20; 43:5f.). The increase in population will be the result either of the return of the scattered Israelites or of the addition of "many nations" (Zech 2:11; 8:20ff.). In any case, the Jerusalem of the present is called to rejoice in the future God has in store. "Sing and rejoice, O daughter of Zion; for lo, I come and I will dwell in the midst of you" (2:10, 13).

The fifth (or sixth, depending on the numbering followed) vision shows a broad, open scroll flying in the sky (5:1–4); on it are written curses against thieves and perjurers. In this way, prior to the time of salvation the community is cleansed of evildoers—does this refer concretely to those who had remained in Israel during the exile and who had appropriated the possessions of the exiles and then refused to restore them to the returnees?

The sixth (or seventh) vision (5:5–11) continues the expectation of the community's purification by God himself and does so in another visible image. The woman (who represents godlessness) sitting in a dry measure in which the guilt of the land has, as it were, been gathered together is carried away by two winged women from Judah to Babylon. There the woman is to stand as an idol on a pedestal in the temple.

The final vision connects with the first, rending the quiet that had there been the occasion for lamentation. Four chariots, each drawn by horses of a different color, come from God, emerging from between two mountains of bronze at the entrance to heaven, and traveling toward the four winds. The carriage traveling northward will "make the spirit of Yahweh descend on the country of the North" (v. 8 JB), not in order to give vent to Yahweh's wrath there but to rouse the exiles to return or even to rouse foreigners to join Israel (see 2:6ff.; 8:7f., 20ff.).

The outermost, or first and last, visions (1:8ff.; 6:1ff.) provide a universalist framework; at the center of the cycle of seven stands the messianic expectation in the fourth, broadly developed vision (4:1–6a, 10b–14). On a golden lampstand are seven lamp bowls, each of which contains seven lips with wicks (therefore forty-nine sources of light in all). The seven bowls stand for the eyes of God, which sweep over the earth; or, in nonsymbolic language, they stand for the omnipotence and omnipresence of the Lord of the universe. Two olive trees to the right and the left of the lampstand are an image of the two "sons of the oil," or anointed ones who are in God's service. According to this vision of the future there is to be a division of powers that had been unknown before the exile; the political and religious or secular and spiritual heads stand side by side with equal rank.

This expectation of a division of powers in the future is heard of again only outside the OT, at Qumran, for in the leadership of the postexilic community the priestly office prevailed. The high priest, too, is henceforth "anointed" (Lev 8:12, 30; etc.).

If Zechariah, son or grandson of Iddo (Zech 1:1; Ezra 5:1; 6:14), is to be identified with the person of the same name in Neh 12:16, then he, like Ezekiel, is from a priestly family. This might explain why Zechariah, unlike Haggai, gives the high priest an important role in the shaping of the future.

The purpose of this central vision (4:14) is developed in a further vision, which reports a symbolic action and sayings. The two men whose names are not given initially (in the central vision) are the high priest Joshua (Jeshua) and Zerubbabel, a descendant of David, to whom Haggai (2:23) had already assigned messianic rank. To the latter, and not to the high priest, a promise is given, in the saying (Zech 4:6b–10) between the fourth (fifth) and fifth (sixth) visions that he will complete the building of the temple: "Not by might, nor by power, but by my Spirit!"

The high priest Joshua, on the other hand, is the central figure in another vision, which is differently structured and was subsequently inserted into the cycle of seven (3:1–7). In the presence of Yahweh's angel, Joshua is charged by Satan, the accuser in heaven (cf. Job 1f.). But Joshua is extricated from his dirty clothes, that is, from guilt, and given new garments; he is even crowned with a turban (see Lev 16:4; also the difficult saying in Zech 3:8f.). On condition that he prove obedient, the high priest is not only entrusted with authority over the sanctuary but is also promised free "access" to God, so that he may intercede for the entire community (3:7; cf. Jer 30:21).

There is a counterpart to this vision in the symbolic action in Zech 6:9ff., which was evidently altered at a later date (and is therefore the subject of divergent interpretation). Like the visions, the symbolic action is told in the first person. Here Zechariah is told to acquire gold and silver from the exiles, to have a crown made of it, and to place the crown on someone's head; according to the text as we now have it the someone is the high priest Joshua. But since Joshua already wears a turban and since the building of the temple is Zerubbabel's task (6:12f.; 4:9f.), the symbolic crowning was probably meant originally for Zerubbabel, and it is he who is proclaimed to be the promised "Branch," under whom "there is to be a branching out" (see Jer 23:5; also Hag 2:23; etc.). The high priest stands at his side (Zech 6:13; 4:14). When the course of history did not confirm this messianic enthronement, the text was corrected (hardly by Zechariah himself), so that the messianic expectation was directed no longer to contemporary history but to the future (6:12).

In his visions Zechariah learned that "the kingdom of God was already prepared in heaven. . . . The eschatological saving orders and offices are already present in the world above" (G. von Rad, *Old Testament Theology*, vol. 2, p. 288).

According to K. Seybold (p. 107), the cycle of visions is "meant as a call to and a prevision of the rebuilding of the temple in Jerusalem, as a proposal and program for the restoration of the cult center on Zion; as such it has the character of a *Hieros Logos* for the new sanctuary." It is remarkable, however, that the temple is mentioned only occasionally in Zechariah and not once in the cycle itself (1:16; 4:9f.; 6:12f.). Moreover, does not the expectation of the dawning of God's reign reach far beyond the immediate occasion?

Chaps. 7f. are of a different kind; they have, to say the least, been enriched with all sorts of later material, although in content they are connected with the continued building of the temple. The question is asked whether liturgies of fasting or mourning are to be celebrated on the anniversary of the destruction of the temple (and on similar commemorative days: 7:3, 5; 8:19). The answer given makes reference to the hardheartedness of the hearers and is initially rather negative. Only on a second approach does the answer turn into a prophecy of salvation: fasting will become a source of joy (8:19). A series of various promises are attached to this expectation of a reversal (see Isa 65:17ff.).

In any event, the subsequent period does not seem to have abandoned the liturgies of fasting but to have continued them (see Mal 2:13; 3:14). In this respect Zechariah's vision of the future remained a hope, but a hope in the victory of God's power in the present world.

3. Chap. 9 begins a section of the book of Zechariah that is new in style and language and in the historical situation it reflects. By means of three uniformly structured superscriptions—"An oracle. The word of the Lord . . ." (9:1; 12:1; Mal 1:1)—the redactors have indicated three collections (each containing three chapters) that form the conclusion to the book of the Twelve Prophets: Zech 9–11; Zech 12–14; and Malachi. The two appendixes to the book of Zechariah are usually attributed to Second Zechariah (9–14), by analogy with the designation in the book of Isaiah. Some, with the content for justification, even distinguish a Second (9–11) and a Third Zechariah (12–14). In any case, the expectation of an assault by the nations in chap. 14 is a separate entity that is close in theme to chap. 12 and yet is different in kind. The texts are therefore not to be attributed to a single author. Very diverse dates in both the preexilic and the postexilic period have been suggested. It is probable that the first and older part is from the time around 300 B.C., the second and more recent part from the third century B.C. The chapters thus originate after the victorious expedition of Alexander the Great around 330 B.C. (see 9:1–8?), that is, at least two centuries after the time of Zechariah's ministry. The Samaritan schism (11:14), the Greeks (9:13), and the successor kingdoms of the Ptolemies in Egypt and the Seleucids in Assyria/Syria (10:10f.; cf. Isa 19:23f.) are mentioned.

What was the justification for attaching these extensive sections to Zech 1–8? As a matter of fact, in addition to certain verbal points of contact (e.g., 2:10 and 9:9, or 2:5 and 9:8) there is a thematic kinship. Chaps. 9–14, too, depict the dawning of the time of salvation, although the literary devices differ: God's care of Jerusalem (9:8, 15f.; 10:6; 12; 14), the return and gathering of the people (9:11f.; 10:6ff., where the northern kingdom is included; cf. Jer 3:12f.; 30f.), liberation from sin (13:1ff.), destruction of the power of the nations (9:13ff.; 11:1ff.; 12; 14), union with Israel (9:7; 14:16ff.), and finally the royal rule of God. "And the Lord will become king over all the earth; on that day the Lord will be one and his name one" (14:9; cf. vv. 16f.; Deut 6:4). When twice attacked by nations (12; 14), Jerusalem will hold its ground the first time (12), but not the second (14). God himself will bring the enemy in and they will once again drag half of the city's population into exile. With this expectation of a purifying judgment (13:7ff.; 14:2ff.) the later prophets continue, though in a different—and partial—

form, the preexilic prophets' announcement of judgment and salvation. Alongside texts whose intention is easily recognizable there are decidedly obscure passages (like the discourse on the shepherds, 11:4ff.). Is the one who has been "pierced" and whom the citizens of Jerusalem mourn (12:10) a messianic figure who must take upon himself the destiny of the Servant of God (Isa 53:5)? In any case, the expectation of a humble king dominates the beginning of Second Zechariah (9:9f.): a king who relies on God for help, rides on an ass instead of a warhorse, and nonetheless brings peace to the entire world through his word.

9	Vv. 1–8	Extension of Yahweh's power to north and west (allusion to the victorious expedition of Alexander the Great?)
	Vv. 9f.	Summons to rejoice over the future king of peace (cf. Matt 21)
	Vv. 11–17	Explanatory oracles of salvation: return, holy war
10	Vv. 1f.	Blessing from God
	Vv. 3–12	War and return (cf. 9:10ff.)
	11:1–3	Taunt-song at exalted things that suffer a fall (cf. Isa 2:12ff.; Jer 25:36ff.)
11:4ff.; 13:7–9		Discourse on shepherds (cf. Jer 23; Ezek 34; Isa 56:9ff.)
	11:4–14, 15–17	Combination of sign action, vision, allegory
		Pasturing of sheep doomed to slaughter
		Two staffs: "Grace" and "Union" (cf. Ezek 37:15ff.)—symbol of the division between Jews and Samaritans
		11:13 Thirty pieces of silver (Matt 27:3ff.)
	13:7ff.	Purification of the remnant (one-third)
	12	Assault on Jerusalem by the nations; they are repulsed
		Outpouring of the Spirit. Lament over "him whom they have pierced" (vv. 10ff.)
	13	Deliverance from uncleanness, idolatry, and (ecstatic) prophesying
	14	Assault by the nations; deliverance only after the taking of the city. Purification of Jerusalem (one half; cf. 13:7ff.). Theophany
		The remnant of the nations worships Yahweh as king (vv. 16ff.)

4. As they stand, the three chapters of the sayings of Malachi form the end of the book of the Twelve Prophets. In addition, by means of the superscription "An oracle. The word of the Lord to Israel by Malachi," these chapter have been combined with Zech 9–11 and Zech 12–14 into a single collection or redactional unit. But in fact Malachi preached about a century before Second Zechariah (9–11),

although after Haggai and Zechariah. There is disagreement about whether "Malachi" is really a personal name or rather a title of an anonymous prophet, "My messenger" (cf. Hag 1:13; Mal 3:1; 2:7).

Just as his name is uncertain, so the time of his ministry can only be approximately determined. Malachi finds himself already compelled to raise his voice (1:6ff.) against abuses in the (second) temple (1:10; 3:1, 10); the (Persian) "governor" is mentioned in order to bring out the point (1:8). The distress caused to Israel by Edom after the destruction of Jerusalem in 587 B.C. seems to have ceased (1:3ff.). The need of regulating marital questions (2:10ff.) and the payment of tithes (3:8ff.) may be taken as placing us roughly in the period of Ezra and Nehemiah (Ezra 9f.; Neh 13:10ff., 23ff.). It is likely then that the prophet to whom the substance of the book of Malachi is to be ascribed, exercised his ministry in the fifth century B.C., in either the first or second half.

The genre of the disputation, which is found occasionally in the earlier prophets and more frequently in Second Isaiah, dominates this book. Characteristic of the genre are questions (1:2f., 6; 2:10; etc.) or citations (2:17; 3:13f.). The prophet takes for his point of departure the (skeptical) views of his hearers and practices a kind of (pastoral) "preaching through conversation," by developing his message in the form of answers to questions.

1:2–5	I love you and hate Edom (cf. Ezek 35; Obadiah; Isa 63)
	Free divine election
1:6–2:9	Accusations (1:6ff.) and announcement of judgment (2:1ff.) on the priests
	Defective, unclean sacrifices (cf. Deut 15:21; Lev 22:20ff.)
	"My name is great among the nations" (1:11)
	The covenant with Levi (cf. Deut 33:8–11) has been broken (2:4–9)
2:10–16	Accusation against the people on account of divorce (vv. 13ff.) and mixed marriages (vv. 11b, 12 probably added; cf. Ezra 9f.; Neh 13)
	"Have we not all one father?" (Mal 2:10; cf. 1:6)
	"I hate divorce" (2:16)
2:17–3:5	Purification of the community (cf. Zech 5)
	Is "every one who does evil ... good in the sight of the Lord" (2:17)?
	God is coming to judge (3:1, 5; cf. 2:3, 9)
	"Behold, I send my messenger to prepare the way before me" (3:1)
	"Who can endure the day of his coming?" (3:2; Joel 2:11)
3:6–12	Conditional promise of blessing
	"Return to me, and I will return to you!" (3:7; Zech 1:3)
3:13–4:3	The "sun of righteousness" shines on those who fear God
	"You have said, 'It is vain to serve God'" (v. 14; cf. Zeph 1:12)

God's book of remembrance (v. 16; cf. Exod 32:32f.; Dan 12:1; Pss
   139:16; 56:8; etc.)
The lot of the righteous and the wicked (vv. 18ff.; cf. Ps 1:6)

4:4, 5f.   Conclusion of the book of the Twelve Prophets
   (Deuteronomistic) admonition to remember the law of Moses (as
     well as the prophets)
   The return of Elijah

In the face of doubt Malachi clings to his belief in the steadfastness
of God's love for his people (1:2). God will prove to Israel that he is
great (1:5) but at the same time he will be mindful of the honor due
to him (1:6; 2:2). Thus Malachi in his turn continues to look for
salvation, but he also announces judgment—although he differs from
the preexilic prophets in limiting the judgment to groups within the
community. The promise of election and salvation is followed by an
indictment of the priests who do not offer the sacrifices in the proper
way. Malachi is here continuing the prophetic criticism of the priesthood (Hos 5:1; Isa 28:7; Jer 2:8; etc.), but he takes proper liturgical
execution very seriously as a form of reverence and obedience to God
(Mal 1:6ff.; 3:6ff., 3f.).

In the conversations, whether these be real or simply rhetorical
devices, we can sense the disillusionment at the delay in the fulfillment
of the promises of a Haggai or a Zechariah. But in the face of all
skepticism Malachi urges trust in the reliability of God's word. God
does not change but holds fast to his promises of blessing and salvation
(Hag 2:9, 16; Zech 8:9ff.), although he makes their fulfillment depend
on obedience and fear of God (Mal 3:6ff., 17ff.). God will eliminate
abuses and cleanse the community of evildoers who do not fear him,
such as sorcerers, adulterers, and perjurers (3:5, 19; cf. Zech 5). On the
other hand, we do not find in Malachi the hope for the humbling of
the nations (but see the universalist, though probably later, expectation
in 1:11).

Prior to the judgment God will send a messenger—hardly the prophet
himself, but some future figure—who will prepare God's way (3:1; cf.
Isa 40:3f.). In the concluding appendix to the book of the Twelve
Prophets this messenger is identified with the returning prophet Elijah,
who will reconcile fathers and children. Is not the unity of the
generations a basic condition for the transmission of the faith (Exod
13:8, 14; etc.)?

§23

JOEL AND JONAH

1. The time when Joel, the son of Pethuel, exercised his ministry is not indicated by a superscription or other source of information and can therefore only be inferred from his message itself. Consequently, the datings differ widely; I shall here mention only the two principal opinions. On the one hand, Joel is dated in the late preexilic period, which makes him a contemporary of Jeremiah and, given his expectation of salvation, an opponent as well. But the political troubles of that period, the distress caused by the Babylonians, and the uneasy lot of the final kings are not reflected in the book. It seems rather that the expectation of judgment upon the nations that have scattered Israel and sold the people as chattels (3:2f., 17) presupposes the catastrophe of 587 B.C. This would mean that the sanctuary in 1:14 and 2:17 is the second temple in a Jerusalem whose wall has already been rebuilt (2:6ff.). Also characteristic of this later period are the many verbal points of contact with the preaching of the earlier prophets.

The correspondences between Joel 3:16, 18 and Amos 1:2; 9:13 were probably the reason for putting the book of Joel ahead of the book of Amos (in the Hebrew text, but not in the Greek where the order is Hosea, Amos, Joel, Obadiah, Jonah). Was the reason that people read the earlier prophets in the light of the later ones, or were they seeking to establish a chronological order as interpreted by the later period?

Unlike the preexilic prophets Joel has a high esteem for the cult and therefore for the priesthood as well (1:9, 13f., 16; 2:14ff.). Was he therefore a "cult-prophet"? It is difficult to give a sure answer to this question, since in the postexilic period the prophets generally, and Malachi in particular, regarded the cult as very important. It seems in fact that Joel's ministry was not too far removed in time from that of Malachi—around 400 or in the fourth century B.C.

The book of Joel falls roughly into two parts (1:1–2:27; 2:28–3:21). Did they always belong together (except for the prose addition in 3:4–8) as the work of a single author? Scholars not infrequently voice doubts on this point. But principal motifs, like the catchword "the day of the Lord," keep recurring (2:1ff.; 2:31; 3:14; cf. also 2:10; 3:15).

283

Above all, each of the two parts closes with a profession of faith (2:27; 3:17), so that the two are linked together in a unity-in-tension. The overall structure forms a kind of liturgical composition made up of laments (1:4–20; 2:1–17) and promises of salvation (2:19ff.; 2:28–3:21). In them Joel takes up the themes familiar in the eschatological expectation of the postexilic prophets: destruction of the nations, blessing, deliverance, and salvation for Jerusalem. Characteristically, however, he takes as his starting point a concrete contemporary peril. Just as Haggai, for example, starts from the adverse economic situation of his time (1:6ff.; 2:16ff.), Joel takes a severe plague of locusts and a drought as the point of departure for his message.

A) 1:1–2:27
    1:2–20   Lament over the plague of locusts and the drought
             Vv. 2f.   Call for transmission of this event to coming generations: distress (v. 4) and deliverance by Yahweh (2:18)
             Vv. 5–14   Call for a national lament
             V. 15   Cry of lamentation: "The day of the Lord is near!" (Zeph 1:7; Isa 13:6; etc.)
             Vv. 16–18 Lament of a "we"-group
             Vv. 19f.   Petition ("Unto thee, O Lord, I cry") by the prophet as leader of prayer
    2   New lament and answer to prayer
             Vv. 1f.   Cry of alarm: The day of the Lord is coming (cf. Zeph 1:14f.)
             Vv. 3–11   Description of the enemy
             Vv. 12–14 Call for repentance
             Vv. 15–17 New call for a national lament
             V. 18   The catastrophe is averted
             Vv. 19f.   God's answer (oracle of answer to prayer): Blessing, dispersal of "the northerner" (the locusts? an army? cf. Jer 1:14f.)
             Vv. 21–24 Call for joy and thanksgiving
             Vv. 25–27 New promise of salvation with a profession of faith in God as its goal (2:27; 3:17)
             The verses in 2:28–3:21 are variously numbered.
B) 2:28–3:21
    2   Outpouring of the Spirit (vv. 28f.)
             Signs in heaven and on earth (vv. 30f.), deliverance in Jerusalem (cf. Obad 7)
    3   Judgment of the nations in Jerusalem (cf. Isa 17:12ff.; 29:5ff.; Ezek 38f.; Zech 12; 14)
             Vv. 4–8   Insertion in prose
             Vv. 18–21 Appendix after the concluding profession of faith in 3:17

A narrative framework (1:4; 2:18f.) provides the setting for a twofold lament with call to repentance. A short introductory account of the peril (1:4) is followed by a somewhat lengthy, organically constructed call for fasting and a national lament (see Zech 7f.; Isa 63). Joel sees the present distress as a "sign of the times," that is, as a harbinger of the final judgment: "The day of the Lord is near!" (1:15; 3:14; cf., earlier, Amos 5:18ff.; Isa 2:12ff.; especially Zeph 1:7ff.). In this eschatological perspective (2:1f., 10f.) Joel calls a second time for a national lament: An enemy spurred on by God is approaching Jerusalem! Here the plague of locusts is described with the help of motifs from the expected assault by the nations (Isa 5:26ff.; Jer 4–6; Ezek 38f.; especially Isa 13) and thus becomes symbolic of an eschatological-apocalyptic event. "The day of the Lord is great and very terrible; who can endure it?" (2:11; 2:31; Mal 3:2). The call for repentance opens up the possibility of deliverance:

> "Rend your hearts and not your garments."
> Return to the Lord, your God,
>   for he is gracious and merciful,
>   slow to anger, and abounding in steadfast love,
>   and repents of evil.
> Who knows whether he will not turn and repent . . . ?
> (2:13f.; cf. Jon 3:8ff.; also Exod 34:6f.; etc.).

Was the call to repentance obeyed as a matter of course? In any case a reversal of the situation did take place and is briefly described. Yahweh "became jealous" (see Zech 1:14; 8:2) out of compassion for his land and his people; he promises deliverance, new blessing, and the replacement of what had been lost. "I will no more make you a reproach among the nations" (2:18f.). The whole sequence depicted here of lament, call to repentance, granting of prayer, and promise of salvation has such an extraordinary impact that it is regarded as worthy of being passed on to the coming generations (1:2f.).

The promises of salvation in the first part (2:19f., 25–27) are given a broad development in the prophecies of the second part of the book (2:28–3:21). The outpouring of the Spirit accords the gift of prophecy—and thus an immediate relationship to God and the declaration of the future—to every person without distinction of age, sex, or social condition:

> And it shall come to pass afterward
>   that I will pour out my spirit on all flesh;
> your sons and your daughters shall prophesy,
>   your old men shall dream dreams,
>   and your young men shall see visions.
> Even upon the menservants and maidservants
>   in those days, I will pour out my spirit (2:28f.;
>   given a universal application in Acts 2).

Because of their sins God will lead the nations to Jerusalem: "I will enter into judgment with them [all the nations] there" (3:2, 12). As the one God (Joel 2:27) puts an end to the plague of locusts and the drought, so too he will protect his sanctuary at the final judgment. "All who call upon the name of the Lord" will be rescued in Jerusalem, which will be inviolable (2:32; 3:16f.; cf. Pss 46; 48).

2. The hope expressed in the approximately contemporary or slightly later book of Jonah reaches much further than that of Joel. In the book of the Twelve Prophets the book of Jonah holds a special place, because it is not a collection of prophetical sayings (see, e.g., 3:4) but a prose story about a prophet. It is attached, at times even verbally, to the tradition of the prewriting prophets, for example, the stories about Elijah, or to the third-person reports in the book of Jeremiah. In its skillful literary form it is close to the story that provides the framework for the book of Job, or to the books of Ruth and Esther. It can, to speak plainly, be called a novella with a didactic purpose, and (especially in chap. 4) it strikes the note of irony.

The book comprises several individual scenes. Three scenes, in which an obstinate Jonah resists Yahweh (1:1–3; 1:17–3:3; 4:1–11), enclose two further scenes in which the prophet encounters pagans and is shamed by their behavior (1:4–16; 3:4–10). The persons and the action show the ideal traits of types. The "wickedness" of Nineveh represents the bustle and activity of the great metropolis (1:2; 3:2f., 8; 4:11; cf. Gen 10:12), and Jonah represents the Israelite hearer or reader who is brought to a realization of God's freely bestowed compassion (4:2) for the pagans.

According to 2 Kgs 14:25 an otherwise unknown prophet named Jonah, the son of Amittai, told Jeroboam II, king of the northern realm (787–747 B.C.), that lost regions would be recovered. In the late postexilic period this "prophet of national salvation" becomes a "hero"—does the name "Jonah," which means "dove," already indicate his fickle or, better, his foolish nature?—in a didactic story of God's mercy to foreigners. Because the earlier Jonah had been approximately a contemporary of the prophet Amos, the little book of Jonah, which originated in the fourth or perhaps even in the third century, was subsequently given its place toward the front of the book of the Twelve Prophets.

There are certain discordances between the two halves of the book (chaps. 1f.; 3f.), for example, in the use of the name of God, which scholars have tried to resolve through literary criticism. But the little book is on the whole a literary unit, although it picks up various earlier traditions and narrative motifs (e.g., the man in the belly of a fish).

Jon 1–2	At sea
1:1–3	Introduction: commission and flight
1:4–16	On board ship: from peril in the storm to calm
1:17–2:10	Jonah three days and nights in the belly of the fish
	Vv. 3–10 Psalm of thanksgiving (probably an addition)
Jon 3–4	On land
3	New commission (vv. 1–3), preaching in Nineveh (v. 4), penitential fast by humans and beasts (vv. 5–9), God's repentance (v. 10)
4	Jonah's anger at God's clemency

A later stratum in the book of Jeremiah reflects on God's attitude to the nations, opposes threat and promise, and reaches a general, though somewhat stereotyped statement of principle; in the case of a threat the principle is as follows: "If at any time I declare concerning a nation or a kingdom, that I will pluck up . . . and destroy it, and if that nation . . . turns from its evil, I will repent of the evil that I intended to do to it" (Jer 18:7f.).

The little book of Jonah illustrates this possibility with an example, while also emphasizing the freedom of God's action quite sharply ("perhaps": 1:6; 3:9) and holding up a mirror in which an overly self-centered Israel may see itself.

God commissions Jonah to preach against the metropolis of Nineveh, because its wickedness has reached up to heaven. But instead of obeying (Amos 3:8), the prophet flees "from the presence of the Lord" by taking a ship to Tarshish (in Spain?), in order to get as far away as he can. But the runaway cannot escape from God (Ps 139:7ff.). The three-cornered relationship of Yahweh—Jonah—Nineveh is prepared for by the scene on the ship; in their colorful assemblage as well as in their reaction the crew anticipates the attitude of the metropolis. The crew responds in an exemplary way when each of them in anxiety and peril "cried to his god" (1:5). In fact, the obstinacy of Jonah in not calling on his God and not admitting his guilt brings the sailors to acknowledge Yahweh and to take Jonah's place, as it were, in confessing the Creator (1:9, 16).

When the crew is able to rescue itself from the raging storm only by throwing Jonah overboard, a "great fish" swallows Jonah at Yahweh's command and after three days and nights vomits him out on the shore (1:17–2:10). When Yahweh's commission reaches Jonah a second time (3:1–3), he has learned from experience and no longer resists, but he delivers his message with astonishing brevity: "Yet forty days, and

Nineveh shall be overthrown!" The city faces the fate of Sodom and Gomorrah, but the unconditional announcement of judgment allows an extension. The threat gives rise to "faith"; even the king (otherwise than in Jer 36) submits to the penitential ritual and summons humans and beasts to fasting and mourning and the renunciation of evil—in the hope that God may perhaps once again cancel the disaster and cease from his wrath, "so that we perish not" (3:9; 1:6; cf. Joel 2:13f.). In this reaction to the prophet's word Nineveh becomes a model unmatched by Israel (cf., e.g., Ezek 3:4ff.).

The effect of his preaching is disconcerting to Jonah. In the final scene, in which he is alone with God in front of the city, he raises an eloquent lament and subsequently justifies the obstinacy he had shown from the outset. In place of God (3:9f.), Jonah is angry, and angry at God's repentance and compassion (4:2). God tries to make the prophet change his mind by means of questions and by means of a shade-giving castor-oil plant, which grows up and then dies. But Jonah remains defiant in the face of God's goodness and wishes he might die (see 1 Kgs 19:4). The story ends with a question; it thus leaves the decision open and requires the hearer or reader to reflect. On the one hand, the little book points out to the people of God: "Not even in Israel have I found such faith" (Matt 8:10; cf. 12:41). On the other, it tries to bring Israel to an understanding of God's mercy toward foreigners.

§24

DANIEL

1. There is probably no piece of OT literature that has elicited so great a response as the book of Daniel with its teaching on the four empires (2; 7) and its expectation of the Son of man (7:13f.). The setting is the period of transition from the Babylonian empire to that of the Medes and Persians. But the historical information given about the period and about the succession of rulers and kingdoms is partially inaccurate and unreliable (5:1, 30f.; 9:1; etc.). However, the information becomes more exact when the book looks forward to events after the expedition of Alexander the Great (11:3f.). In fact, the visionary or historical presentation repeatedly has in mind Antiochus IV Epiphanes (2:41ff.; 7:8, 20ff.; 8:9ff., 23ff.; 9:26ff.; 11:21ff.), who did away with the cult in Jerusalem in 167 B.C. (8:12f.; 9:27; 11:31, 36f.) and tried to hellenize Judaism by force. In this time of desperate straits, when the very survival of the Jewish faith was at stake, the author wrote his book (ca. 164 B.C.). He has experienced the Maccabean uprising (which began in 166) but regards it as affording only "a little help" (11:34), since he looks to God for any decisive deliverance. The rededication of the temple (164 B.C., commemorated by the feast of Hannukah) and the death of Antiochus IV (163 B.C.) are not reflected in the book (see the differently formed prediction in 11:40ff.).

In this time of conflict Judaism was split into sympathizers with Hellenism and groups that remained true to their faith despite persecution (11:32ff.). The author was probably one of the "wise" (11:33; 12:3) among the "devout" (Hasidim, Hasideans, 1 Macc 2:42; 7:13), who were ready to suffer martyrdom if need be (Dan 11:33, 35) but who also hoped for a reversal of the situation, a reversal that would be due entirely to the coming of God's reign, and "by no human hand" (2:34, 45).

The late date of the book's composition explains why it does not have a place in the (Hebrew) canon of the prophets but is listed among the "Writings." The Greek Bible, however, and the translations that follow it put the book of Daniel among the prophetic books (see Matt

24:15), because of a justified sense that in terms of content it belongs
there.

The book of Daniel in the Greek Bible contains four lengthy—apocryphal—
additions. In chap. 3 there are the prayer of Azariah, which is reminiscent of
the communal lament in Dan 9:4ff., and the song of the three young men in
the fiery furnace. Two further additions come at the end of the book—the
story of Bel and the dragon, which mocks every kind of veneration of images,
and the story of Susanna, which glorifies the wisdom of Daniel.

2. The author, who lives at the beginning of the Maccabean period,
makes use, for his portrayal, of a figure who had from time immemorial
been regarded as righteous and wise (Ezek 14:14, 20; 28:3; Daniel is
also known from Ugarit) and has him come on the scene around the
time of the exile, from Nebuchadnezzar to Cyrus. In the first part of
the book, which is made up of stories or legends (chaps. 1–6), we are
told of Daniel in the third person, but in the visions of the second
part (chaps. 7–12) Daniel himself becomes the author and, after short
transitions (7:1; 10:1), speaks of himself in the first person. Thus, there
takes place within the book a passage from anonymity to the pseu-
donymity that is characteristic of (later) apocalyptic (Abraham, Baruch,
Enoch, Ezra [Esdras], and so on). Because the course of history down
to the present time of the apocalyptic writer and into the awaited
future is regarded as made up of a series of events that have long been
foretold and predetermined, the Daniel of the exilic period is bidden
to keep secret his knowledge of the future (12:4, 9; 8:26).

As certain unevennesses in the overall composition still indicate, the author
in the first or "biographical" part of the book is making extensive use of old
narrative material that knows nothing yet of the tribulations in the time of
Antiochus IV. Had this material been circulating in the form of individual
stories (e.g., chaps. 3; 4f.; 6), or had it already been assembled into a collection?
The manner of transmission may explain the striking fact that after the
introductory description of the situation (chap. 1), which is written in Hebrew,
there is an extensive middle section (more or less already in circulation) that
is written in Aramaic (2:4b–7:28). But the author makes use of the shift of
language for his presentation insofar as he makes his transition to Aramaic
precisely at the beginning of a speech (2:4b; cf. Ezra 4:8). In addition, chaps.
2 and 7, which belong together thematically, are also connected, across the
intervening story, by being in the same tongue. (O. Plöger).

The book of Daniel makes frequent use of prophetic traditions—
such as stories, visions, auditions, individual motifs—of the description, reminiscent of Ezekiel, of the prophet's reaction to revelations
(9:3; 10:2f., 8ff., 15). In the visions of Zechariah an angelic interpreter
had come on the scene as mediator between God and the prophet;
now this angelic mediator (4:10; 7:16) has a name, Gabriel (8:15ff.;

9:21ff.). Among the angels of the nations, who are the heavenly representatives of the earthly powers, Michael acts as protector and patron of Israel (10:13, 20f.; 12:1). Above all, Daniel keeps alive the (late) prophetic eschatology, although as used here it seeks to calculate the future in a manner different from that of the prophets. The dating of the imminent end-time, which is to dawn about three and a half years after Antiochus's desecration of the temple, becomes clearer in the course of the visions (7:25; 8:14; 9:24ff.; 12:7), until it undergoes a slight correction (by the author himself? by a third party?) in the light of the actual historical course of events (12:11f.).

3. The book thus continues prophetic traditions, along with sapiential ideas (1:17, 20; 2:20ff.; etc.), and at the same time stands at the beginning of "apocalyptic" literature in the narrower sense of this term. (But perhaps parts of the noncanonical book of Enoch are older.) The name "apocalypse" indicates the main content—"unveiling, revelation" regarding the course of and the end of history. But in any case the transition from later prophecy to apocalyptic is a fluid one, so that no fixed line of demarcation can be clearly drawn. In the prophecy of the collapse and fall of Gog (Ezek 38f.), the nocturnal visions of Zechariah (Zech 1–6), the expectation of the day of Yahweh in Joel and Third Isaiah (cf. Zech 12–14), the hope of a new heaven and a new earth (Isa 65:17; 66:2), and the announcement of a worldwide judgment in the Apocalypse of Isaiah (Isa 24–27) the question is raised of how God's power will win out in this world, and thus the way is prepared for apocalyptic thinking.

Isa 24–27, which is a self-contained, non-Isaianic section appended to the oracles against the nations in the book of Isaiah, is not yet an apocalypse in the strict sense, although certain apocalyptic motifs are already discernible (24:21f.; 26:19; 27:1; etc.). As in postexilic prophecy, the older prophetic writings are presupposed, but they are now actualized in a universalist framework. These chapters of Isaiah are a composition that is not easily intelligible in its details and probably came into existence gradually. At the very least, scholars (since B. Duhm) distinguish between eschatological expectations (Isa 24:1ff., 16ff.; etc.) and songs (24:10ff.; 25:1ff.; 26:1ff.; etc.)— added later?—which to a large extent sing of the downfall of an unnamed city. The element that is of the greatest theological significance is to be found in parts that are perhaps of late origin, 24:21–23; 25:6–8, and that express a hope of God's reign extending to all nations and even to the cosmos. According to an addition that is probably later still (25:8; cf. 26:19), this reign will be victorious even over death.

4. The real theme of the book of Daniel is the relation between worldly rule and the reign of God. The stories in the first part have as their aim the acknowledgment of God's rule in the present (2:46f.;

4:3; 4:22f., 31ff.; 5:18ff.; 6:25ff.; cf. Ps 145:13), while the second part announces the proximate coming of the reign of God, which will put an end to earthly political power (2:44; 7:27; 9:24; 11:40ff.). Here the question of "the end of the days" is the main focus of interest (2:28; 8:17ff.; 10:14; 12:6, 13); for the duration of the world is limited (11:24ff.). In the face of this future, which will radically transform present conditions, the apocalyptic writer seeks to comfort his contemporaries and to urge upon them fidelity in faith, hope, and perseverance.

I. Dan 1–6		Stories or legends about Daniel during three periods
		a) In the time of Nebuchadnezzar
	1	Education of Daniel and his three companions at the Babylonian court
	2	On the end of the empires: Nebuchadnezzar's dream of a statue made of various metals and smashed to pieces by a stone
	3	On constancy in faith: the deliverance of Daniel's three companions from the fiery furnace
	4	On the humbling of the world ruler: Nebuchadnezzar's dream, communicated to everyone, of the tree at the center of the world that is cut down (4:1–37)
		b) In the time of Belshazzar
	5	On the punishment of the ruler: the *mene-tekel* inscription that appears after the temple furnishings have been desecrated at Belshazzar's banquet
		c) In the time of Darius "the Mede"
	6	On Daniel's constancy in faith: deliverance from the lions' den
II. Dan 7–12		Visions in the form of autobiographical accounts by Daniel
		a) Still in the time of Belshazzar
	7	Four beasts, God's judgment, the Son of man
	8	Battle between a ram (Persia) and a he-goat (Alexander the Great)
		b) In the time of Darius "the Mede"
	9	Interpretation of Jeremiah's saying about seventy years as referring to "weeks of years"
		d) In the time of Cyrus, King of Persia
	10–12	Concluding vision
		10 Conversation with the angel by the great river (the Euphrates)
		11 Historical retrospect in the form of a prophecy ranging from Cyrus to Antiochus IV
		Judgment (11:40ff.) and salvation (12:1ff.) in the end-time
		12 Resurrection. Certainty of the end

The book begins its meditation on history in the period in which Israel loses its political independence. In the third year of Jehoiakim (the reference is to the first deportation, in 597 B.C.) Daniel, who is given the name Belteshazzar, is taken from Jerusalem to Babylon. Together with three sagacious friends, Hananiah, Mishael, and Azariah, who in Babylon receive the names Shadrach, Meshach, and Abednego (1:6; 2:26), he is instructed in the language and wisdom of the Chaldeans, that is, the Babylonians, at the court of Nebuchadnezzar. Despite their strict observance of the dietary laws the four prove superior to all others (chap. 1).

When Nebuchadnezzar is troubled by a dream, he demands of his Chaldean sages that they not only interpret his dream but also first tell him what the dream was. At the point when the Chaldean sages are questioned, the language of the book changes to Aramaic (2:4b). The task is too much for them, but Daniel and his friends, thanks to a revelation from the "God in heaven who reveals mysteries" (2:18, 22, 47; 4:9; 5:11ff.; cf. Gen 41:16, 38), are able to perform the double task. The content of the dream was a statue that, beginning at the head and ending with the feet, was made of gold, silver, bronze, and iron or clay, in that order. The statue is "by no human hand" smashed by a stone that became a mountain and "filled the whole earth" (2:31–35). The statue symbolizes four successive empires, which are most likely those of the Babylonians, Medes, Persians, and Ptolemies/Seleucids. (A later interpretation that identified the final empire with Rome was historically influential: Assyrians/Babylonians, Medes/Persians, Greeks, Romans.) The kingdom of God, represented by the mountain, "shall break in pieces all these kingdoms ... and it shall stand for ever" (2:44).

While Daniel's interpretation of the dream anticipates the events of chaps. 4f., the picture of the statue and the intention are strongly reminiscent of chap. 7. The colossal statue represents history (since the exilic period) as a man, and the succession of kingdoms is depicted by the sequence of increasingly less valuable metals. Both here and in the presentation given in chaps. 7 and 8, where the political powers appear as beasts, the book of Daniel is making use of ancient Near Eastern ideas.

Nebuchadnezzar, a foreign ruler, pays homage to the God of Daniel and confers high offices on Daniel and his friends (chap. 2). In the next scene, the three companions, who are representatives and models of Israel in exile, have their fidelity tested as well as their courage in confessing their faith. When they refuse to worship a golden statue erected by Nebuchadnezzar (such worship would be a violation of both the first and second commandments), they are thrown into a fiery furnace. But they are kept safe from burning by a heavenly being who is "like a son of the gods" (3:25). As before, Nebuchadnezzar praises the God "who is able to deliver in this way" (3:17, 29; 6:27).

Because of his experiences with the "Most High God" (4:2f.), Nebuchadnezzar makes known in an edict to all peoples his dream of a world-tree that is cut down so that only a stump is left. This dream, as Daniel interprets it, gives a preview of Nebuchadnezzar's fate. The arrogant (4:30) king will live like a beast until he acknowledges the Lord of heaven, who bestows sovereignty on human beings and exalts them and lays them low (4:32; 5:18f.); then he will regain his power (4:26; 34ff.). And so it happens.

In chap. 4 narrative material pertaining to Nabonidus (see the "Prayer of Nabonidus," discovered at Qumran), the last king of Babylon, who indulged in striking behavior, seems to have been transferred to Nebuchadnezzar. This may explain why Belshazzar (5:1; 7:1; 8:1), who during Nabonidus's absence for many years exercised only the office of regent in Babylon, is regarded in the book of Daniel as king and successor of Nebuchadnezzar. Nothing is said of the intermediate ruler, and a good three decades' passage of time is ignored.

While Nebuchadnezzar regains favor, the same is not true of "King" Belshazzar. At a banquet he decides to drink from the vessels that had been taken from the temple in Jerusalem. As he does so, a mysterious hand writes some words on the wall. The king's wise men are again unable to read and interpret the words (2:5ff.; 4:6f.; 5:8, 15; cf. Exod 9:11 P). Only Daniel can succeed. The words are *mene, mene, tekel,* and *parsin.* These are probably the names of three monetary units, "mina, shekel, half-mina," but they are interpreted to mean "measured, weighed and divided," that is, the end of Babylonian rule is at hand, and the kingdom will be divided among the Medes and Persians (chap. 5).

After the death of Belshazzar power passes to Darius the Mede (6:1). Historically, this man was in fact king of the Persians, not of the Medes. He was the father, not the son, of Xerxes (9:1) and was a successor of Cyrus (10:1). At the persuasion of his court officials, Darius issues a written and therefore irrevocable edict (6:8, 15; Esth 1:19; 8:8), ordering that for a month prayers be offered not to God but only to the divine king. Daniel remains true to his faith and is therefore thrown into the lions' den. But he is delivered, just as his three friends had earlier been delivered from the fiery furnace. Darius then issues an order that throughout the entire realm veneration be paid to "the living God" whose "dominion shall be to the end" (6:26; 4:3; 4:34).

Daniel's vision of the four beasts (chap. 7), who represent the four empires, is reminiscent of the vision in chap. 2. It also forms a transition from the stories to the part of the book that contains a series of visions told in the first person, which are really the heart of the book. Chaps. 2 and 7 are linked not only by the use of Aramaic (which ends with chap. 7) but also by a similarity of theme. The question of the "end," which had surfaced in chap. 2, dominates the second half of the book.

In the vision a lion with eagle's wings, a bear, and a winged leopard are followed by a beast with ten or eleven horns. This last beast is destroyed by a stream of fire that issues from the judgment seat of God, the "ancient of days." The stone that in chap. 2 smashes the colossal statue represents the kingdom of God, which puts an end to worldly kingdoms, and here a manlike figure—in contrast to the beasts—appears only after God's judgment has taken place. "With the clouds of heaven" comes one "like a son of man," and everlasting dominion is given to him (7:13f.). He is presented as an individual and is understood as such both in the book of Enoch and in the NT. But, strange to say, in Daniel's interpretation of the vision, the "son of man" is a collective entity—"the saints of the Most High," to whom the kingdom is given (7:18ff.). Are the "saints" regarded here as heavenly beings or do they represent the chosen people or, possibly, the more limited group of those who are oppressed yet remain true to their faith (7:21, 25)? Regarding the second alternative does not Israel come on the scene as "the people of the saints of the Most High" and, in this role, as participants in the kingdom (7:27)? Perhaps this vision of the future too was revised and reinterpreted. In any case, in its present form it was very much to the point. The series of the ten horns of the fourth beast, that is, the ten kings, leads to the decisive eleventh ruler, Antiochus IV, under whose baneful rule the kingdom of God will dawn.

The images in the next vision seem to be taken from the astral world. Daniel sees a ram with two horns, which represents the kingdom of the Medes and Persians, being trampled by a he-goat with a single horn, which symbolizes Alexander the Great. The single horn is replaced by four others (the successor kingdoms?). From one of these sprouts a further horn (Antiochus IV again) that grows not only toward the south and the east but up to heaven. It desecrates the sanctuary so that no sacrifice is any longer possible—but this state of affairs holds for only a limited time, about three and a half years (8:9ff., 23ff.). After a (subsequently introduced?) penitential prayer with a confession of sins and a petition for deliverance (9:4–20) the prophetic prediction of "seventy years" of judgment upon Israel (Jer 25:11; 29:10; Zech 1:12; 2 Chr 36:20f.) is interpreted for Daniel by Gabriel as referring to the tribulations of his own day and to the end whose proximate coming is hoped for. The angel explains that the years are to be understood as weeks of years (therefore 490 years). This actualization is an example of the meaning the preaching of the prophets had for the apocalyptic writers, and at the same time it shows how they read the tradition as related to the present and the future.

After a lengthy introduction that tells of a meeting with a messenger from God, the final vision (Dan 10–12) likewise leads up to a historical sketch, put in the form of an audition, which has its climax in the time of Antiochus IV and has for its goal the announcement of the end. The expected fall of Antiochus IV in Jerusalem (11:40ff.)—although it did not occur in the way described here—marks the beginning of the end-time, and the punishment of the evildoer signals the reversal of Israel's tribulation. The coming of God's reign means not only domination for Israel (7:27) but also the resurrection of Israel's dead. But only those who have been true to their faith will share in the salvation; the present split within Israel will be confirmed in the final judgment: "Many [i.e., probably all the members of the people of God, or perhaps only the devout, but in any case not humanity as a whole] who sleep in the dust of the earth shall awake, some to everlasting life, and some to shame and everlasting contempt" (12:2).

Thus, the end-time brings the fulfillment both of the prophetic threats of judgment and of the prophetic promises of salvation. God is true to his word.

PART IV

LITURGICAL AND SAPIENTIAL POETRY

§25

THE PSALTER

1. OT poetry includes not only the psalms but also large sections of the prophetic writings and the wisdom literature. Rarely do we find the rudiments of end rhyme (e.g., Jer 1:5; Ps 75:6f.). Alliteration occurs more frequently (Gen 1:1; Amos 5:5; Ps 1:1; etc.). The sentence rhythm is basic, that is, a parallelism or *parallelismus membrorum*, which combines similarity of form with variation in the manner of expression. Since sentence rhythm and thought, form and content ordinarily correspond in Hebrew, the end of the sentence coincides as a rule with the end of the verse.

A verse is formed of half verses, also known as rows, members, stichoi, or cola. A verse is also known as a period or, according as it has two or three members, a distich or tristich, a bicolon or tricolon.

If the metrical lines that belong together as a unit of meaning correspond to one another and express the same thought in different words, we speak of synonymous parallelism:

> Wash me thoroughly from my iniquity,
> and cleanse me from my sin! (Ps 51:2f.;
> cf. 5:1; Isa 1:10; etc.).

If the two members of the verse are in more or less strict contrast, there is an antithetic parallelism:

> The Lord knows the way of the righteous,
> but the way of the wicked will perish
> (Ps 1:6; cf. 27:10; Prov 10:1ff.).

If the second part of the verse or sentence continues the first instead of repeating it in a different form, there is a synthetic "parallelism." This too may be two- or three-membered, but the parallelism in what is said is hardly perceptible:

> The Lord is my light and my salvation;
> whom shall I fear? (Ps 27:1;
> cf. 23:1; 1:3; 103:1f.; Isa 40:31).

299

A special case, distinct from these three basic forms, is parabolic parallelism, in which one half of the verse presents an image, the other half its application:

> As a father pities his children,
>   so the Lord pities those who fear him
>   (Pss 103:11–13; 42:1; Isa 1:3; 55:9–11; Prov 26:14; etc.).

Three-membered verses often use a graduated parallelism, also called climactic, repetitive, or tautological parallelism. In it, key words are repeated but the thought advances. Ancient Near Eastern tradition that is older than Israel is often preserved in this form:

> Mightier than the thunder of many waters,
>   mightier than the waves of the sea,
>   the Lord on high is mighty!
>   (Pss 93:3f.; 24:7f.; 29:1f.; cf. 92:9; etc.).

More of an exception are "short verses," which contain no parallelism but are linked to form series of similar members (Pss 111f.; perhaps also series of laws such as the Decalogue).

Verses are sometimes joined together to form "strophes," which are separated from one another by a refrain (Pss 42f.; 46; Isa 9:8–21; 5:25ff.; etc.) In an alphabetical acrostic the initial letters of the verses or strophes follow in sequence the letters of the alphabet (Pss 9f.; 111f.; 145; Nah 1; Lam 1–4; etc.). Did this stylistic device serve as an aid to memory, or does it rather presuppose that the psalm in question was transmitted in written form, since the alphabetic arrangement is much easier to recognize when written down than when simply spoken?

Hebrew poetry undoubtedly also has a metrical structure, which is based on the succession of stressed and unstressed syllables (not on long and short syllables). According to one view, which reckons with "alternating" syllables, stressed and unstressed syllables follow upon one another in an almost regular fashion. According to the "accentual" system, which is freer and therefore probably more in keeping with the nature of Hebrew verse, a stressed syllable can be followed by several unstressed syllables.

Since the pronunciation of Hebrew changed in the course of time and since pure meters are rarely found, it will be very difficult to find a generally convincing solution to the problem of metrics.

2. From early times Israelites sang songs on widely varying occasions and accompanied these on musical instruments (Exod 15:20f.; Num 21:17f., 27ff.; Judg 5; 2 Sam 1:17ff.; cf. Amos 5:23; etc.). In the historical

books David is already presented as a singer of songs (2 Sam 1; 22f.), and Solomon as the author of proverbs and songs (1 Kgs 4:32). Just about half of the psalms are attributed to David, and two (72; 127) to Solomon.

The much-discussed superscription *lĕdāwīd* is admittedly ambiguous: "by David" or "for David." But it is intelligible only as a description of origin when it is connected with a somewhat detailed description of the situation (Pss 18; 51; etc.).

In any case, the introductory historical notices are later additions and therefore hardly reliable for historical purposes. They tell us less about the origin of the psalm than about the way it was understood at the time when the psalms were formed into a collection. "The Lord is my shepherd" (Ps 23) is hardly a song of confidence from the time of David, nor is Ps 90 really a "prayer of Moses." These secondary historical attributions, which increase in number in the Greek Bible, are the result of an interpretative intention that sought to give a psalm a suitable location in the history of Israel (compare Ps 51:4 with 2 Sam 12:13).

A number of psalms are assigned to various guilds of singers in the postexilic temple; thus Ps 50 and Pss 73–83 are assigned to Asaph (see 1 Chr 15:17, 19). A group of twelve psalms (42–49; 84f.; 87f.) belong to the "hymnal" of the Korahites, whose duty it was "to praise the Lord, the God of Israel, with a very loud voice" (2 Chr 20:19; cf. 35:15; 1 Chr 9:19, 31). These temple singers are hardly to be regarded as the composers of the psalms, but rather as their transmitters. Just as additions were later made to the sayings of the prophets, so in all likelihood older songs were further developed in the later period.

The psalms may be divided into smaller or larger collections on the basis chiefly of the superscriptions and secondarily of shared key words (thus the enthronement psalms, the Hallelujah psalms, and so on; see the outline of the Psalter, below). The existence of a number of doublets (Ps 14 = 53; 40:14ff. = 70; etc.) shows that these collections were originally independent of one another and were only later joined together.

Four times, always at the conclusion of a subcollection (at the end of Pss 41; 72; 89; 106) there is a doxology: "Blessed be the Lord. . . ." These make it possible, at least in retrospect, to regard the Psalter as like the Pentateuch inasmuch as it comprises five books. Ps 150 may be regarded as a concluding hymn for the entire Psalter. Conversely, the invitatory call to salvation in Ps 1 and Ps 2, a royal psalm that is probably interpreted eschatologically, is prefixed to the first book of the Psalter, which contains the extensive and relatively ancient Davidic Psalter (3–41). The second book and in part the third book are occupied by the "Elohist" Psalter (42–89), which is a combination of various smaller collections and in which the name Yahweh was later replaced in large measure by Elohim, "God." Does this substitution result from a strict interpretation of the third commandment, or is the intention rather, as in other more recent literature (Chronicles, Job) to emphasize the distinction between God and humanity?

Arrangement of the Psalter
Book I: Pss 1–41
with concluding doxology, 41:13

Ps 1	Introduction to the entire Psalter: "Salvation" to the reader of the scriptures (the Psalter)
Ps 2	Royal psalm, at one time probably counted as number 1 (see Acts 13:33) and interpreted eschatologically
Pss 3–41	First Davidic Psalter Pss 3–41 (without 33): "Of David"

Book II: Pss 42–72
with concluding doxology, 72:18f.
Book III: Pss 73–89
with concluding doxology, 89:52

Pss 42–83	Elohist Psalter composed of three shorter collections (a–c)
	a) Pss 42–49: "Of the sons of Korah" Subgroups distinguished by their annotations: Pss 42–45; 46; 47–49 Appendix, Ps 50: "Of Asaph"
	b) Pss 51–72: Second Davidic Psalter More specifically: Pss 51–56; 68–70 (LXX, also 67; 71): "Of David" Subgroups distinguished by their annotations: Pss 52–55; 56–60; 62–64; 65; 67f. Appendix, Ps 72: "Of Solomon" (cf. Ps 127; 1 Kgs 4:32) Concluding note in Ps 72:20, "The prayers of David, the son of Jesse, are ended"
	c) Pss 73–83: "Of Asaph"
Pss 84–89	Appendix to the Elohist Psalter Pss 84f.; 87f.: "Of the sons of Korah" Ps 86: "Of David" Ps 88: also "Of Heman the Ezrahite" Ps 89: "Of Ethan the Ezrahite" (cf. 1 Kgs 4:31; 1 Chr 15:17ff.)

Book IV: Pss 90–106
with concluding doxology, 106: 48 (= 1 Chr 16:36)
Book V: Pss 107–150
with concluding doxology, Ps 150 (v. 6)

Ps 90	"Prayer of Moses" (cf. Deut 32f.)
Pss 93; 96–99;	
47	"Enthronement psalms"
Pss 104–106;	Hallelujah psalms (with superscription or signature "Praise
111–117,	the Lord" as response of the community; cf. 106:48)
(without 114?);	
135; 146–150	
Pss 108–110;	
138–145	"Of David"
Pss 120–134	"Pilgrimage" or "Gradual" psalms
	Individual psalms, e.g., the "law-psalm" 119 (cf. 1; 19)

The Greek translation twice combines two psalms into one (Pss 9f., rightly; Ps 114, wrongly), and twice divides two psalms (116; 147). The result is that the numbering differs in the Septuagint, being usually one short.

3. Since antiquity the psalms have been approached from widely diverging points of view.

The eschatological-messianic interpretation goes back to the early Jewish period and was practiced in the Church from the beginning, but it has little basis in the text. The psalms do contain statements about the future, but even in texts that readers would like to interpret eschatologically because of the universalist outlook, the formulas characteristic of the prophetic promises are lacking, namely, "On that day" and similar phrases.

In the nineteenth century the historical interpretation gained acceptance. It endeavors to explain a psalm in terms of its inferred time of origin. But it is hardly possible to determine the historical locus of the psalms, because they translate their concrete occasion in general, more or less formulaic language. They do not describe individual situations as such but typical, exemplary events, so that a given psalm can still be prayed in a changed situation and provide words of lament or praise that the ones praying can make their own. For this reason datings of the psalms are extremely uncertain and disputed. Only Ps 137, "By the waters of Babylon, there we sat down and wept," points with certainty to the exilic period. But the other psalms cannot be regarded as all preexilic (see the commentary of B. Duhm) or as certainly all postexilic. Rather we must settle for some psalms being preexilic (e.g., 2; 24; 29; 45–48; 93; 110), others postexilic.

The form-critical interpretation, which despite some precursors was really the achievement of H. Gunkel, provided the basis on which S. Mowinckel developed his cult-historical interpretation. Mowinckel understood the psalms as cult songs and understood the cult itself as a sacred drama that was centered around an enthronement feast. But a cultic interpretation of the psalms is often uncertain because the basis for it is too weak and our knowledge of Israel's liturgy (Exod 23:14ff.; etc.) too limited for us to be able to bring the two into harmony.

Although most of the psalms are laments or songs of petition, the superscriptions and the doxologies inserted into the text turn them into "songs of praise." This is the justification for describing the Psalter as "the hymnbook of the community of the Second Temple" (J. Wellhausen). But later psalms themselves could hardly have been used solely as songs for (public) worship, but were also used as "private" prayers by individuals (see the Lamentations of Jeremiah). In any case, we must distinguish between a first and a second "home," between origin and later application of a psalm—or, in the case of the postexilic liturgy, of the entire collection of psalms.

The stylistic-literary interpretation (M. Weiss) endeavors to understand the individual psalm as an individual work of art, a linguistic and structural unity. But do we not fail to take into account the heavy influence exercised by tradition when we turn it into a raw material for the creative efforts of a poet?

Scholars are only now beginning to apply to the psalms the traditionhistorical approach, which has been so fruitful in dealing with the Pentateuch and which explains the text in terms of a gradual growth through history, while endeavoring at the same time to distinguish various strata (oral or already written) as resulting from changing situations.

4. Our own public worship still retains, in short liturgical formulas, the two chief ways in which the psalms speak of God: the hymn, which speaks of God in the third person, *Hallelu-jah*, "Praise the Lord!"; and the petition that is addressed directly to God, *Kyrie eleison*, "Lord, have mercy!"

a) The song of Miriam, which sings of Yahweh's victory over the Egyptian pursuers, may be taken as "the simplest and most important basic form of the Israelite hymn" (F. Crüsemann):

Sing to the Lord, for he has triumphed gloriously;
the horse and his (chariot-)rider he has thrown into the sea! (Exod 15:21).

The hymn begins with an invitation to sing or praise, which is directed to a plurality of persons; the main part, introduced by *kî*, ("for") then follows. This main part is both basis and content for the invitation to praise; to praise God means precisely to recount his deeds. This bipartite structure of invitation and main part recurs in the later more lengthy hymns, but it is expanded in various ways and at times stretched to the breaking point (Pss 33; 100; 145–150; etc.). These later hymns may, for example, take over the originally independent hymnic participial style (104:2ff.; 136:3ff.; etc.), or they may contain verses modeled on the invitation itself (103:20ff.; 136:26; etc.). Occasionally God's historical interventions (Pss 135f., and in the "historical psalms," 105f.; 114; 78) or, more frequently, his creative power and goodness (Ps 96, or in the "nature psalms," 8; 19A; 104; cf. 24:1f.; 29) are praised, as in the following phrases, which have already become formulaic: "For he is good; for his steadfast love endures for ever!" (Pss 106:1; 107:1; 118:1ff.; 136:1; etc.).

In his eschatological hymns the prophet Second Isaiah calls for joy even now at the future deeds of God (see 21,2d; cf. Zech 2:10; 9:9f.; etc.). But even individuals can exhort themselves: "Bless the Lord, O my soul [i.e., my self, my being]!" (Pss 103f.; 146; 8; Exod 15). In these forms for the use of individuals, was the hymn gradually breaking its ties with its original life setting, namely, the liturgy (Ps 135:1f.; etc.)?

b) While the hymn with its exhortation is directed immediately to the community, the "lament" is addressed to God and is therefore a prayer in the strict sense: *Hosianna*, "(My God,) help!" (Ps 3:7; etc.), "O Lord God, remember me, be gracious, forgive!" (Judg 16:28; Amos 7:2; also 1 Kgs 18:26 or, in a secular context, 2 Sam 14:4; etc.). The petition with the appeal to God is the key element here, so that "song of petition" would be a more appropriate description. The name "lament" is based on the reasons given for the petition; these consist of an account of the present situation or, in other words, a lament in tribulation.

"There is not a single psalm of lament that stops with the lament. The lament is not an end in itself. . . . The purpose of the lament is not simply a description of suffering and an expression of self-pity; it is rather to obtain an end of the suffering. . . . The real function of the lament is the appeal in which the sufferer turns from himself to the one who can avert the suffering. Seen in this perspective, a lament as such is a movement toward God" (C. Westermann, *Forschung am Alten Testament* II, 1974, pp. 255, 261).

The lament in its developed form is therefore essentially tripartite: invocation, lament, petition. But to these basic components other structural elements (a–e in the following list) are often added, though not in any strict sequence. Communal laments ("we") and individual laments ("I") have a similar structure.

1. Invocation of God, often with a short petition or question added
   "O God, why dost thou cast us off for ever?" (Ps 74:1)
   "My God, my God, why hast thou forsaken me?" (22:1)
   "Out of the depths I cry to thee, O Lord!" (130:1)
   a) Reference to God's earlier saving acts, especially the exodus
   "Thou hast redeemed" (74:2; cf. 44:1–3; 85:1–3; Isa 51:9f.)

2. Lament in the form of a description of distress: sickness, guilt, persecution
   by enemies, abandonment by God—with typical questions,
   "Why?" "How long?"
   "Why should the nations say, 'Where is their God?' " (Pss 79:10; 115:2)
   "How long, O Lord? Wilt thou forget me for ever?" (13:1)
   Laments can be further divided into three parts according to the subjects of
   the sentences (C. Westermann): the enemy, we/I, thou (see 13:1f.)
b) Assertion of innocence
   "If thou triest my heart . . . thou wilt find no wickedness in me" (17:3)
c) Profession of confidence
   "God my king is from of old" (74:12)
   "I have trusted in thy steadfast love" (13:5; cf. 22:19f.; 28:7; 71:6)
   Like the historical retrospect (a) the expression of confidence (c) at the same
   time gives a reason why God should intervene
3. Petition
   "Restore our fortunes, O Lord" (126:4; cf. 80:14)
   "Create in me a clean heart, O God" (51:10f.)
d) Vows of praise, promising praise and thanksgiving after deliverance
   "We . . . will give thanks to thee for ever" (79:13)
   "I will give to the Lord the thanks . . . I will sing praise" (7:17; 13:5)
e) Assurance of being heard
   An oracle of salvation may follow upon the petition. This response from
   the mouth of priest or prophet is present only by allusion in the psalms
   (12:5; 60:6ff.; 85:8ff.; 107:19f.; 119:25, 81; 1 Sam 1:17; Lam 3:57; in the
   form of an answer given to himself by the person praying, Ps 42:5, 11;
   130:5), but explicitly in the message of Second Isaiah (see Isa 50:4; see
   21,2a).
   Such an oracle of salvation seems to be presupposed where the lament ends
   in a "shift of mood," namely, the assurance of having been heard:

> Depart from me, all you workers of evil;
>   for the Lord has heard the sound of my weeping
>   (Ps 6:8ff.; cf. 28:6ff.; 56:9ff.; etc.).

Babylonian lamentations, earlier in date, already show a similar
structure with comparable motifs; these probably became known to
the Israelites through the Canaanites. On other points too there are
all kinds of connections with the prayer literature of the ancient Near
East. The distinguishing mark of the OT psalms is that in them
community and individual alike apply the first commandment in a
concrete way by turning to God alone in time of distress and looking
for help solely from him. He is the true physician (Exod 15:26) who
slays and restores to life (1 Sam 2:6; Deut 32:39; etc.).

The original context for the lament, like the hymn, was the liturgy.
Communal laments were sung at a public celebration of communal
mourning. The people were originally summoned to this kind of "fast"
in times of military pressure, or during a natural catastrophe, or on

some other occasion (1 Kgs 8:33ff.; 21:9ff.; Jer 36:9; Jonah 3:5; Joel 1:5ff.). After the destruction of the temple in 586 B.C. there were regular commemorative days marked by a "fast" (Zech 7:3ff.). This may explain why most of the communal laments in their present form (Pss 44; 74; 79f.; 83; 85; cf. Lam; Isa 63:15ff.; Dan 9) originated in the exilic and postexilic periods.

Of the individual laments (Pss 3; 5–7; 13; 22; and many others) it is likely that the majority originated in a liturgical context; not all of them, however, since they could be prayed far from the sanctuary (Pss 42f.), for example on a sick bed (Isa 38). Since the occasions for prayer or petition to God are many and varied, the laments can hardly have had a single common life setting or *Sitz im Leben*. From the varied references to persecution, imprisonment, sickness, and so on we must conclude rather to a specific background in each case: the situation of one who has been accused (Pss 7; 26; etc.), for example, or that of a sick person (Pss 38f.; 41; etc.) and to corresponding institutions of sacral law, such as the cultic divine judgment or the procedure for reincorporating the sick person into the community (see most recently W. Beyerlin, K. Seybold). But by and large the statements in the psalms are too general and standardized, and insufficiently concrete to allow definitive inferences. Ultimately the psalms ask for the restoration of community with God.

Whatever the original concrete occasion may have been, communal laments and individual laments alike may move beyond it and lament the universal human situation before God; for example, in Ps 90 the transiency of human beings (cf. 103:14ff.; 104:29ff.; etc.). In the penitential psalms (51; 130; 32; cf. 6; 38; 102; 143), instead of a lament over distress the confession of sins and the petition for forgiveness play the dominant role.

The psalm of thanksgiving may be thought of as flowing out of the lament. The ones in distress who utter a lament promise that they will thank God: "I will give to the Lord the thanks due to his righteousness" (Ps 7:17; see above, structural element [d]). Once they have experienced deliverance, they voice this thanks in the sanctuary at the time of sacrifice: "I will pay thee my vows" (Ps 66:13; cf. 116:17; 118:19; Jonah 2:10). But the song of thanksgiving may be separated from the sacrifice of thanksgiving or even be replaced by it (in Hebrew both are called *tôdâ*, Amos 4:5; Ps 50:14). The song of thanksgiving takes over from the individual lament the invocation of God: "I thank thee that thou hast answered me" (Ps 118:21; cf. Isa 12:1; Jonah 2:3).

The heart of the song of thanksgiving is the recounting of God's act of deliverance (Ps 40:1ff.) to the community or to those invited by the one praying (22:22ff.; 66:16; 116:18f.; 118:17). The avowal is passed on so that others may have similar experiences. In the songs of thanksgiving (30; 32; 41; 66:13ff.; 116; 118; Isa 38:10ff.; Jonah 2:3ff.; cf. Ps 18, in the mouth of the king) the account is often expanded by a review of the distress suffered and the lament raised.

The hymn ("Praise, the Lord, for . . .") and the song of thanksgiving ("I thank thee, because . . .") differ in structure and probably in origin as well. It is hardly suitable, therefore to locate both (with C. Westermann) as descriptive and reportorial praise respectively in a single category of "praise" (see F. Crüsemann). Whether there is also a communal song of thanksgiving (Pss 124; 129) is disputed.

Just as the song of thanksgiving follows upon the vow of praise in the lament, so the song of confidence develops the profession of trust in God: "The Lord is the upholder of my life" (Ps 54:4). The expression of confidence, which is a structural element (above [c]) in the lament and also in the song of thanksgiving, has achieved independent existence in the psalm of confidence, whether individual (23; 27) or communal (125; 46; etc.). But the background of distress still makes its presence felt, so that the profession of confidence does not lose touch with reality nor contradict appearances:

> The Lord is my shepherd, I shall not want . . .
> even though I walk through the valley of the shadow
>   of death (Ps 23:1, 4).

c) Three loosely interconnected groups of psalms—royal songs, songs of Zion, enthronement songs—are set apart less on form-critical than on thematic and tradition-historical grounds.

The royal psalms (2; 18; 20f.; 45; 72; 89; 101; 110; 132; 144) differ widely among themselves in form, structure, and probably *Sitz im Leben* as well. "Their internal unity" derives solely from the fact that "all of them deal with kings" (H. Gunkel). The subject of the psalm is the reigning king, usually in the Davidic dynasty (but is the marriage song Ps 45 from the northern kingdom?). But these psalms contain so little concrete contemporary information and are so bent on painting a picture of the "ideal ruler" (justice, long life, worldwide power; see §2c) that it was easy for later generations to interpret them as eschatological and messianic. "Not the king, but God, stands in the foreground. There were apparently no songs glorifying the king, nor did the king boast of his own renown. By the same token, the royal songs in the cult speak less of the king's might and his accomplishments than of God's promises to him, the petitions he addresses to God, and the things for which he gives thanks to God" (G. Fohrer, *Introduction to the Old Testament*, p. 270).

This dependence of the king finds expression in, for example, the fact that dominion and the dignity of a son are promised him only in a (prophetic) oracle (Pss 2; 89; 110) and the fact that the king is in need of prayer or intercession (Pss 20f.; 72; 144). On the one hand, then, the humanity of the king is not forgotten (89:46f.; 144:3f.); on the other, it is not difficult to apply to all what is predicated of the king or, in other words, to "democratize" the royal psalms (Ps 8).

The psalms of Zion, which from a formal standpoint are close to communal songs of confidence (Pss 46; 48; 76; cf. 87; 84; 122; 132; 137:3), give praise to the place where God dwells, namely, Zion. The prophets were already critical (Isa 28:15f.; Mic 3:11f.) of the notion that the "city of God" was impregnable, secure against the sea and the nations (see also Isa 17:12ff.; etc.). Do the psalms of Zion presuppose a liturgical celebration with a procession (Pss 48:12f.; 46:8)?

The question just asked is even more important for an understanding of the more hymnic "enthronement psalms" or psalms of Yahweh's kingship (47; 93; 96–99), which proclaim the royal dominion of God: "Yahweh is king" (JB) or, as it may also be translated, "The Lord reigns" (RSV; 93:1; 96:10; etc.). In its context in Ps 47 (vv. 5, 8) does not this cry suggest a cultic celebration, especially since such a celebration is documented for the enthronement of the earthly king (2 Sam 15:10; 2 Kgs 9:13)? S. Mowinckel (1922; earlier, P. Volz, 1912) has concluded that, analogous to the Babylonian feast of the New Year, at which the struggle with chaos, the creation of the world, and the enthronement of the god Marduk were celebrated, a feast of Yahweh's enthronement was part of the autumn festival. Down to the present time his views have had a following but have also met with tough resistance. The texts do not permit any convincing reconstruction of the liturgical service, although one may think of a procession of the ark, at the entrance of which into the temple God was proclaimed king (see Ps 24:7ff.). Of course, the antiquity of the relevant psalms is disputed, but during the exile Second Isaiah (Isa 52:7–10) presupposes the traditions embodied in the enthronement psalms. Pss 47 and 93 seem to be old, while Pss 96–99 seem to be more recent, perhaps even postexilic. The key elements common to the psalms of this group are the confession of God's universal royal rule and his fidelity to his people (93:5; 99:4ff.).

Just as here and there in these three groups of psalms the celebration of a liturgy can be glimpsed (Pss 2; 110; 46–48), so too in other psalms liturgical elements are to be found (Pss 115; 121; 134; etc.). In particular, it is possible to discern liturgies of entry, connected with entrance into the temple (Pss 15; 24; cf. Mic 6; Ezek 18), liturgies for feasts of thanksgiving (Pss 107; 118), or prophetic judgment speeches during public worship (Pss 50; 81; cf. 95; 82). Liturgical proceedings are similarly reflected in prophetic texts (e.g., Jer 14; Mic 7).

Other psalms (112; 127f.; 133) contain language and ideas from the sapiential sphere. The same can be said of the so-called law-psalms 1; 119 (19B), which praise the way of the righteous; Ps 73 (37; 49), which reflects on the lot of the righteous as compared with the "end" of the godless; and the historical psalm, Ps 78. But sapiential elements are also found far and wide—for example, the petition "Teach us to number our days, that we may get a heart of wisdom" (Ps 90:12; cf. 32:8ff.; 111:10; etc.).

§26

SONG OF SOLOMON, LAMENTATIONS, RUTH, AND ESTHER

The three poetic books, Song of Solomon (or Song of Songs), Lamentations, and Qoheleth/Ecclesiastes (see §28), and the two prose stories, Ruth and Esther, which in our Bible are scattered among the historical (Ruth, Esther), poetic (Qoheleth, Song of Solomon) and prophetic (Lamentations) books, are in the Hebrew Bible gathered into a single group known as the five *Megilloth* or festal "scrolls." The book of Esther had always been connected with the feast of Purim, and Lamentations was used from early times for liturgies of mourning. Only from the Middle Ages on, however, is the liturgical use of the other books attested: the Song of Solomon at Passover (Easter), Ruth for the feast of Weeks (Pentecost), Lamentations at the commemoration of the destruction of the temple, and Qoheleth/Ecclesiastes at the feast of Booths or autumn feast. The five books are arranged partly according to the yearly sequence of feasts and partly in a (supposedly) chronological order, so that the book of Ruth, which is set in the time of the judges, comes first. There was still a certain freedom in the third part of the canon, the "Writings" (see §1a).

The Song of Solomon (and the same can be said of Ruth and Esther) is a good example of how slight the connection of the books with the feasts may be.

1. In any event, the Song of Solomon, or Song of Songs, that is, the song that surpasses all other songs, has been interpreted in diverse ways despite its naturalistic language.

(a) The allegorical interpretation considers the picture given of the relationship between the lovers, that is, bride and bridegroom, to be the same as that found in the figurative speeches of the prophets (Hos 1–3; Jer 2; Ezek 16; 23; also Isa 5) and applies it to Yahweh's relationship with Israel. This interpretation, which goes back to the early Jewish period, was taken over by Christianity in modified form, the relationship in the Song being regarded as symbolic of the relationship of Christ with the Church and even with the individual soul. But the wording of the book itself offers hardly any basis for such an interpretation.

(b) The cultic-mythical interpretation connects the Song in its original, now more or less concealed, sense with the relationship between a god and a goddess; in the background (it is said) is the ritual of the sacred marriage (in the cult of Ishtar and Tammuz), which influenced at least the wording of the Song. There are indeed occasional linguistic points of contact with cultic-mythical texts, but the attempt to explain the Song as a whole in this light is strained and arbitrary.

(c) The "natural," literal interpretation sees the Song as a collection of individual, formerly independent love songs. The order of the collection, which does not form a unified, purposeful whole or a single dramatic entity, was imposed later on, as in the case of the prophetic books. What unity there is is only occasionally thematic; it is based for the most part on accidental and superficial factors, such as the repetition of catchwords (W. Rudolph).

What was the *Sitz im Leben* of these love songs and, at the same time, the reason for their being passed on? Do they sing of "free love"? In fact, most if not all of the songs were probably sung at wedding celebrations that went on for several days and involved music, dancing, and playing. In other words, they hymn the relationship of bridegroom and bride (see 4:9ff.; 1:2ff.; 2:4ff.). As in modern Arabic songs, the bridegroom could be addressed as "king" and even compared with Solomon (1:4, 12; 3:11; 6:8f.; 8:11f.). Perhaps "Shulammite" describes the bride as a prince's daughter who "belongs to Solomon" (6:13f.). In addition, all sorts of particular points can be explained by reference to wedding customs which, though not attested in the OT (see Gen 29:12ff.; Jer 16:8f.; on the king, Ps 45), are for a later period.

Descriptive songs sing of the charm and attractiveness of the bride: "Behold, you are beautiful, my love, behold, you are beautiful!" (4:1ff.; 6:4ff., 13ff.; and of the man, 5:10ff.). The text is full of comparisons and allusions; thus vineyard and garden are symbols of the woman (2:15; 4:12); gathering, eating, and drinking refer to the enjoyment of sex (4:16f.; 8:2; cf. 7:2). The woman, too, speaks with surprising frequency: "My own vineyard I have not kept" (1:6); "My beloved is mine and I am his" (2:16; cf. 6:3; 8:6). Sometimes the man speaks; occasionally there is a dialogue (1:15f.).

As the language shows, the songs came from the late postexilic period, probably from the Jerusalem area (3:10f.; etc.), but they contain older traditional material from the time of the monarchy. The comparison of the bridegroom with Solomon may have suggested the attribution of the collection to the latter. Since Solomon, teacher of wisdom, was also regarded as the author of Proverbs and Ecclesiastes (see 1 Kgs 4:32), we may conclude to a connection between the Song of Songs and the wisdom literature—a connection that takes linguistic shape in individual expressions. These love songs, after all, hardly reflect the simple language of the people; they are artistic, poetic productions and, like the psalms, were not composed for an individual occasion but were intended as patterns and types.

E. Würthwein sums up his views on the origin of the songs in this way: "The poems of the Song of Songs are art-songs from the circle of the postexilic sages in Jerusalem and were meant to be sung during wedding celebrations, which usually lasted for seven days" (HAT I/18, 1969, p. 34).

The "natural" interpretation of the Song of Songs was found to be scandalous later on when the Song had (because of Solomon's authority) already been included among the "Writings." Was the allegorical interpretation an effort to eliminate the scandal? Taken in itself, the Song of Songs speaks with unabashed joy of the beauty of the human person and of nature as well (2:11ff.) and thus of creation—and is there not theological justification for this kind of statement?

2. Lamentations is entirely different in character. Its basic emotion is not joy but sorrow; the laments are not "secular" but are uttered in the presence of God. They describe the situation after the great collapse of 587 B.C., when Jerusalem and the temple were destroyed (2:6ff.); when the king, "the breath of our nostrils, the Lord's anointed, was taken" (4:20); and when the land, "our inheritance," was "turned over to strangers" (5:2). As far as the form and motifs of the laments are concerned, Lamentations combines characteristic elements of the communal lament (especially chap. 5; cf. Ps 44; etc.; and see §25,4b) with elements of the *Qinah* or dirge, which contrasts the brilliant past with the comfortless present and likes to begin with an "Oh!":

> Oh, how lonely she sits,
>   the city once thronged with people,
> as if suddenly widowed.
>   Though once great among the nations . . . .
> Her friends have all betrayed her
>   and become her enemies (1:1f. JB;
>   cf. 2:1; 4:1; Isa 1:21ff.).

This structure has given the songs their name, whether they be called in Hebrew by the introductory "Oh!" and the genre name *qinah* or whether they be called the Book or Scroll of Lamentations. Each of the first four chapters has twenty-two strophes made up of three or (in chap. 4) two lines. Each strophe begins with the next letter of the alphabet (for similar alphabet acrostics, see Pss 9f.; etc.; see also §25,1). The much shorter lamentation in chap. 5 is not alphabetical, but it does have twenty-two verses, and there are twenty-two letters in the Hebrew alphabet.

As the form already indicates, the individual songs were originally independent and were probably only later on combined to form a more or less loosely organized whole. They did originate, however, in the same geographical area, more likely Palestine than Babylon, and at approximately the same time, more or less close to the catastrophe of 587. Perhaps some descriptions (e.g., 4:17ff.) are even based on the experience of eyewitnesses? The Greek and Latin translations of the OT identify this eyewitness by connecting the songs with the book of Jeremiah (a connection still reflected in our modern Bibles) and by regarding the prophet as their author (see 2 Chr 35:25). And in fact Jeremiah was quite familiar with the lament as a form of utterance (8:21f.; etc.). Nonetheless for reasons both of chronology and of content Jeremiah, who was taken off to Egypt soon after the catastrophe, cannot be regarded as the author. It is even uncertain whether Lamentations had one or several authors. The *Sitz im Leben*, on the other hand, is clearer. For though Lamentations (especially the first lament) was perhaps not composed with the liturgy in view, the laments were in any case soon pressed into service in the liturgies of "fasting" or mourning that commemorated at regular intervals the fearful events of 587 (Zech 7f.).

In a manner not unlike that of the Deuteronomistic history, which in its historical retrospect from the standpoint of the exilic period makes confession of Israel's guilt, Lamentations endeavors, in prayer, to explain the situation that has arisen. In an admission of guilt they apply to contemporary Israel the accusations and announcements of judgment that had been uttered by the writing prophets:

> The Lord has done what he purposed,
> has carried out his threat (2:17).

> The Lord has become like an enemy,
> he has destroyed Israel. . . .
> The Lord has scorned his altar,
> disowned his sanctuary (2:5, 7).

In his wrath Yahweh has inflicted disaster (2:1ff.; 3:43ff.), but Israel's own sin is the ultimate reason: "Jerusalem sinned grievously" (1:8; cf. 1:13f.; 3:42; 4:6; 5:7, 16). Much of the blame belongs to the prophets (i.e., the so-called prophets of salvation):

> Your prophets have seen for you
>   false and deceptive visions;
> they have not exposed your iniquity
>   to restore your fortunes (2:14; cf. 4:13).

Just as Lamentations here adds its voice to the attack made by the writing prophets (Jer 23; etc.), so too the laments acknowledge (for example) that the prophetic indictments against Israel's policy of securing safety through treaties are justified (4:17; 5:6f.).

In the midst of afflictions that are described in concrete detail, the lamentations call out to God (1:21; 2:18). There is no one else capable of giving comfort (1:9, 16f., 21). Only he who struck the blow can hear the petition and perhaps grant it. The prayers uttered in the Lamentations are firmly grounded in the conviction that "the Lord will not cast off for ever" (3:31; cf. 3:21ff.; 4:22), but they dare voice this hope only in a restrained manner:

> Restore us to thyself, O Lord, that we may be restored!
>   Renew our days as of old!
> Or hast thou utterly rejected us?
>   Art thou exceedingly angry with us? (5:21f.).

3. The little book of Ruth also speaks of lamentation and of trust in God in time of suffering, but it does so in an entirely different form: the form of a narrative. The individual scenes of this masterful "novella" form a great arch stretching from bitter distress at the beginning to a happy ending.

1:1–7a	Exposition: Prehistory and situation
7b–19a	Conversation of Naomi and Ruth. Their decision
19b–22	Lament back home in Bethlehem: Instead of Naomi, "The gracious one, the sweet one," Mara, "Bitter"
2:1–17	First meeting of Ruth and Boaz in the field at harvest time
18–23	Ruth tells Naomi what happened
3:1–5	Naomi's plan
6–15	Nocturnal meeting of Ruth and Boaz on the threshing floor
16–18	Ruth reports to Naomi
4:1–12	Legal proceedings in the gate. Withdrawal of the "redeemer"
13–17	Boaz marries Ruth. Birth of a son
18–22	(Secondary) list of generations down to David

During the time of the judges a famine forces a man named Elimelech to emigrate to Moab with his wife Naomi and his two sons. After their father's death both sons marry Moabite women. When the sons likewise die, Naomi decides to return home to Bethlehem, but she urges her two daughters-in-law, who are accompanying her, to stay behind in their own native land. One of them, Orpah, goes back "to her people and to her gods," but the other, Ruth, remains determined to "cling" to Naomi and thus also to Yahweh:

> Where you go I will go,
>   and where you lodge I will lodge;
> your people shall be my people,
>   and your God my God;
> where you die I will die,
>   and there will I be buried.
> May the Lord do so to me and more also
>   if even death parts me from you (1:16f.; cf. 2:12).

At home Naomi bemoans the bitter lot Yahweh has chosen for her (1:13, 20f.; cf. Job 1:21). Ruth energetically works to support both women by exercising the right of the poor (Lev 19:9f.; 23:22; Deut 24:19) to glean among the ears of grain in the harvested fields. In doing so, she comes upon the field of Boaz, a relative of Elimelech. Boaz is solicitous for the welfare of the foreign woman, treats her as a relative, and wishes her God's blessing (2:12). When Naomi sees the rich yield of Ruth's work, her lamentation changes into praise of God's goodness (2:20). Naomi is anxious that Ruth should have a "place of rest," that is, a home (3:1; 1:9), and so at the end of the harvest period she advises Ruth to go to Boaz at night on the threshing floor and ask him to enter into a brother-in-law's or Levirate marriage with her: "You have right of redemption over me" (3:9 JB). According to this legal arrangement the nearest relative of a man who has died childless is obliged to marry the widow; the first son born of the new marriage is regarded as a child of the deceased man (see 4:10). Since in the present case there is still living a closer relative than Boaz, who therefore has a prior right of redemption, Boaz waits until the next day in order to attend the legal assembly of full citizens at the city gate (4:1ff.; cf. 2:1; see §3b3) as advocate of the two women. In the presence of ten elders Boaz offers the relative with the prior right the opportunity to "redeem" the property of Elimelech (see Lev 25:25; Jer 32:7ff.), that is, to buy it, and also to marry Elimelech's widowed daughter-in-law. When the man declines, the right is passed on to Boaz in the ancient custom of the transfer of a shoe. Ruth thus becomes the wife of Boaz. A son is born to her who is regarded as a child of Naomi (4:13ff.).

Because of her love for Naomi the foreign daughter-in-law is regarded as more to her "than seven sons."

According to the genealogy that ends the book (4:18ff.) Ruth's firstborn son, Obed, is the father of Jesse and thus the grandfather of David. This genealogy, which reaches far into the past, is borrowed from 1 Chr 2:5, 9ff.; it is out of place stylistically in the narrative setting and is certainly an addition. Does this mean that the entire connection with the family of David was a later addition to the story? Such critical misgivings must, to be maintained, extend also to the name "Obed" (4:17b) and assume that the child originally had a different name. But, then, does not such an excision also do away with the "scandal" of having a Moabite woman among the ancestors of David? Furthermore, the introductory statement about the origin of Elimelech brings us right to David's home: Bethlehem (in the region of) Ephrathah (1:1f.; cf. 1 Sam 17:12; Mic 5:2). Perhaps, too, it is no accident that the good wishes offered to Boaz and Ruth make reference to another ancestor of David, Perez (4:12). Thus it is just as possible that the later genealogy simply renders more explicit a point that the story had always been making.

In any event, such considerations tell us nothing yet about the historical character of the events reported, but only something about the original self-understanding of the "novella." The events narrated are located in the distant past (1:1; 4:7). When the story disregards the law prohibiting Moabites from belonging to the community of Yahweh (Deut 23:3), this may be because it does not yet know of any such prohibition but precedes Deuteronomy and originates in the early monarchic period, or because it originates later and simply pays no heed to the prohibition. It is hardly possible to give an absolute date for the little book of Ruth, but it is more likely that it originated in the later postexilic period, at a time close to that of the "novella" about Jonah, which likewise shows a friendly spirit toward foreigners.

The story of Ruth tells of exemplary behavior, of a sense of duty, concern, and fidelity (see 1:8; 3:10)—fidelity that admittedly stays within the family, but at the same time fidelity on the part of a foreign woman and fidelity to the foreign woman. But in and with the decisions, plans, and actions of human beings God's providence is secretly at work, as with his blessing he directs the action and assures a good ending (1:6, 9; 2:12, 20; 3:10; 4:11, 13f.) to distress and suffering (1:13, 20f.).

4. The book of Esther, which is likewise a "novella" comprising a series of individual scenes, is much more reserved about making

theological statements. The setting is the Persian court at Susa. The first two chapters (1–2) introduce the chief personages and establish the presuppositions for the action proper (in chaps. 3–9). King Ahasuerus (i.e., Xerxes I, 485–465 B.C.) repudiates his wife Vashti for refusing to appear at a banquet (chap. 1). When a replacement is sought for her from among the beautiful young virgins of the country, Esther, a Jewish orphan (whose Hebrew name is Hadassah, "Myrtle"), finds favor with the king and becomes the new queen. Esther's cousin and guardian, Mordecai, succeeds in warning the king about a plot against him; Mordecai's good deed is entered into the records (chap. 2).

Mordecai refuses, however, to bend the knee to the king's favorite, Haman—who, remarkably enough, is not a Persian but an Agagite, that is, a member of the royal family of the Amalekites, which family was hostile to Israel (Exod 17:8ff.; 1 Sam 15). Haman therefore secures an edict decreeing that on the thirteenth of Adar, a day chosen by lot, all the Jews in the entire Persian empire are to be annihilated (chap. 3). Esther, being informed by Mordecai and being convinced, after objections, to intercede (chap. 4), asks the king to invite Haman first to one, then to a second banquet (5:1–8). Meanwhile Haman has a gallows erected for the execution of Mordecai, who still refuses the *proskynēsis* or act of homage (5:9–14). This represents the high point in the power of "the enemy of the Jews" (3:10; etc.), and the change of fortunes begins.

During a sleepless night the king has the book of his chronicles read to him and is reminded of Mordecai's service to him (2:22f.); he determines to reward the man. Haman suggests an appropriate public honor (which he thinks is intended for himself) and then to his horror is obliged to bestow it on Mordecai (chap. 6). At the second banquet Esther confesses her own Jewish ancestry and asks for her life and the deliverance of her people. When the king learns who the persecutor is, Haman throws himself down at Esther's couch and begs for mercy. The king misinterprets Haman's action as importunity and has him hung on the gallows that Haman had intended for Mordecai (chap. 7).

Mordecai now receives the king's signet ring that Haman had worn, and Haman's house is given to Esther. Esther approaches the king again and asks that the decree against the Jews (3:13) be cancelled: "How can I endure to see the calamity that is coming to my people?" (8:6). If the story had told simply of Esther's wish being fulfilled, it would have ended well with the danger being averted and with recompense for the suffering undergone. Why do the persecuted have to become persecutors in their turn? Since a law issued by the king cannot be simply revoked (8:8; 1:19; Dan 6:8f.), the Jews are permitted to ward off their enemies and slay their persecutors. This they do on the thirteenth of Adar and on the following day (9:1–19).

The tripartite epilogue draws a conclusion from these events: On the two days on which "the Jews got relief from their enemies," sorrow was changed into gladness (9:22; 8:15f.), and by the authority of Mordecai and Esther (9:20ff., 29ff.) the feast of Purim was to be celebrated throughout all time. The conclusion once again recalls Mordecai's prestige: he was "next in rank to King Ahasuerus" (10:1–3; cf. 8:2, 15).

The story certainly has a great deal of Persian atmosphere and a good many Persian names (1:10, 14; 9:7ff.), but no concrete historical background can be discovered that corresponds to the story. The course of events and the Jewish triumph over their enemies are not historical, and therefore the book of Esther has also been called a "historical novel." The general situation, however, is indeed historical: Judaism, at this time spread throughout the world, met with rejection and even persecution (cf. Dan 3ff.) because of its alien character (3:8). Did the rumors about the wealth of this people have something to do with it (3:9, 13)? In any case, Jews found it better to keep their Jewish descent a secret if possible (2:10). This situation probably became a reality only in the Hellenistic period, and the story probably arose in the third or second century B.C., probably in the eastern Diaspora.

In its present form the book of Esther leads up to the feast of Purim and is intended to show the basis for the feast. But various doubts have been cast on the unity of the text; 9:20ff. may be an appendix intended to clarify the older concluding remark about the commemoration (9:18f.) and to explain the name Purim as meaning "lot" (cf. 3:7). At least two narrative motifs, represented by Esther (5:1ff.; 7:1ff.; etc.) and Mordecai (3:1ff.; 6:1ff.), have been interwoven (2:5ff., 19f.; etc.). Here and there older forms of the story may show through, which suggest oral narratives rather than an earlier written story. The entire composition is at every point directed toward explaining the feast of Purim.

On the other hand, it seems that only subsequently did the story become the legend explaining the feast, for the feast of Purim was already in existence and was probably taken over by Jews in the Persian or Mesopotamian world to serve as a kind of New Year's feast. Is this the explanation of the names Esther (Persian "star"; cf. Ishtar) and Mordecai ("Worshipper of Marduk")? Was there a reading of destinies on New Year's Day by means of "lots," or is the word Purim to be explained (with G. Gerleman) as meaning "sharing" and referring to the mutual giving of gifts? In any case, the feast has a definitely "secular" character and is marked by joy, the giving of gifts to friends and the poor (9:18f., 22; 8:16f.), and perhaps by fasting as well (9:31). Just as the harvest feasts in the OT are given a justification from the history of salvation (e.g., Lev 23:42f.), so the feast of Purim is given a historical motivation in the story of Esther.

In early Judaism and especially in Christianity doubts arose about whether the book could be regarded as canonical. Mordecai and Esther do indeed cling to their religion in an exemplary way even in a time of danger, but does not the book emphasize too much the superiority of Judaism (6:13)? Why must the deliverance from destruction be prolonged by a triumph over enemies? Retribution administered by their own hand is certainly an understandable desire on the part of those who have been persecuted, but from a theological standpoint it is a wrongful hope. What a different judgment we see passed in the book of Jonah!

The book of Esther avoids using the name of God, but the course of action in it nonetheless supposes that God is secretly in control. When human beings fail to do their duty, "relief and deliverance will rise for the Jews from another quarter" (4:14). Is not the refusal of the *proskynēsis* (3:2; 5:9) an instance of obedience to the first commandment even at danger to one's life (cf. Dan 3)?

§27

PROVERBS

In its first meaning, "wisdom" is less the ability to answer questions of theory and principle than the ability to deal with everyday life and to cope with things and persons. An example of wisdom is the expertise of the craftsman or artist (Exod 31:3ff.; 35:10, 25f., 35; Isa 40:20; etc.), of the ruler or judge (1 Kgs 3; Isa 11:2ff.). "Wisdom" is good sense with regard to living (Prov 6:6); in a word, it is knowledge based on experience. It is grounded in observation of the operations that make up life, in the association of things that are similar, and in the knowledge of the rules. Insight into the existing organization of things, whether in nature or in human relationships, is summed up in language that is imaginative and favors parallelism (see §25,1) and can therefore be retained by the mind. The collection and transmission of experience creates a tradition ("the proverb of the ancients," 1 Sam 24:14) that exercises an authority alongside personal experience (Job 8:8). The purpose of wisdom is to ward off dangers and harm and to show the way to an upright, respected, successful life (Prov 13:14; 15:24).

1. The fact that the wisdom literature is to be found chiefly in the Writings, the third and latest part of the OT canon, gave rise to the view that wisdom was a late phenomenon in Israel. As a matter of fact, however, wisdom was not a specifically Israelite phenomenon, but one found throughout the entire East. Thus there was a Babylonian and a Canaanite wisdom; in Israel the wisdom of the nomadic "sons of the East" was well known (1 Kgs 4:30f.; Job 1:3; etc.). The OT itself mentions foreigners as authors of collections of proverbs (Prov 30:1; 31:1; cf. Job 1:1). Egypt especially seems to have influenced Israelite wisdom. Prov 22:17–23:11 is taken more or less verbatim from the book of the maxims of the Egyptian Amenemophis, but in addition to close agreements this section also contains specifically Israelite material (the theological justifications in 22:19, 23; 23:11). Proverbs, therefore, presents us with "the wisdom of the ancient Near East in its Israelite and Jewish form" (J. Fichtner, 1933).

These connections show that wisdom did not first become known only in postexilic Israel. When the OT tells of the wisdom of Solomon

(1 Kgs 3; 4:29ff.), this tradition is historically reliable at least to the extent that individual proverbs and even shorter collections of them must go back to the early monarchic period. The prophets, too, presuppose the existence of wisdom and take a positive (Amos 6:12; Isa 1:2f.; 11:2; 28:23ff.) or critical (Isa 5:21; 29:14; 44:25; Jer 8:9; etc.) attitude to it.

In any case, sapiential thinking has a long history. It stretches from individual proverbs that express life experience (1 Sam 24:14; Prov 10:1ff.; 25:1ff.) down to the extensive theological reflections in Job or Qohelet and even outside the canon to Sirach and the Wisdom of Solomon. But need the longer sections (Prov 1–9) be later than the shorter ones, or reflect a different *Sitz im Leben*? Is the personification of wisdom (1:20ff.; 8; 9; cf. Job 28) or the linking of wisdom and "law" (Ps 1; etc.) necessarily a late phenomenon? It seems to be such in Israel. In any case, even in the late period Solomon was still the authority to whom people liked to appeal (Proverbs, Qohelet, Song of Songs, the Greek Wisdom of Solomon).

2. There is one group of proverbs that "the men of Hezekiah king of Judah copied" (Prov 25:1). Wisdom was therefore cultivated at the royal court. The king had need of prudent advisers (2 Sam 16:23; Gen 41:33). There may have been a school for officials.

Is not the more original *Sitz im Leben* of wisdom to be found in the family? Here above all was the place where education was given. Not only the father but the mother as well are teachers, and the son listens (Prov 1:8; 4:1ff.; 6:20; 31:26; cf. Exod 12:26; 13:14; etc.); for it behooves a son to honor his parents (Prov 10:1; 20:20; etc.). This makes it understandable that the book of Proverbs contains only a few proverbs about the king (16:10ff.; 25:2ff.), and that unlike the Egyptian bodies of teaching it does not reflect the values of the civil service. Everyone, and not just a particular class, is addressed.

To what extent did the sages of the court simply "copy" (Prov 25:1) or transcribe existing material? To what extent did they give shape to it? In any case wisdom was at home in the school for civil servants (the existence of which school in Israel can only be inferred) and perhaps for priests as well (Jer 8:8f.), and even in the late period it is probable that there was an educational establishment in Jerusalem. The appellations "father" and "son" may reflect the relationship between teacher and pupil (Prov 1:1ff.). In addition to priests and prophets was there a special class of "wise men," who were in a position to give "counsel" (Jer 18:18; cf. Ezek 7:26)? The counsel of a sage was highly regarded (2 Sam 16:23) and could even claim to be based on a revelation (Job 4:12ff.; 32:6ff.). But the term "wise" applies not only to the man able to give counsel and instruct others but also to the man capable of listening to counsel and educating himself.

3. In pursuit of its goal, which is the transmission of experiences, Proverbs uses a variety of kinds of discourse.

a) In the saying—or mashal, sentence, or judgment—the sapiential writers take hold of "the data of reality and declare them in lists and observations" (W. Zimmerli, *Gesammelte Aufsätze*, vol. 1, p. 304). Life is grasped as it really is—as in the case of the consumer:

> "It is bad, it is bad," says the buyer;
> but when he goes away, then he boasts (Prov 20:14).

The writers like to formulate act–consequence connections which show that a person's destiny follows from his or her own behavior:

> He who digs a pit will fall into it,
> and a stone will come back on him who starts it rolling
> (26:27; cf. 1 Sam 24:14; Prov 11:2, 17, 25; 22:8f.).

As a rule, however, the datum is not simply described in a neutral way but evaluated. The judgment often takes the form of a simple contrast: wise man and fool, just man and wicked man, poor and rich, diligent and lazy. A man's behavior turns as it were into an attitude or approach to life that determines his future:

> The hope of the righteous ends in gladness,
> but the expectation of the wicked comes to naught
> (10:28; cf. 11:7, 23; etc.).

Because of its pedagogical orientation wisdom shows a preference for seeing things in black and white. Does this not conceal an easily discernible exhortation to a proper manner of life or, as the case may be, a warning against an imprudent one?

b) In images or similes (the latter indicated by the word "like" or "as") phenomena from various areas, often from the world of nature and the world of humanity, are interrelated. The emphasis in a comparison tends to be on the inference or application:

> As a door turns on its hinges,
> so does a sluggard in his bed (26:14).

> Like a dog that returns to his vomit
> is a fool that repeats his folly
> (26:11; cf. 25:3, 11ff., 26, 28).

Do such comparisons serve simply to render a point more vivid, or do they ultimately suppose an analogy between nature and human life and thus a single order that embraces the entire world? It is more likely that "in Israel at least, there is question not of a universal world-order but of particular things" (H. J. Hermisson, p. 191), of analogies detected here and there. It can hardly be accidental that the *tertium comparationis* or point of comparison, that is, the element common to diverse states of affairs and sequences of actions, can often not be univocally determined but remains ambiguous and even "enigmatic" (riddles: 1 Kgs 10:1; Prov 1:6; Judg 14:12ff.).

c) The same holds for the numerical saying, which may be taken as a special form of the image or simile, because it too correlates diverse phenomena:

> Three things are too wonderful for me;
>   four I do not understand:
> the way of an eagle in the sky,
>   the way of a serpent on a rock,
> the way of a ship on the high seas,
>   and the way of a man with a maiden (30:18f.).

Does the play on the word "way" refer to the way that is not determinable in advance and must be always blazed anew, or on the way that can no longer be retraced in retrospect (as in 30:20)? In any case, the reader gets the impression that "the first three phenomena are introduced only in order to highlight the fourth, which is human behavior" (H. W. Wolff). Proverbs thus offers a "wisdom about nature" (see 1 Kgs 4:33) only as an aid in understanding human nature (see also Ps 104; Job 38ff.).

In addition to "three–four" there are other numerical series ranging from "one–two" to "nine–ten" (Prov 30:15ff.; 6:16ff.); even the prophets may use such sayings (Amos 1:3ff.).

d) A special kind of comparison is to be found in sayings that contrast two phenomena, setting a positive value on the first and a negative on the second:

> Better is a little with fear of the Lord
>   than great treasure and trouble with it.
> Better is a dinner of herbs where love is
>   than a fatted ox and hatred with it
>   (15:16f.; cf. 16:8; 17:1; Eccl 7:1ff.; etc.).

The Hebrew phrase *tôb min*, which is usually translated "better than" is perhaps to be understood not as expressing a weighing of pros and cons but as expressing an exclusion and a contrast: this or that is "good in distinction from and opposition to. . . ." Is not such an interpretation of the phrase more in keeping with sapiential thinking's use of contrasting concepts? In any case, the comparison is meant once again to help persons see their way in life—not only in everyday matters but in the ethical sphere (Prov 19:1, 22) and even in the theological (Ps 118:8f.).

e) The exhortation calls explicitly for a particular kind of behavior, usually adding a justification ("for") or a warning about evil consequences that will otherwise ensue ("lest"). Thus, the act–consequence nexus serves as the basis for an exhortation to circumspection with regard to the wicked:

> Fret not yourself because of evildoers,
>   and be not envious of the wicked;
> for the evil man has no future;
>   the lamp of the wicked will be put out
>   (24:19f.; cf. Ps 37:1f.).

The exhortation, which occurs frequently in the collection made under Egyptian influence (Prov 22:17ff.; also 1:8ff.), also made its way into many other sectors of literature, not least the message of the prophets (see §13b3e).

The book of the Proverbs of Solomon, like the prophetic books or the psalter, consists of individual collections or parts of collections. How otherwise are certain repetitions to be explained (compare 19:1 with 28:6; 11:13 with 20:19; etc.)? The individual sayings are loosely connected with one another by the presence of a common theme (thus the Yahweh sayings, 16:1ff.) but usually only by catchwords (25:2f.) or a similar device. This makes it possible for divergent or even contrasting experiences to be set side by side (26:4f.; 17:27f.); but it is also possible for one saying to shed light on another that precedes it (25:16f.).

Collections are to some extent detectable by reason of a superscription; they are quite diverse in character and also come from various periods. In any case, great reserve must be exercised in trying to determine age with the help of criteria from form or content. The most recent of the extensive principal collections (I, II, and V in the outline below) is set at the beginning as an explanation for the entire book (see 1:7); this is in keeping with a principle often documented in the OT (see Gen 1 P before Gen 2 J). Remarkably enough, the two older collections (II and V) are each followed by appendixes containing non-Israelite material.

I	1–9	"The proverbs of Solomon, son of David, king of Israel" Probably the most recent (postexilic) collection 1:1–7 Superscription for the book as a whole, with the motto: "The fear of the Lord is the beginning of knowledge" (1:7; etc.) Are the longer sections to be explained as instructional discourses, introduced by a call for attention and containing exhortations (1:8ff.; 4:1ff., 10ff., 20ff.; etc.; see B. Lang)? 5–7 (without 6:1–19) Warning against the "loose woman" (cf. 2:16ff.) 1:20ff.; 8; 9 Personification: "Lady Wisdom" (contrasted with the "foolish woman," 9:13ff.) 8:22ff. Hymn to creation: Wisdom as the firstborn of creation and present when the world came into existence (cf. 3:19f.), playing before God; therefore a necessity for human beings (8:32ff.; 2:2ff.)
II	10–22:16	"The proverbs of Solomon"
a	10–15	Along with V one of the oldest collections, probably made up of two parts (*a, b*)
b	16–22:16	In *a* mostly sayings using antithetical parallelism (e.g., 10:1ff.) The behavior and condition of the wise and the foolish, the just and the wicked are frequently contrasted
III	22:17–24:22	"The words of the wise"
a	22:17–23:11	Close dependence on the Book of the Wisdom of the Egyptian Amenemophis (before 1000 B.C.). Primarily exhortations The introductory saying (22:17–21) is followed by ten themes (22:22–23:11)
b	23:12–24:22	Apart from 23:13f. (based on the Assyrian-Aramaic Sayings of Ahikar) and 24:10–12, there is "hardly any foreign influence" but "a strong religious feeling": 23:17; 24:12, 18, 21 (see B. Gemser)
IV	24:23-34	"The following are also taken from the sages"
V	25–29	"Proverbs of Solomon which the men of Hezekiah king of Judah copied"
a	25–27	"The 'most secular' part of Israel's sapiential literature"—and therefore the "most original form" of it (H. H. Schmid, p. 145)? Only 25:2, 22 speak of God
b	28–29	A stronger religious tone Is *a* a "Mirror for Peasants or Craftsmen" and *b* a "Mirror for Rulers" (U. Skladny)?
VI	30:1–14	"The words of Agur" Like VIII, non-Israelite, probably from the Edomite and North Arabian world
VII	30:15–33	Numerical sayings

5. The themes of the Proverbs are many and varied. Wisdom reflects on the use of speech (18:7, 13; 25:11), education (13:24; 29:19), conduct toward parents (10:1; etc.) and king (16:12ff.; 23:1ff.), household and family (12:4; 19:14; 21:9; 31:10ff.), society (11:11, 14; 14:34), the conduct and condition of the wise or upright or devout man (10:20f.; 11:3, 31; 13:25; 14:16; 15:2, 28), etc. Because it is God's concern to maintain or even to establish (10:3, 22; etc.) the connection between act and consequence, certain conclusions follow for human action: commit your work to the Lord (16:3), do not try to exact retribution yourself (20:22; 24:29), do not rejoice at the downfall of your enemies (24:17ff.) but rather help them (25:21f.)! Warnings against contempt for parents (28:24; 30:11, 17; cf. 17:25; 23:24), adultery (6:20ff.; 23:27), false witness (12:19, 22; 19:5; 21:28; cf. 18:5) or the usurpation of another's property (10:2; cf. 16:8; etc.) closely resemble the formulations in the Decalogue.

The oppressed are under the protection of the creator (14:31; 17:5; 15:25). Alongside the exhortation to care for the poor (19:17; 22:9, 22f.; 23:10f.) stands the realization that there are both rich and poor— and both are in God's hand (22:2; 29:13). God can see into the innermost recesses of human beings and weigh them in the balance (15:3, 11; 16:2; 21:2), but God remains free in his actions (16:1, 9; cf. 25:2a). Humans for their part cannot get a clear understanding of themselves and their destiny (20:24; 21:30f.). Since the insight of sages into the order of things (11:24f.) and even into their own hearts (16:1f.) is limited, modesty is in order (16:5, 18f.; 22:4; 26:12). In the final analysis, fear of God, which is at the same time trust in God, is true wisdom (14:26f.; 1:7; 9:10; Job 28:28; Ps 111:10; cf. Jer 9:24f.; etc.).

§28

QOHELETH:
SOLOMON THE PREACHER

Qoheleth or Ecclesiastes (the Greek and Latin version of the name) is a teacher of wisdom; during the Hellenistic period he reflects critically on the fruits of sapiential thinking and in doing so shows surprising independence. The word Qoheleth (which, remarkably enough, is a feminine participle in Hebrew) seems to indicate an office in the assembly (the qāhāl), whether that of the leader who convokes it or a speaker. But the functional description (in 12:8 with the article; cf. 7:27) has become a proper name (1:12; 12:9f.).

Is the proper name in the superscription (1:1) a pseudonym? It identifies Qoheleth with the son of David who is ruling in Jerusalem. Solomon is evidently meant (see 1:16). But the name Solomon occurs nowhere in the text, whereas the book of Proverbs and the Song of Songs expressly claim Solomonic authorship. The authorship of Solomon may have made it easier or perhaps even basically possible for the Song of Songs and Ecclesiastes to have gained acceptance into the OT canon (on the later liturgical use, see §26).

1. Qoheleth probably did not himself put the book together in the form in which we now have it. The evolution of the book can be explained to some extent in light of the framework in which the book is set, that is, the introductory and concluding information, which is given in the third person (1:1–2a; 12:9ff.; cf. 7:27).

The identification of Qoheleth with the son of David (1:1) is probably secondary and made in the light of 1:12: "I the Preacher have been king over Israel in Jerusalem." For in the text only 1:12–2:11, 12 is presented as the words of a king. On the other hand, this "royal fiction" is continued in the first-person language, "I saw, I realized," which runs through the book. The book presents what is said as being personal experience (for this device, see Prov 24:30ff.; Ps 37:25, 35). There are also exhortations addressed to "you" (5:2ff.) and general considerations (3:1ff.; etc.).

At the end of the book two additions—in prose?—may be distinguished, each with a different intention. The first epilogue provides information, approvingly describing Qoheleth as a wise man who "taught the people knowledge" and wrote "words of truth" (12:9–11). The second epilogue, on the other hand, is undoubtedly critical in tone. On the one hand, it warns against the endless composing of books and against exhausting study (12:12), and on the other it exhorts: "Fear God and keep his commandments." God's judgment awaits all human activity, even that which is hidden (12:13f.).

Does this kind of correction from the standpoint of traditional faith also make its presence felt in the book itself? It seems reasonable to regard as additions the statements about God's judgment (11:9b) and equitable retribution (8:12b–13). Other texts (such as 3:17a; 8:5; etc.) are the subject of dispute. Certain unevennesses are due to the material; for Qoheleth is taking traditional sapiential material and interpreting it according to his own critical views, but in doing so he is hardly completely consistent (2:13ff.; 9:4ff.; etc.). In addition, linguistic differences are hard to ascertain. It is likely, therefore, that the book has undergone an "orthodox" revision, but this cannot be shown with certainty.

2. The third-person setting, at beginning and end, contains a further framework, internal to the material and consisting of the repeated programmatic assertion "Vanity of vanities; all is vanity" (1:2; 12:8). Just as the story of creation is interpreted by a superscription and a subscription that sum up everything that will be or has been said (Gen 1:1; 2:4a), so here there is a kind of statement of theme or leitmotiv. Is this a later interpretation that summarizes everything in a "motto"?

It is also possible that the sayings about the succession of generations (1:3–11) and about growing old (11:9–12:7) are deliberately placed at the beginning and the end of the book to serve as statements of principle. If so, the book may have evolved through three stages:

a) The first-person discourse in 1:12ff. may have been the original introduction to the collection of sayings composed by "Qoheleth."

b) The present form of the book is perhaps due to the first epilogist, the author of the concluding remark that recommends Qoheleth (12:9–11). Was he a disciple of Qoheleth?

c) The second epilogist may then have taken the complete book and added his critical remarks (12:12–14).

In any case, the book of Ecclesiastes is not a treatise on a single theme. The book gives no evidence of a logical structure. It is indeed organized into a greater unity than is the book of Proverbs, but on the other hand it is not so much a whole as the book of Job. Individual sayings, some of which are still to be found here and there, have been organized into didactic poems or sets of sentences and reflections. For example, a series of "better than" sayings (7:1ff.) has been introduced into the section that runs from 6:12 to 7:14 and has thus been subordinated to a governing idea. The larger units, however, cannot be clearly marked off from one another. In a number of instances a unit begins with a thesis (3:1; etc.).

The book is given a formal unity by the first-person address, and a material unity by its leading idea, the "nothingness" of human life. Other characteristic catchwords are, for example, toil, vanity (vapor, smoke), breath, striving after wind, folly, gain, under the sun (i.e., on earth, faced with death).

1:1	Superscription
1:2; 12:8	Leitmotiv: "All is vanity"
1:3, 4–11	Return of the same
	"What does a man gain by all the toil at which he toils under the sun?" (1:3)
	"There is nothing new under the sun" (1:9)
1:12–11:8	In this "central section," which is the collection of sayings, the following stand out:
	1:12–2:11 Retrospect of the king
	3:1ff. "For everything there is a season"
11:9–12:7	On growing old
12:9–11, 12, 13f.	Epilogue

3. Qoheleth seems to know the Pentateuch in its completed form (compare 5:4–6 with Deut 23:21ff.), and in his writing he uses a late Hebrew, influenced by Aramaic, into which an occasional Persian word has been absorbed (2:5; 8:11). More precisely, it is reckoned that the book came into existence in Palestine after the age of Persian dominance but a few decades before the Maccabean uprising, toward the middle of the third century B.C. This is the period of early Hellenism.

Qoheleth's thinking shows points of contact with Egyptian and Babylonian wisdom writing, where the critical approach was not unknown (O. Loretz). However, the historical context suggests rather the influence of Greek thinking, although direct borrowings can hardly be demonstrated. In the circumstances, should we not think simply that Qoheleth's critique of wisdom may have been influenced by Greek-Hellenistic skepticism?

4. In style and intellectual stance Qoheleth's associations are with proverbial wisdom; he even takes over its language and insights: "The wise man has eyes in his head, but the fool walks in darkness" (2:14a; cf. 4:13; 8:1; 10:12). In intention, however, Qoheleth is utterly alien from proverbial wisdom (1:17; 7:23ff.; 8:17). He relativizes sapiential knowledge from two basic and interconnected points of view.

The first is that the wise man in the final analysis has no "advantage" (6:8) but dies just as the fool does. The devout and the wicked alike share "one fate"; there is no remembrance of anyone beyond death, and therefore no distinction between humans and beasts (2:14b ff.; 3:19ff.; 9:2ff.). Is Qoheleth also skeptical with regard to the hope of resurrection which was just dawning in his day (3:21; cf. 12:7)?

The second is that there are wise men who fare the same as the wicked, and wicked who fare the same as the wise; the act–consequence nexus does not explain human life (8:14; 7:15; 9:11).

These two chief problems are accompanied by others: the boundless injustice in the world (3:16; 4:1; 5:8; 8:9ff.; cf. 9:16; 10:6ff.), riches (5:10ff.), uncertainty regarding one's heir (2:18f.), the wickedness of humans generally (8:6, 11) and of women in particular (7:27ff.; a different view in 9:9). Even the virtuous person is not without fault (7:20).

For these reasons Qoheleth, unlike the proverbial wisdom, no longer inquires into particular orders within reality but rather about life as a whole (this is especially clear in the comparisons of humanity and nature: Eccl 3:19 vs. Prov 6:6; etc.). Not to have been born is better (4:2f.)—a judgment that is understandable as a heartfelt cry from an individual in great distress (1 Kgs 19:4; Jer 15:10; 20:14f.; Job 3; etc.), but as a statement of principle it is unknown elsewhere in the OT. Life does, of course, have its joys (such as youth or wine: 2:24f.; 3:12f.; 5:18f.; 9:7ff.; 11:9; etc.) and these should be enjoyed as gifts from God (9:7; 3:13; 5:20); but these too are relativized by oncoming death (2:1; 3:22; 8:15).

Despite everything, Qoheleth clings with great assurance to "fear of God" (5:7; 3:14; but see the warning against excess even here, 7:16f.). God gives life and takes it away (5:18; 12:1, 7); he gives both joy and toil, happiness and sorrow (2:24f.; 3:10; 6:2; 7:14). Do we not glimpse here the presence and action of the first commandment? Human beings cannot change what God decides and does (3:14; 6:10; 7:13). God has in fact acted properly in all things, but humans are unable to understand fully God's work (3:11; 8:17; cf. 7:29; 5:2)—and therefore the order that governs life or the connection between act and consequence. Human persons know neither their own time (3:1ff.; cf. 9:1) nor their future (8:7; 9:12; 10:14).

Should we hold it against Qoheleth that he does not mention the name of the God who shows mercy to Israel (Exod 34:6f.)? But the name of Yahweh is little used in the later period generally and in the wisdom literature in particular (cf. Job). Although the book of Ecclesiastes, so alien to the rest of the OT, belongs to the canon, it seems to challenge the reader with a question: Can faith in the God who works in history and who slays and makes alive (1 Sam 2:6) survive in the face of the individual's experience of life and the world?

§29

THE BOOK OF JOB

This book, named after Job, its chief personage, consists of two entirely heterogeneous parts: a frame-story in prose (Prologue, 1:1–2:13; Epilogue, 42:7–17) and a lengthy poetical work in meter. This second part is a dialogue between Job, his friends, and—initially only as a clandestine participant—God (3:1–42:6).

1. The opening sentences are fundamental for both parts of the book; they tell us that Job is a God-fearing, upright, and also rich man. According to the law of act–consequence, misfortune should not come to Job. If calamity were to strike him, the frame-narrative asks, would he retain his faith? But in the dialogue it is hard for the friends of Job to see the point: the problem that calls for a response is not that of suffering in general but of the suffering of a devout and upright person.

Without fault of his own Job loses his possessions and his children (Job 1) and finally his health (Job 2). But even in the face of his wife's provocative words (2:9) he keeps faith; he accepts his lot from God's hand and is even able to praise the creator:

> The Lord gave, and the Lord has taken away;
> blessed be the name of the Lord (1:21).

> Shall we receive good at the hand of God,
> and shall we not receive evil? (2:10).

Because of his fidelity Job is restored to his former prosperity and is in fact even more richly blessed (42:10ff.).

While the Job of the story or legend remains resigned to God's will, the Job of the dialogue rebels, complains, and makes charges. The name of Yahweh, used in the frame-story (1:6ff.), occurs only exceptionally in the dialogue and is probably a later addition (38:1; etc.). The dialogue prefers such names for God as El and Eloah, "God," and Shaddai, "the Almighty." These and other differences show that story and poem are not the work of one and the same author.

The legend of Job was evidently already present in oral tradition; however, in its present form it is hardly to be regarded as a simple "popular saga," but is rather a "didactic wisdom story" written in rhythmic prose (H. P. Müller, pp. 45, 80). It uses the figure of Job to discuss the relationship between virtue and reality or, more precisely, the behavior of a God-fearing person in time of suffering. But story and poem are not simply independent of one another; rather the poem presupposes the story (8:4; etc.). The legend of Job, formerly transmitted as an independent entity, has become the frame-story for the later dialogue and has undergone some revision in the process. How extensive the revision has been is a matter of dispute.

2. The history of the development of the legend is explained in quite different ways because of certain unevennesses in it.

According to one view the two scenes in heaven (1:6–12; 2:1–7) are a later addition. Only in these two scenes does Satan appear as a member of the heavenly court. With God's permission he is allowed to test Job to see whether he will cling selflessly to his faith even amid suffering; Satan is proved wrong in God's sight. But for the act–consequence thinking on which wisdom is based, the scenes in heaven are almost indispensable, since they alone give a reason (hidden from Job himself) why this upright man must suffer; the scenes thus give an interpretation of what is happening.

In addition, it is not possible to excise the scene in heaven from chap. 2 without disturbing the sequence of events (2:7). Of course, according to another view chap. 2 only gives a doublet (added later) of chap. 1. Notably enough, chap. 42 says nothing of Job's being healed (2:7) and is silent about his wife (2:9f.). But is not chap. 1 naturally ordered to chap. 2, inasmuch as the initial reverses (in chap. 1) spare the person of Job himself? Moreover, not only within the scenes in heaven (1:6–8, 11, 12b = 2:1–3a, 5, 7a) but apart from them (1:22 = 2:10b; etc.), the two chapters are closely interconnected. "The narrator shows great artistic skill in using doublets to heighten intensity" (E. Ruprecht, p. 47).

The various unevennesses, then, do allow us to infer stages in the oral transmission of the Job legend, but they hardly provide an adequate basis for challenging the literary unity of the story in its essentials.

There is a further question that is difficult to answer: In addition to the visit from Job's relatives who come to offer sympathy (but only belatedly and at an inappropriate time, in 42:11), did the story always record the visit of the three friends (2:11ff.)? Or was it the poet who introduced them into the story as partners in the ensuing dialogue?

3. The tradition about Job evidently has remote and foreign origins. Job is one of "the people of the east" (1:3; cf. 1 Kgs 4:30) and lives in "the land of Uz," which is probably to be located in the southeast, in

Edomite territory (Lam 4:21). Job's friends, Eliphaz of Teman (in Edom?), Bildad of Shuah (on the Euphrates?), and Zophar of Naamath (in the north) are likewise foreigners. Nonetheless, the story of God-fearing Job hardly arose in Edom or Arabia or elsewhere but in Israel.

On the one hand, the story contains ancient traditions, as when the father of the family himself offers sacrifice as in the time of the patriarchs (1:5). On the other, there are more recent notions, such as the appearance of Satan as tempter or adversary (see Zech 3; 1 Chr 21:1). This means that in its written form the book of Job, like the book of Jonah, probably came into existence only in the postexilic period. When the prophet Ezekiel (14:14, 20) mentions Noah, Daniel, and Job as models of uprightness and virtue who lived in the distant past, he probably has in mind not the present story but only an older oral tradition.

In the currently prevailing view, the book of Job as a whole came into existence between the fifth and the third century, that is, in the Persian or early Hellenistic period; the book is difficult to date with greater preciseness.

4. Changes were subsequently made in the book; two insertions deserve mention.

The most extensive and important accretion is the speeches of the fourth friend, Elihu (chaps. 32–37). He is not mentioned previously or again later in the story (i.e., in 42:7ff.) and receives no response from Job. Above all, the speeches of Elihu break the connection between Job's appeal to God (31:35ff.) and God's answer. The speeches represent a further attempt to bring sapiential views to bear in modified form; it is hardly accidental that unlike the preceding speeches of the three friends the speeches of Elihu frequently cite Job himself (33:8ff.; etc.). In addition to numerous repetitions of thoughts already expressed, the speeches offer the view that suffering is used by God as a warning and a disciplinary measure (33:19; 36:8ff.; cf. 5:17).

The hymn in praise of wisdom (chap. 28) may originally have been an independent composition. It sings of wisdom not as a person (as in Prov 8f.) but as a reified entity. Man can dig for buried treasure but wisdom remains beyond his reach (vv. 13, 21). "But where shall wisdom be found?" runs the refrain (vv. 12, 20). Only God has access to it (vv. 23ff.). The intention in introducing this poem as a speech of Job was surely a critical one: in the final analysis wisdom does not belong to the friends or to Job, but only to God. A more recent addition (v. 28) limits this insight in keeping with Prov 1:7: true wisdom consists in the fear of God.

There are at least two further passages in which the text has been altered.

In the first two sets of speeches the three friends Eliphaz, Bildad, and Zophar take turns speaking, but the third set (chaps. 22-27) is incomplete: Bildad speaks only briefly and Zophar not at all.

The speech given by God (chaps. 38–41) was hardly composed as a single whole but has undergone later expansions. In its present form it has two parts, each of which ends with Job submitting himself (40:3–5; 42:1–6). Originally, there was probably only a single speech—with 40:3–5 (and the transitions, 40:1, 6f.) either being transferred from the end of the speech to the middle of it, or being invented to form a break. In addition, other probably later additions are Behemoth, "hippopotamus" (40:15–24), Leviathan, "crocodile" (41:1–34), and perhaps the ostrich (39:13–18).

We must therefore consider roughly four stages in the evolution of the book of Job:

I. Oral prehistory of the Job story (see Ezek 14:14ff.)
II. The Job story (chaps. 1f.; 42)
III. The poem of Job (chaps. 3–27; 29–31; 38–42:6), which uses the story as a framework
IV. Later additions to the poem of Job (especially chaps. 28; 32–37)

I.	Job 1–2	Frame-story. Prologue
		Job's twofold testing and fidelity
		"Does Job fear God for nought?" (1:9)
		Loss of possessions, children (chap. 1) and health (2)
II.	Job 3–31	Dialogue (three sets of speeches) with Job's soliloquies as framework (3; 29–31)
	3	Job's soliloquy
		Cursing of his birth (cf. Jer 20:14ff.; Eccl 2:17)
	4–27	Three sets of speeches (4–14; 15–21; 22–27)
		with speeches by Eliphaz of Teman (4f.; 15; 22)
		Bildad of Shuah (8; 18; 25)
		Zophar of Naamath (11; 20)
		and speeches by Job (6f.; 9f.; 12–14; 16f.; 19; 21; 23f.; 26f.)
	28	Excursus: hymn in praise of wisdom (cf. Prov 8f.)
	29–31	Job's soliloquy
		with complaint: formerly respected and full of hope (chap. 29),
		now attacked from without and tempted from within (30)
		profession of innocence as oath of purgation (31)
		with a challenge to God (31:35ff.)
III.	Job 32–37	Insertion: speeches by Elihu
IV.	Job 38–42:6	"Theophany." Two speeches by God
		with Job's answer (40:3–5; 42:1–6)
V.	Job 42:7–17	Frame-story. Epilogue

5. While some sapiential elements are to be found in the Job story (2:10; etc.), it is in the dialogue that the wisdom tradition becomes

predominant. It finds expression no longer in individual sayings but, to an even greater extent than in Qoheleth, in longer speeches. But other formal components are also to be found, which are familiar from the Israelite legal system (13:3ff.; 40:8; etc.; cf. H. Richter) or are known to us from Psalms (C. Westermann). Thus in addition to passages closely related to the lament (Job 3; 29f.; etc.) there are hymnic motifs (9:4ff.; 38ff.; etc.).

Like Qoheleth (7:15) and yet in a different manner the author of the dialogue doubts the connection between act and consequence, between virtue and happiness, wrongdoing and suffering. Job challenges this view of life, at least as being applicable in his own case (21:7ff.; etc.), while his friends presuppose it in a remarkably rigid way (4:6ff.; 8:6ff.; 15:20ff.; 20; etc.). Yet these friends realize that in the final analysis no human being is completely upright and faultless in the presence of God's greatness (4:17; 15:14ff.; 25:4ff.); this is the only point on which Job agrees with them.

In the wisdom literature of the ancient Near East there were already a number of texts, quite different among themselves, which resemble the book of Job in form (dialogue) and theme (virtue and suffering); for example, the so-called Sumerian Job, the Babylonian Job—"I will praise the Lord of wisdom"— or the so-called Babylonian theodicy or Babylonian Qoheleth. See, most recently, W. Beyerlin (ed.), *Religionsgeschichtliches Textbuch zum Alten Testament*, 1975, pp. 157ff. (Eng.: *Near Eastern Religious Texts Relating to the Old Testament*, 1978); on the subject, see H. P. Müller, pp. 49ff.

In the OT Ps 73, one of the wisdom psalms, stands closest to Job, although the answer it offers looks beyond the boundary set by death (vv. 23ff.).

6. Since throughout the conversation the friends persist in the viewpoint they have adopted and keep repeating their arguments, any intellectual movement that may exist in their speeches is difficult to discern. In addition, the remarks of the friends on the one side and of Job on the other are only loosely and indirectly related to each other, even when they may be formally linked (16:2ff.; 18:2; 19:2ff.; only chap. 21 directly contradicts chap. 20).

It is therefore not easy to determine whether Job is responding to the friends or whether the friends are reacting to Job (as G. Fohrer maintains). Does the dialogue begin with Eliphaz's speech in chap. 4 or has it already begun in Job's soliloquy of lament in chap. 3?

A further matter of dispute is whether the three friends, while united in their opposition to Job and their acceptance of the "doctrine of retribution," also have each their own style: Eliphaz dignified and circumspect, Zophar brusque, and Bildad somewhere in between.

Nonetheless, the dialogue as a whole does show a certain movement

toward a climax. The friends begin with words of comfort (4:1ff.) and
end up with personal accusation (22:4ff.). Job's course takes him from
cursing his own birth (3:3ff.; cf. 6:8; 10:18ff.), through charges against
God who torments the weak (7:12ff.) and declares the innocent guilty
(9:20ff.), to the hope that God will be his helper. In a process, as it
were, of applying the first commandment to his own lot, Job is thus
led to almost paradoxical assertions about God. Despite his realization
that there is no one to arbitrate between him and God, that is, no
higher and neutral court of appeal (9:32f.), he summons God to the
courtroom (13:3, 18ff.; 23:4ff.). Is Job following the advice of his friends
(5:8f.; 8:5f.; 11:13ff.; 22:21ff.) when, despite his earlier plea "Let me
alone" (7:16; 10:20), he turns to God? He asks God to hide him away
from the divine anger in the kingdom of the dead, where God would
then remember Job kindly (14:13). In other words, against the God
who persecutes him (16:9ff.; 19:6ff.; 21) and has deprived him of rights
(27:2), he appeals to the God who in time of distress stands up for him
and his rights. Against a wrathful, apparently unjust and arbitrary God
Job appeals to the God who intends his good:

> Even now, behold, my witness is in heaven,
>   and he that vouches for me is on high (16:19–21).
> For I know that my Redeemer [Avenger] lives . . . ;
>   then from my flesh I shall see God (19:25f.).

Job is sure that he will find an advocate and that he will even see
God—according to this much disputed passage—in the face of death
or even in death. Are not such confessions rays of hope in the deep
darkness of Job's lament?

While the friends see Job only as a man who suffers and not as one
who is upright, Job himself insists on his innocence (6:24, 28ff.; 9:21;
10:7; 16:17; 23:10ff.). He even vows to remain pure in the future, to
the end of his life (27:2ff.) and ends the conversation with an oath of
purgation asserting that he is not conscious of any guilt in past or
present (31). Again despite his complaint that God does not hear a cry
for help (30:20), Job's protestation of innocence leads him to the cry
"Let the Almighty answer me!"

In the older version of the book of Job, the order of which has now
been disturbed by the intercalated speeches of Elihu, Job's challenge
was immediately followed by God's answer "out of the whirlwind"
(38:1). The answer deals only indirectly with Job's lot. Such questions
as "Where were you when I laid the foundations of the earth? Have
you an arm like God?" (38:4; 40:9) make Job aware of the miracle of
creation and lead him to the realization that humanity is incapable of

creating the world or even of preserving it. The task of maintaining the order found in nature, whether close to human beings or far removed from them (stars, weather, beasts), belongs to God and not to humans with their limited knowledge and power.

By means of rhetorical questions "God turns questioner into respondent and finally into one whose very being is called into question. ... God's speeches set straight the earlier statements about the relationship of God and man, by bringing Job into the presence of the God who makes himself visible in his creation and yet remains incomprehensible." The survey of creation shows humanity "to be limited in time, power, knowledge and ability by comparison with the infinitely superior and incomprehensible God who has been at work in all things since the beginning" (E. Würthwein, p. 215).

God's words are a rebuke to Job (38:2; 40:8) rather than a justification of God. Does Job experience them nonetheless as the act of divine graciousness that he has desired? In any case, Job submits to the Almighty—"Behold, I am of small account; what shall I answer thee?" (40:4)—and renounces his doubts about the order of the world, his complaints against God, and his protestations of innocence:

> I had heard of thee by the hearing of the ear,
>   but now my eye sees thee;
> therefore I despise myself
>   and repent in dust and ashes (42:5f.).

Does this "resolution of the problem of Job" depend on a personal experience of God that transcends and relativizes every explanation of the world and every experience of suffering? When Job "recants," the rebellious Job (of the dialogue) who contends with God becomes once again the submissive Job (of the prologue) who accepts his lot in a spirit of faith (1:21; 2:10). Did the author of the dialogue deliberately keep the frame-story for the profound reason that he intended at the end to bring Job back to where he began? In his very last words Job again adopts an attitude of humility "in dust and ashes" (2:8; 42:6). Has he become a different man, or has he remained the same, though enriched now with new experiences?

After Job's recantation there is need of a divine judgment to render a decision in the dispute between Job (13:7; 27:5; etc.) and his friends (20:3; 22:5; etc.) and to give public notice that Job's acquisition of self-knowledge by no means confirms the theology of the friends. On the contrary, these men live because of Job's intercession for them, for they "have not spoken what is right" about God (42:7–9).

The change in Job's lot as his losses are recompensed in a super-abundant manner is not a presupposition but a consequence of his newfound realization. It is a bonus from God, a confirmation of his judgment (42:10ff.; v. 11 originally belonged to chap. 1f.). Is God thus revalidating the act–consequence nexus that had been interrupted?

§30

FOR AND AGAINST
THE OLD TESTAMENT

The OT has been a treasured and yet controverted book in the Church. From an early date it was both acknowledged and viewed with a critical eye.

1. The primitive Christian community adhered to the OT as a matter of course and applied it to its own situation. In doing so, it was guided by three basic ideas: The God of the OT is the Father of Jesus; Jesus is the promised messiah, the Christ; and the new community is the true, chosen people of God. But while the identity of the OT for the Christian community was thus defined, differences also quickly emerged in a process that was hastened by contemporary events such as the destruction of the temple. The OT sacrifices have been abrogated by the death of Jesus; instead of circumcision, baptism is the sign of membership in the community; the ceremonial and legal prescriptions of the OT have ceased to bind; the law generally has lost its significance as a bond of unity.

In the course of history, especially since the Enlightenment, further distinctions have been recognized and stressed, so that reservations with regard to the OT have been able to develop into outright rejection. For example, when Immanuel Kant, adopting notions of Johann Salomo Semler, discussed this subject almost in passing in his *Religion within the Limits of Reason Alone* (1794[2]; Eng., 1934), he turned the distinction of the two Testaments into a complete break between Judaism and Christianity. Though the Jewish faith "immediately preceded" the founding of the Christian Church, it "stands in no essential connection whatever, that is, in no unity of concepts" with this ecclesiastical faith (p. 116). "General church history, if it is to constitute a system," can only begin with the origin of Christianity "which, completely forsaking the Judaism from which it sprang," is "grounded upon a wholly new principle" (p. 118). The new faith is not in continuity with the old. Historical continuity is thus accompanied by discontinuity of substance.

2. Since the time of Benedict Spinoza or Johann Salomo Semler there have been, at bottom, three motifs that have been repeated over and over again as objections against the OT. These can be summed up in three catchwords:

a) Particularism or nationalism
   OT faith is linked to a particular people; a national religion of this kind seems to be the mark of a limited—and now past—stage of civilization.
b) Legalism
   The OT brings with it the threat that the Christian religion will be infiltrated by legalism.
c) This-worldliness
   The OT contains "no belief in a future life" (Kant, p. 117).
   There is therefore a danger that the Christian understanding of salvation will be secularized under the influence of OT expectations regarding the present world.

If the interpretation of the OT is not simply to shove aside the problems that have arisen from the historical influence exercised by the OT, then these objections must be faced. It is to be observed, however, that such reproaches apply only to certain (more or less broad) areas of the OT and not to the OT as a whole and in all its variety. Especially by reason of its hope the OT succeeds in transcending its own "limitations" (see Isa 2:2ff.; 45:6f.; Jer 31:31ff.; Zeph 2:11; 3:9; Pss 22:27ff.; 73:23ff.; etc.).

3. Given a realization of the peculiar characteristics of the OT, the question of the connection of the two Testaments and even of the unity of biblical tradition becomes an important one. The two texts are part of a common tradition that has many levels. The link is not only one of chronological succession but of linguistic agreement as well. The NT receives from the OT a language that already has a theological dimension and can be used to give expression to new experiences. For example, the phrase "The Lord appeared to . . . ," which goes back to early times, helps primitive, pre-Pauline Christian tradition give linguistic expression to the manifestation of the risen Jesus. In fact, the confession in 1 Cor 15:3f. even makes the connection with the OT an explicit one: "according to the scriptures." The significance is the same for the direct citations of the OT in the NT.

To what extent does the accord at the linguistic level (and at other levels too) reflect a unity of substance? What questions, what answers even, what theological insights persist through the transition from the OT to the New? To what extent does Christian faith have a basis in the OT? In this context, we must reflect before all else on the special character of OT speech about God, as this takes shape in the first commandment. This speech with its manifold variations and multiple resonances is *the* heritage of the OT—and at the same time its continuing challenge—to Christianity. For this reason, too, it is not possible for the so-called young churches to substitute their own national traditions for the OT. If the NT be separated from the OT, is it not too easily open to radical misunderstandings?

4. In the traditional development of Christian dogmatics the influence of the OT shows most clearly in three thematic complexes: the doctrine of God (divine attributes, creation), anthropology (humanity as image of God, creation and responsibility, sin and forgiveness), and eschatology (messianic expectation, etc.). In Christology, moreover, the doctrine of the three offices in particular makes use of elements of OT tradition, while in pneumatology OT texts help give expression to the action of the Spirit.

Should not the prohibition against images, which in the final analysis makes a distinction between speaking about God and representing him in other ways, play a more important role in theology? The OT not only shows how faith is bound up with situation but also provides suggestions for reflecting on the historical character of our understanding of God, the world, and the human person. Wherever people in our world speak of faith in a single God, they do so under the direct or indirect influence of the OT. Ought not this fact lead to new questions regarding the elements common to the religions (Judaism, Islam, Christianity)? The chief impulses from the OT may be those given by its hope, which is not satisfied with present human existence and its afflictions but looks for a new world (Isa 11; 65:17; etc.). But when all is said and done, there cannot be any single answer to the question of the significance of the OT; there are too many sides to the OT itself and to its historical influence.

ABBREVIATIONS

AB	Anchor Bible
AJBI	Annual of the Japanese Biblical Institute
AnBib	Analecta Biblica
AOAT	Alter Orient und Altes Testament
ATANT	Abhandlungen zur Theologie des Alten und Neuen Testaments
ATD	Das Alte Testament Deutsch
AzTh	Arbeiten zur Theologie
BAT	Die Botschaft des Alten Testaments
BBB	Bonner biblische Beiträge
BET	Beiträge zur biblischen Exegese und Theologie
BEvT	Beiträge zur evangelischen Theologie
Bib	*Biblica*
BK	Biblischer Kommentar
BN	*Biblische Notizen*
BSt	Biblische Studien
BTB	*Biblical Theology Bulletin*
BThSt	Biblisch-theologische Studien
BWANT	Beiträge zur Wissenschaft vom Alten und Neuen Testament
BZ	*Biblische Zeitschrift*
BZAW	Beihefte zur *ZAW*
CamBC	Cambridge Bible Commentary
CAT	Commentaire de l'Ancien Testament
CBQ	*Catholic Biblical Quarterly*
CTM	Calwer theologische Monographien
DBSup	*Dictionnaire de la Bible, Supplément*
EB	(Neue) Echter Bibel
EdF	Erträge der Forschung
EntstAT	*Die Entstehung des AT*
ErTS	Erfurter theologische Studien
EvT	*Evangelische Theologie*
FRLANT	Forschung zur Religion und Literatur des Alten und Neuen Testaments
Fs	Festschrift
FzB	Forschung zur Bibel
GesAufs	*Gesammelte Aufsätze*
GesStud	*Gesammelte Studien*
HAT	Handbuch zum Alten Testament
HK	Handkommentar (zum Alten Testament)
HUCA	*Hebrew Union College Annual*
Int	*Interpretation*
JB	Jerusalem Bible
JBL	*Journal of Biblical Literature*
JSS	*Journal of Semitic Studies*
KAT	Kommentar zum Alten Testament
KD	*Kerygma und Dogma*

KHC	Kurzer Hand-Commentar zum Alten Testament
KlSchr	*Kleine Schriften*
NCB	New Century Bible
NICOT	The New International Commentary on the Old Testament
OBO	Orbis Biblicus et Orientalis
OrAnt	*Oriens antiquus*
OTL	Old Testament Library
OTS	*Oudtestamentische Studiën*
PW	*Pauly-Wissowa, Real-Encyclopädie der Klassischen Altertumswissenschaft*
RB	*Revue biblique*
RGG	*Religion in Geschichte und Gegenwart*
SANT	Studien zum Alten und Neuen Testament
SAT	Die Schriften des Alten Testaments
SBB	Stuttgarter biblische Beiträge
SBM	Stuttgarter biblische Monographien
SBS	Stuttgarter Bibelstudien
SBT	Studies in Biblical Theology
ST	*Studia Theologica*
STL	Studia theologica Lundensia
TaI	*Tradition and Interpretation*, ed. G. W. Anderson, 1979
TDNT	G. Kittel and G. Friedrich (eds.), *Theological Dictionary of the New Testament*
TDOT	G. J. Botterweck and H. Ringgren (eds.), *Theological Dictionary of the Old Testament*
THAT	*Theologisches Handwörterbuch zum Alten Testament* I–II, 1971–76
TheolVers	*Theologische Versuche*
TheolViat	*Theologia Viatorum*
ThSt	Theologische Studien
TLZ	*Theologische Literaturzeitung*
TRE	*Theologische Realenzyklopädie*
TRev	*Theologische Revue*
TRu	*Theologische Rundschau*
TTZ	*Trierer Theologische Zeitschrift*
TWAT	*Theologische Wörterbuch zum Alten Testament*
TZ	*Theologische Zeitschrift*
ÜSt	*Überlieferungsgeschichtliche Studien*
VF	*Verkündigung und Forschung*
VT	*Vetus Testamentum*
VTSup	Vetus Testamentum, Supplements
WdF	Wege der Forschung
WMANT	Wissenschaftliche Monographien zum Alten und Neuen Testament
WuB	*Wort und Botschaft des Alten Testaments*, ed. by J. Schreiner, 1967, 1975[3]
WuD	*Wort und Dienst*
ZAW	*Zeitschrift für die alttestamentliche Wissenschaft*
ZBK	Zürcher Bibelkommentar
ZEE	*Zeitschrift für evangelische Ethik*
ZKT	*Zeitschrift für katholische Theologie*
ZTK	*Zeitschrift für Theologie und Kirche*

BIBLIOGRAPHY

§1 The Parts of the Old Testament

Introductions to the OT: O. **Eissfeldt** (1964³, 1976⁴; Eng.: *The Old Testament: An Introduction*, 1965); A. **Weiser** (1966⁶; Eng.: *Introduction to the Old Testament*, 1961); (E. **Sellin-**) G. **Fohrer** (1979¹²; Eng.: *Introduction to the Old Testament*, 1972); O. **Kaiser** (1978⁴; Eng.: *Introduction to the Old Testament*, 1977); R. **Smend**, *Die Entstehung des AT* (= *EntstAT*) (1978); B. S. **Childs**, *Introduction to the Old Testament as Scripture* (1979); J. H. **Hayes**, *An Introduction to Old Testament Study* (1979); J. A. **Soggin**, *Introduction to the Old Testament* (1980).

H. **Haag**, "Kanon," *Bibel-Lexikon* (1968²) 915ff. (bibliog.); H. **Gese**, "Erwägungen zur Einheit der biblischen Theologie" (1970), *Vom Sinai zum Sion* (1974) 11–30; J. **Conrad**, "Zur Frage nach der Rolle des Gesetzes bei der Bildung der alttestamentlichen Kanons," *TheolVers* 11 (1980) 11–19; G. **Wanke**, "Bibel," *TRE* 6 (1980) 1–8 (bibliog.).

§2 The Stages of Israel's History

A. **Alt**, *Kleine Schriften zur Geschichte des Volkes Israel I–III*, (1953–); selection in *Grundfragen zur Geschichte des Volkes Israel* (1969) (an English-language selection: *Essays in Old Testament History and Religion*, 1967); M. **Noth**, *Geschichte Israels* (1954², 1976⁸; Eng.: *The History of Israel*, 1960²); M. **Metzger**, *Grundriss der Geschichte Israels* (1963, 1979⁵); A. H. J. **Gunneweg**, *Geschichte Israels bis Bar Kochba* (1972, 1979³); S. **Herrmann**, *Geschichte Israels in alttestamentlicher Zeit* (1973, 1980²; Eng.: *A History of Israel in Old Testament Times*, 1975; see R. **Smend**, *EvT* 34 [1974] 304–14); A. **Jepsen**, *Von Sinuhe bis Nebukadnezar* (1975, 1979³; with chronological table and ancient Near Eastern courses); G. **Fohrer**, *Geschichte Israels* (1979²); J. H. **Hayes** and J. M. **Miller**, *Israelite and Judaean History* (1977); H. H. **Ben-Sasson** (ed.), *Geschichte des jüdischen Volkes*, I (1978); R. **de Vaux**, *The Early History of Israel* (1978); J. **Bright**, *A History of Israel* (1981³).

§3 Aspects of Social History

Survey of research: W. **Schottroff**, "Soziologie und AT," *VF* 19/2 (1974) 46–66 (bibliog.).

M. **Weber**, *Das antike Judentum* (Gesammelte Aufsätze zur Religionssoziologie III; 1920, 1966⁴; Eng.: *Ancient Judaism*, 1952); L. **Köhler**, *Der hebräische Mensch* (1953; Eng.: *Hebrew Man*, 1957); R. **de Vaux**, *Ancient Israel: Its Life and Institutions* (1961); Y. **Yadin**, *The Art of Warfare in Bible Lands in the Light of Archaeological Discovery*, I (1962); H. **Donner**, "Die soziale Botschaft der Propheten im Lichte der Gesellschaftsordnung Israels," *OrAnt* 2 (1963) 229–45; G. **Buccellati**, *Cities and Nations of Ancient Syria* (1967); H. E. **v. Waldow**, "Social Responsibility and Social Structure," *CBQ* 32 (1970) 182–204; K. **Koch**, "Die Entstehung der sozialen Kritik bei den Profeten," *Fs. G. v. Rad* (1971) 236–57; G. C. **Macholz**, "Die Stellung des Königs in der israelitischen Gerichtsverfassung," *ZAW* 84 (1972) 157–82; G. **Wanke**, "Zu Grundlagen und Absichte prophetischer Sozialkritik," *KD* 18 (1972) 1–17; M. **Fendler**, "Zur Sozialkritik des Amos," *EvT* 33 (1973) 32–53; F. **Stolz**, "Aspekte religiöser und sozialer Ordnung im alten Israel," *ZEE* 17 (1973) 145–59; M. **Schwantes**, *Das Recht der Armen* (BET 4, 1977); F. **Crüsemann**, *Der Widerstand gegen das Königtum* (WMANT 49, 1978); H. G. **Kippenberg**, *Religion und Klassenbildung im antiken Judäa* (1978); W. **Dietrich**, *Israel und Kanaan* (1979); N. K. **Gottwald**, *The Tribes of Yahweh* (1979); W. **Schottroff** and W. **Stegemann** (eds.), *Der Gott der kleinen Leute* I (1979); idem, *Traditionen der Befreiung* I (1980); W. **Thiel**, *Die soziale Entwicklung Israels in vorstaatlicher Zeit* (1980).

§4 The Pentateuch

History of scholarship: H. J. **Kraus**, *Geschichte der historisch-kritischen Forschung des AT* (1969²); E. **Osswald**, *Das Bild des Mose* (1962); R. J. **Thompson**, *Moses and the Law in a Century of Criticism since Graf* (VTSup 19, 1970); R. E. **Clements**, "Pentateuchal Problems," *TaI*, 96–124.

Important monographs: J. **Wellhausen**, *Die Composition des Hexateuchs* (1876f., 1963⁴); idem, *Prolegomena zur Geschichte Israels* (1883, 1905⁶; Eng.: *Prolegomena to the History of Ancient Israel*, 1885, 1957); H. **Holzinger**, *Einleitung in das Hexateuch* (= *EinlHex*) (1893); J. **Estlin Carpenter** and G. **Harford**, *The Composition of the Hexateuch* (1902); S. R. **Driver**, *An Introduction to the Literature of the Old Testament* (1912); O. **Eissfeldt**, *Hexateuch Synopse* (1922, 1962); G. **v. Rad**, "Das formgeschichtliche Problem des Hexateuch" (1938), *GesStud* (1958, 1965³) 9–86; (Eng.: *The Problem of the Hexateuch and Other Essays* (1966); M. **Noth**, *Überlieferungsgeschichte des Pentateuch* (1948, 1966³; Eng.: *A History of Pentateuchal Traditions*, 1972); G. **Hölscher**, *Geschichtsschreibung in Israel* (1952); S. **Mowinckel**, *Erwägungen zur Pentateuch-Quellenfrage* (1964).

Recent works: R. **Rendtorff**, *Das überlieferungsgeschichtliche Problem des Pentateuch* (BZAW 147, 1976); E. **Otto**, "Stehen wir vor einem Umbruch in der Pentateuchkritik?" *VF* 22/1 (1977) 82–97; P. **Weimar**, *Untersuchungen zur Redaktionsgeschichte des Pentateuch* (BZAW 146, 1977); H. Ch. **Schmitt**, *Die nichtpriesterliche Josephsgeschichte* (BZAW 154, 1980, esp. 175ff.); E. **Zenger**, "Wo steht die Pentateuchforschung heute?" *BZ* 24 (1980) 101–16.

Commentaries on Genesis: H. **Gunkel** (HK, 1910³; Eng. of the introduction to this commentary: *The Legends of Genesis: The Biblical Saga and History*, 1901, 1964); O. **Procksch** (KAT, 1924²,³); S. R. **Driver**, *The Book of Genesis* (1926¹²); G. **v. Rad** (ATD, 1953, 1979⁹; Eng.: OTL, 1972); U. **Cassuto**, *Commentary on Genesis*, I (1961); II (1964); E. A. **Speiser** (AB, 1964); N. **Sarna**, *Understanding Genesis* (1966); C. **Westermann** (BK I, 1975²; II, 1977–); W. **Zimmerli** (ZBK I, 1967³; II, 1976); B. **Vawter**, *On Genesis: A New Reading* (1977).

Surveys of research: C. **Westermann**, *Genesis 1–11* (EdF 7, 1972); idem, *Genesis 12–50* (EdF 48, 1975).

Exodus: H. **Holzinger** (KHC, 1900 [Exod, Num]); B. **Baentsch** (HK, 1903 [Exod, Num]); H. **Gressmann**, *Mose und seine Zeit* (1913); G. **Beer** and K. **Galling** (HAT, 1939); M. **Noth** (ATD, 1958, 1978⁶; Eng.: OTL, 1962); G. **Fohrer**, *Überlieferung und Geschichte des Exodus* (BZAW 91, 1964); U. **Cassuto**, *Commentary on Exodus* (1967); J. P. **Hyatt** (NCB, 1971); B. S. **Childs** (OTL, 1974); W. H. **Schmidt** (BK, 1974–); P. **Weimar** and E. **Zenger**, *Exodus* (SBS 75, 1975, bibliog.); J. **Jeremias**, *Theophanie* (WMANT 10, 1977²) 194ff. (bibliog.).

Leviticus: M. **Noth** (ATD, 1962, 1978⁴; Eng.: OTL, 1965, 1977²); N. H. **Snaith** (NCB, 1969 [Lev, Num]); K. **Elliger** (HAT, 1966); G. J. **Wenham** (NICOT, 1979).

Numbers: M. **Noth** (ATD, 1966, 1977³; Eng.: OTL, 1968); J. **de Vaulx** (1972).
Deuteronomy: see §10.

Bibliography 347

§5 Selected Types of Narrative

a) Myth and primeval history

J. **Hempel,** "Glaube, Mythos und Geschichte im AT," *ZAW* 62 (1953) 109–67; B. S. **Childs,** *Myth and Reality in the Old Testament* (1960); B. **Albrektson,** *History and the Gods* (1967); W. H. **Schmidt,** "Mythos im AT," *EvT* 27 (1967) 237–54; A. **Ohler,** *Mythologische Elemente im AT* (1969); W. **Pannenberg,** *Christentum und Mythos* (1972); J. W. **Rogerson,** *Myth in Old Testament Interpretation* (1974); J. J. M. **Roberts,** "Myth Versus History: Relaying the Comparative Foundations," *CBQ* 38 (1976) 1–13; H. P. **Müller,** *Jenseits der Entmythologisierung* (1979²); B. **Otzen** et al., *Myths in the Old Testament* (1980).

Genealogies: C. **Westermann** (BK I, 1974) 8ff.; R. R. **Wilson,** "The Old Testament Genealogies in Recent Research," *JBL* 94 (1975) 169–89; idem, *Genealogy and History in the Biblical World* (1977).

b) The saga as a form of transmission

H. **Gunkel,** *Genesis* (1910³, VIIff.; Eng. translation of the introduction to this commentary: *The Legends of Genesis: The Biblical Saga and History,* 1901, 1964); C. **Westermann,** "Arten der Erzählung in der Genesis," *Forschung am AT* (1964) 9–91 (= "Die Verheissung an die Väter," FRLANT 116 [1976] 9–91); idem, *Genesis 12–50* (EdF 48, 1975) 20ff.; K. **Koch,** *Was ist Formgeschichte?* (1974³) 182ff. (Eng.: *The Growth of the Biblical Tradition: The Form-critical Method,* 1969); J. H. **Wilcoxen,** in J. H. Hayes (ed.), *Old Testament Form Criticism* (1974) 57ff.; H. J. **Hermisson,** in *Enzyklopädie des Märchens* I (1975) 419–41; J. P. **Fokkelman,** *Narrative Art in Genesis* (1975); P. D. **Miller, Jr.,** *Genesis 1–11* (1978); M. **Fishbane,** *Text and Texture: Close Readings of Selected Biblical Texts* (1979); R. **Alter,** *The Art of Biblical Narrative* (1981);

Etiology: S. **Mowinckel,** *Tetrateuch-Pentateuch-Hexateuch* (BZAW 90, 1964) 78ff.; B. O. **Long,** *The Problem of Etiological Narrative in the Old Testament* (BZAW 108, 1968); R. **Smend,** "Elemente alttestamentlichen Geschichtsdenkens," *ThSt* 95 (1968) 15ff.; B. S. **Childs,** "The Etiological Tale Re-examined," *VT* 24 (1974) 387–97; F. W. **Golka,** *VT* 20 (1970) 90–98; 26 (1976) 410–28; 27 (1977) 36–47 (bibliog.); *THAT* II, 945f. (bibliog.).

c) The Joseph novella

L. **Ruppert,** *Die Josephserzählung der Genesis* (1961); D. W. **Redford,** *A Study of the Biblical Story of Joseph* (1970); C. **Westermann,** *Genesis 12–50* (EdF 48, 1975) 56ff.; G. W. **Coats,** *From Canaan to Egypt* (1976); H. **Donner,** *Die literarische Gestalt der alttestamentliche Josephsgeschichte* (1976); E. **Otto,** "Die 'synthetische Lebensauffassung' . . . ," *ZTK* 74 (1977) 387–400; F. **Crüsemann** (§3), 143ff. (bibliog.); H. **Seebass,** *Geschichtliche Zeit und theonome Tradition in der Joseph-Erzählung* (1978); H. Ch. **Schmitt,** *Literarkritische Studien zur nichtpriesterlichen Josephsgeschichte* (above, §4).

§6 The Yahwist History

G. **v. Rad,** *Das formgeschichtliche Problem des Hexateuch* (§4; Eng.); M. L. **Henry,** *Jahwist und Priesterschrift* (1960); H. W. **Wolff,** "Das Kerygma des Jahwisten" (1964), *GesStud* (1964) 345–73 (Eng.: "The Kerygma of the Yahwist," in W. Brueggemann and H. W. Wolff, *The Vitality of Old Testament Traditions* [1975] 41–66); P. F. **Ellis,** *The Yahwist* (1968); L. **Ruppert,** "Der Jahwist—Künder der Heilsgeschichte," *WuB,* 101–20; H. P. **Müller,** *Ursprünge und Strukturen der alttestamentlichen Eschatologie* (BZAW 109, 1969) 50ff.; F. J. **Stendebach,** *Theologische Anthropologie des Jahwisten* (1970; diss. in faculty of Catholic theology, Bonn); V. **Fritz,** *Israel in der Wüste* (1970) 113ff.; O. H.

Steck, *Die Paradieserzählung* (BSt 60, 1970); idem, "Gen 12, 1–3 und die Urgeschichte des Jahwisten," *Fs. G. v. Rad* (1971) 525–54 (bibliog.); E. **Zenger,** *Die Sinaitheophanie* (1971) esp. 138ff.; T. L. **Thompson,** *The Historicity of the Patriarchal Narratives* (1974); J. **Van Seters,** *Abraham in History and Tradition* (1975); idem, *In Search of History* (1983); C. **Westermann** (BK I/1, 1976²) 782ff.; H. H. **Schmid,** *Der sogenannte Jahwist* (1976); R. **Rendtorff,** "Der 'Jahwist' als Theologe?" *Congress Volume Edinburgh* (VTSup 28, 1975); idem (above, §4) 86ff.; L. **Schmidt,** "Überlegungen zum Jahwisten," *EvT* 37 (1977) 230–47 (bibliog.); P. **Weimar,** *Untersuchungen* (above §4); E. **Otto** (above, §4); H. **Vorlaender,** *Die Entstehungszeit des jehovistischen Geschichtswerkes* (1978); H. **Lubscyk,** "Elohim beim Jahwisten," *Congress Volume Göttingen* (VTSup 29, 1978) 226–53; E. **Ruprecht,** ". . . Gen XII, 1–3," *VT* 29 (1979) 171–88, 444–64; W. H. **Schmidt,** "Ein Theologie in salomonischer Zeit? Plädoyer für den Jahwisten," *BZ* 25 (1981) 82–102.

§7 The Elohist History
O. **Procksch,** *Das nordhebräische Sagenbuch. Die Elohimquelle* (1906); P. **Volz** and W. **Rudolph,** *Der Elohist als Erzähler—ein Irrweg der Pentateuchkritik?* (BZAW 63, 1933); W. **Rudolph,** *Der "Elohist" von Exodus bis Josua* (BZAW 68, 1938); J. **Becker,** *Gottesfurcht im AT* (AnBib 25, 1965) 193ff.; L. **Ruppert,** "Der Elohist—Sprecher für Gottes Volk," *WuB,* 121–32; H. W. **Wolff,** "Zur Thematik der elohistischen Fragmente im Pentateuch" (1969), *GesStud* (1973²) 402–17 (Eng.: "The Elohistic Fragments in the Pentateuch," in Brueggemann and Wolff [§6] 67–82); K. **Jaroš,** *Die Stellung des Elohisten zur kanaanäischen Religion* (OBO 4, 1974); J. **Schüpphaus,** "Volk Gottes und Gesetz beim Elohisten," *TZ* 31 (1975) 193–210; F. **Craghan,** "The Elohist in Recent Literature," *BTB* 7 (1977) 25–35; A. W. **Jenks,** *The Elohist and North Israelite Tradition* (1977); H. **Klein,** "Ort und Zeit des Elohisten," *EvT* 37 (1977) 247–60; P. **Weimar** (§4); H. Ch. **Schmidt** (§4); H. **Vorlaender** (§6).

§8 The Priestly Document
T. **Nöldeke,** *Untersuchungen zur Kritik des AT. 1. Die s. g. Grundschrift des Pentateuch* (1869); J. J. P. **Valeton,** "Bedeutung und Stellung des Wortes *berit* im Priesterkodex," *ZAW* 12 (1892) 1–22; G. **v. Rad,** *Die Priesterschrift im Hexateuch* (BWANT 65, 1934; see P. **Humbert,** *ZAW* 58 [1940–41] 30–57); K. **Elliger,** "Sinn und Ursprung der priesterlichen Geschichtserzählung" (1952), *KlSchr zum AT* (1966) 174–98; J. **Hempel** "Priesterkodex" (PW 22, 1954) 1943–67; R. **Rendtorff,** *Die Gesetz in der Priesterschrift* (FRLANT 62, 1954); K. **Koch,** "Die Eigenart der priesterlichen Sinaigesetzgebung," *ZTK* 55 (1958) 36–51; idem, *Die Priesterschrift von Ex 25 bis Lev 16* (FRLANT 71, 1959); idem, "Ŝaddaj," *VT* 26 (1976) 316ff.; M. L. **Henry** (§6); W. **Zimmerli,** "Sinaibund und Abrahambund" (1960), *Gottes Offenbarung* (1963) 205–16; S. R. **Kuelling,** *Zur Datierung der "Genesis-P-Stücke"* (1964); W. H. **Schmidt,** *Die Schöpfungsgeschichte der Priesterschrift* (WMANT 17, 1964, 1973³); A. H. **Gunneweg,** *Leviten und Priester* (FRLANT 89, 1965); R. **Kilian,** "Die Priesterschirft—Hoffnung auf Heimkehr," *WuB,* 243–60; W. **Gross,** "Jakob, der Mann des Segens," *Bib* 49 (1968) 321–44; G. Ch. **Macholz,** *Israel und das Land* (1969, Habilitationsschrift, Heidelberg); J. G. **Vink,** "The Date and Origin of the Priestly Code in the Old Testament," *OTS* 15 (1969) 1–144 (bibliog.); A. **Eitz,** *Studien zum Verhältnis von Priesterschrift und Deuterojesaja* (1970; diss., Heidelberg); D. **Kellermann,** *Die Priesterschrift von Num 1,1 bis 10,10* (BZAW 120, 1970); R. J. **Thompson** (§4); N. **Lohfink,** "Die Ursünden in der priesterlichen Geschichtserzählung," *Fs. H. Schlier* (1970) 38–57 (see also *Unsere grossen Wörter* [1977] 209–24); C. **Westermann,** "Die Herrlichkeit Gottes in der Priesterschrift" (1970), *Forschung am AT* II (1974) 115–37; S. E. **McEvenue,** *The Narrative Style of the Priestly Writer* (AnBib 50, 1971); W. **Brueggemann,** "The Kerygma of the Priestly Writer," *ZAW* 84 (1972) 397–414 (also in Brueggemann and Wolff [§6] 101–13); F. M. **Cross,** *Canaanite Myth and Hebrew Epic* (1973) 293ff.; P. **Weimar,** *Untersuchungen zur priesterlichen Exodusge-*

schichte (FzB 9, 1973); idem, "Aufbau und Struktur der priesterschriftlichen Jakobusgeschichte," *ZAW* 86 (1974) 174–203; A. **Hurvitz,** "The Evidence of Language in Dating the Priestly Code," *RB* 81 (1974) 24–56; E. **Kutsch,** " 'Ich will euer Gott sein,' " *ZTK* 71 (1974) 361–88; E. **Ruprecht,** "Stellung und Bedeutung der Erzählung vom Mannawunder . . . ," *ZAW* 86 (1974) 269–307; O. H. **Steck,** *Der Schöpfungsbericht der Priesterschrift* (FRLANT 115, 1975); J. **Blenkinsopp,** "The Structure of P," *CBQ* 38 (1976) 275–92; R. **Rendtorff** (§4) 112ff.; V. **Fritz,** *Tempel und Zelt* (WMANT 47, 1977); N. **Lohfink,** "Die Priesterschrift und ihre Geschichte," *Congress Volume Göttingen* (VTSup 29, 1978) 189–225 (bibliog.); R. W. **Klein,** *Israel in Exile* (1979) 125–48.

§9 Old Testament Law

Introduction: H. J. **Boecker,** *Recht und Gesetz im Alten Testament und im Alten Orient* (1976, bibliog.).

Survey of research: W. **Schottroff,** "Zum alttestamentlichen Recht," *VF* 22/1 (1977) 3–29 (bibliog.).

A. **Alt,** "Die Ursprünge des israelitischen Rechts" (1934), *KlSchr* I, 278–332 = *Grundfragen* (§2) 203–57 (Eng.: "The Origins of Israelite Law," in *Essays in Old Testament History and Religion* [1967] 101–72); M. **Noth,** "Die Gesetze im Pentateuch" (1940), *GesStud* (1957) 9–141 (Eng.: *The Laws in the Pentateuch, and Other Studies* [1966] 1–107); E. **Gerstenberger,** *Wesen und Herkunft des "apodiktischen Rechts"* (WMANT 20, 1965); R. **Hentschke,** "Erwägungen zur Israelitischen Rechtsgeschichte," *TheolViat* 10 (1965–66) 108–33; W. **Schottroff,** *Der alttestamentliche Fluchspruch* (WMANT 30, 1969); H. **Schulz,** *Das Todesrecht im AT* (BZAW 114, 1969); G. **Liedke,** *Gestalt und Bezeichnung alttestamentlicher Rechtssätze* (WMANT 39, 1971); V. **Wagner,** *Rechtssätze in gebundener Sprache . . .* (BZAW 127, 1972); K. **Koch** (ed.), *Um das Prinzip der Vergeltung in Religion und Recht des AT* (WdF 125, 1972); J. **Bright,** "The Apodictic Prohibition: Some Observations," *JBL* 92 (1973) 185–204; G. **Wallis,** "Der Vollbürgereid in Dtn 27,15–26," *HUCA* 45 (1974) 47–63; J. **Halbe,** *Das Privilegrecht Jahwes Ex 34,10–26* (FRLANT 114, 1975); H. J. **Boecker,** *Recht und Gesetz im AT und im Alten Orient* (1976, bibliog.); W. **Schottroff,** "Zum alttestamentlichen Recht," *VF* 22/1 (1977) 3–29 (bibliog.).

The Decalogue
Surveys of research: L. **Köhler,** "Der Dekalog," *TRu* 1 (1929) 161–84; J. J. **Stamm,** *Der Dekalog im Lichte der neueren Forschung* (1962²), expanded in J. J. **Stamm** and M. E. **Andrews,** *The Ten Commandments in Recent Research* (1967); E. **Zenger,** "Eine Wende in der Dekalogforschung?" *TRev* 64 (1968) 189–98.

H. H. **Rowley,** "Moses and the Decalogue," *Men of God* (1963) 1–36 (bibliog.); G. J. **Botterweck,** "The Form and Growth of the Decalogue," *Concilium,* no. 5 (1965) 58–79; E. **Nielsen,** *Die zehn Gebote* (1965); J. **Schreiner,** *Die zehn Gebote im Leben des Gottesvolkes* (1966); H. **Gese,** "Der Dekalog als Ganzheit betrachtet" (1967), *Vom Sinai zum Zion* (1974) 63–80; A. **Jepsen,** "Beiträge zur Auslegung und Geschichte des Dekalogs" (1967), *Der Herr ist Gott* (1978) 76–95; A. **Phillips,** *Ancient Israel's Criminal Law* (1970); W. H. **Schmidt,** "Überlieferungsgeschichtliche Erwägungen zur Komposition des Dekalogs" (VTSup 22, 1972) 201–20; H. **Schüngel-Straumann,** *Der Dekalog—Gottes Gebot?* (SBS 67, 1973); E. W. **Nicholson,** "The Decalogue as the Direct Address of God," *VT* 27 (1977) 422–33; Sch. **Ben Chorin,** *Die Tafeln des Bundes* (1979).

Book of the Covenant: H. J. **Boecker,** *Recht und Gesetz im AT und im Alten Orient* (1976) 116ff. (bibliog.); F. C. **Fensham,** "The Role of the Lord in the Legal Sections of the Covenant Code," *VT* 26 (1976) 262–74.

Law of Holiness: W. **Thiel,** "Erwägungen zum Alter des Heiligkeitsgesetzes," *ZAW*

350   *Bibliography*

81 (1969) 40–73 (bibliog.); V. **Wagner,** "Zur Existenz des sog. 'Heiligkeitsgesetzes,'"
ZAW 86 (1974) 307–16; A. **Cholewinski,** *Heiligkeitsgesetz und Deuteronomium* (AnBib
66, 1976, bibliog.); G. **Bettenzoli,** *Geist der Heiligkeit* (1979) 51ff.; W. **Zimmerli,**
"'Heiligkeit" nach dem sogenannten Heiligkeitsgesetz," *VT* 30 (1980) 493–512.

§10 Deuteronomy
Commentaries: C. **Steuernagel** (HK, 1923²); G. **v. Rad** (ATD, 1964; Eng.: *Deuteronomy*,
1966); P. C. **Craigie** (NICOT, 1976); A. D. H. **Mayes** (NCB, 1979).

History of scholarship: W. **Baumgartner,** "Der Kampf um das Deuteronomium," *TRu*
1 (1929) 7–25; S. **Loersch,** *Das Deuteronomium und seine Deutungen* (SBS 22, 1967);
H. D. **Preuss,** *Deuteronomium* (planned for EdF).

G. **v. Rad,** "Das Gottesvolk im Deuteronomium" (1929), *GesStud* II (1973) 9–108;
idem, "Deuteronomium-Studien" (1947), *GesStud* II (1973) 109–53 (Eng.: *Studies in
Deuteronomy* [SBT 9, 1953]); F. **Horst,** "Das Privilegrecht Jahwes" (1930), *Gottes Recht*
(1961) 17–154; A. **Alt,** "Die Heimat des Deuteronomiums" (1953), *KlSchr* II, 250–75;
G. **Mendenhall,** *Law and Covenant in Israel and the Ancient Near East* (1955); F.
Dummermuth, "Zur deuteronomischen Kulttheologie und ihren Voraussetzungen,"
ZAW 70 (1958) 59–98; O. **Bächli,** *Israel und die Völker* (ATANT 41, 1962); G. **Minette
de Tillesse,** "Sections 'Tu' et 'vous' . . . ," *VT* 12 (1962) 29–87; N. **Lohfink,** *Das
Hauptgebot* (AnBib 20, 1963); idem, "Botschaft vom Bund," *WuB,* 179–93; H. H. **Schmid,**
"Das Verständnis der Geschichte im Deuteronomium," *ZTK* 64 (1967) 1–15; R. **de
Vaux,** "'Le lieu que Yahvé a choisi,'" *Fs. L. Rost* (1967) 219–28; J. G. **Plöger,**
*Literarkritische, formgeschichtliche und stilkritische Untersuchungen zum Deutero-
nomium* (BBB 26, 1967); R. E. **Clements,** *God's Chosen People* (1968); R. P. **Merendino,**
Das deuteronomische Gesetz (BBB 31, 1969; see A. **Shim,** *Bib* 54 [1973] 452–56); idem,
"Die Zeugnisse . . . ," *Fs. G. J.* **Botterweck** (1977) 185–208; L. **Perlitt,** *Bundestheologie
im AT* (WMANT 36, 1969); D. **Hillers,** *Covenant: The History of a Biblical Idea* (1969);
K. **Baltzer,** *The Covenant Formulary* (1971); S. **Herrmann,** "Die konstruktive Restau-
ration," *Fs. G. v. Rad* (1971) 155–70; G. **Seitz,** *Redaktionsgeschichtliche Studien zum
Deuteronomium* (BWANT 93, 1971); J. **Lindblom,** *Erwägungen zur Herkunft der
josianischen Tempelurkunde* (1971); P. **Diepold,** *Israels Land* (BWANT 95, 1972); D.
McCarthy, *Old Testament Covenant* (1972); idem, *Treaty and Covenant* (1978²); M.
Weinfeld, *Deuteronomy and Deuteronomic School* (1972); S. **Mittmann,** *Deuteronomium 1,1–6,3 . . .* (BZAW 139, 1975; see G. **Braulik,** *Bib* 59 [1978] 351–83); M. **Rose,**
Der Ausschliesslichkeitsanspruch Jahwes (BWANT 106, 1975); H. J. **Boecker** (above,
§9) 154ff.; A. **Cholewiński** (above, §9); E. **Würthwein,** "Die josianische Reform und das
Deuteronomium," *ZTK* 73 (1976) 395–423; R. **Abba,** "Priests and Levites in Deuteronomy," *VT* 27 (1977) 257–67; S. **Amsler,** "La motivation de l'Ethique dans la Parénèse
du Deutéronome," *Fs. W. Zimmerli* (1977) 11–22; E. **Nielsen,** "'Weil Jahwe unser Gott
ein Jahwe ist,'" ibid., 288–301; F. **García-Lopez,** "Analyse littéraire de Deutéronome,"
RB 84 (1977) 481–522; 85 (1978) 5–49.

§11 The Deuteronomistic History
History of scholarship: E. **Jenni,** "Zwei Jahrzehnte Forschung an den Büchern Josua
bis Könige," *TRu* 27 (1961) 1–32, 97–146; A. N. **Radjawane,** "Das deuteronomistische
Geschichtswerk," *TRu* 38 (1974) 177–216.

M. **Noth,** *Überlieferungsgeschichtliche Studien* (1943, 1973⁴; = *ÜSt*); A. **Jepsen,** *Die
Quellen des Königsbuches* (1953, 1956²); G. **v. Rad,** "Die deuteronomistische Ge-
schichtstheologie in den Königsbüchern," *GesStud* I (1958, 1971⁴) 189–204; H. J. **Kraus,**
"Gesetz und Geschichte" (1951), *Biblisch-theologische Aufsätze* (1972) 50–65; O. **Plöger,**

"Reden und Gebete im deuteronomistischen und chronistischen Geschichtswerk" (1957), *Aus der Spätzeit des AT* (1971) 50–66; H. W. **Wolff**, "Das Kerygma des deuteronomistischen Geschichtswerks" (1961), *GesStud* (1964, 1973²) 308–24 [Eng.: "The Kerygma of the Deuteronomic Historical Work," in W. Brueggemann and H. W. Wolff, *The Vitality of Old Testament Traditions* [1975] 83–100; see H. **Timm**, *EvT* 26 [1966] 509–26]; A. **Gamper**, "Die heilsgeschichtliche Bedeutung des salomonischen Tempelwiehgebets," *ZKT* 85 (1963) 55–61; G. **Minette de Tillesse**, "Martin Noth et la 'Redaktionsgeschichte' des livres historiques," *Aux grands carrefours de la révélation et de l'exégèse de l'Ancien Testament* (1966) 51–76; J. **Debus**, *Die Sünde Jeroboams* (FRLANT 93, 1967); N. **Lohfink**, "Bilanz nach der Katastrophe," (*WuB*, 212–25); J. A. **Soggin**, "Deuteronomistische Geschichtsauslegung während des babylonischen Exils," *Fs. O. Cullmann* (1967) 11–17; idem, "Der Entstehungsort des deuteronomistischen Geschichtswerks," *TLZ* 100 (1975) 3–8; O. H. **Steck**, *Israel und das gewaltsame Geschick der Propheten* (WMANT 23, 1967); G. **Sauer**, "Die chronologischen Angaben in den Büchern Dtn bis 2 Kön," *TZ* 24 (1968) 1–14; H. J. **Boecker**, *Die Beurteilung der Anfänge des Königtums in den deuteronomistischen Abschnitten des i. Samuelbuches* (WMANT 31, 1969); G. C. **Macholz** (above, §8); R. **Smend**, "Das Gesetz und die Völker," *Fs. G. v. Rad* (1971) 494–509; idem, *Die Entstehung des AT* (= *EntstAT*) (1978) 111ff.; P. **Diepold** (above, §10); W. **Dietrich**, *Prophetie und Geschichte* (FRLANT 108, 1972); H. **Weippert**, "Die 'deuteronomistische' Beurteilung der Könige . . . ," *Bib* 53 (1972) 301–39 (see M. Weippert, *VT* 23 [1973] 436ff.); F. M. **Cross**, *Canaanite Myth and Hebrew Epic* (1973) 274–89; W. B. **Barrick**, *Bib* 55 (1974) 257ff.; E. **Cortese**, *Bib* 56 (1975) 37ff.; M. **Rose** (above, §10) 146ff.; T. **Veijola**, *Die ewige Dynastie* (1975); idem, *Das Königtum in der Beurteilung der deuteronomistischen Historiographie* (1977); I. L. **Seeligmann**, "Die Auffassung von der Prophetie in der dtr. und chronist. Geschichtsschreibung," *Congress Volume Göttingen* (VTSup 29 [1978] 254–84); H. D. **Hoffmann**, *Reform und Reformen* (ATANT 66, 1980).

Joshua: A. **Alt**, "Josua" (1936), *KlSchr* I, 176ff. (= *Grundfragen*, above, §2) 186ff.; M. **Noth**, (HAT, 1953², 1971³); H. W. **Hertzberg** (ATD, 1954, 1974³ [Joshua, Judges, Ruth]); S. **Mowinckel**, *Tetrateuch–Pentateuch–Hexateuch* (BZAW 90, 1964); J. A. **Soggin** (CAT, 1970; Eng.: OTL, 1972); E. **Otto**, *Das Mazzotfest in Gilgal* (BWANT 107, 1975; bibliog.); R. G. **Boling** and G. E. **Wright** (AB, 1982).

Judges: E. **Jenni**, "Vom Zeugnis des Richterbuches," *TZ* 12 (1956) 257–74; W. **Beyerlin**, "Gattung und Herkunft des Rahmens im Richterbuch," *Fs. A. Weiser* (1963) 1–29; idem, "Geschichtliche und heilsgeschichtliche Traditionsbildung im AT," *VT* 13 (1963) 1–25; W. **Richter**, *Traditionsgeschichtliche Untersuchungen zum Richterbuch* (BBB 18, 1963, 1966²); idem, *Die Bearbeitung des "Retterbuches" in der deuteronomischen Epoche* (BBB 21, 1964); J. **Schlauri**, "W. Richters Beitrag zur Traditionsgeschichte des Richterbuches," *Bib* 54 (1973) 367–403 (bibliog.); *THAT* II, 999ff. (bibliog. on "Richter"); R. G. **Boling** (AB, 1975); A. J. **Hauser**, "The 'Minor Judges,'" *JBL* 94 (1975) 190–200; J. **Blenkinsopp**, "Structure and Style in Judges 13–16," *JBL* (1982) 65–72.

Samuel: L. **Rost**, "Die Überlieferung von der Thronnachfolge Davids" (1926), *Das kleine Credo* (1965) 119–253; H. W. **Hertzberg** (ATD, 1956, 1973⁵; Eng.: OTL, 1964); A. **Weiser**, *Samuel* (FRLANT 81, 1962); R. A. **Carlson**, *David the Chosen King* (1964); J. **Blenkinsopp**, "Theme and Motif in the Succession History (2 Sam XI 2ff) and the Yahwist Corpus," *SVT* 15 (1966) 44–57; G. **Wallis**, *Geschichte und Überlieferung* (1968); R. N. **Whybray**, *The Succession Narrative* (1968); L. **Schmidt**, *Menschlicher Erfolg und Jahwes Initiative* (WMANT 38, 1970); J. H. **Grønbaek**, *Die Geschichte vom Aufstieg Davids* (1971); J. **Mauchline** (NCB, 1971); R. **Rendtorff**, "Beobachtungen zur altisraelitischen Geschichtsschreibung . . . ," *Fs. G. v. Rad* (1971) 428–39; J. W. **Flanagan**, "Court History or Succession Document? A Study of 2 Samuel 9–20 and 1 Kings 1–2," *JBL* 91 (1972) 172–81; H. J. **Stoebe** (KAT I, 1973); A. F. **Campbell**, *The Ark Narrative* (1975); E. **Würthwein**, *Die Erzählung von der Thronnachfolge Davids* (ThSt 115, 1975); B. **Birch**,

352   *Bibliography*

The *Rise of the Israelite Monarchy* (1976); V. **Fritz,** "Die Deutungen des Königtums Sauls . . . ," *ZAW* 88 (1976) 346–62 (bibliog.); F. **Langlamet,** *RB* 83 (1976) 114–37, 321–79, 481, 528; T. D. N. **Mettinger,** *King and Messiah* (1976); W. **Dietrich,** "David in Überlieferung und Geschichte," *VF* 22/1 (1977) 44–64 (bibliog.); J. **Kegler,** *Politisches Geschehen und theologisches Verstehen* (CTM A8, 1977); E. **Otto** (above, §5c) 375ff.; P. D. **Miller, Jr.,** and J. J. M. **Roberts,** *The Hand of the Lord* (1977); C. **Conroy,** *Absalom, Absalom! Narrative and Language in 2 Samuel 13–20* (1978); D. M. **Gunn,** *The Story of King David: Genre and Interpretation* (1978); P. K. **McCarter, Jr.** (AB, 1980); J. P. **Fokkelman,** *Narrative Art and Poetry in the Books of Samuel* (1981).

Kings: J. A. **Montgomery** and H. S. **Gehman** (ICC, 1951); M. **Noth** (BK I, 1968); J. **Gray** (OTL, 1970²); E. **Würthwein** (ATD I, 1977).

Stories about the prophets: see §13.

§12 The Chronicler's History
Surveys of research: E. **Jenni,** "Aus der Literatur zur chronistischen Geschichtsschreibung," *TRu* 45 (1980) 97–108; D. **Mathias,** "Die Geschichte der Chronikforschung im 19. Jh.," *TLZ* 105 (1980) 474f.
G. v. **Rad,** "Die levitische Predigt in den Büchern der Chronik" (1934), *GesStud* (1958) 248–61; M. **Noth,** *ÜSt* (above, §11) 110ff.; K. **Galling,** *Studien zur Geschichte Israels im persischen Zeitalter* (1964); S. **Mowinckel,** *Studien zu dem Buche Esra-Nehemia I–III* (1964–65); J. M. **Myers** (AB, 1965; I Chr; II Chr; Ezra-Neh); U. **Kellermann,** *Nehemia. Quellen, Überlieferung und Geschichte* (BZAW 102, 1967; bibliog.); K.-F. **Pohlmann,** *Studien zum dritten Esra* (FRLANT 104, 1970); T. **Willi,** *Die Chronik als Auslegung* (FRLANT 106, 1972); R. **Mosis,** *Untersuchungen zur Theologie des chronistischen Geschichtswerkes* (1973); P. **Welten,** *Geschichte und Geschichtsdarstellung in den Chronikbüchern* (WMANT 42, 1973); W. Th. **In der Smitten,** *Esra. Quellen, Überlieferung und Geschichte* (1973, bibliog.); K. **Koch,** "Ezra and the Origins of Judaism," *JSS* 19 (1974) 173–97; J. D. **Newsome,** "Toward a New Understanding of the Chronicler and His Purposes," *JBL* 94 (1975) 201–17; H. G. M. **Williamson,** *Israel in the Book of Chronicles* (1977); I. L. **Seeligmann** (above, §11); S. **Japhet,** "Conquest and Settlement in Chronicles," *JBL* 98 (1979) 205–18; F. C. **Fensham** (NICOT, 1982); H. G. M. **Williamson** (NCB, 1982).

§§13–24 The Prophets
Surveys of research: G. **Fohrer,** *TRu* 28 (1962) 1–75, 235–97, 301–74; 40 (1975) 337–77; 41 (1976) 1–12; 45 (1980) 1–39, 109–32, 193–225; B. **Vawter,** "Recent Literature on the Prophets," *Concilium* no. 10 (1965) 112–25; J. **Scharbert,** "Die prophetische Literatur," *Fs. J. Coppens* I (1969) 58–118; J. M. **Schmidt,** "Probleme der Prophetenforschung," *VF* 17/1 (1972) 39–81; idem, "Ausgangspunkt und Ziel prophetischer Verkündigung im 8. Jh.," *VF* 22/1 (1977) 65–82; H. D. **Preuss** (ed.), *Eschatologie im Alten Testament* (1978); P. H. A. **Neumann** (ed.), *Das Prophetenverständnis in der deutschsprachigen Forschung seit H. Ewald* (1979); W. **McKane,** "Prophecy and Prophetic Literature" (*TaI,* 163–88).

Encyclopedia articles: R. **Rendtorff,** *TDNT* 6: 796–812; R. **Meyer,** J. **Fichtner** and A. **Jepsen,** *RGG* 5, (1961³) 613–33; J. **Jeremias,** *THAT* II (1976) 7–26.

General presentations: B. **Duhm,** *Israels Propheten* (1922²); H. **Gunkel,** in H. Schmidt, *Die grossen Propheten* (SAT II/2, 1923²) XVIIff.; M. **Buber,** *The Prophetic Faith* (1949); C. **Kuhl,** *Israels Propheten* (1956); G. v. **Rad,** *Old Testament Theology* II (1965; see also *Die Botschaft der Propheten,* 1977³); J. **Lindblom,** *Prophecy in Ancient Israel* (1962); R. E. **Clements,** *Prophecy and Covenant* (1965); J. **Scharbert,** *Die Propheten Israels bis*

700 v. Chr./um 600 v. Chr. (1965–67); G. **Fohrer**, *Studien zur alttestamentlichen Prophetie* (1967); idem, *Die Propheten des Alten Testament* I–VII (1974–77); J. **Bright**, *Covenant and Promise* (1976); K. **Koch**, *Die Profeten* I–II (1978-80); R. R. **Wilson**, *Prophecy and Society in Ancient Israel* (1980); P. D. **Miller, Jr.**, *Sin and Judgment in the Prophets* (1982).

§13 The Forms of Prophecy

a) Prophetic utterance and prophetic book

b) Main categories of prophetic literature

H. **Gunkel** (above, §§13–24); H. W. **Wolff**, "Die Begründungen des prophetischen Heils- und Unheilssprüche" (1934), *GesStud* (1964) 9–35; C. **Westermann**, *Grundformen prophetischer Rede* (1978⁵; Eng.: *Basic Forms of Prophetic Speech*, 1967); R. **Rendtorff**, "Botenformel und Botenspruch" (1962), *GesStud* (1975) 243–55; K. **Koch**, *Was ist Formgeschichte?* (1974³) 258ff. (Eng.: *The Growth of the Biblical Tradition: The Form-critical Method*, 1969); W. E. **March**, in J. H. Hayes (above, §5b) 141ff. (bibliog.); A. J. **Bjørndalen**, "Zu den Zeitstufen der Zitatformel . . . ," *ZAW* 86 (1974) 393–403; *TWAT* 1:365ff.; 2:108, 119ff.

Stories about the prophets: G. **Fohrer**, *Die symbolischen Handlungen der Propheten* (ATANT 54, 1968²); A. **Rofé**, "The Classification of the Prophetical Stories," *JBL* 89 (1970) 427–40; idem, "Classes in the Prophetical Stories" (VTSup 26, 1974) 143–67; B. O. **Long**, "2 Kings III and Genres of Prophetic Narrative," *VT* 23 (1973) 337–48.

Visions: F. **Horst**, "Die Visionsschilderungen der alttestamentlichen Propheten," *EvT* 20 (1960) 193–205; B. O. **Long**, "Prophetic Call Traditions and Reports of Visions," *ZAW* 84 (1972) 494–500; idem, "Reports of Visions among the Prophets," *JBL* 95 (1976) 353–65; Ch. **Jeremias**, *Die Nachtgesichte des Sacharja* (FRLANT 117, 1977; bibliog.); G. **Bartczek**, *Prophetie und Vermittlung* (1980).

Call narratives: W. **Zimmerli**, *Ezekiel* I (1979); N. **Habel**, "The Form and Significance of the Call Narratives," *ZAW* 77 (1965) 297–323; R. **Kilian**, "Die prophetischen Berufungsberichte," *Theologie im Wandel* (1967) 356–76; W. **Richter**, *Die sog. vorprophetischen Berufungsberichte* (1970); W. H. **Schmidt**, *Exodus* (BK II/2, 1977) 123–29 (bibliog.); B. O. **Long**, "Berufung I," *TRE* 5 (1980) 676–84 (bibliog.).

Judgment speech: G. E. **Wright**, "The Lawsuit of God: A Form-Critical Study of Deuteronomy 32," *Israel's Prophetic Heritage* (1962); H. J. **Boecker**, *Redeformen des Rechtslebens im AT* (WMANT 14, 1970²; bibliog.); E. **Würthwein**, "Kultpolemik oder Kultbescheid?" (1963), *Wort und Existenz* (1970) 144–60; J. **Jeremias**, *Kultprophetie und Gerichtsverkündigung in der späten Königszeit Israels* (WMANT 35, 1970) 151ff. (bibliog.); J. **Blenkinsopp**, "The Prophetic Reproach," *JBL* 90 (1971) 267–78; *THAT* II, 776.

Dirge and woe cry: H. **Jahnow**, *Das hebräische Leichenlied* (BZAW 36, 1923); H. W. **Wolff**, "Der Aufruf zur Volksklage" (1964), *GesStud* (1973²) 392–401; G. **Wanke**, "'ôj und hôj," *ZAW* 78 (1966) 215–18; H. W. **Wolff**, *Joel/Amos* (BK) 284ff. (bibliog.) (Eng.: *Joel and Amos*, 1977); W. **Janzen**, *Mourning Cry and Woe Oracle* (BZAW 125, 1972); H. J. **Kraus**, "hôj als prophetische Leichenklage über das eigene Volk im 8. Jh.," *ZAW* 85 (1973) 15–46; C. **Hardmeier**, *Texttheorie und biblische Exegese* (BEvT 79, 1978; bibliog.); J. J. M. **Roberts**, "Form, Syntax, and Redaction in Isaiah 1:2–20," *The Princeton Seminary Bulletin* (1982) 293–306; D. R. **Hillers**, "Hoy and Hoy-Oracles: A Neglected Syntactic Aspect," *Freedman Festschrift* (1983).

Historical retrospect: J. **Vollmer**, *Geschichtliche Rückblicke und Motive in der Prophetie des Amos, Hosea und Jesaja* (BZAW 119, 1971).

Disputation: J. **Begrich,** *Studien zu Deuterojesaja* (1938, 1963²) 41ff.; H. J. **Hermisson,** "Diskussionsworte bei Deuterojesaja," *EvT* 31 (1971) 665–80 (bibliog.).

Exhortation: H. W. **Wolff,** "Das Thema 'Umkehr' in der alttestamentlichen Prophetie" (1951), *GesStud* (1964) 130–50; W. **Richter,** *Recht und Ethos* (SANT 15, 1966); A. J. **Bjørndalen,** " 'Form' und 'Inhalt' des motivierenden Mahnspruchs," *ZAW* 82 (1970) 347–61; G. **Warmuth,** *Das Mahnwort* (BET 1, 1976; bibliog.); A. Vanlier **Hunter,** *Seek the Lord!* (1982).

Oracle of salvation: see §21; J. **Begrich,** "Das priesterliche Heilsorakel" (1934), *GesStud* (1964) 217–31; C. **Westermann,** "Der Weg der Verheissung durch das AT," *Forschung am AT* II (1974) 230–49.

c) Questions in contemporary study of the prophets

W. H. **Schmidt,** *Zukunftsgewissheit und Gegenwartskritik,* (1973, bibliog.); L. **Markert** and G. **Wanke,** "Die Propheteninterpretation," *KD* 22 (1976) 191–220; J. M. **Schmidt,** "Ausgangspunkt und Ziel prophetischer Verkündigung im 8. Jh.," *VF* 22/1 (1977) 65–82 (bibliog.); H. W. **Wolff,** "Die eigentliche Botschaft der klassischen Propheten," *Fs. W. Zimmerli* (1977) 547–57; W. **Zimmerli,** "Wahrheit und Geschichte in der alttestamentlichen Schriftprophetie," *Congress Volume Göttingen* (VTSup 29 [1978] 1–15).

d) Precursors of the writing prophets

R. **Rendtorff,** "Erwägungen zur Frühgeschichte des Prophetentums" (1962), *GesStud* (1975) 220–42; G. **Fohrer,** *Elia* (ATANT 53, 1968²); O. H. **Steck,** *Überlieferung und Zeitgeschichte in den Elia-Erzählungen* (WMANT 26, 1968); K. H. **Bernhardt,** "Prophetie und Geschichte" (VTSup 22, 1972) 20–46; H. Ch. **Schmitt,** *Elisa* (1972); idem, "Prophetie und Tradition," *ZTK* 74 (1977) 255–72; H. **Schweizer,** *Elisha in den Kriegen* (SANT 37, 1974); R. **Smend,** "Das Wort Jahwes an Elia," *VT* 25 (1975) 525–43; idem, "Der biblische und der historische Elia" (VTSup 28, 1977) 167–84; G. **Hentschel,** *Die Elijaerzählungen* (ErTS 33, 1977).

§14 Amos

Commentaries on the book of the Twelve Prophets: J. **Wellhausen** (1893³, 1963⁴); E. **Sellin** (KAT, 1929–30²,³); T. H. **Robinson** and F. **Horst** (HAT, 1964³); A. **Weiser** and K. **Elliger** (ATD, 1974⁶–1957⁷); H. W. **Wolff** (BK, 1956ff. [Hos–Mic]); W. **Rudolph** (HAT, 1966–76).

Amos: F. **Horst,** "Die Doxologien im Amosbuch" (1929), *Gottes Recht* (1961) 155–66; A. **Weiser,** *Die Profetie des Amos* (BZAW 53, 1929); E. **Würthwein,** "Amos-Studien" (1950), *Wort und Existenz* (1970) 68–110; V. **Maag,** *Text, Wortschatz und Begriffswelt des Buches Amos* (1951); H. Graf **Reventlow,** *Das Amt des Propheten bei Amos* (FRLANT 80, 1962); R. **Smend,** "Das Nein des Amos," *EvT* 23 (1963) 404–23; H. W. **Wolff,** *Amos' geistige Heimat* (WMANT 18, 1964; Eng.: *Amos the Prophet: The Man and His Background,* 1973); W. H. **Schmidt,** *Die deuteronomistische Redaktion des Amosbuches,*" *ZAW* 77 (1965) 168–93; J. L. **Mays,** (OTL, 1969); H. H. **Schmid,** "Amos" (1969), *Altorientalische Welt in der alttestamentlichen Theologie* (1974) 121–44; J. **Vollmer** (above, §13); I. **Willi-Plein,** *Vorformen der Schriftexegese* (BZAW 123, 1971 [Amos, Hosea, Micah]); M. **Krause,** *Das Verhältnis von sozialer Kritik und kommender Katastrophe in den Unheilsprophezeiungen des Amos* (1972; diss., Hamburg); M. **Fendler** (above, §3); W. **Berg,** *Die sogenannten Hymnenfragmente im Amosbuch* (1974); K. **Koch,** "Die Rolle der hymnischen Abschnitte des Amosbuches," *ZAW* 86 (1974) 506–37; idem, *Amos* (AOAT 30/1–3, 1976, bibliog.); L. **Markert,** *Struktur und Bezeichnung* *des Scheltworts* (BZAW 140, 1977); idem, "Amos(buch)," *TRE* 2 (1978) 471–87 (bibliog.); W. **Schottroff**, "Der Prophet Amos," *Der Gott der kleinen Leute* I (above, §3) 39–66; C. I. K. **Story**, "Amos—Prophet of Praise," *VT* 30 (1980) 67–80; G. **Bartczek** (above, §13ab); R. B. **Coote**, *Amos Among the Prophets* (1981).

§15 Hosea
Commentaries: see §14, especially H. W. **Wolff** (1976³; Eng.: *Hosea*, 1974); W. **Rudolph** (1966); J. L. **Mays** (OTL, 1969); F. I. **Andersen** and D. N. **Freedman** (AB, 1980).

G. **Fohrer**, "Umkehr und Erlösung beim Propheten Hosea" (1955); BZAW 99 (1967) 222–41; G. **Östborn**, *Jahwe und Baal* (1956); H. W. **Wolff**, "Hoseas geistige Heimat" (1956), *GesStud* (1964) 232–50; E. **Jacob**, "Der Prophet Hosea und die Geschichte," *EvT* 24 (1964) 281–90; J. **Buss**, *The Prophetic Word of Hosea* (BZAW 111, 1969); J. **Vollmer** (above, §13); I. **Willi-Plein** (above, §14); S. **Bitter**, *Die Ehe des Propheten Hosea* (1975); D. **Klinet**, *Ba'al und Jahwe* (1977); J. **Schreiner**, "Hoseas Ehe, ein Zeichen des Gerichts," *BZ* 21 (1977) 163–83; J. **Jeremias**, "Hosea 4–7," *Fs.* E. **Würthwein** (1979) 47–58; H. **Utzschneider**, *Hosea, Prophet vor dem Ende* (OBO 31, 1980).

§16 Isaiah
Commentaries: G. B. **Gray** (ICC, 1912); B. **Duhm** (HK, 1922⁴, 1968⁵); O. **Procksch** (KAT, 1930); V. **Herntrich** (ATD, 1950); G. **Fohrer** (ZBK, I, II, 1967²; III, 1964); O. **Kaiser** (ATD, I, 1981⁵; II, 1976²; Eng.: OTL, 1974); W. **Eichrodt** (BAT, I, 1976²; II, 1967); H. **Wildberger** (BK, I, 1972; II, 1978; III, 1981 [Isa 1–12; 13–27; 28–39]); W. H. **Irwin**, *Isaiah 28–33: Translation with Philological Notes* (1977); R. E. **Clements**, *Isaiah 1–39* (NCB, 1980).

J. **Fichtner**, *Gottes Weisheit* (1965) 18ff., 27ff., 44ff.; G. **Fohrer**, "Entstehung, Komposition und Überlieferung von Jes 1–39" (1962), BZAW 99 (1967) 113–47; idem, "Wandlungen Jesajas," *Fs.* W. **Eilers** (1967) 58–71; H. W. **Wolff**, *Frieden ohne Ende* (BSt 35, 1962); R. **Fey**, *Amos und Jesaja* (WMANT 12, 1963); H. **Donner**, *Israel unter den Völkern* (VTSup 11, 1964); B. S. **Childs**, *Isaiah and the Assyrian Crisis* (1967); J. **Becker**, *Isaias—der Prophet und sein Buch* (SBS 30, 1968); R. **Kilian** *Der Verheissung Immanuels* (SBS 35, 1968; bibliog.); idem, "Der Verstockungsauftrag Jesajas," *Fs.* G. J. *Botterweck* (1977) 209–25; U. **Stegemann**, "Der Restgedanke bei Isaias," *BZ* 13 (1969) 161–86; G. **Sauer**, "Die Umkehrforderung in der Verkündigung Jesajas," *Fs.* W. *Eichrodt* (1970) 277–95; J. **Vollmer** (above, §13); W. **Zimmerli**, "Verkündigung und Sprache der Botschaft Jesajas" (1970), *GesAufs* II (1974) 73–87; O. H. **Steck**, *BZ* 16 (1972) 188–206; idem, *EvT* 33 (1973) 77–90; idem, *TZ* 29 (1973) 161–78 (on Isa 6–8); H. J. **Hermisson**, "Zukunftserwartung und Gegenwartskritik in der Verkündigung Jesajas," *EvT* 33 (1973) 54–77; J. **Jensen**, *The Use of tôrâ by Isaiah: His Debate with the Wisdom Tradition* (CBQMS 3, 1973); H. W. **Hoffmann**, *Die Intention der Verkündigung Jesajas* (BZAW 136, 1974); J. J. **Stamm**, "Die Immanuel-Perikope," *TZ* 30 (1974) 11–22 (bibliog.); W. **Dietrich**, *Jesaja und die Politik* (BEvT 74, 1976); F. **Huber**, *Jahwe, Juda und die anderen Völker beim Propheten Jesaja* (BZAW 137, 1976); H. **Barth**, *Die Jesaja-Worte in der Josiazeit* (WMANT 48, 1977; bibliog.); W. H. **Schmidt**, "Die Einheit der Verkündigung Jesajas," *EvT* 37 (1977) 260–72; J. **Vermeylen**, *Du prophète Isaïe à l'apocalyptique* (1977); P. R. **Ackroyd**, "Isaiah I–II," *Congress Volume Göttingen* (VTSup 29 [1978] 16-48); W. L. **Holladay**, *Isaiah: Scroll of a Prophetic Heritage* (1978); K. **Nielsen**, "Das Bild des Gerichts in Jes I–XII," *VT* 29 (1979) 309–24; R. E. **Clements**, *Isaiah and the Deliverance of Jerusalem* (1980); idem, "The Unity of the Book of Isaiah," *Int* (April 1982) 117–29; J. J. M. **Roberts**, "Isaiah in Old Testament Theology," *Int* (April 1982) 130–43; M. E. W. **Thompson**, *Situation and Theology: Old Testament Interpretations of the Syro-Ephraimite War* (1982).

§17 Micah

Commentaries: see §14, especially W. **Rudolph** (1975, bibliog.); J. L. **Mays** (OTL, 1976); H. W. **Wolff** (1980–); D. R. **Hillers** (Hermeneia, in press).

W. **Beyerlin,** Die Kulttraditionen Israels in der Verkündigung des Propheten Micha (FRLANT 72, 1959); T. **Lescow,** Micha 6,6–8 (AzTh 25, 1966); idem, "Redaktionsgeschichtliche Analyse . . . ," ZAW 84 (1972) 46–85, 182–212; J. **Jeremias,** "Die Deutung der Gerichtsworte Michas in der Exilszeit," ZAW 83 (1971) 330–54; I. **Willi-Plein** (above, §14); V. **Fritz,** "Das Wort gegen Samaria Mi 1,2–7," ZAW 86 (1974) 316–31; B. **Renauld,** La formation du Livre de Michée (1977); H. W. **Wolff,** Mit Micha reden (1978); idem, "Wie verstand Micha von Moreschet sein prophetisches Amt?" Congress Volume Göttingen (VTSup 29 [1978] 403–17).

§18 Nahum, Habakkuk, Zephaniah, Obadiah

Commentaries: see §14, especially W. **Rudolph** (1975 [Nah, Hab, Zeph]); H. W. **Wolff** (1977 [Obadiah] bibliog.).

Nahum: J. **Jeremias,** Kultprophetie und Gerichtsverkündigung in der späten Königszeit Israels (WMANT 35, 1970 [Nah, Hab]); C. A. **Keller,** "Die theologische Bewältigung der geschichtlichen Wirklichkeit in der Prophetie Nahums," VT 22 (1972) 399–419; K. J. **Cathcart,** Nahum in the Light of Northwest Semitic (1973); H. **Schulz,** Das Buch Nahum (BZAW 129, 1973).

Habakkuk: J. **Jeremias** (see above); P. **Jöcken,** Das Buch Habakuk. Darstellung der Geschichte seiner kritischen Erforschung . . . (1977); E. **Otto** "Die Stellung der Wehe-Worte in der Verkündigung des Propheten Habakuk," ZAW 89 (1977) 73–107.

Zephaniah: A. S. **Kapelrud,** The Message of the Prophet Zephanja (1975); H. **Irsigler,** Gottesgericht und Jahwetag (1977); G. **Krinetzki,** Zephanjastudien (1977).

Obadiah: G. **Fohrer,** "Die Sprüche Obadjas," Fs. Th. C. Vriezen (1966) 81–93.

§19 Jeremiah

Introduction: C. **Westermann,** Jeremia (1967).

Surveys of research: E. **Vogt,** Bib 35 (1954) 357–65; W. **Thiel,** Die deuteronomistische Redaktion von Jer 1–25 (WMANT 41, 1975) 3ff.; S. **Herrmann,** TLZ 102 (1977) 481–90.

Commentaries: B. **Duhm** (KHC, 1901); P. **Volz** (KAT, 1922); J. **Bright** (AB, 1965); W. **Rudolph** (HAT, 1968³); A. **Weiser** (ATD, 1969⁶); J. A. **Thompson** (NICOT, 1980).

S. **Mowinckel,** Zur Komposition des Buches Jeremia (1914); idem, Prophecy and Tradition (1946); W. **Baumgartner,** Die Klagegedichte des Jeremias (BZAW 32, 1917); H. Graf **Reventlow,** Liturgie und prophetisches Ich bei Jeremia (1963; see also idem, ZAW 81 [1969] 315–52 on Jer 7; 26); C. **Rietzschel,** Das Problem der Urrolle (1966); A. H. J. **Gunneweg,** "Konfession oder Interpretation im Jeremiabuch," ZTK 67 (1970) 395–416; E. W. **Nicholson,** Preaching to the Exiles (1970); W. **Schottroff,** "Jeremia 2, 1–3," ZTK 67 (1970) 263–94; G. **Wanke,** Untersuchungen zur sog. Baruchschrift (BZAW 122, 1971); P. **Diepold** (above, §10); W. **Thiel** (see above); idem, Die deuteronomistische Redaktion von Jeremia 26–45 (WMANT 52, 1981; bibliog.); F. L. **Hossfeld** and I. **Meyer,** Prophet gegen Prophet (1973; see also idem, ZAW 86 [1974] 30–50 on Jer 26); H. **Weippert,** Die Prosareden des Jeremiabuches (BZAW 132, 1973; see also idem, VT 29 [1979] 336–51 on Jer 31:31ff.); G. **Münderlein,** Kriterien wahrer und falscher Prophetie (1974, 1979²); J. **Lundbom,** Jeremiah: A Study in Ancient Hebrew Rhetoric (1975); M. **Rose** (above, §10); L. **Schmidt,** "Die Berufung Jeremia," TheolViat 13 (1975–76) 189–

209; S. **Böhmer,** *Heimkehr und neuer Bund* (1976); W. L. **Holladay,** *The Architecture of Jeremiah 1–20* (1976); M. **Weinfeld,** "Jeremiah and the Spiritual Metamorphosis of Israel," *ZAW* 88 (1976) 17–56; C. **Wolf,** *Jeremia im Frühjudentum und Urchristentum* (1976); I. **Meyer,** *Jeremia und die falschen Propheten* (OBO 13, 1977); T. **Seidl,** *Texte und Einheiten in Jer 27–29* (1977); idem, *Formen und Formeln in Jer 27–29* (1978); P. **Welten,** "Leiden und Leidenserfahrung im Buch Jeremia," *ZTK* 74 (1977) 123–50; K. **Pohlmann,** *Studien zum Jeremiabuch* (FRLANT 118, 1978); C. **de Jong,** *De volken bij Jeremia* (1979); F. **Ahuis,** *Der klagende Gerichtsprophet* (diss., Heidelberg, 1973; planned for CTM); N. **Ittmann,** *Die Konfession Jeremias* (diss., Munich, 1977; planned for WMANT); R. P. **Carroll,** *From Chaos to Covenant: Prophecy in the Book of Jeremiah* (1981).

§20 Ezekiel
Introduction: W. **Zimmerli,** *Ezechiel, Gestalt und Botschaft* (BSt 62, 1972).

Commentaries: G. **Fohrer** and K. **Galling** (HAT, 1955); W. **Eichrodt** (ATD, 1966); J. W. **Wevers** (NCB, 1969); K. W. **Carley** (CamBC, 1974); W. **Zimmerli** (BK, 1969, 1978[2]; Eng.: *Ezekiel I* [1–24] 1979).

Surveys of literature: C. **Kuhl,** *TRu* 5 (1933) 92–118; 20 (1952) 1–26; 24 (1956–57) 1–53; H. H. **Rowley,** *Men of God* (1963) 169–210.

H. **Hölscher,** *Hesekiel, der Dichter und das Buch* (BZAW 39, 1924); V. **Herntrich,** *Ezechielprobleme* (BZAW 61, 1933); G. **Fohrer,** *Das Hauptproblem des Buches Ezechiel* (BZAW 72, 1952); H. **Gese,** *Der Verfassungsentwurf des Ezechiel (Kap 40–48)* (1957); H. Graf **Reventlow,** *Wächter über Israel* (BZAW 82, 1962); W. **Zimmerli,** "Deutero-Ezechiel?" *ZAW* 84 (1972) 501–16; idem, "Das Phänomen der 'Fortschreibung' im Buche Ezechiel," *Fs. G. Fohrer* (= BZAW 150, 1980) 174–91; H. **Schulz,** *Das Todesrecht im AT* (BZAW 114, 1969); D. **Baltzer,** *Ezechiel und Deuterojesaja* (BZAW 121, 1971); E. **Vogt,** "Die Lähmung und Stummheit des Propheten Ezechiel," *Fs. W. Eichrodt* (1970) 87–100; J. **Garscha,** *Studien zum Ezechielbuch* (1974); H. **Simian,** *Die theologische Nachgeschichte der Prophetie Ezechiels* (FzB 14, 1974); J. D. **Levenson,** *Theology of the Program of Restoration of Ezekiel 40–48* (1976); C. **Barth,** "Ezechiel 37 als Einheit," *Fs. W. Zimmerli* (1977) 39–52; F. **Hossfeld,** *Untersuchungen zu Komposition und Theologie des Ezechielbuches* (FzB 20, 1977); B. **Lang,** *Kein Aufstand in Jerusalem* (SBB 7, 1978); G. **Bettenzoli** (above, §9); L. **Boadt,** *Ezekiel's Oracles Against Egypt* (1980).

§21 Second Isaiah and Third Isaiah
Introduction: H. D. **Preuss,** *Deuterojesaja* (1976, bibliog.).

Commentaries: B. **Duhm** (HK, 1922[4], 1968[5]); P. **Volz** (KAT, 1932); C. R. **North,** *The Second Isaiah* (1964); G. **Fohrer** (ZBK, 1967[2]); C. **Westermann** (ATD, 1966); P. E. **Bonnard** (1972); R. N. **Whybray** (NCB, 1975); K. **Elliger** (BK, 1978 [Isa 40–45:7]).

L. **Köhler,** *Deuterojesaja stilkritisch untersucht* (BZAW 37, 1923); K. **Elliger,** *Deuterojesaja in seinem Verhältnis zu Tritojesaja* (BWANT 63, 1933); J. **Begrich,** *Studien zu Deuterojesaja* (1938, 1963); H. E. **v. Waldow,** *Anlass und Hintergrund der Verkündigung des Deuterojesajas* (1953; diss., Bonn); R. **Rendtorff,** "Die theologische Stellung des Schöpfungsglaubens bei Deuterojesaja" (1954), *GesStud* (1975) 209–19; E. **Jenni,** "Die Rolle des Kyros bei Deuterojesaja," *TZ* 10 (1954) 241–56; P. A. H. **de Boer,** *Second Isaiah's Message* (1956); C. **Westermann,** "Sprache und Struktur der Prophetie Deuterojesajas," *Forschung am AT* (1964) 92–170 (survey of research); A. **Eitz** (above, §8); O. H. **Steck,** "Deuterojesaja als theologischer Denker," *KD* 15 (1969) 280–93; E. **Nielsen,** "Deuterojesaja," *VT* 20 (1970) 190–205; C. **Stuhlmueller,** *Creative Redemption in Deutero-Isaiah* (1970; see also idem, *CBQ* 42 [1980] 1–29); D. **Baltzer** (above, §20); H. J.

Hermisson (above, §13); A. **Schoors**, *I Am God Your Saviour* (VTSup 24, 1973); E. **Haag**, "Gott als Schöpfer und Erlöser . . . ," *TLZ* 85 (1976) 193–213; R. F. **Melugin**, *The Formation of Isaiah 40–55* (BZAW 141, 1976); F. V. **Reiterer**, *Gerechtigkeit als Heil* (1976); J. M. **Vincent**, *Studien zur literarischen Eigenart und zur geistigen Heimat von Jesaja, Kap. 40–55* (BET 5, 1977); H. Ch. **Schmitt**, "Prophetie und Schultheologie im Deuterojesajabuch," *ZAW* 91 (1979) 43–61; R. P. **Merendino**, *Der Erste und der Letzte. Eine Untersuchung zu Jes 40–48* (VTSup 31, 1981).

Servant songs: W. **Zimmerli**, *TDNT* 5 (1954) 654–77; C. R. **North**, *The Suffering Servant in Deutero-Isaiah* (1956²); H. **Haag**, "Ebed-Jahwe-Forschung 1948–1958," *BZ* 3 (1959) 174–204; O. **Kaiser**, *Der königliche Knecht* (FRLANT 70, 1962²); H. H. **Rowley**, *The Servant of the Lord* (1965²) 1ff.; G. **Sauer**, "Deuterojesaja und die Lieder vom Gottesknecht," *Fs. Evgl.-theol. Fakultät Wien*, Sonderheft, *EvT* (1972) 58–66; K. **Baltzer**, *Die Biographie der Propheten* (1975) 171ff.; J. A. **Soggin**, "Tod und Auferstehung des leidenden Gottesknechts," *ZAW* 87 (1975) 346–55; G. **Gerleman**, "Der Gottesknecht bei Deuterojesaja," *Studien zur alttestamentlichen Theologie* (1980) 38–60; R. P. **Merendino**, "Jes 49, 1–6: ein Gottesknechtlied?" *ZAW* 92 (1980) 236–48.

Third-Isaiah (Isa 56–66): K. **Elliger**, *Die Einheit des Tritojesajas* (BWANT 45, 1928); idem, "Der Prophet Tritojesaja," *ZAW* 49 (1931) 112–41; W. **Zimmerli**, "Die Sprache des Tritojesajas" (1950), *Gottes Offenbarung* (1963) 217–33; D. **Michel**, "Zur Eigenart Tritojesajas," *TheolViat* 10 (1965–66) 213–30; H. J. **Kraus**, "Die ausgebliebene Endtheophanie" (1966), *Biblisch-theologische Aufsätze* (1972) 134–50; F. **Maass**, "Tritojesaja?" *Fs. L. Rost* (1967) 153–63; G. **Wallis**, "Gott und seine Gemeinde," *TZ* 27 (1971) 182–200; K. **Pauritsch**, *Die neue Gemeinde* (AnBib 47, 1971; bibliog.); E. **Sehmsdorf**, "Studien zur Redaktionsgeschichte von Jes 56–66," *ZAW* 84 (1972) 517–76; P. D. **Hanson**, *The Dawn of Apocalyptic* (1975).

§22 Haggai, Zechariah, Second Zechariah, Malachi
Commentaries: see above §14, especially K. **Elliger**, (1975⁷); W. **Rudolph** (1976, bibliog.).

Haggai (and Zechariah): W. A. M. **Beuken**, *Haggai-Sacharja 1–8* (1967); K. **Koch**, "Haggais unreine Volk," *ZAW* 79 (1967) 52–66; O. H. **Steck**, "Zu Hag 1,2–11," *ZAW* 83 (1971) 355–79; K. M. **Beyse**, *Serubbabel und die Königserwartungen der Propheten Haggai und Sacharja* (1972); K. **Seybold**, "Die Königserwartung bei den Propheten Haggai und Sacharja," *Judaica* 28 (1972) 69–78.

Zechariah: also H. **Gese**, "Anfang und Ende der Apokalyptik" (1973), *Vom Sinai zum Zion* (1974) 202–30; K. **Seybold**, *Bilder zum Tempelbau* (SBS 70, 1974); C. **Jeremias** (above, §13ab); G. **Wallis**, "Die Nachtgesichte des Propheten Sacharja," *Congress Volume Göttingen* (VTSup 29 [1978] 377–91).

Second-Zechariah (Zech 9–14): O. **Plöger**, *Theokratie und Eschatologie* (WMANT 2, 1959, 1968³); B. **Otzen**, *Studien über Deuterosacharja* (1964); H. M. **Lutz**, *Jahwe, Jerusalem und die Völker* (WMANT 27, 1968); M. **Saebø**, "Die deuterosacharjanische Frage," *ST* 23 (1969) 115–40; idem, *Sacharja 9–14* (WMANT 34, 1969); I. **Willi-Plein**, *Prophetie am Ende* (BBB 42, 1974).

Malachi: E. **Pfeiffer**, "Die Disputationsworte im Buche Maleachi," *EvT* 19 (1959) 546–68 (see also H. J. **Boecker**, *ZAW* 78 [1966] 78–80); G. **Wallis**, "Wesen und Struktur der Botschaft Maleachis," *Fs. L. Rost* (1967) 229–37; W. **Rudolph**, "Zu Mal 2, 10–16," *ZAW* 93 (1981) 85–90.

§23 Joel and Jonah
Commentaries: see above, §14, especially W. **Rudolph** (1971); H. W. **Wolff**, (1975²; Eng.: *Joel and Amos*, 1977, bibliog.).

Joel: O. **Plöger** (above, §22); E. **Kutsch,** "Heuschreckenplage und Tag Jahwes in Joel 1 und 2," *TZ* 18 (1962) 81–94; H. P. **Müller,** "Prophetie und Apokalyptik bei Joel," *TheolViat* 10 (1965–66) 231–52; G. W. **Ahlström,** *Joel and the Temple Cult* (VTSup 21, 1971); J. **Jeremias,** *Die Reue Gottes* (BSt 65, 1975) 87ff.

Jonah: H. W. **Wolff,** *Studien zum Jonabuch* (BSt 47, 1965, 1975²); G. H. **Cohn,** *Das Buch Jona im Lichte der biblischen Erzählkunst* (1969); A. **Jepsen,** "Anmerkungen zum Buche Jona" (1970), *Der Herr ist Gott* (1978) 163–69; O. **Kaiser,** "Wirklichkeit, Möglichkeit und Vorurteil," *EvT* 33 (1973) 91–103; J. **Jeremias** (above) 98ff.; J. **Magonet,** *Form and Meaning* (BET 2, 1976); L. **Schmidt,** *"De Deo"* (BZAW 143, 1976); T. E. **Fretheim,** *The Message of Jonah* (1977); idem, "Jonah and Theodicy," *ZAW* 90 (1978) 227–37; S. **Schreiner,** "Das Buch Jona . . . ," *TheolVers* 9 (1977) 37–45; G. **Vanoni,** *Das Buch Jona* (1978); H. **Witzenrath,** *Das Buch Jona* (1978).

§24 Daniel
History of scholarship: W. **Baumgartner,** "Ein Vierteljahrhundert Danielforschung," *TRu* 11 (1939) 59–83, 125–44, 201–28; F. **Dexinger,** *Das Buch Daniel und seine Probleme* (SBS 36, 1969; bibliog.); E. **Koch** et al., *Das Buch Daniel* (EdF 144, 1980; bibliog.).

Commentaries: J. A. **Montgomery** (ICC, 1927); A. **Bentzen** (HAT, 1952²); N. W. **Porteous** (OTL, 1965); O. **Plöger** (KAT, 1965); A. **Lacocque** (1976); L. F. **Hartman** and A. A. **DiLella** (AB, 1977).

I. **Willi-Plein,** "Ursprung und Motivation der Apokalyptik im Danielbuch," *TZ* 35 (1979) 265–74.

The Apocalypse of Isaiah (Isa 24–27): W. R. **Millar,** *Isaiah 24–27 and the Origin of Apocalyptic* (1976); H. **Wildberger** (BK X/2, 1978) 855ff. (bibliog.).

§25 The Psalter
Introductions: C. **Barth,** *Einführung in die Psalmen* (BSt 32, 1961); C. **Westermann,** *Der Psalter* (1969²); J. H. **Hayes,** *Understanding the Psalms* (1976); H. **Seidel,** *Auf den Spuren der Beter. Einführung in die Psalmen* (1980).

Surveys of research: M. **Haller,** *TRu* 1 (1929) 378–402; J. J. **Stamm,** *TRu* 23 (1955) 1–68; A. S. **Kapelrud,** *VF* 11/1 (1966) 62–93; E. **Gerstenberger,** *VF* 17/1 (1972) 82–99; 19/2 (1974) 22–45; idem, in J. H. Hayes (above, §5b) 179ff.; J. **Becker,** *Wege der Psalmenexegese* (SBS 78, 1975); P. H. A. **Neumann** (ed.), *Zur neueren Psalmenforschung* (WdF 192, 1976); J. H. **Eaton,** "The Psalms and Israelite Worship," *TaI,* 238–73.

Encyclopedia articles: K. **Galling,** *RGG* 5 (1961³) 672–84, 689–91; E. **Lipinski** et al., *DBSup* IX/48 (1973) 1–214 (bibliog.).

Commentaries: B. **Duhm** (KHC, 1922²); H. **Gunkel** (HK, 1929, 1968⁵); R. **Kittel** (KAT, 1929⁵⁻⁶); H. **Schmidt** (HAT, 1934); A. **Weiser** (ATD, 1973⁸; Eng.: OTL, 1962); H. J. **Kraus** (BK, 1960, 1978⁵; bibliog.); M. J. **Dahood** (AB, 1966–70); A. A. **Anderson** (NCB, 1972 [Pss 1–72; 73–150]); L. **Jacquet** (1975–77); E. **Beaucamp** (1976); P. C. **Craigie** (Word Biblical Commentary, 1983).

H. **Gunkel** and J. **Begrich,** *Einleitung in die Psalmen* (1933, 1975³); S. **Mowinckel,** *Psalmenstudien* I–VI (1921–24); idem, *The Psalms in Israel's Worship* I–II (1962); H. **Schmidt,** *Das Gebet des Angeklagten im AT* (BZAW 49, 1928); C. **Westermann,** *Das Loben Gottes in den Psalmen* (1954; Eng.: *The Praise of God in the Psalms,* 1965; expanded in *Lob und Klage in den Psalmen,* 1975⁵; Eng.: *Praise and Lament in the Psalms,* 1981); G. **Wanke,** *Die Zionstheologie der Korachiten* (BZAW 97, 1966); L. **Delekat,** *Asylie und Schutzorakel am Zionheiligtum* (1967); N. **Füglister,** *Das Psal-*

mengebet (1965); F. **Crüsemann,** *Studien zur Formgeschichte von Hymnus und Danklied in Israel* (WMANT 32, 1969); O. **Keel,** *Feinde und Gottesleugner* (SBM 7, 1969); idem, *The Symbolism of the Biblical World: Ancient Near Eastern Iconography and the Book of Psalms* (1978); W. **Beyerlin,** *Die Rettung des Bedrängten in den Feindpsalmen des Einzelnen . . .* (FRLANT 99, 1970); N. H. **Ridderbos,** *Die Psalmen (Ps 1–41)* (BZAW 117, 1972); J. **Kühlewein,** *Geschichte in den Psalmen* (CTM 2, 1973); L. **Ruppert,** *Der leidende Gerechte* (FzB 5, 1972); K. **Seybold,** *Das Gebet des Kranken im Alten Testament* (BWANT 99, 1973); idem, *Die Wallfahrtspsalmen* (BThSt 3, 1978); B. W. **Anderson,** *Out of the Depths* (1974); H. J. **Kraus,** *Theologie der Psalmen* (BK XV/3, 1979 = *TheolPs*); O. **Loretz,** *Die Psalmen* (1979); A. R. **Johnson,** *The Cultic Prophet and Israel's Psalmody* (1979); E. S. **Gerstenberger,** *Der bittende Mensch* (WMANT 51, 1980).

Royal psalms: K. H. **Bernhardt,** *Das Problem der altorientalischen Königsideologie im Alten Testament* (VTSup 8, 1961; bibliog.); G. **Widengren,** *Religionsphänomenologie* (1969) 360ff. (bibliog.); W. H. **Schmidt,** "Kritik am Königtum," *Fs. G. v. Rad* (1971) 440–61 (452ff.); J. H. **Eaton,** *Kingship and the Psalms* (1976); S. S. **Patro,** *Royal Psalms in Modern Scholarship* (1976, diss., Kiel [history of research]); H. J. **Kraus,** *TheolPs,* 134ff.

Zion psalms: H. **Schmid,** "Jahwe und die Kulttraditionen von Jerusalem," *ZAW* 67 (1955) 168–97; G. **Wanke,** *Die Zionstheologie der Korachiten* (BZAW 97, 1966); J. **Jeremias,** "Lade und Zion," *Fs. G. v. Rad* (1971) 183–98; O. H. **Steck,** *Friedensvorstellungen im alten Jerusalem* (ThSt 111, 1972); W. H. **Schmidt,** *Alttestamentlicher Glaube in seiner Geschichte* (1979³) 206ff. (bibliog.); H. J. **Kraus,** *TheolPs,* 94ff.; J. J. M. **Roberts,** "Zion in the Theology of the Davidic-Solomonic Empire," *Studies in the Period of David and Solomon and Other Essays* (ed. Tomoo Ishida, 1982) 93–108.

Enthronement psalms: P. **Volz,** *Das Neujahrsfest Jahwes* (1912); S. **Mowinckel,** *Psalmenstudien II. Das Thronbesteigungsfest Jahwäs und der Ursprung der Eschatologie* (1922); H. **Gunkel** and J. **Begrich,** *Einleitung in die Psalmen* (above) 94ff.; D. **Michel,** "Studien zu den sog. Thronbesteigungspsalmen" (1956), *Zur neueren Psalmenforschung* (above) 367–99; W. H. **Schmidt,** *Königtum Gottes in Ugarit und Israel* (BZAW 80, 1966²) 74ff.; J. A. **Soggin,** *THAT* I (1971) 914ff. (bibliog.); E. **Lipinski,** *DBSup* IX (1973) 32ff. (bibliog.); E. **Otto** and T. **Schramm,** *Fest und Freude* (1977) 46ff.; J. **Gray,** *The Biblical Doctrine of the Reign of God* (1979); F. **Stolz,** "Erfahrungsdimensionen im Reden von der Herrshaft Gottes," *WuD* 15 (1979) 9–32; H. J. **Kraus,** *TheolPs,* 29ff., 103ff.

§26 Song of Solomon, Lamentations, Ruth, and Esther
Song of Solomon

Commentaries: R. **Gordis,** *The Song of Songs and Lamentations* (1954); H. **Ringgren** (ATD, 1978⁴); W. **Rudolph** (KAT, 1962); G. **Gerleman** (BK, 1962); E. **Würthwein** (HAT, 1969); M. H. **Pope** (AB, 1977); G. **Krinetzki** (EB, 1980).

History of scholarship: C. **Kuhl,** *TRu* 9 (1937) 137–67; E. **Würthwein,** *TRu* 32 (1967) 177–212.

H. **Schmökel,** *Heilige Hochzeit und Hohes Lied* (1956); O. **Loretz,** *Das althebräische Liebeslied* (AOAT 14/1, 1971); J. B. **White,** *A Study of the Language of Love in the Song of Songs and Ancient Egyptian Poetry* (1978); G. **Krinetzki,** *Kommentar zum Hohenlied* (BET 16, 1981).

Lamentations

Commentaries: H. J. **Kraus** (BK, 1956, 1968³); A. **Weiser** (ATD, 1958); W. **Rudolph** (KAT, 1962); O. **Plöger** (HAT, 1969); D. R. **Hillers** (AB, 1972); O. **Kaiser** (ATD, 1979).

N. **Gottwald,** *Studies in the Book of Lamentation* (1962); B. **Albrektson,** *Studies in the Text and Theology of the Book of Lamentations* (STL 21, 1963); T. F. **McDaniel,**

"Philological Studies in Lamentations, I–II," *Bib* 49 (1968) 27–53, 199–220; H. **Gottlieb**, *A Study in the Text of Lamentations* (1978).

Ruth
Commentaries: W. **Rudolph** (KAT, 1962); E. **Würthwein** (HAT, 1969); H. W. **Hertzberger** (ATD, 1974⁵); E. F. **Campbell** (AB, 1975); J. M. **Sasson**, *Ruth: A New Translation with a Philological Commentary and a Formalist-Folklorist Interpretation* (1979); G. **Gerleman** (BK, 1981²).

H. **Witzenrath**, *Das Buch Ruth* (SANT 40, 1975); O. **Loretz**, "Das Verhältnis zwischen Rut-Story und David-Genealogie . . . ," *ZAW* 89 (1977) 124–26; K. K. **Sacon**, "The Book of Ruth," *AJBI* 4 (1978) 3–22; W. S. **Prinsloo**, "The Theology of the Book of Ruth," *VT* 30 (1980) 330–41.

Esther
Commentaries: H. **Ringgren** (ATD, 1958); H. **Bardkte** (KAT, 1963); E. **Würthwein** (HAT, 1969), C. A. **Moore** (AB, 1971); G. **Gerleman** (BK, 1981²; bibliog.); W. **Dommershausen** (EB, 1980).

W. **Dommershausen**, *Die Estherrolle* (SBM 6, 1968); J. C. **Lebram**, "Purimfest und Estherbuch," *VT* 22 (1972) 208–22; A. **Meinhold**, "Die Gattung der Josephsgeschichte und des Estherbuches. Diasporanovelle," *ZAW* 88 (1976) 72–93; idem, "Theologische Erwägungen zum Buch Esther," *TZ* 34 (1978) 321–33; S. B. **Berg**, *The Book of Esther* (1979); J. A. **Loader**, "Esther as a Novel . . . ," *ZAW* 90 (1978) 417–21 (see C. H. Miller, *ZAW* 92 (1980) 145–48).

§27 Proverbs
Introduction: C. **Bauer-Kayatz**, *Einführung in die alttestamentliche Weisheit* (BSt 55, 1969).

Surveys of research: W. **Baumgartner**, *TRu* 5 (1933) 259–88; idem, "The Wisdom Literature," *The Old Testament and Modern Study* (ed. H. H. Rowley, 1951) 210–37; R. **Murphy**, "The Wisdom Literature in the Old Testament," *Concilium* no. 10 (1965) 126–40; E. **Gerstenberger**, *VF* 14/1 (1969) 28–44; R. B. Y. **Scott**, *Int* 24 (1970) 20–45; J. A. **Emerton**, "Wisdom," *TaI*, 214–37.

Lexicon articles: H. **Gese**, *RGG* 6 (1962³) 1574–81; G. **Fohrer**, *TDNT* 7 (1964) 476–96; M. **Saebø**, *THAT* 1 (1971) 557–67; H. P. **Müller**, *TWAT* 2 (1977) 920–44 (bibliog.).

Commentaries: E. **Delitzsch** (1873); B. **Gemser** (HAT, 1963²); H. **Ringgren** (ATD, 1962, 1980³); R. B. Y. **Scott**, *Proverbs/Ecclesiastes* (AB, 1965); E. **McKane** (OTL, 1970); O. **Plöger**, (BK, 1981ff.)

W. **Zimmerli**, "Zur Struktur der alttestamentlichen Weisheit," *ZAW* 51 (1933) 177–204; idem, "Ort und Grenze der Weisheit im Rahmen der alttestamentlichen Theologie," *Gottes Offenbarung* (1963) 300–315; J. **Fichtner**, *Die altorientalische Weisheit in ihrer israelitisch-jüdischen Ausprägung* (BZAW 62, 1933); H. **Gese**, *Lehre und Wirklichkeit in der alten Weisheit* (1958); U. **Skladny**, *Die ältesten Spruchsammlungen in Israel* (1961); W. **McKane**, *Prophets and Wise Men* (1965); C. **Kayetz**, *Studien zu Proverbien 1–9* (WMANT 22, 1966); W. **Richter**, *Recht und Ethos* (1966); H. H. **Schmid**, *Wesen und Geschichte der Weisheit* (BZAW 101, 1966); H. J. **Hermisson**, *Studien zur israelitischen Spruchweisheit* (WMANT 28, 1968); G. **v. Rad**, *Weisheit in Israel* (1970; Eng.: *Wisdom in Israel*, 1972); C. **Westermann**, "Weisheit in Sprichwort" (1971), *Forschung am AT* II (1974) 149–61; B. **Lang**, *Die weisheitliche Lehrrede* (SBS 54, 1972); idem, *Frau Weisheit* (1973); R. N. **Whybray**, *The Intellectual Tradition of the Old Testament*

(BZAW 135, 1974); W. **Bühlmann,** *Vom rechten Reden und Schweigen* (OBO 12, 1976);
J. L. **Crenshaw,** *Studies in Ancient Israelite Wisdom* (1976); L. G. **Purdue,** *Wisdom and Cult* (1977); G. E. **Bryce,** *A Legacy of Wisdom* (1979); M. **Gilbert** (ed.), *La Sagesse de l'Ancien Testament* (1979).

§28 Qoheleth: Solomon the Preacher

Surveys of research: K. **Galling,** "Stand und Aufgabe der Kohelet-Forschung," *TRu* 6 (1934) 355–73; O. **Kaiser,** *Judentum und Hellenismus,* (VF 27/1, 1982).

Commentaries: W. **Zimmerli** (ATD, 1962, 1980³); H. W. **Hertzberg** (KAT, 1963); K. **Galling** (HAT, 1969²); A. **Lauha** (BK, 1978; bibliog.); N. **Lohfink** (EB, 1980).

R. **Gordis,** *Koheleth—The Man and His World* (1951); E. **Wolfel,** *Luther und der Skepsis* (1958); K. **Galling,** "Das Rätsel der Zeit . . . ," *ZTK* 58 (1961) 1–15; H. **Gese,** "Die Krise der Weisheit bei Kohelet" (1963), *Vom Sinai zum Zion* (1974) 168–79; R. **Kroeber,** *Der Prediger* (1963); O. **Loretz,** *Qohelet und der Alte Orient* (1964); H. H. **Schmid** (above, §27) 186ff.; F. **Ellermeier,** *Qohelet I/1* (1967); H. P. **Müller,** "Wie sprach Qohälät von Gott?" *VT* 18 (1968) 507–21; M. **Hengel,** *Judentum und Hellenismus* (1969, 1973²) 210ff. (Eng.: *Judaism and Hellenism,* 1974); M. A. **Kloppenstein,** "Die Skepsis des Qohelet," *TZ* 28 (1972) 97–109; R. **Braun,** *Kohelet und die frühhellenistische Popularphilosophie* (BZAW 130, 1973); A. **Stiglmair,** "Weisheit und Jahweglaube im Buche Kohelet," *TTZ* 83 (1974) 257–83, 339–68; W. **Zimmerli,** "Das Buch Kohelet— Traktat oder Sentenzensammlung?" *VT* 24 (1974) 221–30; D. **Lys,** *L'Ecclésiaste ou Que vaut la vie?* (1977); H. P. **Müller,** "Neige der althebräischen Weisheit," *ZAW* 90 (1978) 238–64; F. **Crüsemann,** "Die unveränderbare Welt," in *Der Gott der kleinen Leute* (above, §3) 80–104; idem, "Hiob und Kohelet," *Fs. C. Westermann* (1980) 373–93; J. A. **Loader,** *Polar Structures in the Book of Qohelet* (BZAW 152, 1979); C. F. **Whitley,** *Koheleth* (BZAW 148, 1978).

§29 The Book of Job

Introduction: A. **Jepsen,** *Das Buch Hiob und seine Deutung* (1963).

Surveys of research: C. **Kuhl,** *TRu* 21 (1953) 163–205, 257–317; 22 (1954) 261–316; H. P. **Müller,** *Das Hiobproblem* (EdF 84, 1978; bibliog.).

Commentaries: G. **Hölscher** (HAT, 1952²); A. **Weiser** (ATD, 1951, 1974⁶); G. **Fohrer** (KAT, 1963); F. **Horst** (BK, 1968 [Job 1–18]); M. H. **Pope** (AB, 1973); H. H. **Rowley** (NCB, 1976); F. **Hesse** (ZBK, 1978).

E. **Würthwein,** "Gott und Mensch in Dialog und Gottesreden des Buches Hiob" (1938), *Wort und Existenz* (1970) 217–92; C. **Westermann,** *Der Aufbau des Buches Hiob* (1956, supplemented by a survey of research in 1977²; Eng.: *The Structure of the Book of Job* [19–]); H. **Richter,** *Studien zu Hiob* (1959); G. **Fohrer,** *Studien zum Buche Hiob* (1963); H. H. Schmid (above, §27) 173ff.; E. **Kutsch,** "Hiob: leidender Gerechter—leidender Mensch," *KD* 19 (1973) 197–214; E. **Ruprecht,** "Leiden und Gerechtigkeit bei Hiob," *ZTK* 73 (1976) 426–45; H. G. **Preuss,** "Jahwes Antwort an Hiob . . . ," *Fs. W. Zimmerli* (1977) 323–43; R. **Gordis,** *The Book of Job* (1978); O. **Keel,** *Jahwes Entgegnung an Ijob* (1978); V. **Kubina,** *Die Gottesreden im Buche Hiob* (1979); F. **Crüsemann** (above, §28); P. **Weimar,** "Literarkritisches zur Ijobnovelle," *BN* 12 (1980) 62–80.

§30 For and Against the Old Testament

C. **Westermann** (ed.), *Essays in Old Testament Hermeneutics* (1963); G. E. **Wright,** *The Old Testament and Theology* (1969); W. H. **Schmidt,** " 'Theologie des Alten

Testament' vor und nach G. v. Rad," *VF* 17/1 (1972) 1–25 (bibliog.); G. F. **Hasel**, *Old Testament Theology* (1972; see E. Osswald, *TLZ* 99 [1974] 641–57); F. M. **Cross** et al., *Magnalia Dei, The Mighty Acts of God* (1976) 455–528; R. E. **Clements**, *Old Testament Theology* (1978); A. H. J. **Gunneweg**, *Understanding the Old Testament* (1978); W. **Zimmerli**, "Biblische Theologie I," *TRE* 6 (1980) 426–55 (bibliog.); H. Graf **Reventlow**, *Hauptprobleme der alttestamentlichen Theologie im 20 Jh.* and *Hauptprobleme der biblischen Theologie im 20 Jh.* (planned for EdF); H. **Seebass**, *Zur biblischen Theologie* (*VF* 27/1, 1982; bibliog.).

INDEX

Aaron, 94, 97
Abraham, 12, 14, 80f., 85f., 88, 104f.
acrostic, 300, 314
Alexander the Great, 161, 295
amphictyony, 18f.
angelic interpreter, 183, 274, 290
announcement, 102, 184f., 189, 231,
    242, 255, 261
anointing, 20, 154, 156
Antiochus IV Epiphanes, 289, 291, 295f.
apocalyptic, 101, 163, 181, 227, 276,
    285, 290ff.
Apocrypha, 4, 8
Aramaic, 12, 21, 23, 27f., 76, 164, 290,
    293, 295, 330
Arameans, 19, 192f., 196
ark, 21, 108, 132, 155
Assyrians, 23ff., 88, 129, 196, 201, 207,
    209, 213, 215, 217f., 221, 226, 230
auditions, 182ff., 260
authenticity (of prophetic oracles), 177ff.
autobiography, 175, 181, 267

Baal, 18, 22, 90, 92, 131, 142, 148, 192,
    206, 230, 243
Babylonia, Babylonians, 26f., 108, 209,
    227ff., 241f., 244, 248, 254, 257, 289,
    293f.
Balaam, 84, 86, 190
Baruch, 234f.
Beersheba, 14, 19, 87
Bethel, 14, 18, 105, 196
biography, 180, 235, 236
blessing, 44, 81f., 89, 96, 113
blood, 102, 104, 118, 130
Book of the Covenant, 16, 87, 110,
    116ff.

call, 180, 214, 242, 248, 253, 260
Canaan, Canaanites, 14f., 17f., 21ff., 35,
    37, 76, 111, 131, 135, 206, 306
canon, 6, 8
Chaldeans, 227
chaos, 104
Chronicler, 140, 161ff., 169
chronology, 94, 137, 158f.

circumcision, 98, 102, 105
clan, 31, 33f.
complaint, 245
connection of act and consequence, 327,
    331, 336, 339
conversion, 145, 190, 255f., 285
creation, 5, 44, 63, 79, 104, 109, 255,
    262ff., 305, 337f., 342
cult, 102, 108, 116, 121, 123, 126ff., 134,
    140, 143, 168ff., 199, 205, 207, 217,
    223, 254, 257f., 272, 283, 303f., 312
curses, 113
Cyrus, 27f., 160, 164, 169f., 209, 257,
    260, 262, 267, 271

David (dynasty of), 20ff., 35, 76, 142,
    153, 156, 168, 213, 219, 221, 225, 255,
    265, 273, 301, 308, 317
Day of the Lord, 214, 229f., 283, 285
Decalogue, 16, 34, 47f., 87, 106, 110,
    114ff., 132, 201, 206, 327
deportation, 24, 26f., 144
Deuteronomist(ic), 57, 87, 118, 120,
    125f., 133, 136f., 139f., 167, 178, 195f.,
    234f., 314
Deuteronomy, 27, 49f., 56, 88, 110, 118,
    120, 167
Diaspora, 27, 145, 319f.
didactic poems, 329
dirge (see qinah)
disputation, 186f., 259, 281
documentary hypothesis, 47, 55
doxology, 195, 301
dream, 91

Edom, 76, 232f., 281
Egypt, 5, 13ff., 25, 27, 36, 74, 107, 207,
    218, 241f., 321
El divinities, 14, 106
election, 133f., 264, 282
Elijah, 180, 191ff., 201, 282
Elisha, 180, 192
Elohist, 22, 24, 50, 55f., 71, 74f., 84, 124,
    201
enthronement psalms, 308f.

365

Also from The Crossroad Publishing Company

J. B. Bauer
Encyclopedia of Biblical Theology
The Complete Sacramentum Verbi

John J. Collins
Between Athens and Jerusalem
Jewish Identity in the Hellenistic Diaspora

Joseph A. Fitzmyer
To Advance the Gospel
New Testament Studies

Elisabeth Schüssler Fiorenza
In Memory of Her
A Feminist Theological Reconstruction of Christian Origins

Erasmus Hort
The Bible Book
Resources for Reading the New Testament

Othmar Keel
The Symbolism of the Biblical World
Ancient Near Eastern Iconography and the Book of Psalms

Jan Lambrecht
Once More Astonished
The Parables of Jesus

Rudolf Schnackenburg
The Gospel According to St John
Volumes 1–3

Charles H. Talbert
Reading Luke
A Literary and Theological Commentary on the Third Gospel

Charles H. Talbert, Editor
Luke–Acts
New Perspectives from the Society of Biblical Literature

Forthcoming

John J. Collins
The Apocalyptic Imagination
An Introduction to the Jewish Matrix of Christianity

Meir Sternberg
The Poetics of Biblical Narrative